MW01257582

1 MONTH OF
FREE
READING

at

www.ForgottenBooks.com

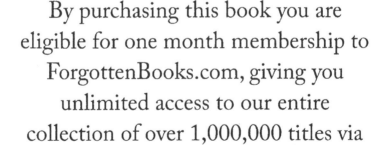

By purchasing this book you are eligible for one month membership to ForgottenBooks.com, giving you unlimited access to our entire collection of over 1,000,000 titles via our web site and mobile apps.

To claim your free month visit:

www.forgottenbooks.com/free174773

ISBN 978-1-5279-8300-7
PIBN 10174773

A DEFENCE
OF ARISTOCRACY

A TEXT BOOK FOR TORIES

BY

ANTHONY M. LUDOVICI

LeRoy Phillips
29A BEACON STREET
BOSTON

DEDICATED

TO THE LOVING MEMORY OF

MY MOTHER

WHO UNTIL HER DEATH REMAINED MY

CHIEF INSPIRER AND FRIEND

"L'Aristocracie m'eût facilement adoré ; aussi bien il m'en fallait une ; c'est le vrai, le seul soutien d'une monarchie, son levier, son point résistant ; l'État sans elle est un vaisseau sans gouvernail, un vrai ballon dans les airs. Or, le bon de l'Aristocracie, sa magie, est dans son ancienneté, dans le temps."—NAPOLÉON.

PREFACE

In three books published during the last five years, the subject of Aristocracy has already formed a no insignificant part of my theme, and in my last book it occupied a position so prominent that most of the criticism directed against that work concerned itself with my treatment of the aristocratic standpoint in Art. Much of this criticism, however, seemed to be provoked by the fact that I had not gone to the pains of defining exhaustively precisely what I meant by the true aristocrat and by true aristocracy in their relation to a people, and in the present work it has been my object not only to do this, and thus to reply to my more hostile critics, but also to offer a practical solution of modern problems which is more fundamental and more feasible than the solution offered by either Democracy or Socialism.

In view of the deep discontent prevailing in the modern world, and of the increasing unhappiness of all classes in Western Europe, it is no longer possible to turn a deaf ear even to the Socialist's plea for a hearing, and thousands of the possessing classes who, prompted by their self-preservative instinct alone, still retort that Socialism is an impossible and romantic Utopia, are beginning to wonder secretly in their innermost hearts whether, after all, this "vulgar" and "proletarian" remedy is not perhaps the only true and practical solution of modern difficulties. Having no other solution to offer, they are beginning to ask themselves, in private, whether this may not be the best way of extricating modern humanity from the tangle of exploitation and privilege, oppression and luxurious hedonism, in which *they*—the top-dogs—seem to be, but *accidentally*, the favoured few. In their

conscience they find no deep reply to Socialism, although
their natural longing to hold what they possess forces
them to cast ridicule and odium upon it.

Now, in the present work, I outline the terms of a
reply to Socialism and Democracy which I venture to hope
is deeper than that usually made by their opponents. I
offer a solution which I believe to be more fundamental,
more consonant with the passions and foibles of human
nature, more practical, and above all more vital and full
of promise for the future, than anything Socialism or
Democracy does and can bring forward.

I have entered exhaustively neither into the Democratic nor into the Socialistic solution of modern evils,
but have confined myself closely to the statement of the
true aristocrat's position, leaving the reader to see how
fundamentally such a statement upsets the claims of both
of the other parties.

Thus the book is not merely an argument in defence
of true aristocracy; for, to all thinking men, who know
it needs no defence, such an argument alone would be
simply platitudinous. It is, in addition, an attempt at
showing wherein hitherto the principles of a true Aristocracy have been misunderstood by the very aristocrats
themselves, and that more than half the criticism directed
against the Aristocratic principle to-day no more applies
to a true Aristocracy than it does to the man in the
moon.

I have called attention to a political and historical fact
which too many writers appear to have overlooked: the
fact that all political struggles, and all the fluctuations of
fortune which have attended the history of aristocracies,
have not consisted actually of a struggle between the
principle of aristocracy and a better, nobler and more
desirable principle, which by its superior virtues has supplanted the former, but of a struggle between the principle
of aristocracy and its representatives, or, in other words,
of Aristocracy *versus* the Aristocrats.

My conclusion that Aristocracy means Life and that

PREFACE

Democracy means Death reveals at once the object with which I undertook to investigate this problem—that is to say, with the object of raising the controversy if possible to a plane higher than mere "matters of opinion" and mere political party; and the impartiality with which I have pointed the finger at the errors and general incompetence of a particular aristocracy should be sufficient to prove the non-political and non-party spirit with which I entered upon the investigation.

The two chapters devoted to Charles I and the Puritan Rebellion, respectively, may seem to some a little irrelevant in a book of this nature; but when it is remembered that I needed a convincing example of the divergence of bad taste from good taste, and that this particular divergence of bad taste from good represents the most imposing instance of the kind which the history of England records—so much so, indeed, that the act of murder committed in 1649 may be regarded as a decisive turning-point in the fortunes of the English people, and a choice of roads which has undoubtedly led to all the evils concerning the origin of which most of us are now consciously or unconsciously inquiring—this excursion into the records of the past, and particularly into the records of the seventeenth century, will perhaps appear more justified and indispensable.

I do not claim to have adduced all the evidence possible for the support of my thesis—most of it, probably, I do not even know—but if I have succeeded in providing at least a stimulating introduction to the point of view taken in these pages, I shall feel that this is not altogether a superfluous book, or one that can be lightly set aside and ignored. For it is not as if the subject of Aristocracy had been discussed *ad nauseam* by a large galaxy of able writers. A glance at the Subject Catalogue of the London Library alone shows how inadequately it has been treated compared with the long list of books which deal with the opposing principle of Democracy. There are in all only nine books mentioned under the heading *Aristocracy* in

PREFACE

the 1909 Edition of the London Library's Catalogue, while the corresponding list under the heading *Democracy* numbers in all eighty-five volumes. When it is remembered that of the nine books above referred to four are purely partisan publications, no one will, I presume, venture to suggest that the author of a new book dealing with the Aristocrat and his life-principle need make half such a profound apologetic bow as he who would add one more volume to the eighty-five dealing with the other subject.

ANTHONY M. LUDOVICI.[1]

[1] The above, together with all the chapters that follow, was written at least a year before even the most prophetic amongst us could have had any premonition of the Great European War. Almost since the very beginning of the war I have been on active service, and not a line of the book has been altered. With regard to the relevancy ot the work at the present juncture I feel that the message my book conveys has by no means been rendered superfluous by recent events. On the contrary, the fluid state that the beliefs, the hopes and the aspirations of the nation are likely to be in at the end of this long trial, allow me to hope that a work marking out so sharp and definite a point of view may not be altogether ineffectual in helping, however slightly, to mould and direct opinion, once we shall have begun to think of other things than submarines and Zeppelins.

A. M. L.

British Expeditionary Force,
France, April 1915.

CONTENTS

CONTENTS

CHAPTER VI

CHAPTER VII

CHAPTER VIII

CHAPTER IX

A DEFENCE OF ARISTOCRACY

CHAPTER I

THE ARISTOCRAT AS THE ESSENTIAL RULER

"Neither Montaigne in writing his essays, nor Des Cartes in building new worlds, nor Burnet in framing an antediluvian earth, no, nor Newton in discovering and establishing the true laws of nature on experiment and a sublime geometry, felt more intellectual joys than he feels who is a real patriot, who bends all the force of his understanding, and directs all his thoughts and actions to the good of his country."—BOLINGBROKE, *On the Spirit of Patriotism*, p. 23.

IT is not my intention in this essay to support any particular aristocracy or aristocrat. I wish merely to throw what light I can upon the principle of aristocracy itself. Often I shall seem as hostile to aristocracies in particular as the most confirmed Radical; albeit, wherever I reveal any abhorrent vice in an individual aristocracy it will be with the object rather of demonstrating how unessential and unnecessary that vice is to the true principle of aristocracy than of stirring up ill-feeling to no purpose.

When one contends that the hereditary principle, as one of the essential conditions of an aristocracy, is a good principle, it is a common thing to hear people reply by calling attention to the number of instances in which it has hopelessly failed. They say, "Look at the Bourbons, the Spanish Hapsburgs, the Braganzas, the House of Osman, the later Stuarts!" Perhaps the reader will follow me and attempt to bear with me for a while, if I preface all my remarks by saying that while I shall make no endeavour to vindicate either the Bourbons, the Spanish

B

Hapsburgs, the Braganzas, the House of Osman or the later Stuarts, I shall, nevertheless, not consider a reference to them relevant as an argument against me, so long as he who mentions them for this purpose has not proved satisfactorily that they did not omit to observe one or other of the rules which are essential to the proper preservation or improvement of a character and type.

I decline to abandon a principle simply because the attempts which have been made to realise it hitherto by most European nations have failed hopelessly. If a principle can be shown to be a good one, then, whatever stigma attaches to it, owing to European failures to approximate to all it can yield, surely reflects more discredit upon those who have shown themselves unequal to it than upon the principle itself.

Moreover, in this question, as in all others, there is a wrong view and a right view. It is not merely a " matter of opinion." That which is merely a " matter of opinion " —as people are wont to say when they want to wash their hands of a thing, or to shirk the responsibility of solving a definite problem in a definite way—that, as I say, which is merely a " matter of opinion " *does not matter* at all. For those things which are merely a matter of opinion can be decided right away by every Tom, Dick and Harry over tea and scones at a cake-shop, and cannot, therefore, be of any consequence.

In all things that really matter, however, there can be but two opinions—the right opinion and the wrong opinion. And on the question of aristocracy the individual point of view of the man in the street simply does not matter.

There is a right way of looking at the question and a wrong way; and to those who look at it in the wrong way—that is to say, to those who are opposed to the principle of aristocracy, and who support the principle of democracy in its stead—all that we who support the principle of aristocracy can say is: that people and nations who believe in and act on our principles will have a longer lease of life, a fuller lease of life, a more flourishing lease of life, than they.

Human life, like all other kinds of life, cannot be the sport of foolish ideals. However nice and pleasant it may sound to say that the brotherhood of mankind, in which every man has a voice in the direction of human affairs, is the state of bliss, we who support the aristocratic ideal know that that state is one of decay, of doubt, of muddle and of mistakes. Now man cannot doubt, cannot be muddled and cannot make mistakes with impunity. Sooner or later he has to pay for these luxurious fads, by losses in the physique and the term of life of his nation.

Look about you now! Observe the myriads of ugly, plain and asymmetrical faces in our streets; observe the illness and the botchedness about you! Note, too, the innumerable societies founded in all the corners of the British Empire, with the object of "reforming" some erroneous policy, or of redressing some grievance. Is it not clear to you, when you see all these things, that something is wrong, and that that something which is wrong cannot be made right by the same class of mind which has given rise to all the muddle and confusion? Is it not clear to you that the men who know, the men of taste and sound instinct, no longer have any say in human affairs?

The principle of aristocracy is, that seeing that human life, like any other kind of life, produces some flourishing and some less flourishing, some fortunate and some less fortunate specimens; in order that flourishing, full and fortunate life may be prolonged, multiplied and, if possible, enhanced on earth, the wants of flourishing life, its optimum of conditions, must be made known and authoritatively imposed upon men by its representatives. Who are its representatives? The fanatics and followers of Science are not its representatives, for their taste is too indefinite; it is often pronounced too late to be of any good and it is not reached by an instinctive bodily impulse, but by long empirical research which often comes to many wrong conclusions before attaining to the right one. It must be clear that the true representatives of flourishing and fortunate life are the artists,[1] the men of taste. The artist, the man of taste—the successful number, so to speak, in the many blanks that human life produces in every generation—is in himself a chip of flourishing life. His own body is. a small synopsis, a diminutive digest of full, flourishing and fortunate life. What he wants, therefore, life wants; what he knows is good, the best kind of life knows is good. His voice is the very voice of full, flourishing and fortunate life. No number of committees or deliberative assemblies, consisting of men less fortunately constituted than he, can possibly form an adequate substitute for him in this. For the voice one has, and the desires and wants it expresses, are not a question of chance or of upbringing, they are a question of the body with which one's ancestors have endowed one. All science, all the known laws of heredity, prove this conclusively.

If one's choice of ways and means, if one's taste, if one's wants, therefore, are such that when they become general wants and general tastes they lead to an ascent in the line of human life, then unconsciously one's body, which is a specimen of flourishing and fortunate life, is uttering the credo of flourishing and fortunate life. If, on the other hand, one's choice of ways and means, if one's tastes and wants are such that when they become general tastes and general wants they lead to a descent in the line of human life, then unconsciously one's body, which is a specimen of mediocre or impoverished life, is pronouncing the doctrine of decline and of Nemesis.

[1] I do not use the word artist here to mean a painter or a musician or an actor. The word artist has been hopelessly vulgarised by the fact that a legion of inartistic painters, musicians and actors have used it as a designation of their ignoble class. By artist I mean a man of taste, a man who unhesitatingly knows what is right and what is wrong. Nowadays there are perhaps only two or three such men in every generation of painters, sculptors, musicians, writers, poets, legislators and actors.

THE ARISTOCRAT

Now, if all this is true—and to us who uphold the aristocratic principle it is the only Divine Truth on earth, and one which Science is bound ultimately to confirm and to prove—then it is obvious that only where the voice of flourishing life is raised to authority can there be any hope of an ascent in the line of life, or even of a level of health and beauty in the line of life.

What do those maintain who stand for the aristocratic principle? They simply hold a finger of warning up to their opponents and say, "Your foolish ideals will have a term; their end will come! You cannot with impunity turn a deaf ear to the voice of flourishing life. You must follow the men who know, the men of taste. If you do not your days are numbered. And the men who know, the men of taste, are simply those examples of flourishing life, those lucky strokes of nature's dice, who, when in authority, lead to the multiplication of flourishing life and an ascent in the line of life. No number of the mediocre or of the botched can hope to fill the place of one or of a few men of taste. Disbelieve in this principle and die. Believe in this principle and live to triumph over all those who do not believe in it!"[1]

This is not a "matter of opinion," it is not a matter concerning which every futile *flâneur* in Fleet Street can have his futile opinion. It is the Divine Truth of life. And the democrat who dares to deny it is not only a blind imbecile, he is not only a corrupt and sickly specimen of manhood, he is a rank blasphemer, whose hands are stained with the blood of his people's future.

[1] The Chinaman, Ku Hung-Ming, in his wonderful little book, *The Story of a Chinese Oxford Movement* (Shanghai, 1910), knew this to be so when, speaking of what the Englishman would discover if he studied the Chinese more carefully, he wrote (p. 60): "In the Chinaman, he (the Englishman) would find Confucianism with 'its way of the superior man' which, little as the Englishman suspects, will one day change the social order and break up the civilisation of Europe." Why? Because the civilisation of Europe is *not* based upon "the way of the superior man."

A DEFENCE OF ARISTOCRACY

Like all particularly fortunate strokes of the dice, these artists, or men of taste and sound judgment, these " superior men," as the creed of Confucianism calls them, do not occur in legions. Their number in a nation is always small. They are the few, and, owing to their highly complex natures, they are often difficult to rear. *" Pauci prudentia honesta ab deterioribus, utilia ab noxiis discernunt, plures aliorum eventis docentur,"*—says Tacitus.[1] But where they are elevated to power—that is to say, wherever they become rulers—the soundest instincts of sound life are made to lead.

For it is not only in the matter of establishing order that good government excels. This might be called the simple " craft " of governing. But it is also in that quality of directing choice, in directing the likes and dislikes of a people, in fact in that great virtue of setting a " good tone " in a nation, that good government distinguishes itself. For to the mediocre, to the less gifted among men, a thousand paths lie open, a thousand goals all beckoning and signing to man to go their way. Many of these paths lead to destruction, a goodly number of these goals mark out the horizon of decadence. Unless, therefore, the taste and judgment of flourishing life intervene, by means of the voice of the superior man, these roads acquire their travellers and these goals obtain their aspirants. It is there, then, that the virtue of that second quality of good rulership can operate—that virtue which sets the tone of a people, gives it a criterion of choice, and guides its passions. And this second virtue of good rulership might be called the " *tutorship* " of governing, as opposed to the " *craft* " above mentioned.

It must be obvious that when no check, coming from " superior man," intervenes between ordinary men and the false roads and false goals that lure them continually;

---

[1] *Annals of Tacitus*, Book IV, cap. 33. Translation by Church and Brodribb (p. 128). " For it is but the few who have the foresight to distinguish right from wrong, or what is sound from what is hurtful, while most men learn wisdom from the fortunes of others."

when, that is to say, "every private man is judge of good and evil actions"—a condition which Hobbes rightly characterised as the "disease of the commonwealth"[1]— not only is the life of a people or of a nation endangered, but human life itself is actually under the threat of destruction. For the voice of mediocre and impoverished life cannot be followed very long without humanity having to pay heavily for its guidance.

I have said that these men of taste and sound judgment are few; hence the high esteem in which an intelligent and life-loving mediocrity will hold them. Hence, too, the honours with which such a mediocrity usually lures them to rulership. For though they, the superior men, may instinctively incline to government, they must find a willing medium for their art, *i.e.* a people able to recognise superiority when it appears, or a people whose moral values actually hold rulership up as the only duty of superiority.

"It is certain," says Bolingbroke, "that the obligations under which we lie to serve our country increase in proportion to the ranks we hold, and the other circumstances of birth, fortune and situation that call us to this service; and above all, to the talents which God has given us to perform it."[2]

In a sound organisation of society, then, superiority implies, as it always should, the power of undertaking responsibilities. "Superior talents, and superior rank amongst our fellow-creatures," says Bolingbroke, "whether acquired by birth or by the course of accidents, and the success of our own industry, are noble prerogatives. Shall he who possesses them repine at the obligation they lay him under, of passing his whole life in the noblest occupation of which human nature is capable? To what higher station, to what greater glory can a mortal aspire than to be, during the whole course

[1] *Leviathan*, Chapter XXIX.
[2] *On the Study of History* (Davies, 1779), pp. 156–157.

7

of his life, the support of good, the controul of bad government, and the guardian of public liberty? " [1]

Thus superiority is inseparable from our idea of the ruler; because the ruler is essentially a protector, and only where men see or experience superiority do they always see and experience protection. Superior power is and always has been the shelter of the weak. Superior strength is and always has been something to cling to; while superior knowledge is and always has been something awakening trust and confidence. It is the marked superiority of the adult in strength, knowledge and power that first captivates and makes a voluntary slave of the child. It is the marked, though momentary, superiority of the Alpine guide which makes the tourists in his charge like unto menials doing his bidding.

Without superiority protection is impossible; it is a pretence, a farce. But to benefit from superiority presupposes an attitude of obedience. Not only does one honour superiority by obeying it, but obedience is actually the only way of using superiority, or of profiting by it.

The obedience which is of value, which is fruitful and which is lasting, is of that kind which redounds in some way to the advantage of those who obey. Where it is simply the outcome of coercing without benefiting the subject, it not only tends to become sterile, but also stands always on the brink of revolt. Great ruling castes have never failed to understand this. No ruling caste, perhaps, ever made a greater number of bloodless and victorious invasions than the Incas of ancient Peru. Again and again the tribes whose territories they overran laid down their arms and submitted to their rule, overcome by the persuasion of their superiority alone. But in support of the contention that the Incas understood, as all great

[1] *On the Spirit of Patriotism* (Davies, 1775), pp. 20–21. Let me also recall Charles I's comment on the Petition of Right, just after he had granted it: " It is my maxim that the people's liberties strengthen the King's prerogative, and the King's prerogative is to defend the people s libertie "

rulers have understood, what the obedience of these subject tribes implied, and what duties they (the Incas) had to perform in return, the anthropologist Letourneau gives us an interesting anecdote.

The Inca, Huay na-Capac, having invaded the territory of a very savage and bestial people, discovered that they had neither covering for their bodies nor homes to live in; that they were addicted to homo-sexual practices, and that they were horribly disfigured by labial ornaments such as the Botocudos of Brazil were wont to wear. He concluded from their habits and their general aspect that they were quite incapable of improvement, far less, therefore, of civilisation; and, turning away from them in disgust, he observed, " Here are a people who do not *deserve* to obey us! " [1]

I need not labour this point. No ruler who did not earnestly believe that obedience to his rule must be an advantage, and must remain an advantage, to those who obeyed him could have used such language. These words were perhaps the finest ever pronounced by a powerful, conquering people, in turning away from an inferior race which it lay in their power to oppress or to exterminate, if not to improve. That one sentence involves a whole cosmogony, very strange to our modern notions; but it also implies an understanding of the relationship of the obedient to the obeyed, which is no less strange to us of the twentieth century than it is likewise unquestionably profound and correct.

As Thomas Hobbes wisely said, " The end of obedience is protection, wheresoever a man seeth it, either in his own or in another's sword, nature applieth his obedience to it, and his endeavour to maintain it." [2]

Thus to disobey is not only to dishonour, but to deny superiority.[3]

---

[1] *L'évolution de l'éducation*, by Ch. Letourneau, p. 209. The italics are mine.—A. M. L.

[2] *Leviathan*, Chapter XXI.

[3] *Ibid.*, Chapter X. " To obey is to honour, because no man obeys

A DEFENCE OF ARISTOCRACY

When all the claims of both the "craft" and the "tutorship" of governing are conscientiously met by rulers, then only can it be truly said that they rule by divine right; and nothing but a *vis major*, such as an earthquake, a devastating flood, a destructive comet or a superior Force, can shake them from their position of power.

Admitting, therefore, that the ability to appreciate superiority is to hand, all insurrections and rebellions, when they are internal troubles and do not arise from sedition introduced from outside by a rival power, are always questions of the heart. They are but rarely even economical in their nature. They are always a sign that rulers have lost their essential quality—superiority—that the "craft" and "tutorship" of governing are inadequately exercised, and that the ruled no longer admit the divine right of those above them.[1] For as Bolingbroke justly observes, "A divine right to govern *ill* is an absurdity: to assert it is blasphemy. A people may raise a bad prince to the throne; but a good king alone can derive his right to govern from God."[2]

---

them whom they think have no power to help or hurt them. And consequently to disobey is to dishonour."

[1] See Disraeli's *Coningsby* (Langdon Davies Edition), p. 290. "I think," said Sidonia, "that there is no error so vulgar as to believe that revolutions are occasioned by economical causes. They come in, doubtless, very often to precipitate a catastrophe, but rarely do they occasion one. I know no period, for example, when physical comfort was more diffused in England than in 1640. England had a moderate population, a very improved agriculture, a rich commerce; yet she was on the eve of the greatest and most violent changes that she has as yet experienced. . . . Admit it, the cause was not physical. The imagination of England rose against the Government. It proves that when that faculty is astir in a nation it will sacrifice even physical comfort to follow its impulses."

[2] *The Idea of a Patriot King* (Davies, 1775), pp. 78–79. See also Thomas Hobbes' *Leviathan*, Chapter XXI. "The obligation of subjects to the sovereign is understood to last as long, and no longer, than the power lasteth by which he is able to protect them." Here Hobbes does not even consider good or bad government, but simply "the power to protect," which, if failing, relieves the inferior of his attitude of subjection.

I have already described the qualities which constitute the chief superiority of the true ruler. I said they were taste and good judgment, arising directly from the promptings of fortunate and flourishing life in the superior man.

Are such men born to a nation? Do men who *know* what flourishing life wants, and who thus stand higher than their fellows—men who are wise enough, strong enough and conscientious enough to undertake the appalling responsibility that ruling implies—come into existence among ordinary mortals?

Most certainly they do. Every nation gets them. Not every nation, however, is wise enough to use them. It is true that they appear more frequently in ages of order and of long tradition than in ages of anarchy and constant change; because their very rule, *which is a reflection of themselves*, must, in order to be good, be the emanation of something square, symmetrical and harmonious. They themselves, therefore, must be something square, symmetrical and harmonious in body and spirit. But how is squareness in body and spirit, symmetry and harmony attained in one man? Only by long tradition, only by the long cultivation, through generations, of the same virtues, the same tastes and the same aversions; only by the steady and unremitting storing and garnering of strength, conscientiousness and honesty. It is only thus that a man can be produced who never hesitates between two alternatives, and whose "conscience" is the definite voice of his ancestors saying "yes" or "no," "we did like this," or "we did not do like this," every time he braces himself for action.

And that is why the true ruler, the true superior man, is always a beautiful man, according to the standard of beauty of his people.[1] Because regular features, strong

[1] According to an early Peruvian legend, the first Incas who acquired a hold upon the uncivilised population of ancient Peru impressed and awed their subject people by their beauty. See Ch. Letourneau, *L'évolution de l'éducation*, p. 196.

features, harmonious features and grace of body are bred only by a regular life lasting over generations, strength of character exercised for generations, harmonious action enduring for generations, and that mastery in action which is the result of long practice for generations, and which leads to ease in action and therefore to grace.

He who doubts that this long tradition produces that beauty of body and grace of countenance and build which, when it expresses itself in the art of ruling or any other kind of art, must produce beauty, harmony and grace, contradicts not only one of the most fundamental beliefs of mankind, but also one of the most fundamental facts of science.

As early as the time of Mencius, one of the most noted of the followers of Confucius, this belief was already pronounced quite categorically, though unscientifically, as follows—

"What belongs by his nature to the superior man are benevolence, righteousness, propriety and knowledge. These are rooted in his heart; their growth and manifestation are a mild harmony appearing in the countenance, a rich fulness in the back, and the character imparted by the four limbs. Those limbs understand to arrange themselves without being told." [1]

And men like Dr. Reibmayr have since shown conclusively with what care and what scrupulous observance of traditional customs and rites the characteristic type of beauty of a race or a tribe, and therefore the superlative beauty of the superior individual in that race or tribe, are attained. [2]

[1] *Chinese Classics*, Vol. II, The Works of Mencius, Book VII, Chap. 21. The Jews also recognised this fact very early in their history. See the laws concerning the beauty of the body, or rather the faults of the body in regard to the ruling priesthood (Leviticus xxi. 16-25), whilst there is an ancient Arab proverb which proves conclusively that the Arabs laid and still lay great store by the message that a face and body reveal. The proverb is : "When you do not know a man's parents look at his appearance."

[2] See his *Inzucht und Vermischung* (Leipzig, 1897).

THE ARISTOCRAT

We know that beauty of design or construction always involves a certain observance of order and balance. Why, then, should the production of beauty in the human race be an exception to this rule? And if bodily beauty is the creation of order lasting over generations, then, since the spirit is but the emanation of the body, a beautiful spirit must likewise depend upon the same laws that govern the production of a beautiful body, and the two are inseparable. None but shallow people deny this. None but those who are hopelessly corrupted by the dangerous errors of democratic disorder and Puritanism ever doubt that beauty of body and spirit must be related. Herbert Spencer is among the philosophers who insisted upon this relationship, and his essay on the subject is, in my opinion, the most valuable treatise he ever wrote.[1]

An ugly or repulsive aristocrat is, therefore, a contradiction in terms? Certainly!

What is the only creed that can be offended at such a doctrine? A creed that maintains not only that body and spirit are distinct, but also that the body is in any case ignoble, and that only a beautiful spirit can sanctify and justify a body, whether it be beautiful or botched.

But the definition of the true superior man or aristocrat which I gave at the beginning of the discussion—that he was a fortunate stroke of nature's dice, a synopsis and digest of flourishing and full life—precludes the very possibility of his being an ill-shaped or ugly man. It was, however, necessary to give a more detailed demonstration of the quality "beauty," as nowadays, strange as it may seem, the attitude I assume in this respect is not exactly taken for granted.

Now, in advancing the proposition that a community of men, whether numbering tens, or hundreds of thousands,

[1] See Vol. II, *Collected Essays*, p. 387, "Personal Beauty." Schopenhauer, in his essay "Zur Physiognomik" (Chapter XXIX of the second volume of the *Parerga and Paralipomena*), also upholds the doctrine of the fundamental agreement of body and spirit. See also p. 317 of this book (Chapter VII).

should be governed only by the few, I am not guilty of very great heterodoxy, even from the purely Liberal standpoint; for even so thorough a Liberal as John Stuart Mill accepted this as a principle, and argued that the most a Popular Parliament could do was to play the part of a supreme Watch Committee.[1] But this amounts to no more than to say that government must always be with the consent of the people—a principle which the Chinese have observed for centuries, although the Chinese people are not actually represented by delegates.

Nobody, however, would cavil at the idea of all government being carried on with the consent of the people. Of course, the people must watch that they are well governed. The very condition of rule by Divine Right, as I have stated above, involves this proviso. And aristocracies who imagine that they can rule hedonistically and egotistically without the consent of the people are bound to fail and to be swept away.

In regard to this matter, it is surely a significant fact that such very profound, though vastly different, thinkers as the Chinaman Mencius and the Italian St. Thomas Aquinas [2]—thinkers separated from each other not only by centuries of time, but also by thousands of leagues of territory—should both have conceded the right of revolution to a badly ruled people. Mencius, that wise follower of Confucius, in addition to justifying regicide in the case of an unjust sovereign,[3] stated as a principle that " if the

---

[1] *Representative Government*, Chapter V. " Instead of the function of governing, for which it is so radically unfit, the proper office of a representative assembly is to watch and control the government ; to throw the light of publicity on its acts ; to compel a full exposition and justification of all of them which any one considers questionable, to censure them if found condemnable, and, if men who compose the government abuse their trust, or fulfil it in a manner which conflicts with the deliberate sense of the nation, to expel them from office, and either expressly or virtually appoint their successors."

[2] See Burckhardt, *Die Kultur der Renaissance in Italien* (10th Ed.), Vol. I, p. 6.

[3] See *The Chinese Classics* (translated by James Legge, D.D.), Vol. II, Book I, Part II, Chap. 8.

Emperor be not benevolent, he cannot preserve the Empire from passing from him. If the sovereign of a state be not benevolent, he cannot preserve his Kingdom." [1]

I wish to lay no stress, therefore, upon the contention that government should be carried on by the few—that seems to be generally accepted by the consensus of intelligent thinkers on this matter. I only wish to emphasise the point that the few who do govern should be of the stamp that I have described above.

Only on that condition can government be successful; for, as I have said, there is not only a "craft," but also a "tutorship," of governing.

I am, therefore, concerned to show that whoever these few may be to whom the government of a nation is entrusted, they should be able not only to manage the practical business of public affairs, but also to direct, inspire and animate the hearts and imagination of the people. The very fact that here in England we already hear some people ignorant and materialistic enough to clamour for a government of merely business men, and that no very great alarm or panic has been caused by the suggestion, shows how very far we have departed from the wise economy that never forgets that there is a "tutorship" as well as a "craft" of governing.

Since men *are* born unequal, and natural distinctions between them as regards nobility, strength, beauty, size, intelligence and elevation of spirit are undeniable, the wisest régime is the one in which these distinctions are not ignored or overlooked, but exploited, placed, used and turned to the best advantage. Admitting that some must and can rule, there will be others who will have to supply the community with the material needs of life, others who will be the servants of these, and so on, until that labourer is reached whose capacities fit him only for the plough or the spade. If, however, the society is to benefit from the rule of the superior man with taste and judgment, a certain spiritual tendency will have to be

[1] *Chinese Classics*, Book IV, Chap. 3.

made to prevail by him, which will direct the manner in which these material supplies must be used, the method and moderation with which the people's passions and desires may be indulged, so that nothing may be misused or abused, and so that no gift of the earth or of the body may turn to a curse and a poison. A certain art of life must, therefore, enter into the community—a certain good taste on which its power and permanence depend.[1] There must be not only producers and consumers; even the lowest in the community must develop a heart, and that heart must be furnished.

"With fear and trembling," said Confucius, "take care of the heart of the people: that is the root of the matter in education—that is the highest education."

And who can supply this furniture of the heart—who can direct and guide mere industry, if not the man of higher judgment, *i. e.* of good taste, who sets, as it were, "the tone" of his people.?

In his *Story of a Chinese Oxford Movement* the China-man Ku Hung-Ming [2] says: "In a healthy and normal state of society in China, the nation has to depend first upon the power of industry of the people or working class to produce food and other necessary commodities for the national well-being. The nation has next to depend upon the power of intelligence of the Chinese literati to train, educate and regulate the power of industry of the people, and properly to distribute the product of that industry. Lastly, and most important of all, the nation has to depend upon the nobility of character of the Manchu Aristocracy

---

[1] See Thomas Hobbes' *Leviathan* (Chapter XXIX). "Though nothing can be immortal which mortals make, yet, if men had the use of reason they pretend to, their commonwealth might be secured at least from perishing from internal disease. For by the nature of their institutions they are designed to live as long as mankind or as the laws of nature, or as justice itself which gives them life. Therefore, when they come to be dissolved, not by external violence but by intestine disorder, the fault is not in men, as they are the 'matter,' but as they are the 'makers' and orderers of men."

[2] p. 4.

to direct—to see that the power of industry of the people is nobly directed, directed to noble purpose, and also that the product of that industry is justly and humanely distributed. In short, the power of industry of the people in China has to produce; the power of intelligence of the Chinese literati has to educate; and the nobility of the Manchu Aristocracy has to direct the power of industry of the people to a noble national life—to a noble civilisation. Foreigners who have travelled in the interior of China and seen the remains of bridges and canals in the country will understand what I mean by noble direction of national life—the direction of the power of industry of the people as regards things material to noble purposes. As for things of the mind, works such as the great K'anghsi dictionary will attest sufficiently to the nobility of character of the early Manchu Emperors, and their ability to direct the power of industry of the mind of the nation to noble purposes."

Hence it seems to be an essential part of the highest utility in a nation that there should be some members of it who stand much higher than the rest, and who can give a meaning and a direction to their inferiors' manual or mental labour. Thus, even admitting that the essential and most difficult task of general legislation has been already satisfactorily accomplished by an artist legislator, I maintain that those who continue the work must be cultured, tasteful and artistic men; otherwise that very humanity which insists upon the man bearing the hardest material burden of the community, being materially content and spiritually well-nourished, will be violated and spurned, to the glory of the Devil and of the Dragon of Anarchy.

But that flourishing life in body and spirit which is the *sine qua non* of the superior man, of the artist ruler, is not bred by struggle, manual labour, strenuous bodily exertions and the neglect of spiritual pursuits. The man who possesses this endowment of superlative vitality in body and spirit will be very largely dependent, as his

father, grandfather and great-grandfather were before
him, upon the industry of the people. He will, therefore,
have to pay for the glory of his exalted calling, not only
by being exploited as a responsible ruler by the mass
beneath him, but by being dependent upon it for his
sustenance and security. That is why it is so preposterous
and unintelligent for a ruler-aristocrat to regard himself
as a mere man of wealth or property, whose means can
be consumed in a round of pleasure or in a life of ease
without any concern about the duties that all golden and
well-fed leisure tacitly implies. It amounts to a miscon-
ception and a debasing of his dignity for him to rank
himself with the ordinary plutocrat, who simply has no
duties because he has no gifts. If he, the ruler-aristocrat,
understands the price of aristocratic leisure, he must know
that it is meditation—meditation upon the profound
problems of the " craft " and " tutorship " of his exalted
calling. He should remember that the mere " business "
or " craft " of his duties will probably be taken for granted
by those he governs. They will not even reckon his
exertions in this respect; for when all goes smoothly, who
suspects that there are pains behind the process?

What they will not take for granted, however, will be
his pains about their heart, if he really does take pains
in this matter. This presupposes a divine element in
him that all men do not possess—it is the element which
distinguishes the true ruler from that other kind of
governor who is efficient only in the business or " craft "
of ruling.

It would seem a perfectly natural thing that the ruler
who was very much in earnest about the *craft* and the
tutorship of his calling could not possibly be a very
happy man, as people understand such a creature nowadays. The ordinary pleasures of common human life
would, by virtue of his very office and of his vast knowledge, fall rather short of his concept of what constituted
happiness. He would have to be content with the secret
joys that attend the artist at his work—that is the utmost

that his life could bring him in the matter of happiness. But as to the rest, as to those joys which constitute the staple diet of the present plutocratic hedonist, he, the ruler, would be a very sad man indeed. For apart from his higher taste in happiness, his very respect for those depending upon him for their security and their guidance would drive his sense of responsibility so high as to keep him ever vigilant, ever thoughtful, and perhaps ever melancholy too.[1] Those who are experienced even in so humble an art as that of keeping children happy will understand what I mean when I say that the hand which dispenses happiness does not necessarily quiver with joy itself.

The fact that this concern about the contentedness and comfort of the man who does the rough work of the State constitutes an important part of that sense of responsibility which all true rulers must feel, finds an excellent formula in one of my favourite anecdotes about Napoleon.

It is given by Emerson in his essay *Napoleon, or the Man of the World*, and is as follows: " When walking with Mrs. Balcombe, some servants carrying heavy boxes passed on the road, and Mrs. Balcombe desired them, in rather an angry tone, to keep back. Napoleon interfered, saying, ' Respect the burden, madam! ' "

" Respect the burden! " This is what all noble and successful rulers have done. A less noble nature, a nature unfitted for the task of ruling, such, for instance, as the

---

[1] See *Madame de Rémusat's Memoires*, Vol. I, p. 101. Speaking of Napoleon she says : " *La gravité était le fond de son caractère ; non celle qui vient de la noblesse et de la dignité des habitudes, mais celle que donne la profondeur des méditations. Dans sa jeunesse il était viveur ; plus tard il devint triste . . .*" See also Bolingbroke, *On the Spirit of Patriotism* (Davies, 1775), pp. 5–6. Speaking of the two kinds of men, the Vulgar and the Few, Bolingbroke says: " The latter come into the world, or at least continue in it after the effects of surprise and inexperience are over, like men who are sent on more important errands. They observe with distinction, they admire with knowledge. They may indulge themselves in pleasure ; but as their industry is not employed about trifles, so their amusements are not made the business of their lives."

nature of most of our English and European aristocrats, past and present, does not understand or pay heed to such a principle. As an example of a vulgar person's behaviour in circumstances almost similar to those described in Emerson's anecdote, hear the following—

"More than forty years ago, a party of six young Englishmen went out for an excursion in the country in the neighbourhood of one of the Treaty Ports [of China]. They were entirely ignorant of Chinese etiquette and custom, and while walking along one of the narrow paths at the side of a paddy-field they met an old man carrying a load, whom they thought very rudely insisted on the path being given up to him and his burden, until he had passed with it. They pushed him out of the way, and struck him with their sticks for his rudeness, entirely unaware that they were the offenders, and gross offenders too. The path being narrow and there being no room for the encumbered and unencumbered to pass at the same time, the Chinese, with commendable common sense, allow the burden-bearer in such cases the right of way, while the unencumbered, who can easily step off the way, do so. . . . The villagers, indignant at the insult, rose, took the young Englishmen into custody, and avenged their wrongs by putting them to death, after some days of imprisonment." [1]

In my opinion, of course, the execution of these six Englishmen was entirely justified. Why? Because they had sinned against a divine precept. Those representatives of flourishing life, Confucius and Napoleon, had taught independently that the burden must be respected. [2] This, then, was a law of flourishing life itself. To flout the

---

[1] *Things Chinese*, by J. Dyer Ball, pp. 253–254.
[2] Petrarch is another good instance of a profound thinker who was no less exacting in the demands he made upon the wise ruler. Addressing his patron, the Lord of Padua, he said : " Thou must not be the master but the father of thy subjects, and must love them as thy children ; yea, as members of thy body." See Burckhardt, op. cit., p. 9.

bidding of flourishing life is, as I have said in the early part of this discussion, rank blasphemy. And blasphemy of that sort deserves death even more than murder does, because it jeopardises not only the life of one man, but the life of a whole nation. You may argue that the six young Englishmen were ignorant of Chinese customs and manners, and had different manners and customs in their own home. But this only makes the matter worse; for it means that instead of being only half-a-dozen isolated dangerous and blaspheming barbarians, they must hail from a land teeming with such blaspheming barbarians, otherwise they would have learnt that fundamental principle of flourishing life at home. The sooner six such dangerous creatures were killed, therefore, the better.

The Chinese burden-bearer was accustomed to live in a country where some true ruler spirit was rife; he, therefore, felt justified in enforcing that principle of flourishing life which reads " Respect the burden." The Englishmen, on the other hand, came from a country where puling sentimental charity towards the burden-bearer went hand in hand with brutal exploitation of him. They were, therefore, dangerous; the blood of millions of burden-bearers was already on their hands before they touched that Chinese workman, and it was right that they should be slaughtered like blasphemers.

The light that the moral of these two anecdotes throws upon the downfall of the aristocracies in Europe is very interesting indeed. The omission to " respect the burden" is a violation not only of the " craft," but also of the " tutorship," of governing.

And what is there that is not included under the head of " respect the burden "? [1] How many problems, socio-

---

[1] Many instances could be given of Napoleon's unswerving adherence to this principle, and, in his *Memoirs to serve for the History of Napoleon I* the Baron de Ménéval (English translation) gives two interesting anecdotes, which, though not important in themselves, reveal the consistency of Napoleon's ruler instincts. The first, on p. 126, is as follows : " M. Amédée Jaubert, who had been General Bonaparte's interpreter

logical, physiological, artistic and political, on whose proper solution the contentedness and comfort of the burden-bearer depend, have not to be faced and mastered before the "respect of the burden" has exacted its last office from the ruler-aristocrat and his peers? No wonder Bolingbroke, when speaking of rulers, was able to say, "They may indulge in pleasure; but as their industry is not employed upon trifles, so their amusements are not made the business of their lives." [1]

Indeed, if rulers take their task to heart, the mere "craft" of governing, apart from the "tutorship" of governing, is enough to tax the energies of the greatest, and to make them pay very, very dearly for the privilege of being at the head of the social pyramid.

There seems to be very convincing evidence to show that the commercial aristocracy of Venice approximated very nearly to the ideal rule of the best.[2] It consisted of men of great taste, courage, honour and intelligence, of men who could be, and were, both rigorous and kind. "Care of the people, in peace as well as in war," says Burckhardt, "was characteristic of this government, and

---

[in the Egyptian campaign], said that one day seeing the General returning from the trenches, harassed with fatigue and dying with thirst, he had told him that a Christian had just brought a skin of wine as a present, and that Bonaparte ordered it to be immediately carried to the ambulance." The second (pp. 127–128) tells how Napoleon, during his sojourn in Cairo, arranged for a military band to play various national airs "every day at noon, on the squares opposite the hospitals," to "inspire the sick with gaiety, and recall to their memory the most beautiful moments of their past campaigns." And here is Méneval's comment on the anecdote : "This mark of interest given to poor sick men, to unhappy wounded soldiers, sad and discouraged at the thought of their distant homes, reveals a delicate attention, a maternal solicitude, as Comte d'Orsay expressed it, and that provident goodness which was the basis of Napoleon's character" See also the Duke of Rovigo's *Memoirs*, which is full of instances of Napoleon's generous good-nature where his inferiors or dependants were concerned.

[1] See note on p. 19.
[2] Interesting confirmation of this view is given by E. A. Freeman in his *Comparative Politics*, p. 266.

its attention to the wounded, even to those of the enemy, excited the admiration of other states. Public institutions of every kind found in Venice their pattern; the pensioning of retired servants was carried out systematically, and included a provision for widows and orphans." [1] And if it had not been for the peculiar instability which constitutes one of the worst evils of a State depending for its existence on trading alone, this remarkable little band of rulers might have given Europe a happy and rare example of permanence and equilibrium.

If a race, or a nation, or a people be blessed with a few such rulers, then its security, comfort and heart will be in safe keeping. And not only will the industry of the people reward the ruler and make him great and powerful, but their character, which is the most important of all, by becoming an approximation to the type dictated by the voice of flourishing life, will constitute a sound and stable basis upon which an almost *permanent creation may be built by the aristocrat if he chooses.*

And the converse of this condition gives the exact formula of decadence and degeneration. For what are decadence and degeneration? Decadence and degeneration are states in a nation's career in which it has forgotten the precepts and values of flourishing life, and in which the voice of flourishing life can no longer make itself heard in its midst. Why, then, are England, France, Germany and almost the whole of Europe decadent to-day? Because for many hundreds of years now the precepts and principles of flourishing life have been neglected, forgotten and even scorned in the Western world. Decadence means practically that the voice of flourishing life has been silenced, that the true aristocrat is dethroned or no longer bred.

You must not, however, suppose that in a decadent or degenerate State the people, the masses, are guided by no taste, by no values. Because nothing could be more plain to-day than the fact that they are so guided or prompted;

[1] Op. cit., p. 67.

But the taste which guides them is confused, uncertain, independent of any higher or wise authority; it is self-made, reared on insufficient knowledge, culture and health. And, therefore, the promptings of their heart, instead of leading them to an ascent in life, lead them to further degeneration. It is bad taste which reigns to-day. All taste which is not the precept of flourishing life must be bad or dangerous taste.

With Guicciardini, Disraeli also realised the importance of this matter of the heart and character of a nation, and in *Coningsby* we read: "A political institution is a machine; the motive power is in the national character —with that it rests whether the machine will benefit society, or destroy it."[1]

Thus all attempts at ruling a people on purely material-istic lines, all attempts at exploiting their industry without tending their heart, their imagination and their character, must and do invariably fail. A people that is going to flourish must be taught a certain fastidiousness in the manner in which it works and spends the fruit of its labour;[2] it must be given a sound taste for discerning good from bad, that which is beneficial from that which is harmful, and healthy, vital conduct from sick, degenerate conduct. I do not mean that they must have that spon-taneous and unerring taste which is the possession of nature's "lucky strokes"—the incarnations of full and flourishing life—who are the true aristocrats; but I mean that they should have a taste founded on likes and dis-likes, points of view and opinions, acquired from a higher,

[1] Langdon Davies Edition, p. 290.

[2] See Ku Hung-Ming, *The Story of a Chinese Oxford Movement*, pp. 13 and 14 : "When the power of industry of a people in a community or nation is nobly directed and not wasted, then the community or nation is truly rich, not in money or possession of big ugly houses, but rich in the health of the body and beauty of the soul of the people. . . . For without these things which Goethe calls the beautiful, there is no nobility of character, and without nobility of character, as we have seen, the power of industry of the people in a nation will be wasted in ignoble and wasteful consumption."

guiding and discriminating authority. "For," as Hobbes says, "the actions of men proceed from their opinions, and in the well-governing of opinions consisteth the well-governing of men's actions." [1]

It is for this reason that I believe that the factor which has largely contributed to the downfall of the European aristocracies has been the relegation of the care of the people's character to a body distinct from and often hostile to the actual governors.[2] For apart from the fact that the credo of this independent body, the Church, happens to be hostile to sharp distinctions between man and man, and irrespective of the undoubted truth that to it all men, whether aristocrats or plebeians, have always appeared more or less as equals, or at least as subordinates who, when the interests of the Church were at stake, might, if necessary, be treated as a mass without distinctions of rank, there is this feature in the influence of the Church which should not be forgotten: it robbed the rulers of that active exercise of the "tutorship" of governing by which the people, as we have seen, lay such great store, and which is the most potent medium for binding a people and their rulers together. Because, as Hobbes says, "Benefits oblige, and obligation is thraldom, and unrequitable obligation perpetual thraldom." [3] And no benefit is more unrequitable than that gift to the heart which makes a man conscious of a higher purpose and aim in life than the mere material round of everyday existence. The idea of an ecclesiastical body ministering to the spiritual wants of the people is not, however, necessarily anti-aristocratic in itself, for the Church might have been conducted and controlled absolutely by the aristocracy, as it was in Venice in the hey-day of her power. It is the fact that it was not so controlled by the majority of aristocracies that proved harmful to them, and Machiavelli

[1] *Leviathan*, Chapter XVIII.
[2] See Palgrave's *History of the Anglo-Saxons,* where the Church is shown to have been "the corner-stone of English liberty."
[3] *Leviathan*, Chapter XI.

is among the most distinguished politicians who understood this.[1]

But the relation of the ecclesiastical body to the people in Europe had another and perhaps still more deleterious influence, though, maybe, it was more indirect than the first. For by undertaking independently to minister to the hearts of the people, not for a national or racial purpose, but for a purpose that lay beyond races and nations, it not only undermined the jealous love of race and nationality which we find so constructive a force in the Greeks of the seventh and sixth centuries B.C., but also gradually divorced the very idea of aristocracy from that noble duty of caring for the hearts of the masses, which was the very task that gave all the gravity and higher responsibility to the calling of the ruler-aristocrat. By doing this, it destroyed in part his conscientiousness and his earnestness, and left him only the "craft" or business of governing, which, as I have pointed out, is much more often taken for granted by a people, even when it is done with the most consummate skill, than that more delicate and artistic duty of firing their imaginations and filling their hearts, which constitutes the divine element of rulership.

"I say it seems to me," says Bolingbroke,[2] "that the Author of nature has thought fit to mingle from time to time, among the societies of men, a few, and but a few of those, on whom He is graciously pleased to bestow a larger proportion of the ethereal spirit than is given in the ordinary course of His providence to the sons of men. These are they who engross almost the whole reason of the species, who are born to instruct, to guide and to preserve; who are designed to be the tutors and the guardians of human kind. When they prove such, they exhibit to us example of the highest virtue and the truest piety; and they deserve to have their festivals kept,

[1] See his reply to Cardinal Rouen in Chapter III of *The Prince*.
[2] *On the Spirit of Patriotism* (Davies, 1775), p. 2.

instead of the pack of *Anachorites* and *Enthusiasts* with whose names the calendar is crowded and disgraced. When these men apply their talents to other purposes, when they strive to be great and despise being good, they commit a most sacrilegious breach of trust; they pervert the means, they defeat as far as in them lies the designs of Providence, and disturb in some sort the system of Infinite Wisdom. To misapply these talents is the most diffused, and therefore the greatest, of crimes in its nature and consequences, but to keep them unexerted and unemployed is a crime too."

And now, apart from the broad and general advantages to which I have already referred, what other real and lasting benefits does human society derive from these divine missionaries sent direct from flourishing life who occasionally descend among us, as Bolingbroke says, and who are much more deserving of a place in the Calendar than all the neurotic, exasperated and bitter saints who now figure there?

By the order and stability they establish, by their instinctive avoidance of those by-paths which lead to degeneration, and their deliberate choice of those highways leading to the ascent of their fellows, they give rise to everything which is of value on earth and which makes life a boon instead of a bane.

Beauty, Art, Will, Conscience and Spiritual Strength to face and to endure even the inevitable pangs and pains of a full life—nay, the very willingness to embrace them, because they are known to have a vital purpose—these are some of the things that can be reared by long tradition and careful discipline alone, and these are some of the things that depend for their existence on the aristocratic rule. For real Beauty is impossible without regular and stable living, lasting over generations; real Art is impossible without surplus health and energy, the outcome of generations of careful storing and garnering of vital forces, and without that direction and purpose which the supreme artist—the tasteful legislator—alone can give to the minor artists, be they painters, architects or musicians, within his realm. Will is impossible without sound instincts getting the mastery of a family or a tribe through generations spent in the rearing of those instincts, and causing that family or tribe passionately to desire one thing more than another; while Conscience and Spiritual Strength depend for their degree of development simply upon the length of the line of ancestors who have systematically built them up for an individual. For what I call conscience is nothing more than the voice of a man's ancestors speaking in him, saying this is right and that is wrong, and uttering this accompanying comment to his deeds, either feebly or powerfully in proportion to the length of the time during which unbroken traditions have lasted in his family. And Spiritual Strength in facing or assailing difficulties or pain is the outcome of the consciousness of being right, which arises from the fact that the comment of one's ancestors in one's breast is heard to be on one's side and with one's cause.

For all these things to be reared, even for the unbroken tradition, on which these things depend, to be established, there must, however, be great stability and permanence in the institutions of a race or a people, and it is the direction of flourishing life, alone, speaking through her representatives, that can reveal the good taste and the good judgment necessary for the preservation of such stability and permanence. For stability and permanence are desired only when beauty is present. When, therefore, we see things constantly changing, as they are to-day, when every day brings a new custom and a new curse, we may feel sure not only that the voice of the real ruler is silent in our midst, but that life is growing conscious of her ugliness. For, like a beautiful woman looking into a mirror, a people who have once achieved beauty, real beauty, and caught a glimpse of this beauty in all the departments of their social life, *must* cry for permanence rather than change, stability rather than flux. It is only then that change is the most dreaded catastrophe of all;

for change threatens to rob the beauty from the face, the limbs and trunk of their civilisation, and their pride and love of its beauty is outraged by the very thought of such vandalism. The permanence and stability of a people's institutions are called by the ugly name of "stagnation" only when these institutions have little or no beauty.

But there is one more problem, and a very important one, which finds its best solution in the rule, not of all men by their equals, but of the mass of men by the aristocrat as I have attempted to sketch him in the preceding pages.

In all civilised human communities there have been and always will be a certain number of menial offices that some have to perform for others—offices which do not necessarily debase, but which may on occasion humiliate. It is, therefore, clear that in order that even the menial office may seem to have a sheen of gold upon it, the personality for whom it is performed must be such as to glorify it and transfigure it in the eyes of the servant. It is not only foolish, it is actually brutal to lose sight of this fact. Look into yourselves and inquire when it is that you feel humiliated by the performance of menial offices. You know perfectly well that for some people you perform them quite cheerfully, willingly; for others you resolutely decline to do so. What makes the difference in your attitude? It is useless to point to the menial office itself, for we can imagine that as remaining the same for all cases. What is it, then, that effects the change in your attitude? Obviously it is the quality of the person for whom the menial office is performed.

When men exist, therefore, whose characters and achievements shed a glamour upon everything that surrounds them, no duty they can impose upon their immediate entourage, no effort they can demand of it, whether it be the bearing of children or the building of a pyramid, can be felt as a humiliation or as an act of oppression. And it is only in such conditions that menial offices are performed daily, year in, year out, century after century, without a suggestion of that rankling spirit of detestation and loathing which, when it ultimately finds a vent, rises up in the form of the black cloud of revolution and revolt, and thunders out the cry of Liberty and Emancipation!

CHAPTER II

"No slavery can be so effectually brought and fixed upon us, as parliamentary slavery."—BOLINGBROKE, *A Dissertation upon Parties*, p. 151.

THE House of Lords has been deprived of much of its power. In the summer of 1911 it stood against the wall and emptied almost all its pockets on demand. With remarkable meekness it even assisted its opponents in fleecing it of its legitimate rights.

It is hard to picture a group of English schoolboys, however unnerved, however out-numbered, yielding passively, without showing fight, to a general raid on their pockets, especially if one or two neutral mates were looking on. And yet we have seen a group of English peers perform this unsporting feat before the eyes of an assembled nation and of the whole world! B. M. S., in the *National Review* for October 1911, spoke of it as " the extraordinary act of cowardice and folly committed in the House of Lords on August the 10th ";[1] but the fact that he ascribed the responsibility of the act to bad leaders, and to Mr. Balfour in particular, does not in the least exonerate the Peers themselves from all blame in regard to the wretched business.

The passing of the Parliament Act was indeed a bloodless revolution of the most fundamental kind. Examine it for an instant in the fierce light which, as Lord Willoughby de Broke pointed out,[2] a certain able writer in

[1] Article : " The Champion Scuttler," p. 214.
[2] *National Review*, " The Tory Tradition," p. 208.

the *Academy* threw upon it, and the extent of its subversive character becomes doubly clear.

The said writer declared—

" In 1909 we had a House of Lords which we regarded as part of the bedrock of our constitution and its impregnable bulwark, whereas all the time it never rested on any more stable basis than this, that a Radical leader had only to come into office, to·bring in a Bill for its abolition, to call upon the Crown to create Peers, and there was an end of its existence. So that, so far from being founded upon rock, it was not even founded upon sand, it was established upon straw."

It was all very well for Lord Willoughby de Broke to say that " the repeal of the Parliament Act . . . is the first duty of the Unionist Party when returned to power," [1] but, as B. M. S. in the same number of the journal rightly observed : " How can the Parliament Bill be repealed when all the machinery of the official Unionist organisation was utilised to induce certain renegade Unionist Peers to vote for it? Repeal in such circumstances will only add infamy to infamy." [2]

Nor did Lord Willoughby de Broke entirely clear matters up when he spoke of the destruction of the House of Lords " as part of the class war that a certain type of Radical has waged for many generations," [3] or of the Radicals themselves as having " the whole field of bribery and corruption and class hatred that we (the Tories) cannot touch." [4]

The best thing the noble Lord did say in his vigorous though to my mind somewhat shallow article, was that Tories should " drink copiously at the fount of Bolingbroke, Pitt and Beaconsfield." [5] In this sentence he really shows that he means business, and that he is vaguely

[1] Op. cit., p. 208.   [2] Op. cit., p. 215.
[3] Op. cit., p. 202.   [4] Op. cit., p. 210.
[5] Op. cit., p. 208. The inclusion of Pitt, however, makes me feel doubtful whether the writer really knew anything about the matter.

conscious of the great flaw in the policy and traditions of his caste.

For, in my opinion, it is inconceivable that a body of men could ever have been induced to connive, even for the purpose of strategy, in depriving themselves of a great and solemn right or privilege, unless a good deal of doubt had prevailed in their own minds concerning the sanctity and unassailability of that right or privilege.

It is true that, when the fell deed was about to be accomplished, a considerable amount of indignation and revolt was to be observed in the ranks of the Unionist Peerage; but the amputating operation was performed notwithstanding, and in a trice we all realised that the aristocrats—that is to say, the *hereditary* rulers of the country—the body of men who might have created a position for themselves so secure and so popular that nothing could have shaken it, had been given a smart *congé*, an unmistakable " Your services are no longer required! " and had been deprived of their full share in the determination of the nation's destiny.

Instinctively they must have felt that they did not deserve to keep the faith of those beneath them, otherwise, as I say, it is inconceivable that they should have shown no fight. They would have preferred to die, as Charles I did, rather than to relinquish an iota of their power, if they had really felt that they were ruling by Divine Right.

The problem which naturally confronts you, when you examine the event in detail is, how did the Lords grow sufficiently weak and doubtful of their superiority, sufficiently disliked and devoid of advocates among the people, to fall such an easy prey to the opposing party? This problem is neither so deep, nor so difficult as it would appear at first sight. If you have eyes to see, you can solve it by walking over Arundel Castle one summer's afternoon; you can solve it by reading the lives of the poets, the great prose-writers, painters, sculptors, politicians and general thinkers of England for the last two hundred years; you can even solve it by looking out into the streets of London, or by analysing the psychology of the Women's Suffrage Movement.

But however you may solve it, whatever your diagnosis may be, your conclusion is sure to be wrong, if, in company with the most stupid among the Tories, you set out with the assumption that class-hatred or class-envy was the starting-point of the recent attack on the Lords. For even supposing we acknowledge that Mr. Lloyd George has been unwarrantably bitter in a number of his speeches, does any reasonable man think that these speeches would have been of any avail if they had been pronounced among a people devoted to their rulers, and conscious of innumerable debts of gratitude to them? Does any one suppose that Mr. Lloyd George's eloquence could ever have succeeded in turning a loving child against its parents? The whole of human experience and human history denies this possibility.

Rulers who maintain their superiority and who make themselves indispensable to, and loved by, the community they rule, or whose beneficent power is so directly felt by the society over which they preside that there can be no doubt as to their value, stand almost quite immune from so-called class-hatred and class-envy; and even if such class-hatred and class-envy do exist among a small minority and lead to conspiracies, these can be treated very lightly.[1] Such rulers are just as immune as the good father from hatred or envy, and against them demagogues and revolutionary agitators can rant and rave to all eternity without succeeding in making a single convert. Rivals may arise against such rulers; but, generally speaking, in healthy communities, a *subject* movement to depose them cannot.

Now, looking at the present condition of England and

---

[1] See Machiavelli, *The Prince*, Chapter XIX. " I consider a prince right to reckon conspiracies of little account when his people hold him in esteem."

at the steps by which it has reached this condition, what is it precisely that we find?

We find a huge population of about forty millions, of which at least two-thirds are dissatisfied and resentful, and suffering from what might be termed genuine fear of what the future may bring; of which at least a third are either semi-sick or seriously sick, and of which at least a ninth are constantly on the threshold of starvation and unemployment. Labour troubles are not by any means the only signs which reveal the restless discontent of the subject masses to-day. These troubles among the workers do indeed show that there is something very seriously wrong; but does not the vast number of reform movements and organisations—from the Salvation Army to the Women's Suffrage societies—prove the same thing? If for the moment we leave the spiritual side, alone, of the Salvation Army out of our reckoning, what can we possibly think of a community in which even the material and practical work of an independent and unofficial organisation such as the Salvation Army, can be urgently needed and readily employed in order to supplement the care which the true rulers should take of their subjects? For it cannot be repeated too often, or too emphatically, that the only possible justification of the non-labouring, non-productive class, lies in their efficient discharge of the duty of protecting and guiding the labouring and productive masses. Any aristocracy that denies this principle is rightly doomed.

In the space of two centuries life in England has grown so complicated, and unrestricted competition in the field of modern capitalistic enterprise has shown that it can grind so many workers down to the level of characterless, spiritless and dependent paupers, that the question which presses continually for an answer is, What has been done by the rulers of the State to regulate, to guide, and *pari passu* to weigh, the value of each item in the incessant inrush of industrial and commercial innovations, and to guard against their evils for the present and the future?

A DEFENCE OF ARISTOCRACY

Any fool can realise a state of muddle, disorder and distress, once it has been created. But who has been wise enough to foresee such a state, to guard against it, or to render its fulfilment impossible?

There is but one answer to this question—Nobody!

According to the doctrine of experience which is sacrosanct in England and all countries like her, it would even have been considered sheer impudence on the part of any thinker to have prophesied, when, for instance, the machine began to show signs of mastering labour, that such and such a state of things would be the result of the innovation.[1]

The whole of the newspaper-reading middle-classes of the British Isles would have cried indignantly, " What is this man saying? Who can tell what the machine's mastery over men may lead to? Possibly the millenium! This thinker is not speaking from experience, how can he tell? "

According to the doctrine of experience one may wait for a whole nation to go stark raving mad before one arrests a development which has not yet been tested by time!

And these people who possess no imagination, no knowledge of true social laws or of human nature, were able to look on with equanimity while the official rulers of England did nothing to guide or direct the tremendous movement, industrial and commercial, of the eighteenth and nineteenth centuries, with its accompanying accumulation of vast urban populations; simply because, like their rulers, they were not people of culture, but creatures reared behind the shop-counter.

There was, however, some excuse for the ignorant middle-classes, upper and lower, if they were able to look on unalarmed at the appalling inrush of ill-considered innovations, especially during the nineteenth century. At

---

One of the few thinkers who did oppose machinery almost from its inception, the spirited William Cobbett, was regarded by those in power as an impudent upstart.

least they were not the aristocrats. Most of them had neither the education, nor the traditions, nor the travelled knowledge, nor above all the leisure of aristocrats. They were simply sheep who were allowed to bleat once at every general election and no more ; and even this influence exercised through the House of Representatives was, at least during the first half of the century, practically negligible. Their brains were cabbage and newspaper fed, and by way of intellectual refreshment all they had were the novels that became popular and the stimulating sermons of their clergy.

But there was absolutely no excuse for the aristocrats. They had a good many of the things which rendered men fit to grapple with problems sprouting up all about them. Moreover, they were once in a position when their word, if they had shown that it was prompted by a "respect for the burden," would have been listened to with interest and reverence. What happened?

They not only neglected the "craft" of governing, which as I have said is more often than not taken for granted by the subjects of a nation, even when they are well governed; but they also scouted the responsibility of the "tutorship" of governing. The character and spirit of the nation were allowed to rot from sheer neglect, or to be ministered to independently by ignorant subject minds (in no way representative of flourishing life), in the form of unguided religious maniacs and incompetent busybodies.

Foolishly, almost blindly, most of the rulers by birth in the British Isles actually regarded themselves merely as plutocrats whose peculiar privileges sent them by God implied no arduous duties, no responsibilities, and no cares beyond those of consolidating their position and rendering it as easy and as pleasurable as possible.

It should, of course, be remembered in this respect that about one half of the existing peerages were created in the nineteenth century, and for three hundred years at least the peers of the realm have been largely recruited from the capitalists. Still, the principle remains the same. However differently a man may feel, who is the descendant of a wealthy alderman or an industrial magnate, from him whose position and wealth come to him through land that has belonged to his family since the Norman conquest, wealth and power ought always to suggest certain responsibilities to their holders. Both are derived ultimately from the nation; both represent leisure obtained through the nation or some portion of it, and to the conscientious man who feels that a life of ease cannot be enjoyed for nothing, both ought to imply certain duties and obligations which cannot devolve upon the masses who are too deeply immersed in the daily struggle for existence to be able to direct this struggle from serene and peaceful heights above, so that it may redound to the credit and not to the shame of the community, so that it may conduce to the glory, permanence and supremacy of a great people, and not to that people's degradation.

But this obligation is all the more binding upon large landowners, seeing that in times past the very condition of land-tenure involved certain duties that could not be neglected with impunity. "The essence of the Feudal polity was that of protector and protected." [1] As Rogers says: "The English landowner of the thirteenth and fourteenth centuries did two things for the savage tenant. He guaranteed the King's peace, that is to say the continuity of the farmer's industry free from the risks of brigandage, and he taught him, by his own example and practice, the best system of agriculture which the age could develop." [2] Thus there was no suggestion of that unlimited possession without return or without proportionate protection or compensation to those not in possession, which is characteristic of the position of many of the landowners and plutocrats of the present day. On the contrary, as the same author argues, " It cannot be doubted,

[1] *Annals of the British Peasantry*, by R. M. Garnier, p. 116.
[2] See *The Industrial and Commercial History of England*, by James E. Thorold Rogers, p. 208.

if the language of those who wrote in early ages on the common law of England has any force whatever, that in theory the largest rights of the private owner of land were very limited and qualified." [1]

When, however, the large private owner of land, accustomed to the conditions of agricultural tenants, suddenly found himself in the late eighteenth and nineteenth centuries the possessor of extensive urban property, he seems to have regarded the changed condition as absolving him altogether from the ordinary duties of ownership, and there seems to have been no attempt on the part of the legislature to outline in any way a return in duty and protection to the urban tenant equivalent to that which was expected from the mediæval landowner. Thus, in the light of this aspect alone, the Parliament Bill of 1911 might well be regarded simply as a belated expression of revolt, on the part of urban populations, against powerful proprietors who had never done anything to justify their position of power over the industrial, commercial and in any case non-agricultural tenants on their estates. They did not even regard it as their incontrovertible duty to apply their thought assiduously to the solution of urban problems or to the guidance and direction of urban tendencies.

The rise of modern capitalism, therefore, with all its cruel lust of gain at all costs, not only met with no check from the legislature, as it had done in earlier Tudor and Stuart times; but it was left practically to perpetrate its worst crimes against the working proletariat under the very noses of the leisured classes, who had themselves degenerated into little more than sweaters and exploiters of labour upon the land. For, if the landowner omitted to perform his duties of protector among the city and town populations, which at least presented new problems, to how much greater a degree had he not already omitted to perform his duties of protector among the rural populations, where the problems were as old and older than his

[1] Op cit., pp. 206-207.

39

ancestors themselves! As we shall see below, the exploitation and cruelty of modern capitalism began on the land.

It takes a long time for such crimes to be realised by
those whom they injure. In addition to the fact that the
struggle for existence among the proletariat is sufficiently
engrossing and preoccupying in itself, subject minds are
much more likely, at first, to ascribe the evils about them
to chance, to inexorable economic laws, to Providential
punishments and to the inevitable scourges of civilisation,
than to trace them to the rulers above. For it requires
both knowledge and insight to trace a state of distress or
oppression to its proper source. In time, however, the
truth will out, and then it is discovered that all the benefits
that these " superior" men have been deriving from their
position of power have in no way recoiled to the advantage
of the inferior, nor driven the former to a sense of the
duties which they ought to perform in return.

Thus, happily, abuses cannot go on for ever, and as
Mr. Arthur Ponsonby says, in a book which, though full
of banalities and by no means profound, contains many
a truth which Tories would do well to consider : " . . . the
suspicion is growing that our aristocratic model is deterior-
ating, that our patricians are inadequately performing the
duties which fall to them, that they are by no means alive
to their responsibilities, and that democracy demands a
higher level of trained, well-informed and, if necessary,
specialised capacity in the agents which are required to
perform its work. There is an increasing impatience
against the existence of a class that merely vegetates, lives
off the fat of the land, and squanders, according to their
whim and fancy, the wealth that others have toiled to
create." [1]

I shall not refer to the obvious and direct crimes of
exploitation, robbery and oppression which have been
committed in the past by exalted and powerful ruling
families, and which it could be easily shown have contributed greatly towards undermining that trust and faith

---

[1] *The Decline of Aristocracy*, by Arthur Ponsonby, M.P. (1912).

in the aristocracy which the proletariat were once capable of feeling. All such crimes, besides being general hackneyed arguments in the mouths of turbulent Radical agitators, may be readily discovered in any history or biographical dictionary. I shall make it my point rather to call attention to the less obvious crimes of omission and commission, which, in my opinion, have tended in a concealed though potent manner to destroy the prestige of the ruling minority in these islands, and which, while being less direct and less deliberate than the former crimes, may nevertheless be brought home to the aristocracy with quite as much justice as crimes of carelessness and neglect against dependent children may be brought home to parents.

Neither shall I refer to individuals. Everybody knows that there are men in the English, Scotch and Irish peerage, who, like those six Englishmen whom I mentioned in the preceding chapter, no more deserve to be put at the head of affairs than a party of South Sea Islanders; and who, by their sins of omission and commission against their dependents have forfeited all right to our respect. But I do not wish to revive bitter memories; though I am quite ready, if challenged, to provide the proof of my contention.

The reason why I condemn these men in a body with warmth and indignation is simply because I regard the evils which they have brought about as in no way essential to an aristocratic *régime*, and because the slur they have thus cast upon a divine institution is all the more difficult to forgive.

For many years now vast changes have been coming over our world. Thanks to the influence of modern capitalistic enterprise and mechanical science, together with the kind of industrialism and commercialism to which they have given birth, new relations have cropped up between man and man; new occupations, some of which are most deleterious both to limb and to character, have been introduced; new ways of living and of spending leisure have been created, new portions of the community have been enlisted in the ranks of the army of labour; innumerable hordes of women have been enticed by wages, however low, to accept employment in the emporiums of commerce and industry, and the population has tended to congregate and to multiply ever more and more in enormous urban centres.

Dr. Cunningham says, " In 1770 there was no Black Country, blighted by the conjunction of coal and iron trades; there were no canals, no railways and no factory towns with their masses of population. The differentiation of town and country had not been carried nearly so far as it is to-day. All the familiar features of our modern life and all its pressing problems have come to the front with the last century and a quarter." [1]

This is very true; but it must not be supposed that the general exodus from the country into the towns was quite so recent in its origin. For hundreds of years there had been a steady flow on the part of the rural population to the urban centres, and it is impossible to separate this steady flow altogether from a certain dissatisfaction on the part of the peasantry with their lot. The number of measures passed during the Middle Ages to make it difficult for the peasant to take up his abode in the town shows that the evil of depopulating the country districts was recognised; but it is a significant fact that the legislation to remedy the evil consisted rather in increasing the constraints upon the peasantry, than in alleviating their lot.[2] Even as early as 1381 Wat Tyler's rising proves that there was already great discontent among the rural labourers; while Jack Cade's rising in Kent in 1450, the Lincolnshire rising in 1538, and Kett's in Norfolk in 1549,[3] furnish further evidence of the same nature. When

---

[1] *The Growth of English Industry and Commerce*, Vol. III, p. 613.

[2] See, for instance, the Statute 7 of Henry IV, cap. 17.

[3] Among Kett's demands there was this significant clause : " That no landlord be allowed to keep flocks and herds for purposes of trade, but merely for the use of his own household."—*Annals of the British Peasantry*, p. 104.

it is remembered that between 1349 and the reign of Elizabeth as many as eight measures were passed to fix wages,[1] and that in each of them it was the object of the legislature to establish a maximum, beyond which it was a crime to rise, rather than to establish a minimum below which it was a crime to descend, we may, perhaps, form some idea of at least a portion of the peasants' grievances; for the rest we have only to recall Wat Tyler's, Cade's and Kett's demand. As Sir G. Nicholls, K.C.B., remarks: " It cannot fail to be observed that in all these enactments for the regulation of wages, the great object of the legislature was to prevent a rise—to fix a maximum, not to assign a minimum—to place a limit on the ascending scale, leaving the descending scale without check or limitation." [2]

Still, as Dr. Cunningham says, at the end of the first half of the eighteenth century, " the differentiation of town and country had not been carried nearly so far as it is to-day." It was effectively completed, however, between 1760 and 1845, when vast numbers of the rural population were dispossessed and herded like sheep into the slums of great towns. And how was this ultimately accomplished? " The misery of the poor," says Thorold Rogers, " was the deliberate act of the legislature, of the Justice's assessments, of the enclosures, the appropriation of commons, and the determination, as Mr. Mill has said, on the part of the landowners to appropriate everything, even the air we breathe, if it could only be brought about." [3]

In the interval between 1770 and the present day huge factories have been erected and vast armies of workers drawn within their gates. With the increasing growth of

[1] See, for instance, the Statute of Labourers, Edward III (1349), 12 Richard II (1388), 4 Henry V, cap. 4 (1416), 6 Henry VI, cap. 3 (1423), 23 Henry VI, cap. 12 (1443), 11 Henry VII, cap. 2, 6 Henry VIII, cap. 3.

[2] See *A History of the English Poor Law*, Vol. I, p. 82.

Op. cit., pp. 54–55.

public companies, the relations of employer and employee have gradually tended to become less and less human, less and less that of a master of flesh and blood to a workman of flesh and blood. Not only on paper, but in actual life, the two have drifted ever further and further apart, and the only circumstances which could bring them face to face were the circumstances of strife. The cruel and lifeless notion of the " Wealth of Nations," the only notion which economists of the last two centuries seem to have been able to form of the measure of a people's prosperity and contentment, fitting in as it did admirably with the growing spirit of greed and gain, left the whole question of the spiritual and physical condition of the country out of the reckoning. It measured the actual degree of flourishing life in the nation by putting its finger into the mass of its pecuniary accumulations or profits. Irrespective of all else it advocated every measure that promoted wealth and deprecated every measure that threatened to reduce it, and thus allowed every kind of inhumanity and shortsighted policy to be practised and pursued which the combined wisdom of the rising modern capitalists might think suitable. It allowed agriculture to be killed, it tolerated the formation of that laziest, stupidest and cruelest of all principles *laissez-faire*, it condoned starvation among the poor, poor-rates in aid of wages, capital punishment for the destruction of machinery, transportation for poaching and for the forming of Trades Unions,[1] and a host of other abuses which will appear in the course of this essay.

The economists' bodiless and abstract concepts Capital and Labour are no longer *virtually*, they are *actually* the only two classes of the community. " Capital," which has taken the place of the old master owner, has become merely a vague concept to the workman; and " Labour," which has taken the place of the old servant workman who was

[1] "In 1834 we transported to Van Diemen's Land six Dorsetshire labourers for forming a Trades Union."—*Annals of the British Peasantry*, p. 417.

part of the master's household, has become but a vague and almost intangible concept to the masters, or owners of capital. And with it all machine after machine has been foisted upon the community without let or hindrance, each machine bringing with it its own particular economic and moral changes. Life's pace has been increased. People no longer feel themselves tied to a given spot, village, town or city. The population has become very largely fluid, and thousands who are here to-day have gone to-morrow.

And now let me put and answer a few questions—

(1) *How many of the hereditary rulers of the country, who had the leisure to meditate upon the problems to which all these innovations gave rise, and who had the opportunity for acquiring the knowledge and the insight for dealing with these problems, have attempted* pari passu *to take up, weigh and judge each change as it came about?*

To this question I shall reply simply in the words of Mr. Arthur Ponsonby, because I deem them substantially correct and susceptible of proof. Mr. Ponsonby says: "To take only the last 300 years, we find the gradual and profound social and economic changes hardly touched the aristocracy in their sheltered position, and passed almost unnoticed by them. Their castle in the sand served their purpose perfectly, and was, in truth, solid enough so long as the tide was far enough out." [1]

(2) *How many of the hereditary rulers have attempted to face the question of capitalistic enterprise and mechanical science and the kind of industrialism and commercialism to which they have given birth, and to guard against their possible evils?*

The answer to this question is obvious. Capitalistic enterprise and mechanical science, together with the kind of industrialism and commercialism to which they have given rise, still flourish in our midst, and nobody in a

[1] *The Decline of Aristocracy*, p. 30.

high quarter has yet questioned whether it is advisable that they should be allowed to hold undisputed sway over the community or not. On the contrary, all attempts that have been made by commoners to limit modern capitalistic methods have always been mistaken by the aristocrats as attacks on property in general, which, it is unfortunately true, they usually have been. But there is absolutely no sense in characterising all reforms which aim at restricting or directing the power of capital beneficently as socialistic, otherwise Elizabeth and Charles I must be classed as Socialists.

"No authoritative attempt," says Dr. Cunningham, "was made to recast the existing regulations so as to suit the changing conditions. . . . In the absence of any enforcement of the old restrictions, in regard to the hours and terms of employment, the difficulties of the transition were intensified; and the labourers, who had never been subjected to such misery under the old *régime*, agitated for a thorough enforcement of the Elizabethan laws. The working classes, for the most part, took their stand on the opinions as to industrial policy which had been traditional in this country, and were embodied in existing legislation. To the demand of the capitalist for perfect freedom for industrial progress, the labourers were inclined to reply by taking an attitude of impracticable conservatism."[1]

But the workman's true protector, the real ruler, who cares for the "heart of the people" and who respects the burden-bearer, was no more. The little of him that had ever existed in England had been successfully exterminated, and the cruel capitalistic cry of "*laissez-faire*" rose like a threat of exploitation, worse than death, throughout the land.

The very formation of the Trades Unions by workmen, as a means of protecting themselves against the exploitation of capitalists and the undue influence of unrestricted competition, shows how necessary it seemed to the indus-

[1] Op. cit., Vol. III, p. 613.

trial proletariat to erect with their own hands and resources some sort of shelter to ward off from their lives, left unsheltered by negligent rulers, the full brunt of an unorganised, unlimited and unrestricted state of *bellum omnium contra omnes*. The fact that these early organisations of workmen were suppressed and their promoters severely punished shows how the rulers resented this usurpation of their right to protect; but what was the good of protesting against such usurpation if no steps were taken to render the provocation or the temptation to this movement null and void? To decline to act as protector, and then to punish those who decided to protect themselves, was obvious folly, and it was soon found that the laws against labour combinations had to be repealed. No Trade Union, however, need necessarily have been formed had the industrial proletariat felt and known that its protection was a thing assured and lasting.

Maybe the problem has now grown so formidable that the possibility of its solution seems beyond the powers of a single generation of thinkers. This, however, does not exonerate those who watched its growth from infancy upwards from all blame in allowing it to attain such unwieldy proportions. Not only the hereditary rulers, therefore, but the political economists of the last century as well, have shown a lack of taste and of fine feeling, the evil results of which are now recoiling upon the nation as a whole in the form of ugliness, vulgarity, squalor and ill-health in every department of its life. Labour troubles can be adjusted, patched up temporarily, and slurred over for a while; but labour troubles will continue until the root of this inhuman system of separation, isolation and so-called independence is eradicated.

Obedience on the part of labour necessarily implies protection on the part of capital. But where labour and capital are both phantoms to each other, where they have only the relationship of cash, where the faith of labour in the protective capacities of capital has been broken by barbarous cruelties in the past, and inhuman practices in

47

the present, all obedience on the part of labour must be sullen, forced, reluctant and resentful, all protection on the part of capital, however splendidly and conscientiously it may be organised, must be heartless, bloodless and *charitable*, when it knows but vaguely whom it protects, to what sort of man, woman or girl it extends its protection, and when it lives in inhuman isolation and seclusion from its dependents. Even the sense of responsibility, both in Labour and Capital, must tend to decline when these divisions in a community are but phantoms to each other; and perhaps not the least of the injuries their respective isolation has wrought is precisely this loss in the feeling of responsibility. And this is quite distinct from that other influence which is hostile to all sense of responsibility—the influence of the peculiar lines on which limited liability companies are run.

If all these evils, all this lack of warm human relationship and responsibility, are inseparable from capitalistic enterprise, then capitalistic enterprise must be wrong, in bad taste and contrary to the dictates of flourishing life. For it is not as if we had had no examples of a contrary tendency. I might almost say that I am at fault in maintaining that the change from the comparatively happy conditions of workmen during the Middle Ages, the Tudors and the early Stuarts [1] was *blindly* allowed to instal itself, without inquisition or protest. There was inquisition and there was protest. Machinery and capitalistic enterprise could never have conquered us if a large and influential portion of the nation had not shown a deliberate preference for, and pronounced taste in favour of, the innovation. Not that I mean to imply that capitalism and the machine, properly controlled and delimited, would

---

See Dr. Cunningham, op. cit., Vol. I, p. 552. "In our time the wealthy capitalist has been spoken of by men of the Manchester School with great enthusiasm as if he were a sort of national benefactor ; in Tudor days he was regarded with grave suspicion." See also Vol. II, pp. 50, 93–94, 170, for particulars concerning the same attitude on the part of the Stuarts.

of their very nature be bad, for the machine and capitalistic enterprise have probably always existed, and will continue to exist. Their worst evils arose when they ceased from being controlled, delimited and guided; when, that is to say, no one arose to prevent them from harming the burden-bearer.

The rule of the machine, or of a system of commerce and industry such as the one termed capitalistic, does not come from Heaven. It is not a visitation of Providence. If it comes at all, if it prevails at all, its ultimate triumph must be due to a deliberate act of taste and judgment on the part of some portion of the nation. The contention that it would have been in the interest of all concerned, and particularly of the landed aristocracy, to resist the ultimate complete triumph of the vulgar tradesman's taste, I for one heartily uphold; and when I look around me to-day and see the ugliness and appalling squalor of our large cities, when I realise that the growing mass of useless dregs in the population, the growing unsavouriness and repulsiveness of mankind, are almost entirely the outcome of a change which is barely 150 years old, I cannot help thinking that those of the governing classes who allowed this change to come about showed a lack of fine feeling and of good judgment, for which they deserve to perish in the general Nemesis which threatens to overtake all societies that allow themselves to become the victims of the engineer's, the shopkeeper's and the stupid person's democratic mind.

The best instincts of the Tudors and the Stuarts were against this transformation of England from a garden into a slum, from " Merrie England "-into a home of canting, snivelling, egotistical, greedy and unscrupulous plutocrats, standing upon a human foundation of half-besotted slaves. The best instincts, too, of the British workman were against the change,[1] and although I do not know of the theory ever having been advanced before from an authoritative source, I have gone sufficiently into this question

---

[1] See Dr. Cunningham, op. cit., Vol. III, p. 611.

49

to feel able to suggest, just as a working hypothesis for better scholars than myself either to substantiate or to explode, that the Grand Rebellion, or the so-called Civil War of the seventeenth century, was as much the first struggle between the new, vulgar spirit of the nation and the old, declining better taste of the nation as it was a contest between Puritan and High Churchman, or of King and Commons. I submit that it was on the battlefields of Edgehill, Marston Moor and Naseby that trade first advanced in open hostility against tradition, quantity against quality, capitalistic industry [1] against agriculture and the old industry of the Guilds, vulgarity against taste, machinery against craftsmanship, grey and mournful Puritanism against cheerful and ruddy Paganism—in fact, plebeian democracy against aristocracy.

For many years the more vulgar and grasping portions of the community had made attempt after attempt to alter the quality and quantity of English industries, but had found in the Tudors and the Stuarts an insuperable barrier to their contemptible schemes. Edward IV and Elizabeth had prohibited the introduction of so-called time and labour saving engines, and James I and Charles I had been equally active in this respect. If all the peers of that day had also been tasteful and thoughtful, and had supported their sovereigns' policy, instead of indolently allowing matters to take their course, the triumph of modern trade and of the machine might have been successfully averted.

It was only after the vulgarest and most grasping of the nation had been driven to desperation by Charles I's constant interference with trade for the benefit of the consumer that things finally assumed a threatening aspect. For the wrath of a thwarted shopman bent on robbing at all costs is mightier than all the political or

---

[1] I say "capitalistic" advisedly here, because the triumph of the machine and the increased expensiveness which it introduced in plant, make machinery and the capitalistic system almost inseparable associates.

religious fervour on earth, though it may adopt a convenient religious disguise.

In a subsequent chapter I shall attempt to throw some light upon this conception of the so-called Civil War; meanwhile, suffice it to say that all the squalor, all the ugliness and all the vulgarity from the sight of which the tasteful people of this nation are suffering at the present day were baptised Puritan and Nonconformist in the blood of the Cavaliers sacrificed on the battlefields of the Grand Rebellion. This was the last stand the old world of taste, consideration and quality made against the new world of vulgarity, unscrupulousness and quantity; and the part that religion played in the ultimate triumph of the baser instincts is one of the most interesting chapters in the history of pious frauds.[1]

(3) *How many of the hereditary rulers have examined new occupations in order, if they were bad, to be able to pronounce a veto upon their introduction? Or investigated the new kind of life and leisure among the masses to tell whether it was good or bad?*

In reply to this question, it may be said that, with the exception of the seventh Earl of Shaftesbury (himself inspired by that noble Tory gentleman, Mr. Michael Thomas Sadler), and later on that other friend of factory legislation, Lord John Russell, not one of the hereditary rulers have ever troubled to examine *pari passu*, as they appeared, all the new occupations flung by unscrupulous inventors and industrials upon the working classes of England. And even the reforms that Shaftesbury instituted were so terribly belated—not owing to his fault, of course—that thousands were maimed, crippled and killed before the evils which he discovered were suppressed.[2]

[1] See Chapter IV.

[2] With the exception of the regulations against truck, the wisdom of which, according to Mr. Russell M. Garnier (op. cit., pp. 415-416) was somewhat doubtful, there was no protection for the miner before 1842, and before 1814 it was not even customary to hold an inquest on miners killed in mines!

And even if the abuses in the textile factories were largely suppressed by the Acts of 1833, it was not until 1864— thirty-one years later—that the miserable facts revealed in unregulated industries, such as earthenware making, lucifer-match making, percussion-cap and cartridge making, paper-staining and fustian-cutting, led to further legislation. And three years later a still larger addition of trades was made to this list.

(4) *How many of the hereditary rulers, when women, girls and children began to be drawn into the mines and factories of England, paused to ask themselves what effect this would have upon the growing generation and the mothers of life in the masses? How many inquired into the effects that the innovation would have on the homes of the masses and therefore on the nursery of the character of the people?*

To this question I can only answer violently, because any moderation in discussing such a topic would mean that I was not only a callous barbarian, but also that I took merely an academic interest in these questions. I have told you the tale of the six young Englishmen who were killed by the Chinese villagers for having overlooked the fundamental ruler principle, "Respect the burden!" But I wonder what punishment a party of Chinamen would have meted out to the savage criminals who, towards the end of the eighteenth and throughout the first three decades of the nineteenth century, were at the head of the cotton mills and collieries of England? I wonder also what punishment a party of Chinamen would have meted out to the hereditary rulers of a country where such savage criminals were allowed to be born and bred and to practise their atrocities? What with the besotted school of *laissez-faire* economists, the lazy indifference of the aristocracy, some of whom were drawing large profits both from the cotton mills and the collieries, and the natural unconcern of the Englishman—who, with all those who are more or less like him on the Continent, has succeeded in turning all such fine things as autocracy, aristocracy, slavery (as it is understood in the East), wealth, leisure and power to shame—the lives of the children and women of the lower classes during the period I have mentioned became one long agony.

It is impossible to exaggerate the brutal treatment that English industrial and commercial men dispensed to their dependents and helpers, or were allowed by their legislatures to dispense to their dependents and helpers, at the time to which I refer. A bald, impartial statement would exceed in horror anything that the imagination could picture, and the wonder is not that the trust of the lower classes in their "superiors" was not for ever broken in those days, but that the spirit of indignation kindled in their breasts did not lead to an implacable desire for vendetta, for revenge, which their progeny might have felt it their sacred duty to carry into effect. A nation that was able to melt into spinsterly tears during the first years of the nineteenth century over the negro slave-trade, a community which in 1824 had founded a Society for the Prevention of Cruelty to Animals,[1] and which in 1833 to 1834 had put an end to negro slavery, was yet able to endure within its midst a form of white slavery, the cruelties and horrors of which, practised as they were upon

---

[1] It is characteristic of the delightfully negative attitude of the Englishman towards humanity that the Society for the Prevention of Cruelty to Children was formed exactly *sixty* years after the foundation of the above-mentioned organisation for the protection of beasts, birds and fishes ; and that at the very time when, in the coal mines, unfortunate infants of six, seven and eight years of age were being made to drag trucks along narrow tunnels on all fours and half naked, the harnessing of dogs to carts was abolished in London (1839) ! It is also characteristic of their dangerous and stupid policy of *laissez-faire* at home and of impudent interference abroad, that while the whole of the Black Country and of the cotton mill districts were the scenes of abuses unparalleled in the history of any other nation, Robert Morrison, of the London Missionary Society, smugly went to China to spread Christianity among the "heathens," and reached Canton in the year 1807—China, the country where we could have learnt at least a few of the principles and precepts of flourishing life !

boys and girls of the tenderest age, exceed anything of the like that universal history can relate.[1] When I think of these things, it often occurs to me that there must be thousands of exceptionally delightful and spirited people in Australia. For the period during which there was a penal station for English criminals at Port Jackson—that is to say, from 1788 to 1839—coincides exactly with the blackest years in the history of English labour. All honour to these men and women who preferred to turn to crime rather than to submit, with their children, to the vulgar, heartless Leviathan which then reigned supreme in the North Country! And when I read that in 1821 there were 22,000 convicts in New South Wales, I cannot help believing that, if any of the descendants of these people still survive, they must be worth meeting and worth befriending. I feel for them and admire them just as much as I feel for and admire those white slaves who were deported to Maryland and Virginia, to lead a life of misery and torture, as a punishment for blasphemy, religious convictions too exalted for their persecutors, and robust living, during the appalling times which the savage Puritans inaugurated immediately before and after the death of that benign ruler, Charles I. Because I know that among these foul Dissenters to-day, among the Methodists, Congregationalists, Baptists, Low Church-men and their like, there are hundreds who would revel in reviving the cruel practices of Cromwell and of their ancestors in his following, if only the law allowed them to send men like myself to a hell on earth, for the simple

[1] See Edwin Hodder's *The Seventh Earl of Shaftesbury, K.G.* (1897), p. 21. " Any one who studies the question of the deep misery of the English poor which commenced after the Peace of Paris, increased to an alarming degree after the Reform Act, and attained its maximum during the first years of the present reign [Queen Victoria] will find ample confirmation in general literature, in the pages of fiction, in poetry and, above all, in the cold, hard statistics of Blue Books, as to the state of women and children who worked in factories and mines, and whose condition was so appalling that it cried for legislation."

crimes of loving life and of detesting their negative, ugly and devitalising creed. But more of this anon.

It is no answer to this charge against the industrial abuses in England to point to similar evils in other countries. For, apart from the fact that two blacks do not make a white, in the first place, these evils never attained to the same proportions either in France or in Germany as they did in England; and secondly, these two last-mentioned countries, which I happen to know very well, do not boast, as England invariably does, of humanity and of humanitarian principles. They are even compared by Englishmen themselves, unfavourably to England, precisely in this respect. And there is another consideration which must not be overlooked. England *led* in the industrial, commercial and mechanical world. She, therefore, set the example. As Dr. Cunningham says: "England was the pioneer of the application of mechanism to industry, and thus became the workshop of the world, so that other countries have been inspired by her example." [1]

Moreover, in so far as the employment of women and children in collieries was concerned, England had under her very nose the constant example of a more humane and more considerate community—the Irish. This was an advantage which other countries did not possess. The Irish, to their credit be it said, allowed neither children of tender years nor females of any age to be employed in underground operations.

But to show how inextricably sorrow and oppression are entangled with the English commercial man and his influence, let me refer you to the evils of the factory system in India at the present day, where apparently it is easier to evade the home laws. [2] Let me also refer you to

---

[1] Op. cit., Vol. III, p. 609.
[2] See the excellent work *Art and Swadeshi*, by that profound Indian writer Ananda R. Coomaraswamy, D.Sc. (p. 20), where, in speaking of the Indian factory system, and after having enumerated its abuses, he says: "It is not that we learn too much from foreign countries. We

the Putomayo rubber atrocities, at the recent inquiry concerning which the British Director pleaded as a justification for some of the most inhuman crimes of his company
that they were under *modern* Peruvian and not under
British law!

But to return to the question under consideration, one
might imagine that these early abuses in our industrial
and mining centres lasted only for a decade—that is to
say, only for so long as it would take to call the attention
of the whole nation to the facts. One might also imagine
that, once the horrible conditions were revealed, they were
immediately swept away by Act of Parliament. Nothing
of the kind! It was a serious outbreak of fever in the
cotton mills near Manchester which first drew widespread
attention to the overwork and ill-treatment of children in
factories in 1784; but it was not until 1833 that the first
really important Factory Act was passed—that is to say,
therefore, only after the brutal and cowardly torture of
helpless children had been *knowingly* tolerated for half a
century. And even when, thanks to the devoted efforts
of Mr. Michael Thomas Sadler, a Tory, and the subsequent untiring work of Lord Ashley, measures were taken
to induce Parliament to pass urgently needed reforms, the
representations of the agitators were met with the most
bitter and most intolerant opposition. And it is interesting to note, *en passant*, that one of Lord Ashley's most
determined opponents in the matter of the Factory Legislation was none other than that canting Nonconformist
Liberal and democrat, enemy of capital punishment,
church-rates and the Irish Established Church, John Bright
—the mill-owner, and the supporter of the Reform Bill
of 1866.[1]

I need hardly reply to the second part of question four.

---

learn too little. If we learnt more, we should not want to repeat the
experiments in *laissez-faire* of early Victorian England."

[1] Among Lord Ashley's other opponents were: Sir James Graham,
Lord Brougham (who, by the by, had taken an active part in the
abolition of negro slavery), Mr. Gladstone and Richard Cobden!

For it is obvious that in a country where women, girls and children were allowed to be overworked and brutally ill-treated in factories and mines there was very little chance of any one inquiring into the moral effect on the home of such employment. In fact, this question still remains open at the present day. The effects of female labour upon the home of the workman and the so-called lower middle-class business man still have to be investigated. That they are evil must be obvious from the appreciable decline in ability among the young women of the nation in the arts of cooking, nursing, needlework and general domestic thrift and industry. But no one has yet felt that these evils are of any great consequence. How, indeed, could the decline of the art of preparing food be regarded as an evil in a country in which Puritans have persistently taught that the things of the body do not matter?

(5) *How many of the hereditary rulers attempted to calculate the desirability or the reverse of the new type which was bound to be developed among the new and unwieldy urban masses?*

In reply to this question, we all know what has happened. Nothing has happened! It is only just recently, with the formation of the Eugenic Society—inspired and organised by commoners—that the question has arisen as to whether the type that is being bred by modern industrial and commercial conditions is a desirable or even promising one. It is only just recently—since, that is to say, Darwin's Evolutionary Hypothesis awakened general interest in such questions as Heredity, Race and Survival —that the grave question of Breeding under unfavourable conditions has so much as been mooted. Almost every one of the hereditary rulers, or people of power in the nation, watched with equanimity the gradual transformation of England from an agricultural and more or less home-industrial nation into a nation of giant cities and factories. (I say " or people of power" in this case because I would entirely endorse the statement of Captain Thomas Drummond, Under-Secretary for Ireland in 1839, to the effect that "property had its duties as well as its rights.") Not a strong, earnest word of protest was raised. And it is only now, in the early years of the twentieth century, that we are beginning to wonder whether the kind of man that is bred and reared among urban and modern industrial conditions is a creature of promise or of danger for the nation.

The subject of the depopulation of rural districts, its causes, and the grave consequences it involved for the spirit and health of the nation, is too vast to be entered into here in any detail. To any one who has studied the history of the English peasant not only in the Statutes of the Realm, but also in the works of such writers as Garnier, Rogers, Sir Frederick Eden, Sir George Nicholls and others, the long story will have seemed painful and tragic enough. But what must strike him with ever greater force, the more he reads, is the levity, the appalling frivolity, with which a life so healthy, so conducive to fine, manly courage, perseverance and spirit, and, in short, so fruitful in all the most desirable qualities that a nation could desire, should have been allowed to be forsaken by millions of the nations best people for a life which is known to lead in every respect to the reverse of these qualities. And for this change, for this loss in exchange, nobody is more responsible than the British landowner and legislator.

Garnier says: "If the ethnic idiosyncrasies of the Anglo-Saxon had been identical with those of the African, it is not to be doubted that he would have been more uniformly comfortable under the cordial relationship existing betwixt an indulgent master and a faithful slave, than under that modern business etiquette which now freezes the sympathies between employer and employé." [1] This may be so. It may be true that the Englishman, whether peasant or potentate, has within him that fatal element of

[1] Op. cit., p. 28.

recalcitrant, liberty-loving independence which makes him a bad and unreliable servant, and a selfish and unthinking master, even in the best patriarchal conditions—and if this be so, then all hope of settlement between servant and master must be for ever abandoned in this country. But I doubt whether even Garnier's study of the British Peasantry itself justifies this conclusion. For what does Garnier himself tell us was the cause of Wat Tyler's peasant rising in 1381? Agrarian oppression.[1] And of Jack Cade's in 1450? Agrarian oppression.[2] And of Kett's in 1549? Again agrarian oppression![3] Whether it was the slavery of our manorial rents, or the labour laws of the fourteenth century which "tied a man down to starve on a particular spot at a day's wage fixed lower than the current price of his day's bread";[4] whether it was that farms had been engrossed, "stuff and purveyance for the king's household had not been paid for," "feigned indictments had been brought against poor and simple folk 'that used not hunting,'" and common lands had been enclosed;[5] or that encroachments had been made on the common arable field, lands converted from tillage to pasture, and homes of husbandry pulled down; throughout the Middle Ages and the Tudor period, especially after Henry VIII's ruffianly favourites were cast like wolves upon the land, the peasant always seems to have been groaning under some grievance which was more material and more concrete than the mere abstract longing for that liberty and enfranchisement which became a plain and definite cry in recent times. Certain it is that, from the time of Edward VI to the present day, the capitalistic and greedy element in the landed gentry and aristocracy has steadily increased.[6]

---

[1] Op. cit., pp. 59–60.
[2] Op. cit., p. 63.
[3] Op. cit., Chapter VIII.
[4] Op. cit., p. 60.
[5] Op. cit., pp. 62–63.
[6] "The fresh owners of the Church lands (in Henry VIII's reign) had introduced a commercial spirit into the English soil. . . . Our landed gentry had never before and never since sunk so low in public estimation.

Why, then, seek so far as the "ethnic idiosyncrasy" of the Anglo-Saxon in order to account for the gradual death agony of those happy relations between peasant and landlord which, if continued, might have meant that England's rural districts would still be thickly populated by an industrious and healthy peasantry, dreading like poison the swollen urban cysts ("wens") which, however, might be considered good enough for the weaklings and undersized sharpers who would naturally congregate there? I am ready to acknowledge that, in the heart of the English working man, there is a certain limited and extremely passive spark of liberty-loving independence; but on historical grounds, I refuse to believe that it alone could have been ardent enough to kindle the many conflagrations which have ultimately led to the decline of the rustic populations and their industry, had it not been wantonly fanned into flame by a class of people who again and again have shown themselves utterly unworthy of property, power or leadership. For if things are otherwise, if this subversive ethnic partiality for liberty were all that Garnier and the bulk of English historians think it is, it would be impossible to account for the astonishingly protracted periods during which the lower orders have, time and again, patiently endured the most intolerable abuses without immediate and spirited protest. That is why I cannot help feeling that, in spite of many faults, which are doubtless inseparable from the Englishman's nature, the blame for at least three-quarters of the discord between master and man in the British Isles, with all those provoked reactions which we call riots, Trades Unions, strikes and their concomitant distrust, ill-feeling and hatred, ought from every point of view, historical, psychological, ethnic and the rest, to attach to the people who to-day, as well as in the past, have shown themselves incapable of being

---

A class or an individual is in dire circumstances when society considers them past praying for. But in the reign of Edward VI the landowners had arrived at that still more desperate stage when they had to be prayed against."—Garnier, op. cit., p. 90.

leaders and lovers of men. The English gentleman as a rule understands how to rear the menial; but he seldom understands how to rear and preserve the minion. It takes an artist to convert a menial into a minion, and unless that artist is plentiful in the governing classes of the country there can be little hope either of stability or happiness in the relations between master and man.

For, to come to more recent times, do we find things very much better?

What whim, what passing fancy, are we to suppose led a fine English peasant like William Cobbett to say in the early years of the nineteenth century: "There is in the men calling themselves English country gentlemen ' something' superlatively base. They are, I sincerely believe, the most cruel, the most unfeeling, the most brutally insolent: but I know, I can prove, I can safely take my oath, that they are the most base of all the creatures that God ever suffered to disgrace the human shape." [1]

Cobbett was not a demagogue; neither was he a Radical Reformer. He was a plain, level-headed English Tory who believed, as I do, in aristocracy, and in a landed aristocracy into the bargain. He was a man who could honestly say of himself: "My whole life has been a life of sobriety and labour. . . . I have invariably shown that I loved and honoured my country, and that I preferred its greatness and happiness far beyond my own." [2] And yet, after a most painstaking and exhaustive examination of the condition of the rural districts during the early years of the nineteenth century, he was able to say on September 29, 1826: "Of all the mean, all the cowardly reptiles that ever crawled on the face of the earth, the *English landowners* are the most mean and most cowardly." [3] In his *Rural Rides* he undertakes to supply the elaborate proof of this statement, but to the inquiring reader such proof is also abundantly accessible in the works

[1] *Rural Rides* (Edition Dent), Vol. II, p. 46.
[2] *Ibid.*, Vol. II, p. 187. [3] *Ibid.*, pp. 121–123.

of men whom he may consider more impartial, in the Governmental Reports and Returns of the period, and in the evidence given before State Commissions.

Let me, however, quote what Garnier says concerning the same period. And let it be remembered that if Garnier may be suspected of any bias at all, that bias is in favour of the landed proprietors rather than against them. In his *Annals of the British Peasantry* the author says: " In fact, towards the close of the last century, he (the peasant) was starving amidst plenty, unable to live except by becoming a beggar, and unable to combine and agitate for higher pay except by becoming a criminal. Not the least bitter drop in his cup of woe was to see on all sides of him his employers enjoying the luxuries of an abnormal prosperity." [1]

It was thus that these men, the very heart of the British Empire, were treated!—the men who won our victories at Crécy and Poictiers, and later at Trafalgar and Vittoria; for, as Garnier says, " the spirit of the peasant at both epochs was the subject of mingled dread and admiration throughout the armies of Europe. . . . The men-at-arms, who came of the mediæval common fields, carried a quiver which, in the language of Scripture, was an open sepulchre. The man-of-war's man, kidnapped by the press-gang from amidst some group of parochial roundsmen, wielded his cutlass with no less deadly results." [2] These were not the men to clamour for a two-to-one standard against a foreign Power. Their food, and therefore their independence, lay in the land which they cultivated. England required to be populated by a herd of non-producing, undersized clerks and shopmen before this cry of a two-to-one standard in ships of war could become a loud one in the land.

And now listen to the stirring words of good old Cobbett on the same subject. In addressing a " Landlord Distress Meeting " in Norwich on December 22, 1821, he spoke as follows—

" What a thing to contemplate, gentlemen! What a

[1] p. 70.   [2] Op. cit., p. 31.

scene is here! A set of men, occupiers of the land; producers of all that we eat, drink, wear, and of all that forms the buildings that shelter us; a set of men industrious and careful by habit, cool, thoughtful and sensible from the instructions of nature; a set of men provident above all others, and engaged in pursuits in their nature stable as the very earth they till; to see a set of men like this plunged into anxiety, embarrassment, jeopardy not to be described; and when the particular individuals before me were famed for their superior skill in this great and solid pursuit, and were blessed with soil and other circumstances to make them prosperous and happy: to behold this sight would have been more than sufficient to sink my heart within me, had I not been upheld by the reflection that I had done all in my power to prevent these calamities, and that I still had in reserve that which, with the assistance of the sufferers themselves, would restore them and the nation to happiness." [1]

No wonder poor Cobbett thought, as I think, that the nobility were "in a long trance," [2] and no wonder he cried in despair, "What a system it must be to make people wretched in a country like this!" [3]

For, in spite of that which this grand old man said he "still had in reserve," [4] there is nothing to show that his teaching was followed. In the end, as we know, the starvation of the millions was relieved by a capitalistic solution, the Repeal of the Corn Laws; and this was not the triumph, but the defeat, of the farming classes, to the advantage of uncontrolled Industry and Commerce [5]— that is to say, to the advantage of a type of life and a type of man which never has and never can build up a great empire, although it *may* accumulate great temporary wealth upon the foundations of a great empire, once the latter has been built up by other and sounder men.

And though we might suppose that by now the govern-

---

[1] Op. cit., Vol. I, pp. 55–56.   [2] Op. cit., Vol. I, p. 67.
[3] Op. cit., Vol. I, p. 52.   [4] Op. cit., Vol. I, p. 55.
[5] See Garnier, Op. cit., p. 338.

ing classes had learnt their lesson, and were using every endeavour to revive this ebbing life of the best of England, the agricultural population, nothing could be more disappointing or more exasperating than to examine the present state of things in this quarter. For one has only to peruse the works of a writer such as Mr. F. E. Green in order to be convinced that the state of affairs still cries urgently for drastic reform. I know of nothing more harrowing than his book, *The Tyranny of the Country Side*, more particularly to one like myself who firmly believes that nothing stable, nothing great, nothing imposing, and certainly nothing creative, free and independent can ever be constructed on a purely usurious, commercial, office-bred and ledger-wed population.

"It would be hard to say," says Mr. F. E. Green, "whether it is the large farmer, in his desire to add field to field and to prevent the agricultural labourer from getting land or living in cottages independent of him as landlord; or the huge landowner, in his insatiable lust to obtain huge pheasant preserves, vast deer forests and multitudinous rabbit warrens, who has done the greater harm to our most virile class of workers, and through them struck a blow at the heart of our Empire." [1] And Mr. Green concludes a book in which he rightly lays claim to having "established beyond a doubt that agricultural labour is a sweated industry" [2] with the following words of warning : " If reform does not come quickly to repeople our empty country-side, either we shall lose our bold peasantry altogether, and with it our virility as a race, or a swift retribution will overtake the governing classes."

Like William Cobbett, Mr. Green also deprecates very strongly the cowardice of the professional classes—country lawyers, parsons and doctors. He shows, just as Cobbett had shown before him (though Cobbett dealt only with the ecclesiastical gentlemen), how sneakishly these public-school-bred and cricket-field-trained " gentlemen " grovel before the potentates of the land, and prefer to allow the

[1] Op. cit., p. 17.   [2] Op. cit., p. 249.

most crying evils to remain unredressed among their poorer and more destitute fellows, rather than run the risk of a hostile encounter with their wealthy patrons.[1] For, as Mr. Green aptly observes, the lawyer's children, "like those of the parson, must go to a public school," [2] and where should the money come from if not from these wealthy patrons?

So thus it goes on, year after year. True ruling grows more and more scarce, greed and gain tend more and more to become the only motives actuating all classes of the community, and nobody asks, nobody cares, how the spirit and the physique of the nation is faring. For if what doctors tell us be a fact—that, after three generations, born and bred cockneys become sterile—then it requires no more words of mine to remind the reader of the essential relationship between good rule and the voice of flourishing life, on which I laid such stress in my first chapter. No good rule leads to death. When death is the outcome of any system of government or life, it is a sure sign that the voice of flourishing life is no longer audible or obeyed in a nation; it means, therefore, that there is no longer any true aristocracy, and that there has not been any true aristocracy in the land for many years past.

(6) *How many of the hereditary rulers foresaw the dehumanising and besotting influence of the machine and the modern factory upon the workman? How many of them attempted to "place" the machine—to determine the limits of its healthy development, or to warn the nation against its abuse?*

The same unsatisfactory reply must be given to this question. In a very interesting article by Mr. Edward Spencer, entitled "The Use and Abuse of Machinery," in the *Fortnightly Review* of November 1911, the author argues that the condition of affairs at the present day ought to have been foreseen and provided against by the

---

[1] See *The Tyranny of the Country Side*, pp. 25–26 and all Chapter IX.
[2] Op. cit., p. 25.

disciples and friends of such a man as Adam Smith, "for upon the ground plan of an estimate of human nature and its needs such as we find taken for granted in the *Wealth of Nations*, it would be unreasonable to expect a better or indeed a different superstructure than that of the present capitalistic system." And then he proceeds to say that "the earlier economists, like ourselves, were hypnotised by the spectacle of the extreme poverty prevailing in the lower ranks of labour, and, as a result, they were induced to pursue comfort and hygiene *as if they were ends in themselves*,[1] and as if the whole industrial problem were to be discovered in their attainment."

Of course these economists were "hypnotised" by the distress in the lower ranks of labour; for they possessed subject minds and could not possibly see deeper than the distress itself.

When we read in the Majority Report of the Poor Law Commission that the total cost of poor relief per annum in the British Isles amounts to £60,000,000, and when we hear that, excluding the sick, the aged, the insane and the very young, 50,000 able-bodied indoor paupers are supported throughout the year at a cost of about £1,387,239,[2] and that the number of these able-bodied paupers is rather increasing than decreasing; furthermore, when we learn that these paupers are mostly depraved, undisciplined and hopeless, how can we, as thinking men, divorce their condition entirely from their antecedents? How can we exonerate ourselves, and those of our predecessors who had the requisite leisure and the knowledge for facing problems and solving them—how, I say, can we exonerate ourselves and our predecessors from all blame in regard to the lives led by the parents, grandparents and great-grandparents of these characterless and poor-spirited people? How can we forget the besotting, the dehumanising, influence of turning a lever all day from

[1] The italics are mine.—A. M. L.

[2] My figures are taken from the *Nineteenth Century* of November 1911. Article : "The Idle Poor."

left to right or from right to left in a factory? Or of folding, cutting and preparing the same material for the same machine from one year's end to the other? Who has cared for the character of these people? Who has seen that their spirit should not be hunted out of them through the generations? [1]

For, as Mr. Edward Spencer rightly and profoundly observes in the article already quoted, the *machine*, with all the inestimable advantages it was supposed to bring to the community at large, has not yet been "placed," either by economists or by the rulers of this nation; and, he adds very wisely, "to place it to the best human advantage, it is necessary to start from a sound estimate of human character, its needs and its capacities."

In fact, for nearly two centuries now the lower classes have been absolutely at the mercy of science, and particularly mechanical science, both of which have been working quite unscrupulously and indiscriminately, without the suggestion of a ruler-mind at their backs. My quarrel with modern science, and modern mechanical science particularly, is not based upon the mere fact that they are complicating life without beautifying or improving it, but that, once more, behind science, and mechanical science above all, there is no ruler-spirit which is able to say, with the full knowledge of the limits of a certain collective human scheme, what place and what power they are to take in our midst.

If at any moment an unscrupulous inventor appeared who had discovered a means of making us travel at fifty times our present maximum speed, not a single voice would be raised to say, " Before we accept this man's idea,

[1] See W. Cobbett, op. cit., Vol. I, p. 179, where the author, referring to the workers in the factories in the early years of the last century, expresses himself as follows : " Talk of *vassals!* Talk of *villains!* Talk of *serfs!* Are there any of these, or did feudal times ever see any of them, so debased, so absolutely slaves, as the poor creatures who, in the ' enlightened ' north, are compelled to work fourteen hours in a day, in a heat of eighty-four degrees ; and who are liable to punishment for looking out at a window of the factory ! "

do we know the full consequences that such an invention will be likely to have upon the national character and the national physique, and are these consequences desirable? "

Unquestioningly, unhesitatingly, almost with the assurance and self-composure of complete knowledge, practically all innovations introduced since Tudor and Stuart times [1] have been acquiesced in as if they must necessarily be improvements. Again and again mere change has falsely been welcomed as Progress; mechanical revolutions have falsely been embraced as desirable evolutions, and uncontrolled new tendencies have been falsely acclaimed as inevitable developments. Only when it was too late, only when the evil results of novelties became strikingly obvious, did these novelties begin to be problems. And all this muddle and confusion were sanctified by the doctrine of "experience," which treats as impudence any presbyopic or prophetic glance into the near or distant future. Ananda K. Coomaraswamy says hopefully: "Already it is being recognised in Europe that the general substitution of machines for men must invariably lower the whole intellectual and moral status of the working population, and we need not hope to avoid this result by tinkering at compulsory education." [2] But I question very much whether this is not far too optimistic a statement of the case. It is very doubtful whether even the sociological thinkers, not to speak of the peoples of Western Europe themselves, are more than half aware of the gravity of this question; and to suppose that they would have the courage to solve it as it ought to be solved, even granting they ever faced it fairly and squarely, is quite unwarrantable. For there is a terrible feeling abroad that things have already gone too far. [3]

---

[1] See Dr. Cunningham, op. cit., Vol. II, p. 295. " Machinery was viewed (in Tudor and Stuart times) with suspicion, not only on account of the quality of the work done, but because of its injurious effects upon handicraftsmen."

[2] *Art and Swadeshi*, p. 19.

[3] The first thinker to express this fear that things had already gone

Nor is there the excuse that the legislators had had no warning, nothing to call their attention to the matter. Cobbett's was not the only voice that was raised in England against the evils of machinery. The workmen themselves rebelled, and in a very active manner indeed. During the autumn and winter of 1811, the so-called "Luddite" riots, which broke out among the stocking weavers of Nottingham, and during which machinery was broken up and destroyed wherever the rioters could reach it, ought to have been sufficient to show every thinker among the statesmen of the time that here at least was a problem that ought not to be passed over without profound reflection. Even supposing they could have been quite impartial in approaching this question, in any case it was not of a nature to be judged purely in terms of wealth, or of immediate profit or loss. For the men who fought in these riots were grim and determined, and hundreds of them were actually starving. There was a psychology of the question, a sociology of the question, apart from its surface aspect as a blow to prosperous industry and commerce. What happened? Early in 1812 a Bill was passed making frame-breaking a capital offence,

---

too far where machinery was concerned was Samuel Butler. See his letter to "The Press" (Christchurch, N.Z., June 13, 1863), from which I take the following passage. "Day by day, however, the machines are gaining ground upon us; day by day, we are becoming more subservient to them; more men are daily bound down as slaves to tend them, more men are daily devoting the energies of their whole lives to the development of mechanical life. The upshot is simply a question of time, but that the time will come when the machines will hold the real supremacy over the world and its inhabitants is what no person of a truly philosophical mind can for a moment question. Our opinion is that war to the death should be instantly proclaimed against them. Every machine of every sort should be destroyed by the well-wisher of his species. Let there be no exceptions made, no quarter shown. . . . If it be urged that this is impossible under the present conditions of human affairs, this at once proves that the mischief is already done, that our servitude has commenced in good earnest, that we have raised a race of beings whom it is beyond our power to destroy, and that we are not only enslaved, but absolutely acquiescent in our bondage."

and in November of that year sixteen "Luddites" were executed by sentence of a special Court sitting at York.[1]

But in regard to this matter it would be unfair to the aristocratic class I am criticising were I to omit all mention of the wonderful speech Lord Byron delivered in the House of Lords on February 27, 1812, while opposing the measure making frame-breaking a capital offence introduced by that cold-blooded and matter-of-fact lawyer Lord Erskine. This speech was one of the only three Lord Byron ever delivered in the higher legislative chamber, and it was certainly the best of the three.

After explaining the difficulties of the unfortunate workmen concerned in these riots—for Lord Byron had recently visited the scene of the trouble in order to acquire first-hand knowledge—and after laying stress upon the poor quality of the work done by the machines, he proceeded—

"You call these men a mob, degenerate, dangerous and ignorant, and seem to think that the only way to quiet the *Bellua multorum capitum* is to lop off a few of its superfluous heads. But even a mob may be better reduced to reason by a mixture of conciliation and firmness than by additional and redoubled penalties. Are we aware of our obligations to that mob? It is the mob that labour in the fields and serve in your houses, that man your navy and recruit your army, that have enabled you to defy all the world, and can also defy you when neglect and calamity have driven them to despair. You may call the people a mob, but do not forget that a mob too often speaks the sentiments of the people."[2]

To their credit be it said that Lord Holland, Lord Grosvenor and Lord Grenville supported Lord Byron in opposing the Bill; but, as we have seen, the measure became law notwithstanding, and the harshness of its

---

[1] See *The Political History of England*, Vol. XI (by the Hon. George C. Brodrick, D.C.L.), p. 83.

[2] *Hansard's Parliamentary Debates*, Vol. XXI, pp. 966-969.

application effectually ended the disturbances for a time.

(7) *In the face of the acceleration of life's pace, in the face of the fact that the population was becoming fluid, how many hereditary legislators were cautious enough to foretell that when a population became fluid—since "local" public opinion is the severest censor of conduct —morality, however stern and rigid it might be, would also tend to become fluid and therefore lax?*

In answer to this question, it may be said that bustle and hurry to nowhere, to nothing, was arrested neither by the hereditary rulers nor by the spiritual guardians of the nation. On the contrary, frantic and meaningless haste became the order of the day. People never halted to think or to consider; they merely followed the shortest road to the main chance. Presbyopic views, views concerning the morrow or the future, began to yield before the immediate concern about the best trick, the most expedient ruse, wherewith men could outwit or oust their neighbours. Motion became more rapid; the very increase of motion began to be looked upon as "progress," and to deny this was tantamount to confessing oneself insane.

"Every one, indeed," says Mr. Ponsonby, "supposes he is 'doing more' because he can move more rapidly. Whereas it would be nearer the truth to say we accomplish less, because our nervous energy and vitality are being seriously impaired by the whirl and rush of ceaseless mechanical motion." [1]

And it must not be supposed that this feverish rush is characteristic only of the lower classes, where, at least, it is excusable; for, to slaves, time is indeed money. On the contrary, once rapid movement became the ideal, the means to move soon led to moves being made for the sheer love of moving, and the richer you became the faster you moved. The mushroom success achieved by the motor-car is a proof of this. In a better, nobler,

[1] *The Decline of Aristocracy*, p. 80.

A DEFENCE OF ARISTOCRACY

healthier and more stable age either the motor-car would
have remained an undeveloped plaything, or it would
have been relegated to trade, where sheer speed is often
a means of success. In a vulgar age, however, it arrived
sufficiently opportunely to be a huge success, and its
adoption by the powerful and the wealthy proves how
absurdly vulgar and stupid these people had become.

"There are people of the highest rank in the England
of to-day," says Mr. Ponsonby, "whose existence is as
much nomadic as that of Red Indians in the reserved
territories of North America. . . . The existence of a
monk in a cloister, of a prisoner in a fortress, is more
favourable to the intellect than theirs." [1]

Not one of the members of the governing classes, and
least of all the Church, halted in order to inquire what
influence this fluid condition of society would tend to
exercise over morality, over the sounder traditions of the
nation, and over families and other ties. The profound
value of local opinion and local censure in maintaining
the customs and virtues of a nation was utterly forgotten.
Again, from the standpoint of experience, mere travelling
was regarded as a good thing in itself. No thought was
given to the fact that to a man without backbone or balance
and without rigorous principles travelling and varied
experience are the unsoundest things of all.[2] On the
contrary, everybody applauded, everybody cried "Progress!" everybody got drunk with the mere sensation of
speed—until nothing became too stupid, too preposterous
or too insane for society to think or to do. Hedonism,
blatant and unscrupulous, was left as the refuge of the
prosperous—and to the poor, Revolt!

[1] *The Decline of Aristocracy*, p. 140.
[2] See W. Cobbett, op. cit., Vol. II, p. 31, where the author says
he is "convinced that the *facilities* which now exist of moving human
bodies from place to place are amongst the curses of the country, the
destroyers of industry, of morals, and, of course, of happiness. It is a
great error to suppose that people are rendered stupid by remaining
always in the same place." And Cobbett wrote this on August 27,
1826! What would he say to-day!

Unfortunately, however, nothing fruitful ever came or ever can come of democratic revolt. Inevitable, reasonable, well-founded as it is, the desire on the part of the proletariat to get the direction of affairs as much as possible into their own hands cannot and will not be any more fruitful than the plutocracy's Hedonism. For it is a mere reaction following upon incompetence in higher quarters. It is not the outcome of the conscious possession of a sound and far-sighted scheme of organisation, which is the creation of profound ruler wisdom and ruler power. Democratic revolt and cynical Hedonism are but the reverse and obverse of the same medal, and that medal is the sterile fact of impoverished and degenerate life.

The difference between the two orders of society which are now ranged against one another is, unfortunately, merely a difference of balance at the bank. Give the indignant masses, groaning under the traditional yoke of modern industry, the banking account of those against whom they inveigh, and what would happen? We all know what would happen. Certainly no constructive or regenerating policy or *régime* would ensue. The whole crowd would simply rush to provide themselves with cars and cards, and whirl and play away their existence in a round of pleasure. No longer a mere section of society, no longer a mere privileged minority, but everybody would play golf, everybody would sup at the Carlton and the Savoy, and everybody would attend the winter sports in Switzerland. While even from those who were more sober in the enjoyment of their newly acquired leisure, nothing of permanent or genuine value could be expected. And for the simple reason that at the present moment there is nothing to induce one to believe that the voice of flourishing life—which is the only voice that can possibly lead in the proper direction—is any more alive in the struggling and oppressed masses than it is in the leisured classes. If it is silent above, it is pretty hopeless to seek for it below; because, as I pointed out in the preceding chapter, the conditions below are the very last to create or to cultivate it. In a subsequent chapter I will give an outline of the conditions under which superior spirits may be found or cultivated among the sub-orders of a society, and then it will be seen how few of these conditions are already to hand among the labouring masses. Thus to say that you trust the " People " with a capital P, to put your hand to your heart and shout hopefully that the worm is turning *ruler*, when it merely *turns* under pressure, is to be guilty of a kind of optimism which is as empty and foolish as it is romantic; and all those who feel inclined with the modern democrat to declare, " The People are at the helm, all's well with the world! " not only misunderstand the very principle of prosperous and successful rule as outlined in my first chapter, but also utterly mistake the true nature of even the healthiest and happiest People.

But apart from the fact that there is nothing—absolutely nothing either in history, anthropology or psychology— to show that when a people get the rule into their own hands they can be, and are, a substitute for those rare spokesmen of flourishing life whose taste knows what and how to choose; apart from the fact, therefore, that you cannot supply the place of a few artists by a number, however large, of people who are not artists, what grounds are there for supposing that the rule of the people would even be more beneficent than that of the aristocrats— beneficent, I mean, towards those whom they have in their power? Because I take it that the rule of a people by themselves always must be the rule of a community, different sections of which are pursuing different aims and different interests, although the whole may be animated by a national idea when an enemy comes on the scene. It may come to pass, therefore, that one section, considering its own interests, as the governing classes have for many generations done in this country, will have power over the other section, or over several other sections. Are there any reasonable grounds for supposing that such a section, simply because they are of the people, would exercise their power more beneficently than a pseudo-aristocratic section has done? Seeing that the people may justly be regarded as the working and busy portion of the population, immersed in the struggle for existence and animated by its keenness, how can they be regarded as a body sufficiently leisured, sufficiently instructed and sufficiently presbyopic to be guided only by those far-sighted and broadly altruistic motives which glance over a whole scheme, over a whole future and over the whole of the claims of the present and of posterity before acting? Conceding, as I readily do, that the pseudo-aristocracy which has ruled England since the time of Henry VIII has shown, more or less, all the faults of the non-leisured, non-instructed, non-presbyopic or short-sighted body who are immersed in the struggle for existence, what sense is there in supposing that that very body itself will do any better?

Hear what that philosophic demagogue John Stuart Mill said on this very question—

"Experience, however, proves that the depositories of power who are mere delegates of the people—that is, of the majority—are quite as ready (when they think they can count on popular support) as any organs of oligarchy to assume arbitrary power, and encroach unduly on the liberty of private life. The public collectively is abundantly ready to impose, not only its generally narrow views of its interests, but its abstract opinions, and even its tastes, as laws binding upon individuals." [1]

These words, coming as they do from such an inveterate democrat as the writer of *Liberty*, are particularly significant, and ought to make every one pause before he speaks too eloquently or too sentimentally about all being well with the world because the People are at the helm!

Herbert Spencer held the same view. In his *Essay on Parliamentary Reform* [2] he says: "While we do not

[1] *Principles of Political Economy* (Ed. 1865), Book V, Chapter XI, p. 570.
[2] First published in *The Westminster Review* for April 1860.

see reason to think that the lower classes are intrinsically less conscientious than the upper classes, we do not see reason to think that they are more conscientious. Holding, as we do, that in each society and in each age the morality is, on the average, the same throughout all ranks, it seems to us clear that if the rich, when they have the opportunity, make laws which unduly favour themselves, the poor, if their power was in excess, will do the like in similar ways and to a similar extent. Without knowingly enacting injustice, they will be unconsciously biased by personal considerations, and our legislation will err as much in a new direction as it has hitherto done in the old."

Here there is no mention of the born artist-ruler, the spokesman of flourishing life. But we should scarcely expect such an idea from Herbert Spencer. Still, the passage shows the hopeless dilemma a nation is in when it has to choose only between its top and its bottom dogs, when there is none superior to the dog in the whole population.

I, however, maintain that every nation always produces a crop of those who are superior to the top and the bottom dogs, if only those values and those selective means are prevalent within it which lead to the recognition and promotion of such superior men. Confucius knew this fact, and with his doctrine of the superior man he paved the way to its general acceptation by the whole world.

I am, however, digressing. These considerations belong to another chapter, and for the present I must continue my criticism of the English governing classes, but on another and higher plane, *i. e.* in the Tutorship of Ruling.

CHAPTER III

THE ENGLISH ARISTOCRAT AS A FAILURE IN THE TUTORSHIP OF RULING

"The true image of a free people governed by a Patriot King is that of a patriarchal family, where the head and all the members are united by one common interest, and animated by one common spirit."— BOLINGBROKE, *The Idea of a Patriot King*, pp. 140–141.

WHAT purpose can I serve by enumerating any more of the sins of omission that can be laid at the door of our governing classes, not to mention that of the Established Church? To any one who is familiar with the history of the English people during the last three hundred years, the little handful of facts that I have collected for my indictment of the governing classes of this country will seem meagre and perhaps somewhat inadequate evidence with which to prove my case. I am, however, not an historian. I wish to refer to these things only in order to acquire sufficient warrant to proceed with my general discussion. What concern is it of mine that the kind of fact I have adduced in support of my contention might be multiplied a hundredfold? I simply wish to urge the point that further facts could but substantiate my claims the more.

In replying to my seven questions, I think I have shown satisfactorily that the rulers of this country have failed time and again in the "craft" of their calling; but in making this point I have also had occasion to refer to their neglect of the "tutorship" of governing. Now, however, in my reply to my next question, I shall be concerned chiefly with this "tutorship" of governing, and with the almost total neglect of this pre-eminently important element in the art of ruling.

If, then, to use the phraseology of that brilliant Chinaman Ku Hung-Ming, I ask what the governing classes of England have done to guide the taste of the people, and to direct their industry so that it might not be wasted and disheartened in a purely futile accumulation of wealth for mere Hedonists to squander; if I ask what the governing classes of England have done to " set the tone " in their nation, so that the wholly material industry of the masses might be given a higher purpose and aim, what is the only honest reply that can be given?

I have not expatiated at any length upon the simple fact that these governors have failed hopelessly in the plain " craft " of their calling—that they have failed in their duty of protecting and, with their superior wisdom, of controlling for everybody's good the burden bearers of the country. I have taken this point as proved in the main by the few facts I have adduced—facts which, as I say, can be multiplied to any extent. When, however, we come to the question of " tutorship " in governing, the charge against them seems to me to be even more severe than the previous one.

Speaking of the aristocrats of Great Britain, Mr. Arthur Ponsonby says, " They have never been superior, they have ceased to be governing; is there any reason that they should continue to be noble? " [1]

There is bitterness in this manner of putting the case, but it is not without some foundation. There can be no doubt that for centuries, almost, the Lords have neglected, or completely forgotten, the principle of flourishing life which reads, " Respect the burden "; and in the rebuff which they received in the summer of 1911, they felt the revenge of Life herself upon those who scorn her fundamental principles. I would go further and would say definitely that since the middle of the eighteenth century, but for a few brilliant exceptions, such as the seventh Earl

[1] *The Decline of Aristocracy*, p. 128.

of Shaftesbury, the voice of flourishing life has been entirely silent in England; and all the confusion and doubt which we now see about us, all the ugliness, vulgarity, misery and uncontrolled Hedonism which now prevail, are nothing but the inevitable outcome of the fact that the voice of impoverished life, of inferior life, has been practically the only guiding voice in our island for one hundred and fifty years.

There is a misery prevalent to-day which is blacker and more hopeless than any misery that has ever existed on earth before. It is not only the misery of ignoble work, disease and poverty, for that infests all orders of society; but, in the lower orders, it is the misery of countless masses who do menial, characterless and distasteful labour without anything to justify it, or to shed a ray of gold upon it from a height up towards which that work might be looked upon as but a necessary step. And, in the superior orders, it is the misery of those who have lost all sense of a higher aim, all consciousness of a purpose, a goal, or a grand scheme of life, and who are beginning to feel literally uncomfortable and mystified in their position of merely *material* superiority; because no noble or worthy unravelment seems to be promised them for the tangled knot of exploitation, privilege, wretchedness, luxury, pleasure, squalor, comfort, starvation and plenty, which now characterises modern life, and in which they happen to be simply fortunate accidents.

The terrible cynicism of modern times leads many of these materially superior people to say or think, "*Après nous le déluge!*" But the more thoughtful and more sensitive among them are torn in two by doubt and misgivings, and are beginning to wonder what is the purpose of it all—of their privileges and of their less fortunate fellows' thraldom.

Beginning with the former kind of misery, and starting out from first principles, let it be thoroughly understood that nobody—no man, woman or child from any rank of society—would instinctively recoil before the performance of any office, however mean, if the value, power and human fascination alone, of him who demanded it, seemed to justify or glorify that office. Nor does the loving and reverent menial recoil even before pain, if a higher life or a nobler life gives this pain at least some lofty meaning or some lofty purpose. This is the experience of all those patriarchal spirits who have the art of inspiring devotion in their subordinates, and who know it to be one of the duties of ruling to *take a tender care of the hearts of their inferiors and to make minions of menials.* The burden that is borne in these circumstances by the man below seems to become light through its very significance, through its very human beauty. His labour is glorified by being a fraction of popular endeavour and endurance, helping forward a grand general movement or supporting a grand life, the virtues and achievements of which are sufficiently beyond his power to command his admiration without provoking his envy. This is human. This is positive. This the meanest understand at once. It is part of the most magnificent traditions of mankind. A certain good taste, a certain understanding of the springs of human action, ought even to incline all those for whom menial offices are performed actually to cultivate and preserve that modicum of genuine superiority which alone can permit them to look on without offending their servants while the menial office is being performed.

But what do we see to-day? Endless toil, endless misery, black squalor, disease and disgust, without anything or any one great enough to justify them or shed a ray of glory upon them, even if they were inevitable. Not only is there nothing—no grand purpose or grand caste— to give present burden-bearers the feeling that they have something worth living and toiling for; but the very people for whom the meanest and most characterless tasks are performed nowadays are never even seen by the wretched underlings who perform these tasks for them. In this way the menial office is robbed of all its human sanction, beauty and depth, and it becomes merely what it actually is in scientific fact, without emotional glorifi-cation—a dirty job which no money, no pecuniary rewards can cleanse.

For, even supposing that, like foolish and idealistic Utopians, we could fancy a state of affairs from which hard toil and misery were entirely absent, and in which nothing in the shape of squalor or sordidness necessarily formed part of the lives of the lowest strata of society; nevertheless we could not conceive of a community in which no menial office would have to be performed, for some one or something, were it only the cleaning of a machine. Where, then, could we seek that person or persons who would make us perform even that menial office cheerfully, with love and without rankling indig-nation? Where could you or I, to-day, hope to find the man for whom we would willingly perform the meanest office?

A commercial and industrial age, by founding every-thing upon a money basis, forgot that there was humanity and not machinery behind the exchange of coin for care; and that all the money in the world cannot build up heart, conscience, desire, love, good cheer and contentedness, in the way that a healthy, inspiring and inspiriting human relationship can.

That is why our *domestic* servants, that is to say all those servants who come into the closest contact with their superiors, will be the last to revolt, especially against those of us who have still preserved enough of the patriarchal spirit to make them feel that they get more than their money for their work. The action of domestic servants in regard to Mr. Lloyd George's Insurance Act was signi-ficant in this respect. That clause in the Insurance Act which referred to them was a legislative attempt to make the breach which already separates them from the patri-archal care of their employers even wider than previous legislation had already made it; and behind all the economic arguments that were raised against this new negative measure, there was a great deal of conscious and unconscious opposition to the anti-patriarchal spirit which animated it, as many of the letters addressed by servants to the Press actually proved.

Still, what an infinitesimal portion of labour is accounted for by domestic servants alone! And what a vast army of people who work for us lie without our gates, where neither our eye nor our voice can reach them, where not even a knowledge either of our purpose, of our aspirations, or of the justification of it all, can ever cheer them; simply because at present there is no such purpose, aspiration or justification. Even the religious meaning of their lives is rapidly departing from them; though this is certainly of less value as a cohering and uniting force than that other meaning which is given them by having glory shed on their lives by the loftiness, the equilibrium, the wisdom and the beauty of those whom they serve.

That is why the misery of to-day is blacker than any misery that has ever been seen on earth before; that is why the hopelessness and hate of to-day are more real and more profound than all the hopelessness and hate that have ever existed in human life until now; and that is why all forces which at present are tending to make the breach between man and servant greater; all forces, whether demagogic, religious, social or educational, which incline to further and greater separation and personal strangeness between the leisured and the working classes, are the most infernal and most devilish forces of the age. "For," as Bolingbroke said, "to divide can never be an expedient for good purposes, any more than to corrupt; since the peace and prosperity of a nation will always depend upon uniting, as far as possible, the heads, hearts and hands of the whole people, and on improving, not debauching morals." [1]

Thus the minister who rules by dividing, who acquires power by separative and disturbing means, ought by that

---

[1] *A Dissertation upon Parties* (Davies, 1775), p. xxiii of Dedication. See also Disraeli in *Coningsby* (Langdon Davis Edition), p. 289, where the author ascribes the decline of public virtues to the fact that the various classes-of the country are arrayed against each other.

one act alone to earn the odium and contempt of all parties. To divide is the incompetence of rule, to separate is the cowardice of the desperate legislator.

And now to speak of the second kind of misery. The *material* superiors of the present age, the top-dogs—" the upper ten thousand," as they are called—are fully aware of the horrors and terrors at the base of the social edifice; they are also fully conscious of the fact that neither their lives, nor their functions, nor the direction and nature of modern life in general, justify these horrors and terrors; and in consequence of this knowledge they are profoundly ill at ease and their consciences feel intolerably heavy.

Nobody knows better than the sensitive unit of this upper ten thousand that for many generations now the heart of the people has been spurned and neglected, and its character mutilated.

The old conscience-stiller, the scientific " Mother Siegel's Soothing Syrup " which Darwin and his school flung to these conscience-stricken " upper ten," by telling them that all this aching misery and cruel struggle at the base led inevitably to the " survival of the fittest," has ceased at last from soothing them, because it is no longer believed. As Thorold Rogers says, " It was inexpressibly soothing to those who had brought about the situation, for it seemed to show that nature, not man, was the cause of it, that it was the result of an inexorable law, and in no sense the result of positive and partial legislation." [1] But it was soon discovered that misery, as Adam Smith had foreseen, was not even the check on population that it was supposed to be; for with Rogers we have discovered that " oppressed people become reckless." Thus the terrible fact gradually came to light that the fittest to survive in this stew of plunder against plunder, exploitation against exploitation, and greed against greed, which is called " unrestricted competition " and " *laissez-faire* " (literally : let

1 *The Industrial and Commercial History of England*, p. 57. For a very interesting refutation of the belief that the paupers' struggle with one another leads to anything, see pp. 56–61 of Rogers' book.

the capitalistic trader have his way, unguided and un-limited) was neither a very desirable nor a very admirable specimen, and the comforting thought that things can be left to themselves—which, by-the-bye, seems to have animated all Victorian thinkers up to the time of Herbert Spencer—is now, thank Heaven! in its death agony.

With the general decline of this belief, it was only natural that charity, which hitherto had been either sporadic or traditionally virtuous, should become feverish, system-atic, methodical, eager and astoundingly munificent. For if charity be a flower, then its most powerful forcing manure is most certainly neither the altruism of spotless innocence nor of guileless simplicity, but the excrementa of an uneasy conscience, or of a vain and purse-proud heart.

Munificent charity and boundless benevolence are, however, no cure for evils in the social organism. They do not even skim the surface of the fundamental causes of these evils. They do accomplish one thing though; they help to abate the awful self-accusations which tend to rack the hearts of any class or caste which has ceased to be aware of any genuine justification for its peculiar privi-leges, or of any grand scheme of life or politics which might, at a pinch, help it to consider the burden borne by those below it as useful, as necessary, or as sanctified.

When social evils are prevalent and potent, charity and benevolence are not the counter-agents chosen by rulers or deep thinkers. They are essentially the counter-agents which occur to the shallowest and least thoughtful minds. Given the necessary means, any man can be a philan-thropist in the ordinary "charitable" sense, any man can endow hospitals or homes for incurables, or refuges for waifs and strays, or asylums for the blind, the crippled and the sick. These are "cures" that any vain fool with a banking account can dispense as long as his money lasts. But to attack these evils as enemies, to revise the scheme that has brought them about, to uproot the first principles from which they spring, and to institute such reforms (not patchwork readjustments) as will render their continuance impossible or their justification a thing recognised by all—even the sufferers themselves—requires something more than money can purchase. It requires ruler qualities of the highest order, knowledge covering the widest range, and thought of the deepest kind, correlated with all the leisure that would render these possessions fruitful and operative.

The fact that the ignorant plutocratic solution of social evils neither impresses the masses nor anybody else, is proved by the irrefutable truth that it is precisely in this very age when, according to all accounts, philanthropic and charitable undertakings absorb greater sums of money than they have ever absorbed before, that Socialism, class-hatred and ingratitude are most rampant and most bitter.

These ignorant or "subject" methods of redressing wrongs do not therefore command respect; for there is nothing so sensitive to the touch of the experienced hand as the subordinate, whether he be a horse or an inferior unit in a great nation.

It is important not to overlook this, more particularly when we feel inclined to explain such difficult and recondite matters as the action of the people in regard to the Parliament Act of 1911, by referring in a leisurely and easy manner to *artificially* stirred-up hatred.

The quantity of subject movements, alone, which are on foot at present is literally bewildering—announcements of them come with every post, and they show how conscious even the unimaginative and unthinking men in the street, even the dull-witted spinsters with their small modicum of learning and leisure, are becoming of the disorder, the misrule and the incompetence in higher spheres to-day. For if you look into these movements, started and supported by the subject mind, whether of an old maid or of an old colonel, you will find that they are chiefly corrective in their nature—that is to say, calculated to patch up certain flaws in the existing social edifice.

A DEFENCE OF ARISTOCRACY

The Eugenic[1] and the Ethical movements are cases in point, as are also all the societies and institutions for the prevention or promotion of this or that; as are also all charitable and benevolent bodies. Any individual subject who happens to recognise what he, from his back parlour, conceives to be an evil, is at liberty to gather a few of his neighbours around him and to set to work to put it right.

And since the uninitiated subject is, in the majority of cases, neither a deep student of human nature nor a deep thinker in legislative and sociological science, and as there is no general plan or direction prescribed to him from above, he is generally satisfied with effecting certain minor changes which he would call " improvements in the welfare of the submerged, by increasing their material comfort."

No superior purpose or general idea governs all these subject movements, so that their combined efforts may help to consummate a perfectly definite and preconceived plan. No superior power exists which, with profound knowledge to support it, can lay down its hand and say emphatically " No! " to any organisation or institution which seems in its purpose to diverge too materially from the general scheme laid down for the nation's collective weal and glory—and for the simple reason that there is no such general scheme!

But we should not expect the mind of the subject to do any more than it is doing. We should not expect the mind of the subject to behave like the mind of the ruler. How could a subject mind create a co-ordinating and regenerating scheme? How could it do more than patch and plaster when things go wrong? A nation ought to be only too glad when each of its subject members is so conscious of the specialised knowledge and capabilities required for his own particular business as positively to repudiate any concern with matters beyond, or merely outside, his sphere of power. But what we may and do

[1] For a criticism of the aims and methods of this movement see Chapter VII.

expect is that some one in the position of a ruler, with the knowledge, the traditions, and the leisure of a ruler, should apply his mind to questions of State, and exert it with all the earnestness that the solemnity of the matter would seem to inspire. I am not forgetting the many blots which such ordinary people as Howard, Wilberforce, Romilly, Miss Carpenter, Sheriff Watson and others removed from our legal system; I merely maintain that such work is patchwork, and has no creative value at all.

Unfortunately, it is precisely when the subject mind, with all its other multifarious and often purely self-preservative preoccupations, is left to concern itself with these questions that things get into such a hopeless muddle; and only correctives or antidotes are prescribed, when a fundamental general scheme or plan alone, which would sweep away the necessity for any correctives and antidotes, is the crying need.

England, with her long Protestant tradition, is admittedly the land of Amateurism *par excellence*. What does a false note or a false value in politics matter, when we are brought up amid false notes and false values, perpetrated daily in our immediate circle by a legion of amateur singers, pianists, painters and writers? I say, "England with her long Protestant tradition," because the influence of this last factor in promoting the spirit of Amateurism should not be forgotten. When an Englishman says, "Every man has a right to his own opinion," he little knows how truly Protestant or anarchical this remark is. Apart from its being merely an impudent and foolish platitude, however, it is dangerously untrue. And any one who requires this contention of mine to be supported had better stop reading this book here and turn his mind to more compatible matter. In any case I shall not waste time in supporting it. To those people who really concern me, my attitude on this point will be quite plain. Suffice it, therefore, to say, that the heart of Protestantism and Protestant tradition is this presumptuous and swollen-headed notion that every man has a right to have his say in all things.[1] The very foundation of Luther's attitude of revolt against a higher authority on Church doctrine, which was the belief that the profoundest things can be made questions for the "individual conscience" to decide, received its highest sanction from that great apostle of anarchy and revolt—St. Paul.

"Do ye not know," said St. Paul to the Corinthians, "that the saints shall judge the world? and if the world shall be judged by you, are ye unworthy to judge the smallest matters?" (1 Cor. vi. 2). No Protestant who was allowed by his Church to become acquainted with this inflammatory doctrine ever doubted that he *could* judge the smallest matters. And St. Paul proceeds, "Know ye not that ye shall judge angels? How much more things that pertain to this life?" There is no limit to such impudence, and once it becomes thoroughly absorbed by a nation, there is no limit to Amateurism. Who would dare to set the affairs of earthly government, the affairs of sociology, politics and general state-craft above the judging of angels? Consequently, if later on we are going to judge angels, sociology, politics and state-craft must surely be child's play now! This is the logic at the root of political Amateurism or Democracy. And Matthew Arnold might have inveighed against this logic until Doomsday, he would never have succeeded in refuting it

---

[1] This spirit reaches its zenith in Puritanism and its first cousin Scotch Presbyterianism. James I saw this perfectly well, and when he was asked whether he would tolerate a diversity of religious ceremonies—a toleration favourable to the Presbyterians, he said : " A Scottish presbytery agreeth as well with a monarchy as God and the devil. Then Jack and Tom and Will and Dick shall meet, and at their pleasure censure me and my councils and all our proceedings. . . . Stay, I pray you, for one seven years, before you demand that from me, and if then you find me pursy and fat, and my windpipes stuffed, I will perhaps hearken to you ; for let that government be once set up, I am sure I shall be kept in breath ; then shall we all of us have work enough . . ."—meaning, of course, that anarchy would be rife.— S. R. Gardiner, *The First Two Stuarts and the Puritan Revolution* (1905), pp. 14–15.

had he not first overcome its procreator—the Pauline impudence of the New Testament.

But although England has gone very far indeed in the realisation of this fatal doctrine, although her evil example is now being followed, just as it was in industry and commerce, by the whole of the civilised world—since she was the first to prepare the machinery for the evil—why should she not be the first to put her foot down and declare an end to it? For, despite the fact that the modern democratic state counts—nay, insists upon—an amateur in politics (the average voter) raising his voice as high as that of the serious and deeply thoughtful student of the question; in England, at least, we have been able to preserve a class of men who are placed in an exceptionally ideal position for the task of ruling and, therefore, of guiding with paternal solicitude the voices (the suffrages) of these amateur politicians and legislators whom the State condemns to incompetent meddling. In the landed aristocracy we had the good fortune to possess a body of men who had all the opportunity, the leisure and the self-preservative impulses for becoming deeply human and deeply wise rulers. We, therefore, possessed at least the machinery for that desirable counter-check to the evils that were bound to arise from proletarian politics, in the form of a caste which, by its example, its wise counsel and forethought, its careful scrutiny and censorship of the mental food of the people, its fatherly protection and superior knowledge, and its presbyopic altruism, might ultimately have convinced us of its indispensability, value and power.

Is it to be supposed, despite the germ of separative anarchy that is thought by some to lie in all Englishmen's hearts, that such a caste, with all the privileges of leisure and wealth it enjoyed—privileges which must be granted if deep study and profound thought are to be made possible—is it to be supposed, I say, that such a caste would have been overthrown if it had shown its fitness for the lofty task tradition had bequeathed to it?

A DEFENCE OF ARISTOCRACY

It is impossible to conceive of such a revolution when a caste so placed fulfils all that its inferiors have a right to expect from it. In the simple act of giving to the rest of their fellows a direction, a general purpose or aspiration, alone, such a body of men would have found the means of making themselves both loved and respected. For, as Disraeli observed, " Man is only truly great when he acts from the passions; never irresistible but when he appeals to the imagination." [1]

But, far from giving them a general purpose, direction or aspiration, they did not even see to it that the people should cultivate or even preserve the character that is required in order to be able to profit from such things when they were given. It is no idle statement to say that such a vast organisation as the Salvation Army (whatever its actual merits or demerits may be) would have been a superfluous and preposterous piece of subject meddle-someness if the governing classes of England had " with fear and trembling taken care of the heart of the people." And how many other subject movements are there whose aims are similiar to those of the Salvation Army!

When factories arose, when the age and youth of the nation began to be herded into the slums and lower middle-class streets of large cities, how many were there among the ruling classes who attempted to organise their social life in such a manner that the deleterious influence of their occupations upon their mind and body might be either neutralised or at least mitigated? Simultaneously with the employment of women and children in factories and mines, how many of our rulers saw to it that the precious links in the traditional culture of the home which join grandmother, mother and daughter together in healthy and normal families, should not be cruelly sun-

---

[1] *Coningsby* (Langdon Davies), p. 292. Even that dry-as-dust econo-mist, John Stuart Mill, made a most unexpected admission on this point. He said, " It is very shallow, even in pure economics, to take no account of the influence of imagination."—*Political Economy*, Book II, Chapter X, p. 202.

dered? How many fought to preserve the arts of the needle, of the saucepan, and of the besom and wash-tub, when capitalistic sweating threatened to poison all such arts, and all desire for such arts, in the characters of the working masses? Whereas a stupid subject movement under the banner of Temperance was of course made to suppress the drink evil, how many rulers thought of keeping the working man at home by preserving the workman's womenfolk from deterioration? Naturally, stupid subject movements arose for improving the homes of the working classes; but how many of these understood or militated against the root of the evil? How many of the ruling classes sought to shelter the labouring proletariat *not only from the cruel and unfair competition,*[1] but also from the frequently vitiating moral and political influence of all the ruck and scum of Europe, who were allowed to settle down among our fellow-countrymen in the poorer districts of our urban centres? Who foresaw that *thrift* would gradually be hunted from the character of the so-called submerged, if for generations they were disheartened, demoralised and rendered reckless by a heartlessness and a hopelessness which they could neither understand nor oppose?

How many of the ostensible protectors of the people took care to ascertain that even the literature which reached the masses should not be in bad taste or demoralising? I do not mean "demoralising" in the Puritan sense; for, according to the Puritan, you can perpetrate any piece of literary or intellectual vulgarity in your books, so long as you do not refer, save with horror, to the joy and beauty of sex. I mean "demoralising" in the sense of destroying right and proper ideas concerning humanity, human aims, human prestige and human relationship.

Who saw to it, then, that if the people had any mental

---

[1] As this cruel competition was tolerated as a source of profit by the capitalists, the latter must be held directly responsible for all the grave incidental evils that have resulted from the enormous alien population in our midst.

culture at all, it should be of a healthy character- and nerve-strengthening kind? In asking all these questions I am not forgetting the many charitable attempts that were made to meet and mitigate the evils consequent upon the last hundred and fifty years of " Progress "; because, as I have pointed out, these were all subject efforts and were not only absurdly inadequate, but constantly very stupid and superficial. What I mean is that as fast as the evils, or threats of evils, arose, which gave the impetus to charitable *subject* efforts, no *ruler* mind appeared who questioned the whole system at the root of these evils, or who dared to slam the door in the face of an innovation which, togged out in the infernally deceptive garb of " Progress," yet unscrupulously preyed upon the spirit and character of a great nation's social foundation—the working classes.

To take the question of education alone, let us see what light it can throw upon this stage in the examination of the principle of aristocracy. Before I proceed, however, I should like the reader thoroughly to understand two things: (1) That I do *not* approve of the present system of education. (2) That I only select it for scrutiny because it is one of the chief departments of state administration which is concerned with caring for the hearts of the people, and, therefore, despite its misguidedness, as far as method is concerned, presents a measure according to which we can gauge the earnestness of the governing classes in entering upon the task of caring for the hearts of the people.

To begin with, then, the whole system of National Education in England before the Act of 1870 was a matter merely of state-aided voluntary effort; and in order that the precise extent of this state aid may be realised, the following figures, though few, may be sufficient to support my indictment of those who, during the first seventy years of the last century, were in charge of the nation's character and mind. I should like to caution the reader against believing that I approve of a cash or quantity test in matters of this sort; but, since it is the only available test we have, it must be used simply as a means of measuring the warmth, not necessarily the efficiency or profundity of statesmen's dealings with this matter; while we must also bear in mind that this cash test is so far reliable seeing that it reveals *all* that the statesmen concerned with it undertook to do in the matter of caring for the character and mind of the people.

Previous to 1833, Parliament appears to have made no grant whatsoever, save in Ireland,[1] to the independent voluntary bodies who, in a *subject* manner, were trying to solve the problem of national education to the best of their limited ability. And even the *subject* attempts at grappling with the problem were shown by Henry Brougham's Commission, started in 1816, to be greatly hampered and rendered inoperative by the landlords and clergy of the different parishes. For it was discovered that the charity schools throughout the country were not only monopolised by these gentlemen, but also *that the latter were actually embezzling the ample revenues provided for the upkeep of these institutions!* In 1833, "after a long controversy as to whether the Government had any right at all to interfere with education" (!),[2] with a population of about 14,000,000 in England and Wales alone, the first grant of £20,000 was made to the *subject* voluntary schools. In 1839, with a population of about 15,000,000, this grant was increased to £30,000; in 1846, with a population of about 16,000,000, it grew to £100,000; in 1851, with a population of 17,927,609 it was £150,000; in 1853, with a population of about 18,000,000, it became £396,000; in 1858, with a population of about 19,000,000, it stood at £663,400; in 1861, with a population of 20,066,224, it was £813,400; in 1865, with a population of about 21,500,000, it was only £636,800; in 1870, with a population of about 22,500,000, it rose again to £894,000; in 1876, with a population of about 23,200,000, it was

---

1 And this was due to anti-Catholic feeling and bitterness.

2 *A Text-Book in the History of Education*, by Paul Monroe, Ph.D., p. 733.

£1,600,000; and in 1878, with a population of 24,000,000, it was £2,200,000.

Taking this system as we find it without further criticism, the absurd inadequacy of these grants may be realised by comparing them with the present expenses of the Educational Department of State in relation to the population. But the most preposterous feature in this question, from a ruler standpoint, was the manner in which the supposed rulers of the nation slothfully and incompetently preferred to avail themselves of individual subject effort and initiative, rather than to face the difficulty and devise, establish and run an educational organisation of their own. But the action of the English governing classes in regard to this question must not be considered as exceptional. It is characteristic of their whole attitude towards internal politics for the last two hundred and thirty years; and when Sir Joshua Fitch speaks of the provision for the education of the people of England as being practically the product of a haphazard happy-go-lucky system of muddling through somehow, without either mastery or profound understanding,[1] he simply provides the formula for a criticism of almost everything that has been done in this country for the last hundred years in the matter of solving social problems.

In a nation where so little was done for the hearts of the people, it ought to surprise no one to find that next to nothing was done for the care of their bodies. If trade and capitalistic exploitation of the labourer had been allowed to deteriorate the mind and character of the masses, it could not be hoped that in a Christian country, which places spirit above body, anything would be done to preserve their bodies from similiar evils. No one

[1] His actual words are : " The public provision for the education of the people of England is not the product of any theory or plan formulated beforehand by statesmen or philosophers ; it has come into existence through a long course of experiments, compromises, traditions, successes, failures and religious controversies." See *Encycl. Britannica* (10th Edition), Article : " Education."

moved a finger to prevent the deterioration of the bodies of the lower classes through the gradual deterioration of the mothers of these classes. It was soon found that among urban factory girls, for instance, confinements were frequently attended not only with great difficulty but also with great danger. This evil alone ought to have suggested not merely a patchwork remedy, but a questioning of the whole system which gave rise to it. Nothing fundamental was done! With romantic levity it was fondly imagined that a great nation might be maintained on sickly bodies. Even to this day, the problem of the body and its pre-eminent importance has not yet been faced fairly and squarely. Meanwhile, however, we have the impudence to continue sending missionaries to China—the country in whose Book of Rites even the essential qualities of a wet-nurse (for cases in which such a domestic auxiliary cannot be dispensed with) are carefully prescribed for the community, and have been so prescribed for centuries by the presbyopic legislators of the nation. This is true education. All education that does not begin with the suckling's body and its requirements is little more than romantic fooling—*dangerous* romantic fooling. And when this dangerous romantic fooling is more or less rendered sacrosanct by Puritanical contempt for the body; when it is condoned by the highest sanction of all—the sanction of the State religion, which argues that the salvation of the soul can be impeded or prevented neither by physical disability nor any sickness of the body, however bungled, however botched, inodorous or gangrenous that body may be; but rather that sickness, botchedness, or crippledom are often a passport to Heaven, because they are a trial and a chastisement sent by a loving Providence—then an undue importance is attached to the so-called " soul," beside which the body sinks into perilous insignificance. Sooner or later when such doctrines prevail their consequence must be brought home to those professing them in a manner which is as ugly as it is inevitable. In modern Europe we are rapidly approaching a point at which it will be too late, too hopeless, too appalling to do anything to arrest the decadent torrent. Is there a panic at this thought? Are our leaders already solemn with dread at the prospect? Nothing of the kind! The majority are too used to sickness to see that there is anything abnormal in its prevalence. The minority are too near to sickness, too much compromised by its contact and its culture, any longer to feel that instinctive abhorrence which was undermined once for all when healthy mankind were taught that a pure soul could sanctify anything—even foul breath. And, meanwhile, everything is allowed to drift and drift, while rulers studiously ignore all dangers, all grievances and all morbid tendencies which are not pressed upon their attention by a subject agitation.

What can possibly be expected from such a manner of dealing with vital questions? We can expect only what we see—a nation seething with discontent, a nation packed to overflowing with characterless, spiritless, ugly and degenerate people, and a host of amateur political surgeons and physicians at work day and night, plastering and patching up the tottering though luxurious social organism, while it learns to forget that numbers and wealth are no measure of a great nation, but only a deceptive feature, if its heart, character and body are degraded.

All this time, however, we have had a caste—a superior, leisured, educated and wealthy class—who enjoyed the privileges of rulers, and who ought to have felt it their duty not to enjoy those privileges for nothing. Every consideration that ever influenced the minds of rulers ought to have conduced to make them face these problems one by one as fast as they appeared, and to meditate upon them until, to use Mr. Edward Spencer's words, they would have " foreseen and provided against " evils which were bound to result from the untested and untried innovations pouring in anarchically from all sides. Remembering that they were a privileged caste in an ostensibly democratic community, their instinct of self-preservation alone, much more therefore their instinct of perfection, beauty and order, ought to have told them that by neglecting to dwell thoughtfully upon the character and spirit of the people, and by neglecting to preserve that character and spirit from deterioration, they were simply condemning the coming *true* democracy itself, as well as themselves, to utter ruin. There was no excuse for this neglect; for had not Disraeli, their greatest teacher, told them early in the nineteenth century, "that there is something to be considered beyond forms of government— national character"; whereupon he proceeds, "and herein should we repose our hopes. If a nation be led to aim at the good and great, depend upon it, whatever be its form, the government will respond to its convictions and its sentiments." [1]

The fact that this has not been done in all these years, the fact that these problems are not even regarded as problems yet, cannot possibly recoil half so heavily upon the subject's as upon the ruler's head. With but few exceptions, the Lords, in their heart of hearts, have all been democrats and plebeians throughout. A small handful of rare ones apart, among whom it is a joy and a solace to think of the seventh Earl of Shaftesbury, they have said like the greedy underman who is a constitutional pauper, "I want everything for nothing!" But they ought to have known that their life of pleasure could be no justification for the burdens the lower orders bore. Only a life spent in ruling with a deep concern for the welfare, character and safety of the burden-bearer, only a lifetime spent in the promotion of the glory and good taste of their nation, could be a justification of the burdens of those beneath them.

It never occurred to them, however, to give something in return (not in kind, but in thought, forethought, meditation and wise ruling), for the priceless privileges they enjoyed; and thus they not merely lost the confidence of the community and all confidence in themselves, but also

[1] *Coningsby*, p. 427.

brought the great order to which they belonged into dis-
repute—an act for which all those who, like myself,
fervently believe in aristocratic rule, will have some
difficulty in forgiving them.

For this tutorship of ruling, of which I have spoken in
the present chapter, involves among the other duties mentioned, one tremendous responsibility. It involves the
responsibility of building up a healthy culture, a culture
alluring and powerful enough to knit a whole people
together, a culture sufficiently imposing in its grandeur
to render its spread over the face of the earth a boon and
not a bane to other subject peoples, and one so self-
evidently superior as to be able to achieve its victories
almost without contest, just as the culture of the ancient
Incas conquered and spread.

It is a great culture that makes a people, or that creates
a people out of a hotch-potch of peoples,[1] and leads them
to regard themselves as one huge organism to be defended
and upheld against barbarians. And it is the superior
men alone of a nation who can undertake, and who have
always undertaken, this task of creating that miraculous
leaven and tonic, a great Culture. And what is the sort
of culture we at present have to hand on to a people whom
we draw or force into our sphere of power? It is at most
the culture of the commercial city and of an exploded
superstition; it is at most a culture in which we ourselves
are rapidly losing all faith, and which spreads ill-health
and misery wherever it goes.

It is so devoid of all true and self-evident superiority
that for over a century now a whole nation like the inhabitants of the East Indies have held aloof from it and are

[1] See J. K. Bluntschli, *The Theory of the State* (3rd Edition of
Authorised Translation), p. 87. "A mere arbitrary combination or
collection of men has never given rise to a People. Even the voluntary
agreement and social contract of a number of persons cannot create
one. To form a People, the experiences and fortunes of several generations must co-operate, and its permanence is never secured until a
succession of families handing down its accumulated culture from
generation to generation has made its characteristics hereditary."

growing to despise it ever more and more. It is so lacking in convincing value that we ourselves have not the heart to impose it on any one. It is so anarchical and feeble that it has lost all power of persuasion even over ourselves. The Christian portion of it has been assailed again and again; and having been found not only wanting in healthy values, but also untenable in more than one particular, is gradually tottering to its fall and is rapidly losing its power as a moral force. If such a thing as a culture of doubt and indifference be possible in any sense whatever, this is the culture we now possess; and the only definite principles it contains are principles drawn from the struggle for material success, material comfort and the mechanical complication and acceleration of life. Nothing has been done or even attempted by the actual governing classes to create another culture on the moribund body of the expiring one. And when we look in their direction for help in this respect, it is rather with despair than with hope that we ultimately turn away.

The first principle of every sound and healthy morality ought to be this: " Thou shalt not sacrifice the greater to the less; but, if need be, the less to the greater."

In these three first chapters it may appear to the superficial Nietzschean that in laying all the stress upon the duties of the governing classes to the working people, I am subverting this first principle of a sound and healthy morality. This, however, is not the case. At a time when the leisured classes simply live in ease upon the labour of their inferiors without undertaking any of those arduous and profound duties which, as I have tried to show in these three chapters, can be performed only by them (the privileged class), they cease from being the *greater* portion of a people. And if we are to speak of sacrifice, then it is they who should be the victims. In the eyes of a philosopher, the sacrifice of inferiors, when the ostensible superiors are simply parasites, or very nearly so, is an intolerable evil. It is only when the superiors are leading a grand march, the benefits of which must inevitably conduce to a greater degree of healthy, flourishing and beautiful life—it is only then that the sacrifice of inferiors can for an instant be˜tolerated or condoned. It is only then that the weak and those devoid of power, if the necessity should arise, may with the clean conscience of the community, be left to perish by the wayside, or be exploited for the profit of life, the intensity and excellence of life.

When, therefore, the governing or proprietary classes become mere hedonists, spending their lives in a round of pleasure and neglecting those material and spiritual duties which all power should suggest to the healthy mind; when this happens, you are sacrificing the greater to the less, if one single individual of the labouring inferiors dies through any hardship or sickness which can be ascribed to the system under which he is yoked, and which cannot be traced to his own independent choice or crime.

Let historical pedants and Greek scholars say what they may, the rule of our landed aristocracy in England had every one of the essentials for being the rule of the best. They were the best in so far as material and spiritual circumstances went, and they were the best in respect of opportunity. In order to make themselves intrinsically the best spiritually and physically in the nation, all they required to do was to discipline and refresh or augment their stock with more discrimination and to avail themselves of their exceptional chances to acquire that deep intellectual[1] and bodily culture which is denied to the parvenu. At one time their prestige alone lent weight to their wildest utterances, and the dignity of their position was in itself a sufficient guarantee of their worthiness. What a history of neglect and wilful squandering of golden chances *their* "progress" must have been, for it to be possible for a recent writer with some plausibility to say

[1] See Ku Hung-Ming, op. cit., p. 58. "Without deep intellectual culture, you cannot have true ideas ; you cannot distinguish false from true ideas. Again, without ideas you cannot interpret facts."

of them : " They seldom rise above the level of mediocrity. Physically, morally and intellectually they are a species in a steady decline, and there is reason to believe that they are conscious of it." [1]

If they had been a healthy thinking nobility, an intellectual, inquiring and conscientious nobility; if, instead of falling in with the general commercial and industrial stampede for riches and plunder, they had halted to think of the consequences of it all to the national character and capacity, and if only they had paused to give an example of prudence and of ruling wisdom to the less favoured and less cultured among their fellows, how incalculable would their rewards have been to-day!

You may reply that, had they done so, they would only have perished like martyrs, after the fashion of their predecessors the Cavaliers, slain by the overwhelming hordes of the vulgar and tasteless upstarts who ushered in all the extremely questionable innovations of the late eighteenth and the early nineteenth centuries. I do not believe that there is a single cogent argument to support this view; for in the nineteenth, unlike the seventeenth century, they would have had the people on their side. It was not known, at least to the well-to-do people in the seventeenth century, that in fighting on the side of Cromwell and so-called " Liberty," they were opening their arms to a race of capitalistic and unscrupulous oppressors. But in the nineteenth many more people than in the seventeenth century would have realised that any portion of the nation that insisted upon respect for the burden, any part of the community who tested, weighed and judged every innovation as it arose, must be on their side. Or, if they did not know that, they would soon have learnt it. The Liberals of the nineteenth century, then as now, like the Parliamentary party of Cromwell's time, may be regarded entirely as people who are " on the make"; their legislation in itself , capitalistic as it always has been, is entirely against the people, however much, on the surface, it may

1 See Arthur Ponsonby, M.P., *The Decline of Aristocracy*, p. 141.

seem in their favour.[1] Thus during the nineteenth century and after, the Tories have had the chance of their lives. Behind them they had the fact, the knowledge of which Charles I's Cavaliers did not possess—the fact that "as the power of the Crown has diminished, the privileges of the people have disappeared; till at length the Sceptre has become a pageant, and its subject has degenerated again into a serf."[2] They could have taken the place of the Crown in England as the patriarchal rulers of the community, and they could have proved that other contention of Disraeli's that "power has only one duty: to secure the social welfare of the People."[3]

But they missed their opportunity. Probably they did not even see it. For there are some of them even to-day who will be found to declare that such statements as I have just quoted from Disraeli are *Radical*, and not susceptible of adoption by Tories in any way whatsoever! Thus they allowed things to go their own way, and obeyed the stupid indolent behest "*laissez-faire*"; and though I say it without bitterness or resentment—for I am myself an ardent supporter of an hereditary noble caste—the fate with which the Lords met in the autumn of 1911 was not unmerited. They even deserved to appear as cowards before the eyes of the whole world. And their best friends, rather than conceal the real truth from them, ought to prefer to prove their friendship by telling them the whole of it and showing them how, even at this late hour, their lost reputation may be retrieved.

[1] This point has been so ably explained by Mr. J. M. Kennedy in his *Tory Democracy* that I need scarcely burden my pages with a repeated explanation.

[2] Disraeli's *Sybil*, p. 488 (Longmans, Green and Co., 1899).

[3] *Ibid.*, p. 312.

CHAPTER IV

PURITANISM, TRADE AND VULGARITY

" Commerce, Opulence, Luxury, Effeminacy, Cowardice, Slavery : these are the stages of national degradation."—WILLIAM COBBETT, *The Register* (August 1805).

To the Englishman of average culture, even when he is not biassed by any party or religious feeling, Charles I is little more than a captivating figure of misguided royalty, possessing a considerable measure of romantic charm. With his long hair, his velvet suit, lace collar and long-maned charger, it is his exterior, and, perhaps, his all too violent death as well, that chiefly endears this unhappy monarch of the seventeenth century to the sentimental Englishman.

If, however, you say to such an Englishman that there is much more than romantic charm in Charles I's character and rule, he will immediately smile upon you with indulgent incredulity, and regard you as a fanatic who is suffering even more severely than he is himself from the seductiveness of bygone dramas and their principal heroes. Indeed, so convinced is he that it is rather the glamour than the sterling quality of Charles, that claims attention, that if this monarch could return to life to-morrow, the only change in his exalted fate that the Englishman, with becoming twentieth-century softness, would make, would consist in deporting the great Stuart to St. Helena, or perhaps to Trinidad, and in sparing his handsome head.

Not long ago, for instance, I had the honour of meeting a certain gentleman who is well known in the literary world of London, and who, moreover, enjoys the distinction of being at the head of one of our greatest publishing firms. He informed me that he, too, was a convinced convert to this romantic cult of the most fascinating figure of the seventeenth century, and smiled almost tearfully over the thought that his son, in whom he had implanted a strong adoration for our beheaded sovereign, had once solemnly raised his hat in the presence of Charles I's golden armour in the Tower of London.

Hoping, at the moment, that there was something more fundamental and more solid in this gentleman's hero-worship than mere sentimentality and the love of a picturesque prince, I suggested to him that there were many rational and very sound reasons for his admiration. In an instant the incredulous smile I had so often seen, and which I confess I had half-dreaded on this occasion too, again spread over the features, even of this hopeful fellow-worshipper, and I was overcome with disappointment. " My son is now fourteen," he said, " and he has been studying history at school. And the other day he declared that I must have been ' pulling his leg ' about Charles I; for he had now learnt to esteem this despicable despot at his proper value! " I protested. But I was merely met by a wave of the hand and a deprecating simper of urbane scepticism. His admiration of Charles I was sartorial, romantic, sentimental, school-girlish—in fact, it was merely a foolish and empty pose!

Apparently it had never occurred to him, despite his undoubted erudition and experience, to ask himself whether, in an age which is in every respect the creation of Charles I's maligners and murderers, a public school history class were precisely the best place in which to hear the truth concerning the Stuart King. Seemingly, he had never inquired whether, at a time when vulgarity, trade and hedonism are paramount, a sober judgment— not to speak of a friendly one—could possibly be formed on this vital question. Without hesitation, without a moment's doubt or shrewd suspicion, this apparently sceptical person had accepted the verdict of a most deceptive and unreliable age, concerning a man who had so little in common with its principles, that in a hopeless endeavour to oppose and defy them, he had heroically given up his life.

And yet the evidence of this fact is accessible to all. The proof of it can be read by everybody and anybody, at any hour, any day. Only a bias that is friendly to the evils of this age, only a prepossession in favour of our materialistic, mechanical, unscrupulous and supinely irresponsible civilisation of "Progress," could so distort the facts as to make Charles I appear as the felon, and the ignoble band of grasping, bigoted and filthy-minded Puritans as the just accusers, in this historical trial and tragedy.

For in spite of all that the school history book may say, Charles I fought for a cause very much more vital and more fundamental than that of despotism. He fought for the cause of flourishing life against the growing, but already powerful forces of modern capitalistic trade, of democracy, and of mere quantity as distinct from quality. He himself, the whole of his government, and his lieutenants were inspired by the watchword "Respect the Burden." Their downfall can be ascribed to the fact that they were no respecters of persons, that they upheld the oppressed against their oppressors, and that they tried, wherever possible, to arrest that vile greed of gain and accumulation, at the mercy of which the lower classes were to be left for evermore, after the opening of the Grand Rebellion. This is not fancy or exaggeration; it is a plain statement of fact.

But Charles I had the most dishonest and most unscrupulous opponents that a man can have. He had to contend with mercenary, vulgar and heartless tradespeople, or with avaricious and unscrupulous men of power among the landed lords and gentry, both of which parties did not hesitate to raise a specious cry of liberty and religious ardour to conceal their true and more material motives. Imagine yourself, for a moment, at war with the most narrow-minded Nonconformists of the present day, on the one hand, and with greedy plutocrats, on the other. If the two groups together marked you as their quarry, what chance do you suppose you could have? What quarter do you suppose they would allow you? Have you ever lived with Puritans, with Nonconformists, with plutocrats? I have! Have you ever tried to thwart them? Have you ever shown them how much you despise them? Only then can you realise who Charles I's enemies were. Only then can you realise the quandary a distinguished and true aristocrat was in, who attempted to reveal the filth and squalor beneath their brazen cries of liberty and religious ardour. I will show in due course what this liberty and religious ardour were worth; for the time being let it suffice to point out that to oppose the ignominious herd who decked their low designs with these inflated war-cries, was to run the risk of appearing as a Papist and a slave-driver when a man was neither the one nor the other.

We know the end of Cæsar Borgia, who attempted to rid the Romagna of its oppressors, and to free the people from the bondage of insufferable tyrants. We know how the escort of Colbert's hearse had to grope secretly through the dark streets of Paris in the dead of night, because the corpse of this great man would otherwise have been torn from its shell, by the very mob to whom he had devoted his whole life, in a vain attempt at emancipating it from an insufferable yoke. We also know the fate of Strafford, who was murdered in cold blood without a single voice of alarm or protest being raised among the lower orders he had protected and succoured all his life. It would seem as if the very attempt to protect the people against un-scrupulous oppressors were foredoomed to failure, owing sometimes to the ignorance of the former, and always to the latter's inordinate power of wealth which triumphs as easily over good taste as it ultimately triumphs over all other obstacles. But, as we shall see, the people are not always ungrateful.

Who, however, are Cæsar Borgia, Colbert and Thomas

Wentworth compared with Charles I? All four fought greed and oppressive opulence for the sake of the people, and three of them died spurned by their protégés. But Charles staked the highest stake in the cause. He was a king, a crowned and powerful monarch—not a mere illegitimate Jew and itinerant preacher, who had nothing to lose and whose antecedents were, to say the least, not of the most distinguished order—but a sovereign who, if he had liked, could have sided with the winning party, the tradesmen and grasping landed nobility, at the cost of the masses for whom he died.

And now that the tradesmen and landed nobility have triumphed for over two hundred and fifty years, what could be more natural than that Charles I should be. the most reviled of monarchs? What could be more feasible than the fact that Thomas Carlyle, that utterly Puritanical and obtuse romanticist and ranter, of the stupidest and vulgarest age in history, should have spoken of this great King's death as follows—

" Thus ends the second Civil War. In Regicide, in a Commonwealth and Keepers of the Liberties of England. In punishment of Delinquents, in abolition of Cobwebs; if it be possible, in a Government of Heroism and Veracity; at the lowest of Anti-Flunkeyism, Anti-Cant, and the endeavour after Heroism and Veracity.[1]

It will be the burden of this chapter to show that this paragraph is a piece of the most utter nonsense and misrepresentation that any sentimental scoundrel has ever written. It will be the object of the facts adduced to show not only that Carlyle lied, but that he must have lied knowingly and deliberately in writing these words, and that, if it were not for the fact that his opinion, as that of a eunuch, must be taken with pity rather than with censure, the above half-dozen lines ought to be sufficient to discredit him for ever in the minds of all conscientious readers of history.

[1] See *Cromwell's Letters and Speeches* (Ward, Lock and Bowden), p. 260.

A DEFENCE OF ARISTOCRACY

And it was this worst kind of Caledonian fool who, at the very time when the poor of England were groaning under their crushing burden of unredressed wrongs, and crying for an able and fearless spokesman, spent his time spluttering peevishly, bombastically, and above all uselessly, through several volumes, over an aristocracy that was beyond all help or repair and had been punished and sufficiently chastised by the very events he set himself to relate.

Is it not, however, a most significant comment on the Puritan and Mercenary Rebellion, that this eunuch takes sides with it *against* the King? What could such a man know of Basilican virtue, not to speak of obelisks and such virile things!

Charles I was unfortunate in his predecessors, and still more unfortunate in his contemporaries. We have seen that the upstart owners of the Church lands, forced upon the country by that unscrupulous Bluebeard, Henry VIII, had introduced a commercial spirit into the English soil. These parvenus, the majority of whom had been obsequious sycophants in the entourage of that most outrageous specimen of English royalty, were now quite settled on their estates, and were running them on purely mercenary lines with a view to reaping the maximum amount of gain possible irrespective of the comfort or happiness of the inhabitants.[1]

[1] For some of the indirect evils of this change, apart from the direct evils resulting from the oppression of the people's friends, the monks, see Garnier, op. cit., pp. 90, 91, *et seq.*, while on p. 94 we find this passage : " The dissolution of the monasteries must have rendered home-life unbearable to many of the rural poor in the times under our notice. Rents were increased, cottagers' rents among others . . . The Tudor crofter's or Tudor cotter's messuage was required for the wants of the sheep-hold. Husbands, wives, woful mothers and fatherless babes had to make way for the ewe and lamb, and so the simple goods which had taken the savings of more than one generation to collect, had to be disposed of at a forced sale, and their owners turned out to starve or steal in the highways. If this occasionally was the heartless practice of the feudal lords, what wide-spread misery must there not have been when it became the general practice of the fresh landowners."

But there was also another class, that of the successful tradesman, which was now invading the rural districts and buying estates in all parts of the country. This element tended only to intensify the commercial spirit which was now spreading over the whole land and transforming its customs just as much as its temper;[1] while in the towns themselves a great and powerful middle class was rising into prominence, thanks to the fortunes which were constantly being amassed in home and over-sea trade.

The destructive influence which these changes brought to bear upon the patriarchal relationship between the lower and the higher orders—a relationship which, though it was never complete or hearty and never worked smoothly, at least had qualities infinitely superior to those of the new *régime*—this destructive influence, together with the abolition of the monasteries, and that still more heinous crime, the appropriation and confiscation of the Guild funds and lands, gave rise to widespread discontent and considerable unrelieved poverty. The fact that Henry VIII alone put 72,000 thieves to death in his own reign, shows the extremes to which desperate indigence had been driven even in his time. Edward VI and Elizabeth had infinite trouble with the poor, and we have only to examine the numerous statutes dealing with the problem of poverty, passed in the latter's reign, in order to realise the extent to which the evil must have been increasing.[2]

Now Rogers tells us that "there is no period in English history in which the English were poorer and more unenterprising than during the last fifty years of the sixteenth and the first forty years of the seventeenth centuries."[3] It is important, for my purpose, to note that the last fifteen years of this period constitute the first fifteen years of Charles I's reign. Moreover Parliament,

---

[1] See Garnier, *History of the English Landed Interest*, Vol. I, pp. 258 *et seq.*

[2] See Sir G. Nicholls, K.C.B., op. cit., Vol. I, pp. 164 *et seq.*

[3] *The Industrial and Commercial History of England*, p. 12.

which, during James's reign had become practised in hostile tactics against the Crown, was now recruiting a large proportion of its members from the new and mercenary class of small landed proprietors, who, as Garnier says, "combined both the haughty pride of the old Norman aristocracy and the cool calculation and shrewd foresight of the merchant."[1]

The poverty laws passed in the previous reigns, tentative and imperfect as they were, yet constituted a fairly adequate piece of State machinery to deal with the difficulties they were calculated to mitigate. It often happened, however, that the very men who were entrusted with the administration of these laws, were rapacious creatures whose interests were in conflict with the means of relief which these laws prescribed, or persons who were too fearful of offending the great landowners of their neighbourhood to dare to complain of their carelessness or actual negligence in regard to the laws in question. Abuses were general; and though beneficent individuals were to be found, a sharp eye had to be kept on the whole of the administrative body, lest the burden-bearers should go wanting, despite the legislation which existed for their special succour. The ruler of a nation, in these circumstances, required to be a man who was no respecter of persons. Now Charles was precisely such a man. If he had been different, he would have found more powerful friends in the hour of his trial. His two greatest ministers, Wentworth and Laud, were also no respecters of persons; they made enemies among the highest, through their absolutely rigid sense of justice and of duty. But, as might have been expected, all three—Charles and his two lieutenants—lost their lives in this quixotic struggle against a mob of unscrupulous shopkeepers, and in the end, as we shall see, only the loyal nobles and the poor clustered round their King to defend him.

Before I go into the details of this struggle between taste and rapacity, duty to the burden-bearer and the

[1] *History of the English Landed Interests*, Vol. I, p. 331.

reckless oppression of him, there is, however, one other sign of the times I would fain discuss. I refer to the rising forces of Puritanism. Concerning who the Puritans were and the scheme of life for which they stood, I shall, in the eyes of some readers perhaps have more than sufficient to say in the next chapter; for the moment I should like to lay stress only upon the close connection which the commercial element in the nation bore to Puritanism. In addition to the wealthy tradesmen who had wandered into the country in search of a pastoral and gentlemanly existence, and the large number of landowners, after the style of Cromwell himself, whose Puritanism was almost a conscientious justification of their being in possession of lands which had once belonged to the Holy Church, London, in which at that time nearly the whole trade of the kingdom was concentrated, was almost entirely Puritan; [1] whilst practically the only two important towns in the west which ultimately opposed Charles in the great struggle, I refer to Bristol and Gloucester, were both likewise strong in trade and in Puritanical opinions. It should also be remembered that East Anglia, Kent and other southern counties, had recently been overrun by Flemish refugees and French Huguenots, and although many of these aliens were at first not necessarily extreme Puritans, as tradesmen and manufacturers they threw in their lot with the Puritan party against the King, and thereby revealed that their sympathy with the religious views of the Parliamentary forces was deeper than with those of the Cavaliers.

This relationship of trade to religion was a most important factor in the struggle between the King and his more powerful subjects. Even in our analytical times it is difficult enough to find people who are sufficiently honest to see clearly into the springs of their actions and desires; but in those days, in which mankind was scarcely conscious

---

[1] *The Political History of England*, Vol. VII, by F. C. Montague, p. 172. For the attachment of London to the Parliamentary party see also Leopold von Ranke, *History of England* (Oxford), Vol. II, p. 209.

at all of the multiplicity of motives that may sometimes conduce to bring about an action which has all the appear-. ance of having sprung from a single desire or aspiration, it was easy—nay, almost inevitable—for the Puritan trades-men to marshal all their mercenary objections to Charles and his lieutenants' paternal and protective government, his beneficent interference with trade, and the check he put upon their rapacious oppression of the lower orders, under two such high-sounding and empty terms as "Liberty" and "No Popery." In this way they appro-priated from the start the two most deceptive and most attractive war-cries which could possibly have been found, to appeal to the masses. And the fact that, despite these seductively alluring devices upon their banner, they failed to draw the non-commercial and poorer classes of the community over to their side, only shows the extent to which Charles I's rule must have endeared him to these portions of the population.

Speaking of the powerful phalanx of saints or zealots in the Commons in 1625, Lingard says—

"They deemed it the first of their duties to eradicate Popery, which like a phantom haunted their imaginations by day and night; wherever they turned they saw it stalk-ing before them; they discovered it even in the gaieties and revelries of the Court, the distinction of rank in the hierarchy, the ceremonies of the Church, and the existence of pluralities among the clergy." [1] And then he proceeds : "What rendered the union of the two parties [the zealots and the country party] more formidable, was the specious colour given to their pretences. They combated for pure religion and civil liberty : to oppose them was to court the imputation of superstition and of slavery." [2]

With the impudent effrontery of extreme Protestants, these people who supposed that the Almighty was always hobnobbing with them and standing perpetually at their elbow, just as the Low Churchmen, Methodists and other

[1] John Lingard, D.D., *History of England*, Vol. VII, p. 286.
[2] *Ibid.*, p. 287.

Nonconformists believe to-day, were not the sort of persons to respect an earthly King, however great. They had harassed poor Elizabeth, who detested them. But, not being strong enough during her reign to defy her openly, they had contented themselves with creeping into corners, allowing their resentment to ferment, and growling that she was an "idle slut" and an "untamed heifer." [1]

The Puritans were people capable of intolerance so cruel and relentless, that the colonies they formed in America became the scenes of the most shocking abuses and oppression that the world has ever experienced. So bitter were they and so resentful towards those who doubted their bigoted and negative creed, that the inhuman tortures they practised upon their opponents when they fell into their power, equals in brutality anything of a similar nature that history records. But I am anticipating. I have yet to bring forth the proofs of these allegations, and these proofs I am reserving for another chapter.

Charles I, who was a man of great intelligence as well as insight, detested the animosity and bitterness which arose from discussions of which his minister Laud subsequently remarked that "no human power could decide." He realised the futility of religious controversy, and did all in his power to effect a peaceful settlement between all the various creeds in his realm. In the proclamation for the peace of the Church issued on June 16, 1626, as also in the Declaration issued in November 1628, the idea was "to secure at least outward peace, by enjoining silence in the pulpits on those points on which men never had been and never will be agreed." [2] The proclamation, so Dean Hook tells us, "was carefully worded and was valued by the King for its impartiality."

[1] *Commentaries on the Life and Reign of Charles I*, by Isaac Disraeli, Vol. I, p. 474.
[2] See *William Laud*, by W. Holden Hutton, p. 59. See also p. 65 for evidence of the fact that even in his instructions to the bishops in December 1629, the King intended "restraint on both sides."

A DEFENCE OF ARISTOCRACY

As Gardiner says, "Charles provided for liberty of opinion,"[1] and when Laud became his principal ecclesiastical official, both he and his master always endeavoured impartially to quell religious agitations, and to do everything in their power to smooth all asperities. "In their attempts to close [religious] discussions for ever," Gardiner observes, "Charles and Laud were, at least, impartial. In vain Dr. Brooke, the Master of Trinity at Cambridge, implored permission to publish a book, which, as he affirmed, would crush the Puritans and reconcile all difficulties at issue." Its publication was forbidden by Laud and the King, and the book never reached the press.[2] In the case of the self-styled Bishop of Chalcedon also, as well as of Montague's book, *Apello Cæsarem*, Mainwaring's Sermons, Dr. Potter and Archbishop Abbot, Charles and his adviser's attitude was one of strict and unbiassed justice.[3]

Many other instances could be given of Charles's impartiality and of his pacific attitude towards the creeds; but the cruelest and most unscrupulous claim that the Puritans put upon him, and one which, in his impartiality and sense of duty to the laws of his nation, he did not evade (save in so far as capital punishment was concerned), was the demand for the severe enforcement of the Elizabethan laws against Catholics. Indeed, he went so far as to instruct all magistrates to put the penal laws in force, and appointed a commission to demand the fines from the recusants. Catholic priests and missionaries were ordered to leave the kingdom, and even the Catholic peers were, on the advice of his Council, disarmed—an act which naturally very much embittered many powerful families.

Seeing that Charles had just married a young Catholic

[1] *The Personal Government of Charles I*, by S. R. Gardiner (1877), Vol. I, p. 21.
[2] *Ibid.*, p. 164.
[3] *Lives of the Archbishops of Canterbury*, by Dr. W. F. Hook, Vol. XI, pp. 182, 183.

wife, it was the acme of brutality to wring this concession from him. But his Royal letters issued against Papists and Puritans, December 15, 1625, show how early in his reign he tried to embody in a communication to each of the extreme parties, that principle of justice to all, together with a firm and legal support of the Church of England, which remained the chief characteristic of his religious position throughout his reign.

Every Parliament he met clamoured for ever more severe measures against the hated Papists. The Commons interrupted the discussion on the state of the finances in the First Parliament, to present the King with a "pious petition," praying him to put in force the penal Statutes against Catholics. They behaved in precisely the same way in the Second Parliament when they formed themselves into three committees, one for religion, a second to consider grievances and a third to discuss evils. And the Committee of Religion once more resolved to enact still more rigorous laws against Popery. The Third Parliament, as Isaac Disraeli observes, was simply "a committee sitting for religion."[1] They declared that "the business of the King of this Earth should give place to the business of the King of Heaven!" and, in addition to the severe enforcement of the laws against Catholics, they were content with demanding nothing short of the immediate death of any priest returning from banishment abroad. In vain did Charles plead that if at any time he had granted indulgence to the Romanists, he had done so in the hope that foreign princes would extend similar indulgences to Protestant subjects. These men were irreconcilable. In spite of the many proofs he had given of his earnest desire to stand firm by the Protestant Church of England, as defined in the statutes, the Puritans looked with a jealous eye upon his Catholic wife, and though her influence in religious matters, far from prevailing with him, never showed signs even of affecting his conduct in the slightest degree, they never ceased from suspecting him and his

[1] Op. cit., p. 308.

ministers of Popery.[1] But what could be expected of a
class of men who were barefaced enough to charge Laud
with Papist leanings, and whose ultimate leader, Oliver
Cromwell, had the audacity to accuse the Archbishop of
" flat Popery! "—a lie so flagrant and so unjustified, that
a mere perusal of history, apart from the evidence of
Laud's own diary, private correspondence and public deeds,
is sufficient to refute it? [2] Is it to be supposed that so
high and impartial an authority as Professor Gardiner
would not have recorded some facts in support of these
suspicions against Laud, if they had been well-founded?
But if the reader still feels any doubt upon this point, let
him refer to Hutton's excellent and compendious
biography of Laud or to the work by Dean Hook or
Heylin. There he will find positive proofs which I cannot
give him in this small space, of the unscrupulous shifts
to which these Puritans resorted, in order to bring their
quarry to earth, and in order to poison the public mind
against the King and those who tried for a while to assist
him in ruling for the benefit of the subject.

I have referred to all these matters, not so much because I wished here to state a case for Charles I in the
matter of religion, but rather because I desired to give a

[1] Dean Hook argues that inasmuch as all that the Puritans wanted
was to be able to fan into flame the feeling of alarm roused in the
first instance by the presence of Charles I's Catholic wife : " It was
unfortunate for them that Charles did not give any sign of preference to
the Church of Rome. He remained steady to the principles of the
Church of England."—Op. cit., p. 92.

[2] On the matter of the alleged Catholic leanings of Charles I, Wentworth and Laud, that great and impartial foreign historian, Leopold
von Ranke, is perfectly plain and emphatic. In his *History of
England*, Vol. II, p. 52, he writes : " The Lord Deputy [Wentworth]
can be as little accused as the King or the Archbishop of wishing to pave
the way for Catholicism. Wentworth was known as a very staunch
Protestant. Their thoughts were only directed to the development of
Anglicanism expressed in its most rigid form." While on p. 63, he also
says: " It was not that Charles I had thought of subjecting himself to
the Papacy. We know how far his soul was averse to this." See also
p. 81 of the same volume.

brief account of the temper of the Commons previous to Charles's eleven years of personal government. For it is well to bear in mind that although at first the two parties —the zealots and the so-called patriots—were not entirely united, neither party scrupled to make use of the claims of the other, or to conceal their own personal motives beneath the aspirations of the other, whenever it suited their purpose. Thus Pym, who was very far from being a Puritan, as every one admits, did not recoil from associating himself with the Puritans when he saw that it served his own ends so to do.[1]

And what was it that the so-called Patriots particularly desired beneath their cry for the liberty of the subject?

As Professor Gardiner observes, Wentworth foresaw what the transference of all power to Parliament, as it was then constituted, would lead to. "The rule of the House of Commons meant for him—not altogether without truth —the rule of the landowner and the lawyer at the expense of the poor."[2] And the same author continues: "It is certain that to transfer supremacy to the House of Commons on the terms on which Eliot wished to transfer it, would have been to establish a gross tyranny"[3]—a tyranny, that is to say, of capitalists and tradesmen—the kind of tyranny that grew up and became supreme after Charles I's assassination.

Now it should be remembered that Charles had the opportunity—nay, that he actually received the advice— to manœuvre the return of a number of his own sup-

[1] Isaac Disraeli, in the work already quoted, gives the following enlightening and interesting anecdote concerning Pym (p. 513, Vol. I): "When on one occasion it was observed that the affairs of religion seemed not so desperate that they should wholly engross their days, Pym replied that they must not abate their ardour for the true religion, that being the most certain end to obtain their purpose and maintain their influence." To a similar observation Hampden replied: "If it were not for this reiterated cry about religion, they would never be certain of keeping the people on their side" (pp. 330-331).
[2] *The First Two Stuarts and the Puritan Rebellion* (1905), p. 76.
[3] *Ibid.*, p. 73.

porters to his first Parliament, but that he stalwartly ignored both the opportunity and the advice. " The Lord-Keeper [Williams] observed that it had been usual to take certain precautionary measures to allow the King's trustiest friends to deal with the counties, cities and boroughs where they were known, to procure a promise for their elections. The King refused the counsel, and Buckingham opposed Williams. With the generous earnestness of his age, Charles had resolved to throw himself unreservedly into the arms of his Parliament." [1] Gardiner praises Charles for having refused to look up to a man " so shifty " as Williams [2];—would that he had maintained this attitude until the end of his reign!

It is, however, interesting to observe how curiously Charles's conduct in regard to this refusal to fill Parliament with his friends, contrasts with the conduct of a later King—George III. The money George III spent in corruption in order to get his own friends into the Commons must have amounted, during the whole of his reign, to some hundreds of thousands of pounds. George III, however, was not beheaded—why? He met with no powerful Puritan opposition. How was this? Obviously because the moneyed interests of his day, the sharks in the city and on the land, did not find in him so powerful an antagonist to their greed, as their ancestors had found in Charles in the first half of the seventeenth century.

For Charles I's concept of a King's duties may well be summed up in the words of his chief lieutenant, Wentworth, spoken before the Council of the North on December 30, 1628—

" Princes are to be indulgent, nursing fathers to their people; their modest liberties, their sober rights ought to be precious in their eyes, the branches of their government be for shadow for habitation, the comfort of life." [3]

---

[1] Isaac Disraeli, op. cit., Vol. I, p. 125.
[2] *The Personal Government of Charles I*, Vol. I, p. 13.
[3] H. D. Traill, *Lord Strafford*, p. 49.

PURITANISM, TRADE AND VULGARITY

There is no greater modern authority than Professor Gardiner on this period of English history. What is his conception of Charles's idea of kingly rule? He tells us it is expounded in the first part of the Lord Keeper's speech to the judges before they left London for the Summer Assizes on June 17, 1635: "He spoke to the judges of the care which it behoved them to take to do equal justice between rich and poor, to guard against 'the corruptions of sheriffs and their deputies, the partiality of jurors, the bearing and siding with men of countenance and power in their country,' to make 'strict inquiry after depopulations and enclosures, an oppression of a high nature and commonly done by the greatest persons that keep the juries under and in awe, which was the cause there are no more presented and brought in question.' To maintain the right of the weak against the strong was, according to Coventry, the special glory of the Crown." [1]

And was this only an ideal, or was it actually carried into practice? As we shall see, it was very much more than an ideal; it was the mainspring of all Charles's rule, and with it he inspired his ministers. But that it was "unpopular" in the eyes of the wealthy minority may easily be understood. For Charles never seems to have succeeded in convincing more than a very select few of the soundness of this principle of government, and the

[1] *The Personal Government of Charles I*, Vol. II, p. 173. The speech here referred to, which occupies five pages of Rushworth's Historical Collections (Part 2, Vol. I, pp. 294–298) is certainly a remarkable piece of evidence in support of the contention that Charles I's rule considered primarily the welfare of the masses. In addition to the points alluded to above in the passage from Gardiner, this clause is worth noticing (p. 295): "Next unto this, let those that be Licensed, be held strictly according to the Law. It hath been observed, and very truly, that in the Taverns, Inns, and Ale-Houses in *England*, by the falsehood of their measure, and unjust prices, they have drawn more from the guest, than out of the sizes of Ale and Beer is exacted by the States in Holland. A strange thing! that People for a publick Work, for anything that is Good, should be loth to part with anything ; and yet with open eyes see themselves deceived by such base and lewd people."

courtiers who attended at his poor court and who had only a small chance of increasing their wealth at the public expense, were naturally the last to admire a system of rule which proved so unprofitable to themselves.

It was to these courtiers and others who infested the city in the hope of sharing in some of the glamour of the royal presence, that Charles appealed when he published that Proclamation to the gentry in 1632, commanding them " to keepe their Residence at their mansions in the Country," and the terms of the Proclamation have an interesting bearing upon my present contention.

" For where by their residence and abiding in the severall Countreys whence their means ariseth," says this document, " they served the King in severall places according to their degrees and Rankes in ayde of the Government, whereby and by their House-keeping in those parts, the Realme was defended, and the meaner sort of people were *guided, directed and relieved*,[1] but by their residence in the said Cities and parts adjoining they have not employment, but live without doing any service to His Majestie or His people," etc., etc. After which it urges them not to earn their substance in one part and spend it in the cities, in luxury and futile amusement; and threatens severe measures to those who disobeyed.[2]

It should be borne in mind by those who are too ready to charge the King with " oppressing " his subjects, that nothing of the sort ever really took place at all. England was never so lightly taxed as during the personal government of Charles I. The accusation his opponents were reduced to bringing against him, was not oppressive taxation, but taxation levied without Parliamentary sanction. For even Ship-money was never crushing, and every halfpenny of it was spent upon the Navy.[3] Nor

---

[1] The italics are mine.—A. M. L.
[2] British Museum Proclamations, 506, h. 12 (8).
[3] Isaac Disraeli, who, in his *Commentaries on the Life and Reign of Charles I*, went to great pains in order to discover the human motive behind all the ostensible patriotism of the so-called patriots,

should it be forgotten that many of the ships which were provided by this detested tax must subsequently have seen action in our "glorious" naval victories under Cromwell.

The basis of the King's unpopularity among the rich and powerful was, of course, in the first place, ostensibly of a religious nature. Sir Edmund Verney was deluded enough to suppose that the religious question was fundamental even in bringing about the rebellion; and Dr. Hutton holds a similar opinion to-day. The true reason, the genuine, though often unconscious, reason was neither a religious one, nor due to the fact that the King's taxation was illegal or levied without the consent of the Commons. An essential part of the real grievance was that the weight of this taxation fell entirely upon the trading and wealthy classes. It reduced the profits of the tradesman and took a percentage from the incomes of the landed gentry. The taxes on food, on the poor man's sustenance, were to be the innovation of a free Parliament a few years later. But Charles was content to tax the profits of trade, and, for the rest, to demand a contribution

---

suggested that when John Hampden, in 1637, refused to pay the Ship-money demanded of him at his estate in Buckinghamshire, he was actuated more by his feelings of hostility to the local Sheriff (the outcome of a long-standing feud) than by patriotism. For this suggestion he was violently attacked by Lord Nugent in his book, *Some Memorials of John Hampden, his Party and his Times.* Lord Nugent pointed out that there was no such feud as the one alleged between the local Sheriff and Hampden, and challenged Disraeli to show his proofs. In a little pamphlet called *Eliot, Hampden and Pym* (1832) Disraeli replies to this (pp. 20-24) and other attacks by Lord Nugent, acknowledges the error about the Sheriff, which he ascribes to a slip, and says that it was the Treasurer of Buckinghamshire with whom Hampden was at loggerheads. And he declared that he derived his information from a gentleman who, among other papers in his possession, had once been the owner of the diary or journal of the Treasurer in question. Certainly the ridiculously small sum demanded from Hampden for this tax (20/-) lends some colour to Disraeli's contention. For Hampden was a very rich man, and he would surely not have been so anxious to oppose the tax as many a less wealthy and equally energetic man.

to the expenses of government from the wealthy landed classes.

The nobler among Charles's wealthy subjects understood and accepted it. They saw the King daily making sacrifices himself, in order to rule beneficently. They knew that he had pledged the Crown jewels and plate, and sold property to the City of London to the extent of £120,000, at the very moment when he was appealing to the clergy to help him, early in his reign. And they saw that he did not spend this money in idle merriment or wasteful extravagance.

Nor were his most trusted ministers, Laud and Wentworth, very far behind him in their readiness to spend their own private money in the public service. The former presented his most precious treasures during his lifetime to public libraries and to friends; spent over £1,200 himself on the work of restoring St. Paul's; endowed a Professorship of Arabic at Oxford, and, but for grants of timber from the King, defrayed the whole cost of the building of St. John's entirely alone. As Dr. Hutton observes, " He was a poor man : no Archbishop for centuries, it was said, had ever been so poor." [1]

As for Wentworth's personal contributions to the expenses of his and the King's administration—they are proverbial. When it was a matter of organising his troops in Ireland, " he was able to boast of having sunk £6000 [out of his own pocket] in horses, furniture and arms"; [2] in order to help and promote the Irish linen industry, " he had imported flax seed of a superior quality from Holland at his own expense, and busied himself in bringing over the most expert workmen from France and the Low Countries; " [3] while towards the expenses of the expedi-

---

[1] *William Laud*, p. 227. For a list of Laud's gifts to St. John's and to the Bodleian Library see p. 107 of Hutton's book ; while for a list of the Acts of Bounty projected by Dr. Laud, Bishop of London, and most of them performed in his lifetime, see Rushworth's *Historical Collections*, Part 2, Vol. I, p. 74.

[2] H. D. Traill, op. cit., p. 138.   [3] *Ibid.*, p. 137–138.

tion against Scotland in 1640 he generously subscribed the handsome sum of £20,000 of his own money.

But all this exceptional disinterestedness was of little avail in the sight of enemies who had *reasons*, more self-centred than patriotic, for overthrowing this unusual administration of men who were obviously " spoiling the game " for others, and who were apparently too foolish to profit by their position of power.

For all historians are unanimous, at least in one particular, and that is, that Strafford and Laud never once sacrificed the public weal to their own interests. There was peculation and malversation enough among the men in high places, who surrounded Charles I; but neither Strafford nor Laud can be accused of either crime. As Laud truly wrote to Strafford, " I am alone in those things which draw not private profit after them." [1] " Their ends were not the advancement of private interests," says Dean Hook of the two friends, " but the promotion of the public good." [2] Professor Gardiner says of Laud, " For himself he had no private ends in view, no desire of pelf or vainglory, no family to provide for, or state to keep up." [3] And as for the noble Strafford, whom Ranke declares, " was indisputably one of the greatest of the administrators who rose up among the English before they gained possession of India," [4] no historian, however hostile, has yet been able to accuse him of defrauding or robbing the people in his charge, either for his master's ends or for his own. Macaulay stupidly refers to him as " this great, brave, bad man;" [5] but even with such a prejudiced Puritan as the pompous Thomas Babington, it is not for Strafford's dishonesty in the public service that this absurd epithet " bad " is applied in the case of so noble a nature, but, rather, for his so-called

[1] W. Holden Hutton, op. cit., p. 51.
[2] Op. cit., p. 259. In regard to Strafford see also pp. 259 and 260.
[3] *Personal Government of Charles I*, Vol. II, p. 163.
[4] Op. cit., p. 184.
[5] Article on John Hampden, *Edinburgh Review*, December 1831.

"apostasy." When, however, I began to enumerate some of Laud's and Strafford's deeds, the present contention that they were both honest, self-sacrificing and incorruptible officials, in an age when occupiers of high places were anything but honest and incorrupt, will be found to be more than adequately substantiated. For the present I must return to the consideration of their great master.

As I make no pretence in this work of recounting all the incidents of Charles I's reign, enough has been said to give the reader some idea of the spirit of the Commons during the whole of the three sessions which preceded Charles's personal rule. It would have been impossible for any responsible ruler—and no ruler was more keenly alive to his responsibility than Charles I—I say it would have been impossible for any responsible ruler to have dared to hand over to Parliament at that time all the power and influence it demanded. The leaders of the Commons were not in a temper for tolerance; they were by no means ready to exercise their power beneficently—nor does history, from 1649 to the present day, prove that their successors were ready for it even hundreds of years after Charles's time—and they were too self-seeking and too unfeeling to be let loose as rulers upon the country. No monarch desirous of protecting *the people*, would ever have consented to hand his subjects over to the mercy of a body which was led by men of the stamp of Sir John Eliot. And as soon as Charles felt himself supported in his attitude by a man of such insight and intelligence as Wentworth, it was only natural that he should venture upon the hazardous plan of dispensing with such a turbulent, subversive and vindictive assembly.

Speaking of the Parliament of those days, Professor Gardiner says: " In Wentworth's eyes it only partially represented the nation, if it represented it at all. The lawyers and country gentlemen of whom it was composed were not to be trusted to govern England. The lawyers, with their quirks and formulas, too often stood in the way

PURITANISM, TRADE AND VULGARITY

of substantial justice. The country gentlemen, too, often
misused the opportunities of their wealth to tyrannise over
their poorer neighbours. Wentworth, therefore, would
appeal to the nation outside the House of Commons. . . .
The King was to do judgment and justice fairly and
equally for rich and poor. So would come the day when
Parliament would meet again." [1]

This is a fair statement of the resolve with which the
King in March 1629 embarked upon his career of a British
Sovereign ruling without a Parliament. And we have no
better proofs of the earnestness of this resolve than the
attitude and quality of the two ministers whom he chose
to elect as his principal advisers, almost from the very
moment when he abandoned all hope of working in
harmony with the Commons. [2] In one of his communica-
tions, so Traill tells us, Wentworth " pledges himself, not
only not to fail in any point of his duty to his master,
but fully to 'comply with that public and common protection which good kings afford their good people.' " [3]
And of Laud, Dr. Hutton says, " the benefit of the
governed was the thought that underlay all his statements
of political doctrine." [4]

What was Charles to do? He refused to leave his
people to the tender mercies of their oppressors, as they
were to be left by later sovereigns. Nothing, however, but
cruel intolerance and bigoted persecution and exaction
would please the Commons, therefore the Parliament
which refused to grant Charles even the means for carrying on his government without his making concession after

[1] *Personal Government of Charles I*, Vol. I, pp. 168, 169.
[2] Gardiner further declares (p. 281) : " It was one day to be the
evil attendant upon the victory of the Parliamentary system, that the
territorial aristocracy were to make use of the forms of the constitution
to fill their own pockets at the expense of the nation, and to heap
honours and rewards upon their own heads. Against such a degradation
of the functions of the State, Wentworth struggled with all his might.
The depository of the national authority, he held, must be above all
persons and all parties, that he might dispense justice to all alike."
[3] Op. cit., p. 60.   [4] Op. cit., p. 125.

125

concession to their avarice and their hatred of all sects save their own—this Parliament and all like it must end.[1]

We know the words of one of his last appeals to his Third Parliament—

" Every man must now do according to his conscience; wherefore if you (which God forbid) should not do your duties in contributing what this state at this time needs, I must, in discharge of my conscience, use those other means which God hath put into my hands to save that which the follies of other men may otherwise hazard to lose. Take not this as threatening (I scorn to threaten any but my equals), but as an admonition from him that both out of nature and duty hath most care of your preservation and prosperities: and hopes (though I thus speak) that your demeanours at this time will be such as shall not only make me approve your former counsels, but lay on me such obligations as shall bind me by way of thankfulness to meet often with you: for, be assured that nothing can be more pleasing unto me, than to keep a good correspondency with you." [2]

And how did the Commons respond to this fine appeal? They forthwith entered upon a debate on the old topic of grievances, then supplies, and finally prepared a petition to enforce the laws against recusants!

[1] The comment upon this decision, made in the *Cambridge Modern History*, is of great interest. On p. 274, Vol. IV, we read : " To later observers this appears a hazardous, even a hopeless, experiment ; it did not seem so then. Long periods had elapsed in Elizabeth's reign without Parliaments ; longer still in the reign of James I. The parliamentary system was far from being regarded as essential to good government. In Spain it had practically disappeared. In France the States General had not met since 1614, and was not to meet again till 1789. In Germany the Diet was already little more than a diplomatic council. Holland was a Republic, and therefore out of court. Why should not England follow the way of France and Spain ? All that seemed requisite was the adoption of a pacific policy abroad, the improvement of administration at home, and the gradual extension of autocratic control over the national sources of supply. Such was the policy which the Government now attempted to carry out."

[2] See *Parliamentary History of England*, Vol. II, p. 218.

They did everything in their power to harass and to thwart their sovereign. Not understanding him in the least, regarding his artistic tastes as mere foppery, longing to confirm their base and utterly false suspicions concerning his leanings to Popery, and detesting his patriarchal concern for the welfare of the people, to oppress whom they thirsted for "*liberty*" and a free Parliament, they could not forgive a man who, while he was discerning enough to dismiss a cad like Williams and to befriend an honest genius like Wentworth, was yet not sufficiently penetrating to see that if only he would join them—them, the elect of God, the possessors of almost all the wealth of the nation, and the backbone of all the trade—he would be safe and sound as the Georges were ultimately to be; *but* upon the rotten foundation of a crushed though patient people.

When, therefore, Professor Gardiner says of Strafford, "there can be no doubt that he had thrown himself on the wrong side in the great struggle of his day," [1] surely a curious note is struck by this great and otherwise impartial historian. If the unsuccessful side is always going to be the *wrong* side; if the loser in a struggle is, on that account alone, always to be the delinquent, then of a certainty nobility and heroism are at an end. For where success is the sole measure of value—which, I admit, it unfortunately is to-day—then martyrdoms, crucifixions and heroic sacrifices are indeed quite valueless. I am only surprised that Professor Gardiner should have given his great authority—as he seems to have done in the above passage—to so regrettable a credo.

Thus, although Charles was reduced to unparliamentary means for the collection of at least some of the expenses of State, he did not flinch for one moment from the task of pursuing his bold and patriarchal policy. He realised then the truth which Cromwell was to acknowledge later (in 1655, for instance), that the England of his time could be properly governed only by a single ruler capable of

[1] *The First Two Stuarts and the Puritan Rebellion*, p. 109.

127

directing able assistants.[1] In all directions the doctrine was re-echoed, that there was to be no respecting of persons but only justice done. Church lands and property illegally and greedily appropriated by his powerful subjects, poor-funds filched by unscrupulous nobles and country magnates, were restored as far as possible to their proper owners and applied to their proper purposes. In Ireland the King, by gra t   to the clergy all the Crown impropriation, himself set angoble example to his subjects which seems, in some instances, to have borne fruit. Following in his father's footsteps, he turned his attention to Scotland, and resorted to drastic measures for mitigating the "grave social and political evils attendant upon the vast absorption of Church revenues by the high nobility,"[2] and upon the rapacious nature of the tithe-owners. The fortuitous and salutary arrangement which he was ultimately able to effect "weakened," as Professor Gardiner tells us, "the power of the nobility, and strengthened the prerogative in the only way in which the prerogative deserved to be strengthened, by the popularity it gained through carrying into effect a wise and beneficent reform. Every landowner who was freed from the perpetual annoyance of the tithe gatherer, every minister whose income had been increased and rendered more certain than by James's arrangement, knew well to whom the change was owing."[3]

Naturally such a policy created powerful enemies, and when Charles sought to impose Laud's conformity upon Scotland, it cannot be doubted that such of his formidable opponents as the Earls of Rothes and Loudoun, were

[1] Dr. W. F. Hook, in speaking of Cromwell's sagacity, says : " That same sagacity led Cromwell to see that, as the country then existed, it must be subjected to the rule of one. He himself became that one, but by doing so he endorses, to a certain extent, the policy for upholding which Charles, Strafford, and Laud were brought to the block." —Op. cit., Vol. XI, p. 357.

[2] Gardiner, *Personal Government of Charles I*, Vol. I, p. 347. For a full account of the king's good work in Scotland see pp. 330-362.

[3] *Ibid.*, Vol. I, p. 351.

actuated by the memory of these beneficent reforms of the King.

At home Commissioners were appointed to inquire into the laws for the relief of the poor. They were to see that the country Justices of the Peace did their duty, and did not omit to act in accordance with the law, even where their duties clashed with their own interests. Abuses were to cease. Reports were demanded periodically, and local magnates were constrained to maintain a high standard in the administration of their authority.[1]

A body of Commissioners was also appointed to come to terms with the creditors of prisoners imprisoned for debts amounting to less than £200, and whom the judge who had tried them regarded as cases deserving of mercy. And yet another Commission was appointed " to inquire touching Depopulations and conversions of Lands to Pasture,"—an evil which, as we have already seen, pressed heavily upon the poorer inhabitants of all rural districts. Charles was very severe upon this class of delinquency, and Sir Anthony Roper was fined no less than £30,000 for committing Depopulations.[2]

The King was, however, just as solicitous of the welfare of the spirit as of the body of the people, and wherever he was able he firmly resisted all Puritanical attempts at depressing the national temper. The first act of his first Parliament had been to suppress all games on Sunday, on penalty of a fine, and to insist on Sunday observance. Again, owing to the influence of the Puritans, in 1628, by the Act 3 Charles I, cap. 2, all carriers, waggoners, wainmen and drivers were prohibited from travelling on Sunday. In 1633 Charles I, to the intense annoyance of the Puritans, repealed the Sunday observance laws, which he felt were taking the spirit out of the working people, who had but that day upon which to play and enjoy themselves, and he ordained that, after attending

---

[1] For a full account of the work of this Commission see Sir G. Nicholls, K.C.B., op. cit., Vol. I, pp. 252–255.

[2] Rushworth's *Historical Collections*, Part II, Vol. I, p. 333.

evening prayers, everybody should be allowed to amuse himself in any decent way he might choose.

As a matter of fact, in doing this he did-but re-issue his father's *Book of Sports*, which was first published in 1618. On his return from Scotland in 1617 James I had had a petition presented to him by the people, chiefly consisting of the lower classes, who were desirous of having Sunday amusements; and· in spite of opposition from the clergy and the middle classes, the King had granted them their wish.

In his preamble to the re-issue of this declaration, Charles I said : " Our Deare Father of blessed memory, in his return from Scotland, coming through Lancashire, found that his subjects were debarred from Lawful Recreations upon Sundayes after evening Prayers ended, and upon Holydays. And he prudently considered, that if these times were taken from them, the meaner sort who labour all the weeke, should have no Recreations at all to refresh their spirits." And from the concluding passage I take the following : " Now out of a like pious Care for the service of God, and for the suppressing of any humours that oppose trueth, and for the Ease, Comfort and Recreation of Our well deserving People, We doe ratify and publish this Our blessed Father's Declaration : The rather because of late in some Counties of· Our Kingdom We find that under pretence of taking away abuses, that there hath been a generall forbidding, not only of ordinary meetings, but of the feasts of the Dedication of Churches, commonly called Wakes." [1]

Charles was no less active in other directions in trying to secure the welfare of his people. In addition to combating the fighters for parliamentary supremacy, which, as we have seen, was simply coveted for the liberty which it gave to those in power to indulge their lusts of *private gain* and *private greed*, undeterred by a ruler who, while standing apart from all factions, could rule for the benefit

[1] King Charles I's Declaration to his Subjects concerning Lawful Sports to be used on Sundays (October 18, 1633).

of all; there were two other forces which were beginning to make themselves felt at this time—*mechanical science*, with its contrivances of all kinds calculated to increase the rapidity of production without concerning itself in any way about the character of the workmen who were to control these contrivances or machines; and *capitalistic industry*, which had begun to rear its head as early as the sixteenth century, and which, with the unscrupulous stress it laid upon the mere gain of the producer, and the lack of responsibility it often allowed to the moneyed employer, heeded neither the people it employed nor the consumers for whom it catered. While, correlated with the rise of mechanical science and capitalistic industry, there was that growing hostility to beauty, love of life, good spirits, joy and abundant health, all of which qualities, when they are regarded as inviolate and sacred, tend to become formidable obstacles in the path of the two forces in question.

With regard to this hostility to beauty, love of life, good spirits, joy and abundant health, I shall, in the opinion of some people, deal more than adequately in my next chapter. For the present I shall concern myself only with the rise of the two forces just described.

It is well known that the Tudors were consistently opposed to the introduction of all engines and machines which tended to prove injurious to handicraftsmen, or to deteriorate the quality of the articles produced.[1] Edward VI and Elizabeth were both equally vigorous in their attitude towards mechanical innovations, and the case of the gig-mills in the former's reign and that of Mr. Lee's stocking loom in the latter's reign, are too well known to be dwelt upon here. The course which these two

[1] See Garnier, *Annals of the British Peasantry*, p. 176. "The Government for a long period seems to have regarded machinery with the same hostile views as did the Luddites in subsequent times. Inventive genius was termed 'subtle imagination,' and any substitute for the 'manufacture by hands and feet' was regarded as conducive to the 'final undoing of the industry concerned.' For this reason, the fulling mill in 1482, the newly-invented gig mill in 1551, and the tucking mill in 1555 were discountenanced."

monarchs had inaugurated, however, James and Charles continued with even greater vigour. But, in the reigns of the last two monarchs, the men who firmly believed that mechanical innovations *per se*, quite irrespective of whether they improved or deteriorated *man*, constituted " Progress," were beginning to lose patience and to grow in number. They could no longer brook this paternal control from on high. To them any thought of directing or limiting the march of mechanical science amounted to intolerable interference, insufferable tyranny. They scoffed when James I prohibited the use of a machine for making needles; but they scoffed still more when Charles reinforced the Tudor enactments, and also upheld his father's attitude in this struggle against the besotting machine. Their surprise, however, must have been great when the noblest of the Stuarts, on June 15, 1634, not only issued a proclamation against " that great annoyance of smoak which is so obnoxious to our City of London," but also carried his concern about the beauty and happiness of this city so far as actually to recommend the use of a new and special furnace calculated to mitigate the evil.

Incidentally, it is obvious from this royal proclamation that the great Stuart King was not blindly suspicious of innovations as such; [1] otherwise he would have looked askance even at a furnace calculated to mitigate the evil of smoke.

As Dr. Cunningham observes : " The chief object which James and Charles set before themselves in regard to the industry of the country, was not the introduction of new

---

[1] As another proof of this contention, Charles's attitude towards the Commons in the matter of the constructional reforms in London is very interesting. Among the grievances of the Commons in 1625 there is a complaint about the building of all houses in London in one uniform way, with a face of brick towards the street. (Bricks had recently been introduced for building by the Earl of Arundel.) To this complaint Charles replied that this reform in building was a good reform, and he was determined to allow the work to proceed.

PURITANISM, TRADE AND VULGARITY

forms of skill; they were much more occupied in providing for the supervision of the existing industries, so that the wares produced might be of good quality." [1]

But one does not require to be a deep student of the vulgar and unthinking class of mechanical innovators, to understand the kind of exasperation to which such an attitude on the part of the ruler would soon give rise in their ranks. Big-sounding, bombastic phrases, such as the " Forward March of Humanity," " The Progress of the Race," welled up in their foolish and sentimental throats and caused them to look with rankling indignation at that superb figure in lace and velvet whose consummate taste preferred to cling devotedly to Beauty rather than to their absurd and inhuman idea of advancement!

There was, however, a deeper and perhaps more unconscious hatred in Charles I and his father against mechanical innovations than the mere hatred of their threatened deterioration of both the handicraftsman and the quality of the goods produced. There was the profound suspicion that machinery implied *expensive and elaborate* installations which must necessarily lead to the extinction of the poor home-worker, or even of the artisan of moderate means, and the yielding up of his liberty, his power and his gifts to a more unscrupulous and less desirable taskmaster than the buying public, *i. e.* the capitalistic traders, out for personal gain. For machinery and capitalism are plighted mates and are necessarily allies.

The strongest objection advanced against this attitude towards machinery can be stated in a few words. It is this: Man is essentially a machine- and instrument-using animal. All his advancement, if advancement it may be called, is due to the fact that he was the only one, among all the species of quadrumana, to realise that there is no limit to the extra external organs he can create for himself. Thus an arrow, as a machine for death, is more formidable, more treacherous and more efficacious than all the stealthy and sheathed lions' claws, and all the reptilian

[1] *The Growth of English Industry and Commerce*, Vol. II, p. 295.

poison on earth. As an extra organ added to man's structure, the arrow with the bow that drives it becomes a magnificent step from a position of subjection to beasts of prey, to a position of mastery over them. From the arrow to the locomotive is a long jump; still, it is difficult to draw the line anywhere, and you cannot point your finger at any particular stage in the evolution of machinery and say, "Here it should have stopped and proceeded no further."

All this is perfectly true, but for the last passage, and my reply to that is, that I can and do put my finger upon a particular stage in mechanical evolution, and that I do cry: "Here it should have stopped and proceeded no further." That is to say, I do undertake to perform what the average Englishman always regards as a task too difficult even to approach, namely, "to draw the line somewhere." *I say that the line of demarcation between beneficent and deleterious machinery is to be found at that point where machines begin to cease from developing desirable qualities in the characters and bodies of those who use them, or where they begin to develop positively bad qualities.*

This I believe to have been the Stuart and the Tudor view, and it is absolutely unassailable from every standpoint.

Now turning to the second force, that of rising capitalistic industry—again we find that the Tudors preceded the Stuarts in their hostility to the spirit of greed and gain which seems to have characterised this form of industry from the very first.

As Dr. Cunningham assures us, "Edward VI was quite prepared to oppose that anybody should ' eat up another through greediness,' " [1] and Garnier declares that, "the aim of Elizabeth's advisers was to disperse and distribute the national wealth, instead of allowing it to accumulate in a few hands." [2] The necessary concomitant of greed—

[1] Op. cit., Vol. I, p. 560.
[2] *Annals of the British Peasantry*, p. 98.

the tendency, that is to say, of neglecting quality in workmanship so long as a rapid and plentiful supply can be produced to meet the demands of the market, was also opposed by the Tudor sovereigns, and their assiduous supervision of manufactures, such, for instance, as the pewterer's, brasier's and cooper's trades, shows the extent to which they carried this principle into effect.[1]

" The Tudor government," says the reverend historian of English industry, " backed by public opinion, took a very strong line as to the duty of capitalists, either as merchants or employers under such circumstances [fluctuations of trade]; it was thought only right that they should bear the risk of loss, which arose from increasing their stocks while there was no sale abroad, rather than condemn the workmen to enforced idleness." [2]

But the attitude that the Tudors only initiated the Stuarts maintained with their customary energy and augmented zeal. They regarded speculation with suspicion, and considered it as mere " private gain " accruing to individuals who performed no public service in return for their advantage. And in 1622 and 1623, during the great depression in the clothing industry, James insisted by proclamation upon the clothiers continuing to employ the weavers as they had done at the time when trade flourished. In 1629, again, under Charles I, the Justices came to the rescue of the Essex weavers, and forced their employers to give them better terms than those to which the mere automatic action of " free competition " gave rise.

The measures resorted to after the bad harvest of 1630 were also very characteristic of Charles and his whole policy. Every possible step was taken to prevent any rise in the price of corn. Unlike the Georges, Charles could not bear the thought that one or two individuals should speculate and grow rich upon the starving bodies of the poor and their children; and, like Cobbett, who was

[1] See Cunningham, op. cit., Vol. I, p. 513.
[2] *Ibid.*, op. cit., Vol. II, p. 50.

subsequently to express his loathing of the wretched Quakers who drew profit in times of scarcity from having kept back large stores of grain,[1] Charles went to elaborate pains in the crisis to prevent anything of the sort occurring. The Irish, who had not suffered from any dearth, were requested to send to England all the grain that was not absolutely required for their own purposes; Justices of the Peace in counties where there happened to be a sufficiency of corn were instructed to provide for their less fortunate neighbours. Nobody was allowed to sell wheat at more than seven shillings a bushel, and the storing of grain for re-sale was prohibited. Even starch-makers and maltsters were reminded that their produce was not so necessary to human life as was the raw material of their industry.[2] And thus the crisis was overcome without either too much hardship or too much disorder.

Another instance of the same attitude on the part of Charles I is to be found in the proclamation of May 4, 1633, affecting the price of victuals, and directed " against the intolerable avarice of Bakers, Brewers, Innholders and Butchers, who not contented with a reasonable profit in uttering and selling Victuall within Our Dominions, and especially within the Verge of our household, unlawfully exact and demand unreasonable and extreame prizes for Victuals, Housemeat, Lodging, and other necessaries, above the prizes they were sold at before our coming to those parts." [3]

Concurrently with this vigilance in regard to the growing spirit of greed and gain in the country, Charles was, moreover, persistently interfering in trade, whenever and wherever abuses were practised by those engaged in it. At one time he is found legislating against frauds in the sale and packing of butter,[4] at another against fraud in the drapery trade,[5] and anon against the abuses of the

---

[1] Op. cit., Vol. I, pp. 163–164.
[2] Gardiner, *Personal Government of Charles I*, Vol. I, p. 199.
[3] British Museum Proclamations, 506, h. 12.
[4] November 13, 1634.   [5] April 16, 1633.

Gardeners [1] of London, or the makers and purveyors of counterfeit jewellery.[2]

Much capital has been made by the Puritan opponents of this great monarch out of the scandal of his government's interference with the soap trade; but, as Gardiner points out, it was Portland who was responsible for this. It was Portland who enriched his friends at the cost of the soap-makers, and Laud was horrified enough when he discovered the dishonesty of the whole affair.[3]

In any case, as far as Charles was concerned, it was his earnest endeavour to preserve a good standard in the quality of the goods produced by the manufacturers among his subjects, and though his interferences naturally gave rise to discontent, more particularly among the rapacious Dissenting mercantile classes of London, he never refrained from enforcing his high standard of quality and honesty whenever he felt justified in so doing. The case of the silk trade is a good instance of his perseverance in this respect. Three times did Charles attempt to suppress the frauds and adulterations in this trade. He began by incorporating the silkmen in 1632 for the purpose of supervising one another. As this company, however, upheld the abuses, he placed the responsibility of search in the hands of the London Company of Dyers. These, it was found, also connived at the frauds, and in 1639 Charles accordingly established a government office, where the silk was inspected, stamped and declared to be of an adequately good quality.[4] After which matters seem to have proceeded more satisfactorily.

As Cunningham observes: " Under the Stuarts, strenuous efforts were made to organise a system of industrial supervision on national lines, and thus to maintain a high standard of quality for goods of every kind, manufactured for sale either at home or abroad."[5] But it will be readily

---

[1] December 3, 1634.   [2] April 18, 1636.
[3] *Personal Government of Charles I*, pp. 165-169.
[4] See Cunningham, op. cit., Vol. II, p. 300.
[5] Vol. II, p. 296.

understood that such action on the part of a sovereign, in the midst of a nation which was rapidly moving towards the vulgar shopkeeping ideal, was not of a kind to breed good-will between the government and the governed.

The traders of London were all savage at this arbitrary imposition of the virtues of honesty and the love of quality upon themselves and their fellows.[1] Such ideals were incompatible with greed and gain; they were, moreover, irreconcilable with the stout-hearted British love of "Liberty!" and a "Free Parliament!"

And, in truth, when we begin to enumerate in a single passage all the deeds of Charles's patriarchal and popular government—his opposition to the grasping Lords and country gentry; his intolerance of the filching of the Church and poor-funds by provincial magnates in England, Scotland and Ireland; his firm resolve to maintain the spirit of the labouring classes and to keep the Puritans from depressing them; his hostility to the introduction of besotting machinery; his determined stand against the growing lust of gain and profit at all costs; not to mention his love of beauty, flourishing life, and the rest—we are

---

[1] Among other interferences in trade not already mentioned, I may refer to Charles's proclamation of June 20, 1629, concerning the making of starch and avoiding annoyance thereby ; his proclamation of June 7, 1631, for preventing "Deceipt in the Importation of Madder" ; his proclamation of January 12, 1632, for regulating the buckle-making trade ; his proclamations of February 18, 1632, of January 20, 1633, of January 20, 1634, of February 1, 1635, and of January 20, 1636, for the "Prizing of Wines" ; his proclamation of March 14, 1634, for dealing with the supply of salt ; his proclamation affecting the fisheries and forbidding the use of an engine called a Trawle, April 2, 1635 ; his proclamation of September 6, 1635, for the prevention of abuses by lawyers and lawyers' clerks ; and his proclamation of July 9, 1636, for the "due execution of the office of Clarke of the Market of Our Houshold, and throwout Our Realme of England and Dominion of Wales : And for the surveying and seeling of the constant Rule appointed to be used by all Clothiers, and workers in cloth and yarn ; and for the increase of the poores wages labouring therein."—British Museum Proclamations, 506 (Rushworth's *Historical Collections*, Part 2, Vol. I).

less surprised at his tragic end than at the fact that it came so extraordinarily late. To behave as he behaved at the time when he reigned, required not only insight, but dauntless courage and a fearless and almost desperate sense of duty.[1] His conduct aggravated his opponents the more because he gave them no handle, either in his private life or his public deeds, wherewith to bring him more rapidly into their power. The only accusation they could bring against him during his eleven years of personal government, was the levying of taxes, which, by the by, were never oppressive, without the consent of Parliament—a last shift to which they themselves had forced him. And even this they could not have regarded as so terribly remiss, seeing that they were quite willing to overlook the whole of this apparently "awful" crime in the Short Parliament. But of this anon. I must now say a few words concerning Charles's ministers.

In Chapter XXIII of his *Prince*, Machiavelli says: "Therefore it must be inferred that good counsels, whencesoever they come, are born of the wisdom of the prince, and not the wisdom of the prince from good counsels."

[1] The character that F. C. Montague gives of Charles in *The Political History of England*, Vol. VII, p. 126, is worth quoting in this connection as the opinion of an important historian who, on the whole, is as fair as any one can expect in his estimate of the Stuart period. Mr. Montague says : " Charles was personally brave, and he had many of the virtues that dignify private life. By his strict fidelity to his queen he set an example as rare as it was praiseworthy among the sovereigns of that time. He was sincerely religious without the theological pedantry of his father. He was industrious in the routine of kingship." Leopold von Ranke, as a foreign historian of considerable weight, is also worth reference on this point. On p. 65, Vol. II, of his *History of England*, the author says : " In the world which surrounded him Charles always passed for a man without a fault, who committed no excesses, had no vices, possessed cultivation and knowledge to the fullest extent, without wishing to make a show in consequence ; not, however, devoid of severity which, however, he tempered with feelings of humanity . . . Since the death of Buckingham he appeared to choose his ministers by merits and capacity and no longer by favouritism."

A DEFENCE OF ARISTOCRACY

Personally I am content to regard this statement of Machiavelli's as an axiom. I am perfectly content to believe that the wisdom of a prince's advisers is *always* the prince's wisdom, in cases in which he has had to choose his counsellors from among the public servants surrounding his person. But there is this obvious difficulty to be remembered, namely, that " to be honest, as this world goes, is to be one man picked out of a thousand," and that, after all, when a wise prince has exhausted the small crop of honest men in his entourage, no " choosing," no " discrimination " on his part can possibly create honest men where there are none, especially when we remember that the range of men who are prepared to undertake a public duty is always limited.

To Charles's credit, be it said, that he selected for his closest and most trusted advisers two of the most honest men that England then contained, Wentworth and Laud; but for the rest, like poor Napoleon with his admirals, he had to do the best he could with the material that a merciful though sparing Providence placed in his hands.

Men such as Portland, Cottington, Windebanke, Weston, though necessarily used and required by Charles, never attained to that high degree of disinterested devotion to their duties which characterised both Laud and Wentworth. There can be no doubt—in fact the proof of it appears again and again—that all four practised peculation on a small or large scale, according to their opportunities, and always sought their own interests before those either of the King or the people. Still, it is impossible to conceive how Charles could have got on without them; and if, as is no doubt the case, they contributed in no small degree towards making his government fail, it should be borne in mind that where they departed from the path of strict honesty and justice, they were neither in sympathy with Charles's main policy, nor inspired by his precept and example.

The best proof of this lies in the fact that the ministers who were nearest and dearest to Charles, were as disinterested as he himself was in promoting the cause of the governed, and no act of corruption, malversation or peculation was ever proved, even by their bitterest foes, against either of them. I speak, of course, of Laud and Wentworth.

Inspired by the King and the only men of his period who were worthy of him, these two ministers pursued with undaunted courage the policy which he set up as his ideal; and when ultimately they were brought to the block it was by the enemies they had bravely created in their suppression of abuses practised by the powerful and the mercenary. For, like Charles, they were neither of them respecters of persons.

Of Laud Professor Gardiner says: "His hand was everywhere. Rich and poor, high and low, alike felt its weight. . . . Nothing angered him so much as the claim of a great man to escape a penalty which would fall on others. Nothing brought him into such disfavour with the great as his refusal to admit that the punishment which had raised no outcry when it was meted out to the weak and helpless, should be spared in the case of the powerful and wealthy offender." [1]

No bishop or archbishop before or after him was ever more zealous in discovering and punishing abuses against Church property; and as these were plentiful, and always the acts of powerful people, the enemies poor Laud ultimately had to meet were numerous and formidable indeed.

His eye, too, was always fixed with honest reproach upon the immediate entourage of his master; and the frequent acts of corruption and peculation which he had to witness caused him no small amount of sadness. Unfortunately, in trying to suppress some of the wholesale robbery that was constantly being practised close to the throne, he embittered some of the most powerful men of the kingdom against himself. As Dean Hook observes, his hostility to the avaricious and unscrupulous courtiers

[1] *Personal Government of Charles I*, Vol. II, p. 205.

"who robbed the King to enrich themselves," resulted in the fact that "he [Laud] found among the courtiers adversaries as bitter, though for fear of offending the King not so openly abusive, as he had found among the Puritans."[1]

His life work, as an able Anglican Churchman, was a noble struggle against the growing anarchy in religion. The Puritans, with their impudent assumption of omniscience, were rising in all directions. They *knew* what God felt, liked, wanted and appreciated, just as the Dissenters and Low Churchmen *know* these things to-day. They even had the downright insolence to declare that Christ himself was one of them—a Puritan! No one knew better than they the path to Paradise. And they were prepared to murder, mutilate, sell into slavery, torture, burn or poison, any one who dared to doubt their extravagantly impertinent claims and creed.

Laud saw through their impudent theology. He foresaw the anarchy that must necessarily follow their triumph, and with a patient tolerance, that did him and all his sympathisers great honour, while he defended the legal attitude of the Church of England, he was never either oppressive or cruelly hostile to these revolutionaries.

There is no finer appeal against the anarchy of settling deep religious questions by the individual conscience than his letter to Sir Kenelm Digby, quoted in full in Dean Hook's biography.[2] But the words of this letter are not those of a narrow fanatic; nor are they the words of an implacable and resentful foe. They express the sentiments of an earnest, scholarly and highly intelligent man who was anxious to establish order where chaos threatened to reign.

I have already alluded to Charles I's fairness in his treatment of all the religious agitators of his reign.

[1] Op. cit., p. 355. See also p. 226. "The courtiers whose peculations he [Laud] had resisted, were enemies to him, almost as bitter as the Puritans."

[2] See pp. 274–281.

PURITANISM, TRADE AND VULGARITY

But in this fairness he was ably seconded by his ecclesiastical lieutenant. I have referred to the just manner in which controversy was quelled—that is to say, that *both* sides were silenced, and not merely the side opposed to the Church of England. And I have attempted to show that this attitude towards controversy was far more the outcome of a desire for peace and order than of a fanatical dislike of the enlightenment that may come from discussion. For Charles was neither a pedant nor a fanatic. Laud, however, was equally just in his efforts to quell factious preaching. As Dean Hook observes, these efforts of Laud's were "not all on one side : and the Calvinists had no just ground for their assertion that none but they were prohibited, or that the opposite party went off unpunished." [1]

It is ridiculous to charge this man with bigotry and narrow-minded bitterness as some have done. A man who could deplore the violent discussions concerning religion, because "few things in religion are demonstrable," [2] was not a man to entrench himself behind a rigid dogmatic defence, when it was a matter of vindicating his position.

But Laud sinned in the same way that Charles sinned, and in the same way as Wentworth sinned. He was no respecter of persons. Although he was no more active than any of his colleagues in the sentencing and punishment of culprits brought up before the High Commission Court, the very names of those who were arraigned by this assembly during his term of office for acts of immorality that no healthy State could afford to overlook, reveal how strongly the fearless influence of Charles made itself felt.

"Persons of honour and great quality," says Dr. Hutton, "of the Court and of the country, were every day cited into the High Commission Court, upon the fame of

[1] Op. cit., p. 194.
[2] Words used in the magnificent letter to Sir Kenelm Digby, to which reference has already been made.

143

their incontinence, or other scandal in their lives, and were there prosecuted to their shame and punishment." [1]

Among those of high position who were thus cited, I may mention Frances Coke, the wife of Lord Purbeck, Sir Giles Alington, Lady Eleanor Davies and Bishop Williams—the latter for subornation, perjury, and for revealing the King's secrets, contrary to his oath as a councillor.

The treatment Laud received at the hands of the Long Parliament and their vile instrument Prynne, surpasses anything that can be imagined in brutality, injustice and dishonesty.[2] I cannot enter here into all the nauseating details of the long trial and imprisonment of this honest man. Suffice it to say, that the charge against him was a mass of the grossest falsehoods that all his enemies together were able to concoct, and that they were naturally quite unable to substantiate a single clause of the indictment. In spite of this, they sentenced him to death, tormenting him until the end, and even sent Sir John Clatworthy to bully and irritate him on the scaffold.[3]

A significant and touching clause is to be found in his will, which shows more than any words of mine could how devoted this simple man still remained in adversity to the great master in whose service he had met his death—

"I take the boldness to give my dear and dread Sovereign King Charles (whom God bless) £1000, and I do forgive him the debt which he owes me, being £2000, and require that the two tallies for it be given up."

I now turn to Thomas Wentworth, Earl of Strafford. But I might as well save myself the pains: for all historians, of any worth at all, are unanimous in their praise

---

[1] Op. cit.

[2] Dr. Hutton (op. cit., p. 207) declares that "never in English history, it may truly be said, was there a more monstrous violation of justice and good feeling in the trial of a capital charge."

[3] For details of this last act of villainy see Dean Hook's biography, p. 381.

of this great man. Like Charles and Laud, he sinned in
a way which the rapacious, vulgar and heartless spirit
of the times could ill forgive. He was determined to
administer justice, suppress abuses and alleviate the
oppression of the people,[1] without any regard for the rank
or wealth of the individuals he opposed; and as one of the
splendid triumvirate which once ruled over the destinies
of England, he pursued his policy with the greatest degree
of ability, pertinacity and courage.

Even his bitterest opponents ultimately had to acknowledge the magnificent gifts of this dazzling personality,
and more than half of the anger and hostility created by
his conversion to the King's cause in 1628 was the outcome of his late colleagues' profound appreciation of his
powers. No group of men ever accuse another person
rancorously of apostasy if, on leaving their party, he does
not impoverish it. On the contrary, they are only too
glad that the counsels of a fool should jeopardise their
opponents' cause. Do but read, therefore, of the anger
that Wentworth's desertion of his party roused, and you
will be able to form an approximate estimate of his
value.

Like Charles, Wentworth was a handsome man. Compare Charles's face with Cromwell's, and Wentworth's[2]
with Hampden's,[3] and if you are a believer, as every
great people and most great men have been, in the message
of the face and body, you will be able to dispense with
all historical inquiry, and to conclude immediately that
Charles and his friend Wentworth were on the *right* side,
and not, as Gardiner seems to suppose, on the *wrong* side,
of the great struggle of the seventeenth century.

---

[1] "His accession to the Privy Council," says Professor Gardiner,
"was followed by a series of measures aiming at the benefit of the
people in general, and the protection of the helpless against the pressure
caused by the self-interest of particular classes."—*Personal Government of
Charles I*, Vol. I, p. 197.

[2] I refer to the portrait belonging to the Duke of Portland.

[3] The portrait belonging to Earl Spencer.

This evidence of the features and of the body is, however, insufficient nowadays to convince the average European possessed only of moderate health and spirits: that is partly why I have written this essay.

I shall not enter into the question of Wentworth's so-called apostasy. Nothing definite seems to be known about it, and it is just as much open to the Puritans to say that he was bribed by honours to join the King's party —a thing they do not hesitate to assert concerning this noble man—as it is for me to declare that Wentworth, after fourteen years of close association with the Puritan party, was at last forced, in spite of his honest nature, not prone to suspect evil in others, to recognise the absolute unworthiness and prurience of his whilom comrades. At any rate he was never a Puritan;[1] and, in view of the hold Puritanism began to take of the Parliamentary party in the struggle with the King in 1628, I can see nothing surprising in the fact that a man of Wentworth's stamp should suddenly be caught at the throat with a feeling of uncontrollable nausea, and should seek purer and more congenial air in the neighbourhood of a sovereign such as Charles I.

It is true that Charles employed him in high and responsible duties almost immediately; but then, as Traill has shown, Charles had liked and admired Wentworth long before the act of so-called apostasy was even contemplated. There are not now, and there were not then, so many men in England of Wentworth's singular ability as to leave a monarch for long in hesitation as to whom he should entrust his highest charges. Once, therefore, Wentworth had declared himself on the King's side, it is not surprising that he should have been almost immediately given the most exalted duties. Charles has been accused of many things, but he was certainly no fool. He

---

[1] See *The Political History of England*, Vol. VII, by F. C. Montague, p. 155, where the author, speaking of the so-called popular party in the Commons, says: "They were Puritans, but Wentworth was not, and he therefore lacked the strongest bond of sympathy with his fellows."

had the old-world trust in the message of the face and the body, and his discerning eye would not have missed the reading of Wentworth's character from the look of the man.

The choice was, at all events, not a bad one. For, as President of the Council of the North and as Lord Deputy in Ireland, Wentworth was soon to distinguish himself as a ruler not merely beneficent, but also extremely able.

Speaking of Strafford, Gardiner says : " Justice without respect of persons might have been the motto of his life. Nothing called forth his bitter indignation like the claims of the rich to special consideration or favour." [1] And it must not be supposed that he was a mere upstart or a demagogue who held the modern socialistic view of wealth. He was the descendant of a very old family, which had been seated on the manor of Wentworth in Yorkshire since the Conquest, and he was, moreover, for his time, exceedingly rich. He knew that wealth, like any other form of power, involved sacred duties, and he hated to see it used as an instrument of oppression or of injustice.

There is no doubt that he had the greatest contempt for the body of upstarts that the rising commercial class and the new landed " gentry " had imposed upon the nation; and when he spoke of the " Prynnes, Pyms and Bens, with the rest of that generation of odd names and natures," [2] it was not with the acerbity of a jealous rival, but rather with the natural proud disdain of a gentleman of ancient lineage.

Like the King, he was loath to see the people handed over to the mercy of this upstart rabble of lawyers and country " gentry "; and, like his master and Laud, he met his doom trying to protect the Crown, the Church and the people from spoliation by these sharks.

As he said in his defence before the Privy Council in 1636, when he was called upon to justify his conduct in

[1] *The First Two Stuarts and the Puritan Rebellion*, p. 76.
[2] *Life of the Earl of Strafford*, by John Forster, p. 194.

Ireland owing to the clamour of protest that had been raised by those who before his time had been allowed to rob and filch in perfect peace: "For where I found a Crown, a Church and a people spoiled, I could not imagine to redeem them from under the pressure with gracious smiles and gentle looks; it would cost warmer water than so." [1]

And, indeed, it did cost "warmer water than so." In dispensing justice and restoring robbed treasure he had to meet and oppose the most powerful in the land. In addition to the host of minor military and civil officials whom, owing to their incompetence, he weeded out of the service to make way for better men, among the persons of real influence whom he reduced to reluctant and savage submission was the Earl of Cork, whom he discovered to have misappropriated large tracts of Church lands. And, incidentally, in fearlessly attacking Cork he estranged both the Earl of Pembroke and the Earl of Salisbury, who did "their best to save Lord Cork." [2] Lord Wilmot was another magnate whom he brought to justice for "taking Crown property to his own use," while Lord Clanricarde and his son, Lord Tunbridge, were full of rankling hatred for the honest Lord Deputy who had expropriated them from estates filched from the Church.

The case of Lord Mountmorris is too well known to be discussed in detail here; suffice it, therefore, to say that it was his constant petty peculations and malversations as Vice-Treasurer of Ireland that originally incensed Wentworth against him. And it was certainly Wentworth's intolerable vigilance and irksome disinterestedness that first incensed Mountmorris against his superior

When we remember that these Irish noblemen had friends in England, it can easily be seen that the extent and power of the hostility generated against the Lord Deputy of Ireland was formidable indeed. For if Lord Clanricarde's case alone could account for the hatred

[1] *The Earl of Strafford's Letters and Despatches*, Vol. II, p. 20.
[2] Gardiner, *Personal Government of Charles I*, p. 132.

inspired in the Earl of Essex for Wentworth, how can we reckon the legion of lesser men than Essex who also were friends of "gentlemen" suffering from the Lord Deputy's zealous honesty in Ireland? [1]

The fact that Wentworth's rule proved to be a miracle of beneficent reform in a country that for many years had been the bugbear of all British statesmen is not contested by any historian of note. Under his stewardship the finances were put in order. The annual deficit of £24,000 was converted into a surplus of £85,000, and in three years the revenue was increased by £180,000.

The depredations of pirates which harassed all the shipping on the coast were not only abated, they were totally suppressed. As regards the manufactures of the country, through the encouragement already referred to above, the prosperity of the linen industry was, as we know, promoted and perfected. Meanwhile, " justice was dispensed 'without acceptation of persons,'" and "the poor knew where to seek and to have relief without being afraid to appeal to His Majesty's Catholic justice against the great subject." [2] Nor was the Army or the Church neglected. I have already referred to the Church; and Gardiner, speaking of the Army, says: "The officers were startled to find that the new Lord Deputy, who, unlike his predecessors, was General of the Army as well as Governor of the State, actually expected them to attend to their duties. His own troop of horse soon became a model for the rest of the Army." [3]

To the students of human nature, however, it will not be difficult to see that all this honest zeal and untiring energy demanded from people who hitherto had indolently

[1] See *The Political History of England*, Vol. VII, by F. C. Montague, p. 198. Speaking of Wentworth's administration in Ireland, the author says : " Courtiers, parasites and place-hunters found at last a lord deputy who could and would balk their appetites. The revenue which he had so greatly increased he expended honestly and frugally."

[2] Traill, op. cit., p. 139.

[3] *Personal Government of Charles I*, Vol. II, p. 123.

allowed things to go along pretty well as they liked, provided they themselves were not the losers—it will not be difficult to see, I say, that all this did not tend to make the Lord Deputy popular, save with that uninfluential portion of the community, the labouring masses, whose voice cannot save their protector once he is assailed by more powerful agents. As Gardiner observes: "Privy Councillors and officers of various kinds looked upon their posts as property to be used for the best advantage, and would turn sharply upon the man who required from them the zealous activity which he himself displayed." [1]

As we know, they did "turn sharply upon the man," and with just as little mercy for his honesty as he had shown for their despicable villainy. Lingard calls the impeachment of Strafford "the vengeance of his enemies." [2] It was undoubtedly no more and no less than this; for not only were the sorest sufferers under his honest rule—men like the Earl of Cork and Lord Mountmorris—called to bear witness against him, but the very charge which in the end proved most damning to his case (the charge of having urged the King to employ an Irish army to reduce England to submission) depended upon an arbitrary interpretation of words which he was alleged to have used in Committee of the Privy Council, when all the while the words themselves were attested by only one witness, and not confirmed by any other member present at the Committee before which they were alleged to have been uttered. When, moreover, we find that this member was a man who bore Strafford no small amount of ill-will, we cannot help feeling, with Traill, that this piece of evidence was of a kind which "any judge at *nisi prius* would have unhesitatingly directed a jury to disregard." [3] All other members present at the Committee, including the King himself, denied having heard the words, although they distinctly recollected the other portions of Strafford's speech; and we must remem-

[1] *Personal Government of Charles I*, Vol II, p. 118.
[2] *History of England*, Vol. VII, p. 470.   [3] Op. cit., p. 180.

ber that there was one man present when the fatal words
were supposed to have been uttered who, next to Laud
and Strafford, was the most honest personage in England
at the time—Bishop Juxon.

But Sir Henry Vane, who loathed Strafford with all the
loathing that a mediocre creature always feels for that
brilliant exception, the man of genius, declared that he
had heard the words, and this was enough for the body
of irate religious Tartuffes who then filled the benches of
the House of Commons.

What mattered it that Sir Henry Vane had coveted the
Barony of Raby at the time when it had been conferred
upon Strafford? What mattered it that Sir Henry Vane
was still full of rankling hatred against Strafford, because
the latter, recognising Vane's mediocrity, had once opposed
his promotion to the Secretaryship of State?

The Long Parliament was not a body of decent men,
it was merely a pack of mercenary Puritans. They understood and sympathised with rankling hatred as none but
Puritans can. Sir Henry Vane's evidence was embraced
with alacrity. It was twisted into a charge of treason
against the unfortunate victim of the now powerful party,
and nothing but a death sentence would satisfy them.

Strafford's judges, however, would not pass this sentence. They refused to admit that the charge of treason
had been proved. They had looked on unmoved at a
trial which had been refined in the cruelty meted out to
the prisoner by the committee of managers; they had
allowed Strafford, broken in health as he was, to be tor-
mented, harassed and baited in a manner unprecedented
in the annals of English justice; but to this last act of
savage unfairness they would not go.

What did the Commons do? They dropped the
Impeachment, feeling that it was hopeless to compass
Strafford's death in that manner, and they proceeded
against him by Bill of Attainder.[1]

[1] Lingard (op. cit., p. 477) makes an interesting comment on this
stage of Wentworth's misfortunes : "It is singular," he says, "that

A DEFENCE OF ARISTOCRACY

Nothing more nauseating and utterly base could possibly be imagined than this running of the noble Wentworth to earth by a pack of hypocritical villains who, until the end, endeavoured to conceal their all too personal "reasons" beneath a semblance of legal procedure. They had not the honesty of an Italian tyranny; they had not the daring villainy to kill him outright with poison, or even with a stab in the back. No; they must consummate his doom with the cold-blooded deliberation of toads with guilty consciences.

Lord Digby, who was himself one of the managers of the impeachment, and who, moreover, as a son of the Earl of Bristol, had "reasons" for being hostile to the Court party, rose in the House of Commons, and, in a fine speech full of an honesty and manly courage which did him credit, declared that he could not vote for the Bill.

"God keep me," he exclaimed, "from giving judgment of death on any man, and of ruin to his innocent posterity, on a law made *a posteriori.*"[1]

But even this hostility to the Bill on the part of one of the former managers did not impress the brutal Puritans, and this scandalous measure was passed. At its third reading before the House of Lords only forty-five members were present; to the rest the work of murder was still either too distasteful or the danger of openly opposing it seemed too great;[2] and the measure became law by a small majority of seven.

these ardent champions in the cause of freedom should have selected for their pattern Henry VIII, the most arbitrary of our monarchs. They even improved on the iniquity of the precedents which he had left them ; for the moment that the result became doubtful they abandoned the impeachment which they had originated themselves, and to insure the fate of their victim, proceeded by Bill of Attainder."

[1] Rushworth, *The Tryall of Thomas Earl of Strafford* (1680), p. 52.

[2] The latter alternative seems more probable. Cobbett tells us in his *State Trials* (Vol. III, p. 1,514) : "The greatest part of his friends absented themselves upon pretence (whether true or suppositious) that they feared the multitude, otherwise his suffrages had more than counterpoised the voters for his death."

And now I come to the saddest part of this terrible tragedy. I should have mentioned that nine days previously the King had made a personal appeal to the House of Lords, denying the charges against his friend Strafford, and, in the hope of saving him, going so far as to pledge himself never to employ the late Lord Deputy again, even as a constable. It must have cost the King a good deal thus to humble himself, even before the noble rabble of the House of Lords, on behalf of an old and trusted friend, and why almost all historians condemn him for doing this I cannot understand. No one, save perhaps Juxon, ever knew what Charles must have gone through at this time. Even if we suppose that this personal appeal was a mistake, it was at least the sort of mistake which only a loving and faithful friend would have ventured upon in a moment of acute and intolerable anxiety.

Meanwhile, however, the Puritans, these past-masters at rousing artificial agitations, had fomented all the ruck and scum of London, in order that a popular clamour might be raised for Strafford's head. Leopold von Ranke shows how they used even the pulpits of the metropolis to prejudice the minds of the people against the Earl,[1] with the result that a threatening mob soon mustered outside the Houses of Parliament and in Palace Yard, shouting for " Justice! "—justice, after all that had happened!

How the King was ultimately persuaded by the disreputable Bishop of Lincoln to sign a commission for giving the Royal Assent to the Bill is now too well known to be discussed here. But why is it that so much stress has been laid on this jesuitical argument on the part of Williams? I feel convinced myself that no sophistry of which a man like Williams was capable would ever have moved a man of Charles's character. But with the clamour outside, with the convincing though bogus pageant of London's "righteous indignation" beneath his very windows, and the consciousness of the fact that everything

[1] Op. cit., Vol. II, p. 265.

was tottering to its doom—for the mob did not hesitate to cry, "Strafford's head or the King's!"—it is more than probable that Charles was well convinced not only of the necessity for Strafford's death, but for his own as well.

Staggered by the diabolical malice of the rising so-called popular party, he must have felt that his time had indeed come. And, severed from every one whom he could trust, save the honest Juxon, it must have been with a feeling of fateful hopelessness that he consented to the murder of his great comrade and supporter. As it was, he would willingly have died, there and then, with Strafford, if he had only been able to convince himself that his act of self-sacrifice would affect him alone.

"If my own person only were in danger," he said, with tears in his eyes, as he announced his resolution to the Council, "I would willingly venture it to save Lord Strafford's life. . . . My Lord of Strafford's condition is more happy than mine." [1]

I could not conclude this short sketch of Strafford's career in a manner more fitting than by quoting the last words of the noble Earl's appeal to the King to sign the death warrant. They are a tribute alike to their author and to him for whom they were written. For to write such a letter one must be a great man, but to inspire it one must be an even greater one. [2]

"With much sadness," wrote Strafford, "I am come to a resolution of that which I take to be the best becoming me, to look upon that which is most principal in itself, which, doubtless, is the prosperity of your sacred person

[1] Gardiner, *History of England*, Vol. IX, pp. 366–367.

[2] As a proof of what the *true* feeling of the masses was, towards the rule of the great triumvirate, it is interesting, pending the more substantial demonstration I shall give later, to refer to John Forster's account of Strafford's progress to the scaffold. John Forster is not by any means partial to the Court party ; yet, in his biography of Strafford he says : "Strafford, in his walk, took off his hat frequently and saluted them [the people, 10,000 of whom were gathered on Tower Hill] and received not a word of insult or reproach," p. 409.

and the common wealth, infinitely before any man's private interest.

"And, therefore, in a few words, as I feel myself wholly upon the honour and justice of my peers, so clearly as to beseech your majesty might pleased to have spared that declaration of yours on Saturday last, and entirely have left me to their lordships; so now, to set your majesty's conscience, etc. at liberty, I do most humbly beseech you, for the prevention of such mischief as may happen by your refusal, to pass the bill, by this means to remove, praised be God, I cannot say this accursed, but, I confess, this unfortunate thing forth of the way towards that blessed agreement, which God, I trust, shall ever establish between you and your subjects.

"Sir, my consent herein shall more acquit you to God, than all the world can do besides: To a willing mind is no injury done; and as, by God's grace, I forgive all the world, so, sir, I can give up the life of this world with all cheerfulness imaginable, in the just acknowledgment of your exceeding favour; and only beg, that, in your goodness, you would vouchsafe to cast your gracious regard upon my poor son and his sisters, less or more, and no otherwise than their unfortunate father shall appear more or less guilty of his death. God long preserve your majesty.

"Your majesty's most humble,
"most faithful subject and servant,
"STRAFFORD." [1]

I now come to the concluding scene of this harrowing tragedy, in which, as I have shown, Taste, quality and the most genuine aristocratic tradition of ideal rulership were pitted in an unequal struggle against the overwhelming and ruthless forces of rapacious vulgarity, quantity and trade. I have gone to some pains to show how intolerable Charles and his two leading ministers had made themselves

[1] Rushworth, *The Tryall of Thomas Earl of Strafford* (1680), pp. 743-744.

to the party which was going to effect the fatal turning-
point in England's social history, and to stamp her spirit
and her physique until this very day with its loathsome
mark. I have endeavoured to demonstrate how surely
but resolutely the road was made clear by these advocates
of " Liberty " and a " Free Parliament " for all that heartless oppression and high-handed robbery and corruption
which reached its high-water mark at the beginning of
the nineteenth century; and now I have only to record,
in a few short sentences, the most salient features in the
last phase of this ghastly drama.

It is quite certain that when the Short Parliament was
called in 1640, the less estimable portion of the country
—that part of it which is the direct parent of all our
present chaos, misery, ugliness and ill-health—was exasperated beyond endurance with the policy Charles, Laud
and Wentworth had pursued. The determined stand
which these three men had made against greed and the
lust of gain, against quantity as opposed to quality, and
against vulgarity, cant and that myopic selfish hedonism
which has been so characteristic of the governing classes
ever since—this determined stand must be suppressed at
all costs! Nevertheless, at the time of the calling of the
Short Parliament, the consciousness of Charles's beneficent
rule was still a little too strong to render a violently
hostile attitude to the Court quite plausible. Before
agitators like Pym, Cromwell, Hampden, Vane, Essex,
Bedford, Holland and Prynne could engineer a genuine
public upheaval, something a little more reprehensible
than mere patriarchal government must be included in
their charge against the Court. For as Mr. F. C. Montague says in speaking of Charles I's eleven years of
personal government—

" England enjoyed profound peace; taxation was not
heavy; justice was fairly administered as between man and
man; and the government showed reasonable consideration for the welfare of the common people. Trade still
flourished, large tracts of the fens were reclaimed, and

the tokens of wealth and luxury were seen on every side." [1]

It is true that the most was made of Ship Money; but even this imposition the Short Parliament were ready to overlook, provided only that Charles would consent never to levy it again without their leave, and they went so far as to offer to grant supplies if he pledged himself to this arrangement. In fact, it is quite certain that not only was Charles quite willing and even desirous of coming to terms with his Parliament, but also that the majority in the Commons in April 1640 were quite prepared to come to terms with him. Such an agreement, however, would never have suited the extremists of the so-called popular party, and there is every reason to believe that Vane the elder, who, as we have seen, had only one desire —the compassing of Wentworth's doom—was the chief instrument in wrecking the promised happy relations between the King and Parliament.

By his messages, as Secretary, to the Commons from the King, and by his reports to the King of progress in the Commons, with an ingenuity which was monstrous in its diabolical selfishness and malice—for it finally put an end to all hope of peace between the Court and the Commons—he so contrived to embitter the King against Parliament, and *vice versâ*, that in the end, to the consternation of all the more moderate members of the so-called popular party, Charles I dissolved the Short Parliament on May 5. [2]

Here, then, together with the religious trouble up in Scotland, was a sufficient grievance to inflame the less

---

[1] *The Political History of England*, Vol. VII, p. 202.

[2] An interesting and illuminating account of this Parliament and of the dastardly part that Vane played in wrecking it, is to be found in Traill's *Biography of Strafford* (pp. 162–166). For a confirmation of Traill's account of Vane's perfidy and of the manner in which he opposed Wentworth's sober advice to Charles, with the object of rendering all agreement between Parliament and the King impossible, see Gardiner's *History of England*, Vol. IX, p. 113. For Vane's lie to the King about the temper of Parliament, see especially p. 117.

vindictive members of the so-called popular party against the King; and, in the hands of able intriguers and agitators, it was wrought into a superb ˗weapon of sedition.

When the Long Parliament met on November 3, 1640, there was no longer any question of an agreement between the King and the popular leaders, and step by step all the powerful men on the King's side were either murdered or forced to flee the country.

The Commons now became supreme in the land, and an end was put to that patriarchal rule which, if it had only been able to inspire a larger number of the noblemen of the period, would have been the means of altering the whole face of history from that time forward, and the aristocracy of England would still be standing, not as a suspected and semi-impotent body of rulers, but as a caste enjoying the accumulated popular gratitude of two centuries, and a prestige second not even to that of the ancient Incas of Peru.

It is true that in the final struggle a majority of the House of Lords joined the King's side; we know, however, that many took this step reluctantly, and we must also not overlook the fact that when war was ultimately declared a very different situation was created from that which had existed when Charles, Wentworth' and Laud were ruling England. At the opening of the Grand Rebellion many of the aristocracy felt that they stood or fell with Royalty, and in their extremity joined the King's side. During Charles's personal government, however, when every opportunity was at hand for joining the King in preserving and protecting the rights, the health, the spirits and the happiness of the people, they showed an indifference and often a hostility to the Court policy which must have given great encouragement to the baser sort in the Commons to press forward their ignominious designs.

One thing, however, is perfectly certain, and that is that the poorer people, the masses who had felt the warmth and paternal care of Charles's government, joined the King whole-heartedly in the struggle with the Party which most histories have the impudence to declare was fighting for the people's liberties!

What is liberty to the working man if it is not freedom from undue oppression and molestation, while he earns his living and rears his family   What can the working man care for this " liberty " which the Parliamentary forces purchased on the fields of Edgehill, Marston Moor and Naseby, if there is no one to protect his health, to preserve his creature comforts, and to see that he is not robbed of the wherewithal to rear his children? [1]   Read English history from the time of the Grand Rebellion, and see the appalling misery this so-called liberty conferred upon the working masses!   •

Even that inveterate democrat Jeremy Bentham could detect the cant of this cry of liberty when it was raised in a country in which the burden-bearers were respected. " Many persons," he says, " do not enquire if a State be well administered, if the laws protect property and persons, if the ·people are happy.   What they require, without giving attention to anything else, is political liberty— that is, the most equal distribution of political power. Wherever they do not see the form of government to which they are attached they see nothing but slavery, and if these pretended slaves are well satisfied with their condition, if they do not desire to change it, they despise and insult them.   In their fanaticism they are always ready to stake all the happiness of a nation upon civil war for the sake of transferring power into the hands of those whom an invincible ignorance will not permit to use it except for their own destruction." [2]

---

[1] In his *Autobiography* Gibbon makes a shrewd remark relative to this very point.   He says : "While the aristocracy of Berne protects the happiness it is superfluous to enquire whether it be founded in the rights of man."—*The World's Classics Edition* (Henry Frowde), p. 217.

[2] *An Introduction to the Principles of Morals and Legislation*, quoted by Tom Mann in a speech delivered before Parliament, May 3, 1895.

But we know that this cry for "Liberty!" was only cant, unless it meant "liberty to oppress the people." For the one fact that stands out with almost amazing inconsistency in this last phase of Charles I's unhappy career is that in a struggle against the monarchy which was ostensibly to reclaim the liberties of the people, the real uncorrupted people themselves, whose "trade" interests had not been threatened by a tasteful patriarchal ruler, sided with the King.

"In the struggle between Charles and his Parliament," says Thorold Rogers,[1] "a line drawn from Scarborough to Southampton would give a fair indication of the locality in which the opposing forces were ranged. The eastern district, of course including London, was on the side of Parliament, the western, with the exception of some important towns, such as Bristol and Gloucester, was for the King. The resources of the Parliamentary division were incomparably greater than those of the Royal region."[2]

Thus it is quite obvious that the poorest counties, which were the northern and the western, espoused the Royal cause, while the wealthier, including the trading districts, were in league with Parliament. Garnier, commenting on this fact, says, "it is a curious circumstance."[3] But surely, after what we have seen, it is exceedingly comprehensible. Two other facts, however, should be borne in mind: first, that East Anglia and Kent, which were for the Parliament, had recently been flooded with Flemish and French refugees, who were all engrossed in trade, and who cared little either for the King or for the fate of the country of their adoption, provided only that they could

---

[1] *A History of Agriculture and Prices in England*, Vol. V, p. 11.

[2] The continuation of this passage is worth quoting, as throwing further light upon the course of the Grand Rebellion: "The military resources of the King were far superior to those of his rivals, except in one important particular, the means of paying his troops. Cromwell, by the new model, soon trained his soldiers, and the resources of Eastern England enabled him to pay them regularly." See also pp. 73 and 159–160 of this same work, Vol. V.

[3] *History of the English Landed Interests*, Vol. I, p. 333.

accumulate wealth in peace; and, secondly, that of the landed gentry, it was the recently imported and more mercenary blood that joined the Parliament,[1] while the older families sided with the King.

In the Grand Rebellion, therefore, we see the curious anomaly of a powerful minority of agitators, supported by a large contingent of aliens, landed upstarts, town tradesmen and thousands of deluded followers fighting against the poorer people [2] and the King, for the "liberties of the people." Only unsuspecting spinsters or modern democrats, however, could ever believe such a tale; and, when we know what followed, when we read of the oppression and slavery to which the victory of the Parliamentary party prepared the way; when, moreover, we keep steadily before us the facts of Charles I's reign, we not only suspect, we *know*, that there were other, more personal, less disinterested and far less savoury motives behind the so-called popular party, than a desire to vindicate the "liberties of the people."

The triumph of Parliament did not mean the triumph of the liberties of the people. It meant the triumph of a new morality, a new outlook on life, and a new under-

---

[1] Gardiner gives an interesting remark of Windebank's relative to this element in the Parliamentary forces. Speaking to Ponzani in 1635, Windebank said: "O, the great judgments of God. He ever punishes men with those means by which they have offended. That pig of a Henry VIII committed such sacrilege by profaning so many ecclesiastical benefices in order to give their goods to those who being so rewarded might stand firmly for the King in the Lower House; and now the King's greatest enemies are those who are enriched by these benefices."—*Personal Government of Charles I*, Vol. II, p. 241.

[2] When one considers that the poorer districts, as I have shown, were for the Royal cause, with the bulk of the non-industrial and non-mercantile population, one may well speak of the *English people* as being on the side of the King; for all the pure characteristics of England's noble peasantry were there, and no distortion of the facts can ever prove that the new middle-class, Puritan, trade and alien element, which constituted the forces of the other side, possessed the then-vaunted virtues of the English nation, although they are certainly typical of the Englishman now.

standing of what life was worth. It meant the triumph, of the morality of unrestricted competition, of uncontrolled and unguided trade, and of a policy of neglect in regard to all things that really mattered.

Rogers tells us that "the war between King and Parliament is the beginning of the modern system of finance," but it was more than that.

"The success of Puritanism," says Cunningham, "meant the triumph of the new commercial morality, which held good among moneyed men; capitalists had established their right to secure a return for their money, and there was no authority to insist upon any correlative duty, when they organised industrial undertakings and obtained a control of the means of production." [1]

This was what the Grand Rebellion achieved, and this, in the main, was the sole object of the Grand Rebellion. With consummate craft and ingenuity, transcendental motives were woven into the general scheme to blind the eye and to distract the detective glance of critics; and it might even be said that in a large number of cases the cry of religion from the Puritan side was raised with a sincerity which baffled even the most suspicious. But it must be remembered how readily ignorant and grasping men involve their deity in their own quarrels, and how unconsciously they confound the injuries done to their own interests with injuries done to their God. This phenomenon had occurred before. The Old Testament is full of examples of God being on the side of a party who had something to gain in a war. The sincerity of some, at least, of the Puritans need not, therefore, surprise us. Only clean and thoroughly lucid minds can be accused of insincerity when they mix up religious with mercenary motives. But the commercial canaille that fought under Cromwell and Hampden were quite capable of being sincere in their religious cry, without being in the least conscious of the mercenary motives that inspired them to raise it.

[1] Op. cit., Vol. II, p. 206.

PURITANISM, TRADE AND VULGARITY

In any case, as Cunningham says: "The victory of the Parliamentary forces over Charles I turned out to be an important step in the direction of *laissez-faire;*"[1] and from that time forward the vulgar spirit concerned with gain and greed as ends in themselves was unloosed on this unhappy island, never to be effectually controlled or held in check again. And Charles I knew that this would be so. He actually said as much, and he certainly felt as much.

Dr. Hutton would have it that Charles died a martyr to religion. He writes, "when the last struggle came he [Charles] still refused to save his life, as there can be little doubt he could have done, by surrendering and deserting the Church of his fathers. In this sense it is that Charles was, and that Laud made him, a martyr."[2]

Now I should not like to be thought to have anything but the sincerest respect for Dr. Hutton's judgment—I have quoted him sufficiently often to show the reliance I place on it—but really, on this one point, I feel that I must disagree. I am perfectly willing to admit that Charles might have saved his life in the end, by renouncing something so loathsome to the Puritans as the Church of England; but surely this, though an important matter, was not the only point at stake. A far greater issue depended upon whether Charles yielded or maintained his ground, and this was, whether the governing classes in Parliament, unfit as they were for the duty, were to become the sole masters of the destinies of the people, or whether the latter were still to find in one who was above all self-interest, a protector, a tasteful, paternal guide and a friend solicitous of their welfare.

This was the issue. The question of the Church was only part of it. And while in support of my view I can point to the whole of Charles I's and Wentworth's policy, I also have Charles's own words on the scaffold. Surely these can no longer leave us in any doubt upon this one point; and with these noble sentences I shall draw the present essay to a close.

[1] Op. cit., Vol. II, p. 18. [2] Op. cit., p. 236.

" For the people," said the King, " and truly I desire
their Liberty and Freedom as much as any Body whom-
soever, but I must tell you, that their Liberty and Freedom
consists in having of Government, those laws by which
their Life and their Goods may be most their own. . . .
Sirs, it was for this that now I come here. If I would
have given way to an Arbitrary Way, for to have all Laws
changed according to the Power of the Sword, I needed
not to have come here; and therefore I tell you (and I
pray God it be not laid to your charge) that I am the
martyr of the people." [1]

[1] Rushworth, Part IV, Vol. II, p. 1,429. See also part of his speech
before the Court that sentenced him to death : "This many a day all
things have been taken away from me, but that that I call dearer to
me than my Life, which is my Conscience and my Honour. And if
I had a respect to my Life more than the Peace of the Kingdom, and
the Liberty of the Subject, certainly I should have made a particular
Defence for myself; for by that at leastwise I might have delayed an
ugly Sentence, which I believe will pass upon me. Therefore certainly,
Sir, as a Man that hath some understanding, some knowledge of the
World, if that my true Zeal to my Country had not overborn the care
that I have for my own preservation, I should have gone another way
to work than I have done."—*Ibid.*, p. 1,422.

CHAPTER V

"Beautie is no helpe nor furtherance, but a great impediment unto chastitie."—W. PRYNNE : *The Unlovelinesse of Lovelockes,* 1628.

IT will seem to some, perhaps, that I have dealt at unnecessary length with Charles I and his system of government. It is, however, difficult in a work intended for the general reader to avoid doing this, particularly when it is a matter of emphasising and substantiating a point of view which is neither universally taught, nor universally held, concerning this great Stuart monarch. For, despite what many may consider to be a fair criticism of this and the foregoing chapter, I myself can never regard them as an attempt to "whitewash" Charles I, as the journalistic jargon has it.

I had a much more important purpose to serve in writing them than the mere "whitewashing" of a man, however great, who has been dead for well over two centuries. For what purpose these acts of "whitewashing" are ever accomplished I cannot understand, unless, belike, they slake a sentimental thirst in the "whitewasher's" throat for justice on behalf of a dead hero.

I, at all events, am moved by no such empty purpose. I care little for the reader's opinion of Charles I as a hero or as a martyr. My chief concern, however, the matter which I really do take to heart, is rather to call attention to the last stand which was made in England against everything which to-day makes life so ugly, so wretched, so spiritless and so unhealthy. It is not my object to urge

165

admiration for our beheaded sovereign, but to show that his death meant also the death of a hundred things for which we are madly hungering to-day, and which all the ingenuity of the finest legislator would find it difficult to restore to us, after all these years, during which they have been absent from our midst. And among these coveted treasures of a bygone generation, of which all trace has now vanished, I refer to taste, the love of quality above quantity, the care of health and spirit and the hatred of such empty aims as mere wealth, speed, "pleasure" and change, where no culture, no superior purpose or aspiration guides them for the general weal or even for the true elevation and glorification of a worthy minority.

It was my object in writing this and the preceding chapter to give at least the outlines of an answer to a question which will soon be on all people's lips, the question as to when all the muddle and futility of our present civilisation began: what it was that has made it possible for every Englishman of to-day contentedly to point only to the exports and imports of his country, and not to her national beauty, culture, health, spirit or character, when called upon to indicate wherein her greatness lies. Apart from the fact that almost all this beauty, culture, health, spirit and character are dead, why is it that it would never occur to the average sane Englishman to imagine that it is necessary to refer to something more than trade returns to prove a nation's greatness?

The answer to this question involves the wielding of such enormous masses of material that it would be absurd for me to pretend to give them all here. But that the bare outlines of it are drawn in these two chapters is certainly my earnest hope; while the fact that these outlines not only throw light on the principle of aristocracy, but also necessitate the discussion of questions kindred and essential to it, is an adequate excuse for giving them at this stage in the present work.

By far the most impressive feature of our modern civilisation in England, is the unanimity with which certain opinions concerning the greatness of a nation, are held. It is not only the Londoner, or the inhabitant of a large provincial city, who measures England's greatness by the square-mileage of her colonies and the huge figures of her imports and exports—*every* Englishman does this, whether he be a scholar, a painter, a doctor, a lawyer, a grocer, or a farmer. Those Englishmen who do not do this, constitute the exceptions, and they, as a rule, withdraw to the English colony in Florence, Bruges or some other continental city, if they have the means. If they are poor, they sit at home and bewail the fact that they were not born in another age.

For this unanimity of opinion to have been imposed like a religion upon a nation, something in the nature of a grand feat of sacerdotal ingenuity must have been practised upon the English people. For, it should be borne in mind that the bulk of a nation do not create opinions, they simply accept them ready made. If, therefore, for the time being, we imagine a large priesthood deliberately inculcating upon a submissive people the doctrine that large trade figures and large colonies, alone, are the essential attributes of a great nation, under what circumstances are we to suppose that such a doctrine was submissively accepted?

It is one thing to say that opinions are not created by the majority of a people, but merely accepted by them, and quite another matter to suppose that *all* opinions once created are accepted by the bulk of the people. The first proposition is true, the second is false. For, the essential pre-requisite to the general acceptance of an opinion, is the readiness of the mental soil on which it is to be planted. Preach it, on the other hand, to a nation of women whose men are unworthy of the smallest sacrifice or of the smallest honour, and even if these women are free from undue arrogance or impudent self-esteem, their hearts will prove an unfavourable soil for this new moral plant. Preach it, on the other hand, to a nation of women thoroughly convinced of the genuine superiority, high value and inestimable worthiness of their men, and it will spread and be accepted very rapidly.[1]

Before, therefore, the doctrine could be accepted that mere bulk and large trade-figures alone constituted the *greatness* of a nation, the mental soil of a people had to be prepared, tilled, manured and broken up, in a manner calculated to enable it to accept and prove favourable to this doctrine. Not only that, but the political attitude of mind which is favourable to the doctrine had also to be reared. For this doctrine is not one which is natural to healthy mankind. It is much more natural to healthy mankind to admire beauty, greatness of character, strength of will, spirit and body. It is much more natural to healthy and spirited mankind to admire health, grace, prowess and skill.

The peasants who fought and won Crécy, Poictiers and Agincourt would have been completely at a loss to understand what you meant had you told them that England was great because she could count her trade returns in so many hundreds of millions, and because the sun never set on her Empire. They would have felt that while such things might constitute greatness, if the ideals, the hearts, the health and the spirit of the nation were not great as well, they would mean nothing apart from these other attributes.

To-day, however, we can look on our vulgar culture of automobiles and general " smartness," we can contemplate our weak-kneed, lantern-jawed, pale-faced clerks and typists, we can inspect the ugliness of our huge cities, our slums, our hospitals, our factories and our lunatic asylums, and still say that England is great. Why is England

---

[1] In regard to this question of the Suttee, it is interesting to note why and how it was prohibited by the English rulers of India. To the modern European it is rightly inconceivable that he should constitute so magic, so great, so valuable a part of any woman's life, that her self-immolation on his tomb could ever be a justifiable act of desperate sacrifice. Thus, to him, all such self-immolations of women on their husbands' tombs must be bad and unjustifiable. Therefore he rules the custom out of existence, as a futile superstition, because in his part of the world it would indeed be a futile superstition.

great under these circumstances? "Because," says the glib modern man, "she is the market of the world, the counting-house of Europe, the workshop of five continents, the wealthiest nation on earth!"

"But," objects the man of taste, the man who knows, "these things do not last, they are not necessarily great, and they do not lead to a powerful race." To-day, however, the man of taste has not only a powerful minority to contend with, as Charles I had, he has a whole nation, which knows its lesson so well, that every 'bus-conductor, cobbler, peer, duke, stockbroker, priest, artist, doctor, grocer, butcher, or architect, in it, says the same thing and believes the same thing about this doctrine of trade and bulk and wealth.

As I say, this unanimity of opinion is impressive. Can it be possible that it is the outcome of something in the nature of a religious faith?

It has often been said, and, I believe, with some reason, that the true religious spirit resides in the East, that the genuine religious founder is essentially an Oriental, and that the Occident understands little of the machinery needful for establishing a creed in the hearts of a people. Certainly, if we examine the methods of Manu, Moses and Mahommed—those arch-geniuses in the art of the *pia fraus*—we are amazed at the thoroughness and subtlety with which they contrived to weave a religion into the food and hygiene of a people so as literally to build up a fresh human physique that might with justice be called either a true Brahman, a true Israelite, or a true Mahommedan. No detail is overlooked. The follower of the true religion has everything prescribed for him, even his meditations.

And I think it would be quite wrong to suppose that the pious fraud was in each case a conscious deception. It is far more probable, in fact, certain, that Manu, Moses and Mahommed were unconscious of the twist they were giving to the weapon religion, and to the disciplinary thought of God, when they used both in order to separate

169

the goats from the sheep, the great from the small, the unhealthy from the healthy, the work-day from the holy-day, the desirable food from the undesirable, and the good man (or the ideal man of the race) from the bad man (the degenerate or incompatible man). And this unconscious use of religion and of God to effect a deep racial or sociological act of consolidation is all the more potent and all the more irresistible from the very fact of being unconscious.

I do not mean to suggest, as Wilkinson does, that the pious fraud as practised upon the people by the ancient Egyptian priesthood, was wrong or necessarily reprehen-sible because it was conscious, or that, on the other hand, the unconscious pious fraud is always right and proper simply because it is unconscious.[1] I merely submit that there are many reasons for supposing that in the majority of cases the pious frauds of the past have been uncon-scious, and that they were all the stronger and all the more irresistible for being so. The characteristic which has always been common to them all, however, apart from their consciousness or unconsciousness, has invariably been that their object was to consolidate some race, community or group of communities, and to bind it by an internal relationship, based upon the most elaborate prescriptions for general conduct, diet, hygiene and spiritual occupa-tion, until ultimately this internal relationship was stamped upon the faces and the bodies of the people.

Now it is precisely this art of the *pia fraus* which is said to be indigenous to the Orient, and which some would deny to the Occident in any form whatsoever.

It will be the object of this chapter, however, to prove, not only that the art of the *pia fraus* has also been practised with consummate skill in the West, but that this strange event happened as recently as the seventeenth century, here in England. Whether it was completely unconscious or not, I should not like to say, as I believe it would be possible to show that some of the greatest among its per-

[1] *The Manners and Customs of the Ancient Egyptians*, Vol. I, p. 178.

petrators, such men, I mean, as Pym and Cromwell, were the most abandoned hypocrites. But that, on the whole, the rough work of effecting the pious fraud was wrought entirely by unconscious agents, believing themselves to be wholly in the service of God, I do not doubt. It is precisely this element that gave the last pious fraud on a grand scale which has been perpetrated in modern times all its formidable power and irresistible momentum.

For, in this particular instance, it was again a matter of consolidating a scattered and more or less disorganised body of men, and of forming them into a solid phalanx which could not only wring submission from the rest of the nation, but also *convert* the rest of the nation to its own persuasion.

Thus, if the Anglo-Saxon becomes famous at all, and not merely egregious to posterity, it will be as a man of such religious ingenuity, of such mastery in the art of establishing a creed in the hearts and the bodies of a people, that his compeers will have to be sought among those very geniuses of exalted falsehood, such as Manu, Mahōmmed, Moses, and the rest of that ilk, who hitherto have enjoyed an exclusive and uncontested position of supremacy in the art of framing a lasting faith.

For a great problem presented itself to the soul of the British nation during the sixteenth and even more during the seventeenth century—a problem with which *conscious* legislation battled and strove in vain, and one over which, in my private opinion, our greatest monarch, Charles I, forfeited his head.

The question to be decided was not only whether it was good to transform England from a land of agriculture and of homecrafts, into a capitalistic, commercial and factory-ridden country; but it was also necessary to discover a method whereby the people could be reconciled to the change most satisfactorily and thoroughly. We have seen how the Tudors and Stuarts fought against the first signs of the change, and how they sought to suppress the unscrupulous spirit of gain and of greed which sought to promote it. And we have seen how enthusiastically the people supported them.

But it was as if the most powerful element in the nation were bent upon having this new life, this new ideal—the ideal of the giant urban population, with its smoky factories, its slums, its exploitation and its misery. And it was as if the old guardian angel of Great Britain forsook her for a while, in order to leave her to the tender mercies of the new religionists, the new fashioners of her fate, the Puritanical Traders.

For, if I dare to place these unconscious leaders beside Manu, Moses and Mohammed, it is because the object which their religion accomplished, could have been achieved by no other means.

It was a matter of making trade, commercialism, factories, capitalism and general shop-keeping, as we now know them, paramount and triumphant. To effect this change, however, it was essential that legions among the population of the British Isles should be depressed, reduced in body and spirit, rendered pusillanimous, weak, servile, anæmic, asexual, and in fact sick. It was necessary to have a vast army of willing slaves who would not be merely satisfied and content, not merely pleased and happy, but who would actually reach the topmost wave of their being, so to speak, in balancing themselves all day long, like stylite saints, upon office stools, in turning over the leaves of ledgers, invoice books and registers, or in manipulating the lever of a punching, a cutting, a rolling or a rocking machine.

Not only must their highest aspirations be towards asceticism, their very bodies must be converted into machines " below par " in vigour, sanguinity, energy and sexuality. Their ideals, their pleasures, their love of life must be transposed to a lower, sadder, more stoical and less spirited key. Work—will-less, unattractive, thankless work, must be mechanically performed, without hope, without joy and without respite; save on the miserable and soul-deadening sabbath. They must learn that beauty which leads and lures to life, to the joy in life and to the multiplication of life, is neither essential nor helpful either to the factory, the office, the mine, the slum or the tin chapel; therefore beauty, by being merely an irrelevant disturber of the daily round, is *bad*, and to be connected only with fast women, fornication and hell-fire.

Now, even in the towns, the population was still too spirited, too healthy and too tasteful, to accept with heart and soul the conditions necessary for creating modernity, as we modern Europeans know and understand it. While among the agricultural population, large numbers of whom were soon to be forced into the cities, things were even worse, from the standpoint of the new desiderata.

What, then, was the profound problem with which England began blindly to grapple in the seventeenth century? In essence it was this: to discover the religion essentially allied to trade and commerce! Which was the religion whose prescriptions concerning conduct, diet and hygiene, dovetailed most naturally with the requirements of the triumph of capitalistic industry? All great religions hitherto had, by means of a system of conduct, diet and hygiene, consolidated a certain scattered race, community or tribe. Which was the religion that would consolidate the masters and rear the slaves for that form of trade which is the characteristic creation of the last two centuries?

With the marvellous insight of the unconscious religious founder, the solution was discovered in the whole-hearted, acceptance and promotion of Puritanism.

For though Puritanism had existed long before the middle of the seventeenth century—though, indeed, it might be said that it had always existed, sporadically, locally and individually, all over the world like a disease or a mental idiosyncrasy—it was not until the seventeenth century in England that the circumstances of life were propitious to its identification and union with a certain well-defined and perfectly distinct class of men and occupation—the rising employers and employees engaged

in the trade and manufactures which were destined to
stamp the face of the future.

And it was certainly more than mere chance which led
to this union and identification of mechanical manufacture
and trade pursued merely for gain and greed with Puritanism. For trade and mechanical manufacture, unguided
and uncontrolled, have many ideals in common with
Puritanism, and even if the events of the seventeenth
century had turned out differently, the union of these
two elements in the nation could not have been long
delayed.

Strictly speaking, although the modern factory does
not necessarily covet sickly, ugly and spiritless creatures
for its working hands, robust health, beauty and high,
unbendable spirits are not at all essential to its requirements; in fact, they may very often thwart its purpose,
seeing that beauty lures very strongly to preoccupations
quite irrelevant to the hopeless drudgery of ministering
to machinery; while high spirits and robust health are
notoriously hostile to that demand for meek submission
and to confined and stuffy industry which the exigencies
of a factory imply.

It is quite unessential to this demonstration to refer
to the thousands and thousands of healthy English families
among the proletariat who actually have been rendered
sickly, and sometimes crippled, through factory work. All
I need show is that the work of the factory and the ideals
of the factory are as little concerned with the sacredness
of beauty, robust health and high spirits, as are the ideals
of the little tin chapel. It matters not to the employer,
who is out for gain, and who has an almost unlimited
supply of unskilled labour from which to draw his factory
hands—it matters not to such a man what the actual
physical and spiritual conditions of his employees are like,
provided only that they are just able to do his work.
Neither is he concerned with the kind of children they
bring into the world. The unskilled labouring proletariat
—and even the skilled, for that matter—are but so much

material which he uses *pro tem.* to amass his wealth. If, under the system of *laissez-faire*, he is uncontrolled and unguided in his use of this material, who is to say that the ideals of beauty, health and high spirits must necessarily guide him in the selection of his life-principles and in his treatment of the life that is in his power? The working people belong to another class than that to which he belongs; to all appearances, they belong to another race. Under anything but a patriarchal government, such as that which was overthrown by the Puritan Rebellion against Charles I, who is to prevent him from fostering those very ideals concerning beauty, robust health and high spirits which are most inimical to the true welfare and the true prosperity of the race?

For a whole body of people to submit to the awful ugliness, unhealthiness, hopelessness and squalor of town, coupled with factory life, it is almost a necessity that their spirits should be broken, that their best instincts with regard to beauty, the joy of life, the love of life, and the sacredness of robust health should have been corrupted or completely suppressed. They must not even taste of the happiness of a real, full and inspiriting existence; even their rest days must be gloomy, colourless, silent, shorn of beauty, bereft of high spirits and generally depressing; so that their appalling drudgery may not seem too intolerable by comparison. But a substantial portion of high spirits and of energy and vigour lies in the sex instinct, and in all the efforts and passions to which it gives rise. Sexuality, therefore, must not be either encouraged or fostered or even preserved in these working slaves; on the contrary, they must be taught that sex is horrible, that even dancing is, as Calvin taught, a crime equal to adultery.

And doctrines which apply to the factory or to the mine hand hold good with even greater force in the case of the office-clerk, the book-keeper, the office-worm! To these men who have to perch on a leather-covered stool all day, and the top wave of whose being is attained in turning over the pages of a ledger or an invoice book, robust health, beauty and high spirits would not only be a hindrance, they would be a pronounced source of dis-, comfort. While a high degree of healthy sexuality would be an obstacle so fatal that it would mean the renouncement of a business life. Observe all these moist-fingered, pale-faced, round-shouldered men who work side by side with girls in the big counting-houses of large stores, in the large emporiums of the linen-drapery trade, and in factories. Do you suppose that a strong sexual instinct would be any good to them? It would prove their undoing! The basic instinct of all life would be a source of infinite trouble to them, if it were powerful or even moderately healthy.

I do not require any outside confirmation for this description of the spiritual and physical pre-requisites of the factory and office slave; for the evidence of what I have written lies all about us to-day, and we need move very little further than to the High Street of our particular town or city, or city quarter, in order to realise to the full the unquestionable truth of the above statements. Still, an interesting and absolutely independent confirmation of my views came into my hands the other day, and as it raised no murmur of protest in the paper in which it was published, I have decided to quote it here—not, mark you, as an authoritative substantiation of my attitude in this matter, but rather as evidence of the fact that my contention is not disputed even by the friends of commerce and capitalistic industry themselves.

In *Reynolds's Newspaper* of February 16, 1913, Mr. Herbert Kaufmann wrote as follows—

" Cromwell was one of the ugliest men of his time. Pierpont Morgan has never been mistaken for Apollo.

" We don't look for achievement [we know what these business men mean by ' achievement '] in pink cheeks and classic features.

" We are pleased to behold clean and attractive men— but we can't declare dividends on pulchritude.

" All things being equal, we prefer handsome employees, but when we scan the weekly balance sheet and check accounts the only thing we can see is results [mark you! the only thing these business men can see is " results "], *and then a squinting hunchback who shows an improvement in his department seems beautiful in contrast with a Beau Brummel who hasn't earned his salt.*"

This requires little comment. It is perfectly comprehensible. Certainly "a squinting hunchback " is more lovable to the business man than a handsome, well-built, healthy youth. Health, beauty and the high spirits that usually accompany them are difficult to reconcile with the requirements of a hideous office and its emasculating work. But the already emasculated cripple is a predestined plant for such an environment. And is the average anæmic, round-shouldered and moist-fingered clerk so very far removed from the emasculated cripple?

And now let us turn to Puritanism in order that we may see at a glance how veritably it is the plighted mate of the industry and commerce of the modern world. In order to do this satisfactorily, however, it would be useful, in the first place, to understand who and what the Puritan is.

The Puritan is primarily and essentially a man " below par " either in vigour, in health, in sound instinct or in bodily wholeness; and that is why I say that, although Puritanism did not become an organised and powerful force until the seventeenth century in England, the Puritan, as such, has always existed sporadically, individually and locally, just as sick animals represent a certain percentage of all the animals born every year.

There are two conditions in which a man may be suspicious and distrustful of life, and in which, therefore, he may enter into existence with a bodily prejudice against life. These two conditions are: first, ill-health and any kind of physiological botchedness; and, secondly, a state of disharmony, discord, violent disunion or anarchy of the passions.

N

Let us examine these two conditions separately.

The Puritan, as a *sick* man, is the man who, after having discovered by self-examination that the taking of any share in the full life of the passions, with all its violent thrilling joys and appetites, invariably leads to a state of painful debility and self-reproach (for morbid physical fatigue and a sickly condition of the body after any indulgence in the full joys of life are always interpreted by the mind of the sufferer in the terms of moral self-reproach), transfers this *self*-reproach to the whole of humanity, by arriving at the simple though erroneous dictum that "the joys of the flesh are bad."

He has not the healthy honesty to say "the joys of the flesh are bad for me"; he says more bitterly and more vindictively—for there is a spark of envy in every invalid —"the joys of the flesh are bad for all!" With the incredible selfishness of a sick, plague-stricken crow, he suspects the whole world of possessing his impoverished blood and vigour, and lays down the law for the universe, when the law in question applies only to his own repulsive body and to those that are like it.

Calvin, for instance, who did so much to entrench the power of Puritan Nonconformity after the Reformation, and who complained so bitterly to the Duke of Somerset concerning the "impurities" and "vices" of delightful, voluptuous, sleek and, alas! irretrievable "Merrie England," was a miserable, god-forsaken invalid who, racked with fevers, asthma, gout and the stone, dragged his foul body through this life as if the world were a mausoleum, and himself the gangrenous symbol of the death of all human joys.

What could such a belching, dyspeptic and badly functioning human wreck know about what was impure and what was vicious? To him any indulgence of the healthy and life-giving instincts, however slight, was a danger he dared not approach. To him all love must be the vilest and most deadly fornication; all healthy eating and drinking, the most loathsome of vices; and all merriness and joy, all dancing and singing, a barefaced outrage against the God of the sick, the bungled and the botched!

And now let me turn to the other kind of Puritan, *i. e.* to the man who, though apparently in good health and possessed of a robust and vigorous frame, still suspects life and casts the blight of his distrust upon it.

This is a man who, like Socrates, is conscious of having a whole host of evil demons pent up in his breast, and who has had neither the traditions of culture and of control, nor the necessary antecedents of regular living and healthy harmony, which would be favourable to imposing a measure upon his instincts. This is the man who has no practice, no bodily skill in imposing a limit, a sort of " no-further-shalt-thou-go! " upon his passions, and who, therefore, can see no difference between ordinary indulgence and excess. And, indeed, to him there is no difference between ordinary indulgence and excess; because he has not the wherewithal in his system to draw the line between the two. He has not the taste and instinctive discrimination of the healthy man which say " Stop! " when he has enough. His cure, then, his remedy, his only resource, in fact, if he would survive, is inhibition, prohibition, castration, or its equivalent in a milder form—the blue ribbon of abstinence. Instinctively he joins hands with the first kind of Puritan who brings him his credo and morality cut and dried; and thus, in spite of his apparent health and vigour, you see him stalking through history, arm in arm with the sick Puritan and the man who is *beneath* all share in the joys of life. But the interesting point and the one which really concerns us here is that, from two totally different starting places, these two kinds of men arrive at precisely the same conclusion; and as in a nation as recently raised from barbarism as England was in the seventeenth century there is bound to be a very large number of men of the kind I have just described, it will easily be seen that once the more intelligent and more penetrating sick animals, like Calvin, took the lead and expounded the credo, the second order of Puritans—those who were apparently healthy, but had no long tradition or culture behind them to enable them to harmonise their instincts—were quick to follow suit and join their anæmic and less vigorous brethren.

The mental characteristics of the second kind of Puritan are these: like Maeterlinck, he is unable to portray a feast that is not an exhibition of the most uncontrolled gluttony; therefore, all feasting must be bad. Like Knox, he will be unable to think of women without picturing all the degradation and pollution to which excessive sexual intercourse leads; therefore all women must be bad. Like Maeterlinck, again, he will be unable to think of laughter and revelry without seeing the addled, imbecile condition to which excessive merriment may lead; therefore all merriment is bad. And like the Long Parliament of the seventeenth century, he will want to make man virtuous by legislation and by forbidding all those things which, while they make life worth living, do not belong to the category of pleasures in which the members themselves could indulge without making hogs of themselves.

The second kind of Puritan, therefore, is essentially a hog who has acquired a moral standard of judgment, and who wishes to transfer the necessary constraints he puts upon his unbridled passions to the whole of mankind. And in this he differs fundamentally from the man of sound and cultured tradition, whose instincts are both healthy and controlled, who can even allow himself, and *does* allow himself, a certain margin for feasts and bouts, and even orgies, at times; because he knows full well that his inner balance, his inner harmony, which is the outcome of generations of regular and disciplined living, will recover completely from any such occasional luxury. To this man there is nothing evil in the joys of the flesh. He incurs no danger when he indulges his natural appetites, and it is difficult for him to understand the frenzied hatred of the flesh which characterises the attitude of the Puritan.

METAMORPHOSIS OF THE ENGLISHMAN

It was obviously inevitable that the two kinds of Puritan described above should unite and constitute the breath and body of a single religious creed; and when, in addition to the physical factors which determined their union, there also arose the interests of the private purse and of the counting-house, their coalescence became so complete as almost to defy analysis.

The fact which it is essential for every one to remember, however, is that, springing though they did from two totally different causes—in the one case ill-health, and in the other a lack of harmony in the instincts—they both agreed in suspecting life, and in casting a slur upon even the healthy manifestation of her most fundamental instincts. And, as a result of this attitude, they naturally despised all such things as beauty, gaiety, high spirits and voluptuousness, which lure to life and to her joys, and which stimulate the functions of her most fundamental instincts.

Nor did they confine this hostility to the manifestation of beauty in the human body alone. They were literally incapable of any appreciation of beauty in the productions of the human mind and hand. Too ignorant to know how deeply high art and social order and permanence are related, and too tasteless in human matters to have any regard for things merely accessory to human life, the love of beautiful things was to them an incomprehensible vice, a morbid mania. Charles I, whose thoroughness in the art of governing found its inevitable counterpart in his nature in a consummate refinement of discrimination where artistic matters were concerned, was to them a monstrosity—a dangerous eccentric. It has been said with reason that Charles "had a better taste in the fine arts and in elegant literature than any King of England before or since." [1] In any case it is certain that whatever power England has shown in the graphic arts has been due entirely to his initiative, and the pictures and statues which he was never tired of collecting throughout his

---

[1] *The Political History of England*, Vol. VII, p. 126.

anxious reign formed the first grand art treasure that this nation has ever possessed. The fact that it was dispersed after his murder by the Puritan party shows how slight could have been the latter's sympathy even with the King's hobbies. There can also be no doubt that had Whitehall Palace been completed as it was contemplated by Charles and conceived by Inigo Jones, "the Louvre and the Escurial would have found in our calumniated island a more magnificent rival";[1] while even the exceptional beauty of men and women's dress after the reign of James I has been ascribed by one historian, Dr. Traill, to Charles I's refined taste.[2] But to all those who would like fuller, stronger and more convincing evidence of Charles's taste and knowledge in sculpture, architecture, music, literature and painting, I cannot do better than recommend the chapter on the Royal Martyr in Blaikie Murdock's wonderful little book[3] on the Stuarts, and Chapter XXXI of Isaac Disraeli's profound work on Charles I.[4]

No wonder, however, that this aspect of Charles's character made no appeal to his enemies. For men who could cast a picture by Rubens into the Thames, who could smash the glorious painted windows and the images of Westminster Abbey and St. Margaret's, and perform other untold deeds of barbarous iconoclasm all over the country, were scarcely the sort to ask themselves whether a monarch with taste were a rarity worth keeping. And the Puritan who in 1651 published the book called *The Non-such Charles* probably expressed the general impression, when he accused Charles of having squandered his money on "braveries and vanities, on old rotten pictures and broken-nosed marbles."

Now it requires no subtle ingenuity nor wilful bias to recognise the peculiar sympathy, the basic relationship,

---

[1] Isaac Disraeli, op. cit., Vol. I, p. 400.
[2] See *Social England* (edit. 1903), Vol. IV, pp. 229–230.
[3] *The Royal Stuarts in their Connection with Art and Letters.*
[4] Op. cit. See also pp. 56–58, Vol. I, of Ranke's *History of England.*

which, from the beginning, must have drawn the Puritanical outlook on the world into close and intimate touch with that view of life which is essential to the kind of industry and commerce now prevalent and triumphant among us, and it would be absurd to suppose that it is due merely to coincidence that Birmingham, for instance, in the time of Charles I, should have been noted for its ironworks as well as its Puritanism.

We have seen no less an authority than Dr. Cunningham proclaim the Puritan rebellion as the beginning of the commercial morality which is still supreme in the modern world, and I need only refer the reader back to my enumeration of the aims of this commercial morality for him to realise how inevitably it became and remained united with the morality of Puritanism.

Think of how much they had in common! A profound suspicion of flourishing, irrepressible, healthy and robust life; indifference and even antagonism to beauty—whether in the human body or in art; hostility to strong sexuality and the high spirits it involves; a preference for mildness, meekness, inferiority of vigour, vitality and general viability; and above all a deteriorated love of life and of the joy of life, which would render millions not merely resigned and submissive, but actually content in town, factory and office surroundings.

With these elements in common, and with the unconscious desire behind them to pursue gain and wealth undisturbed by any higher, more tasteful or more national considerations, how could they help but wed, and fight hand in hand to exterminate the last vestige of patriarchal beauty, culture and solicitude for the people's welfare, which still clung to the social organisation of expiring Merrie England?

But it is when we examine one by one the leaders and some of the most important agitators at the back of the Puritan Rebellion that we become convinced of this infallible association of Calvinistic proclivities with the shop, the factory, the warehouse or the office. For, although we have seen how Charles was opposed by the upstart landed gentry, townsmen, alien merchants and manufacturers, native tradesmen and other office offal, marching under the banner of Puritanism, we have not yet become personally acquainted with this grasping and counterjumping rabble.

Allow me to introduce them to you!

From two sources—*Buckle's History of Civilisation in England*, Vol. II,[1] and an old volume, published in 1665, called *The Loyall Martyrology*,[2] by William Winstanley —I have been able to collect a few names among the leaders of the Parliamentary and Puritanical party, together with the occupations their owners pursued, which, in addition to substantiating my contentions, ought to prove of interest to the reader; and these I shall now proceed to enumerate without any too elaborate comment—

Joyce, highly respected in the army, had been a common tailor. He ultimately captured the King.[3]

Colonel Pride was a drayman,[4] ultimately became a brewer.[5]

Venner, one of the most distinguished of the powerful party after Charles's death, was a wine-cooper.[6]

Tuffnel, distinguished like Venner, was a carpenter.[7]

Okey had been a stoker in an Islington brewery,[8] and later on was a chandler near Bishopsgate.[9]

Cromwell, as every one knows, was a brewer.

Colonel Jones, a serving man (brother-in-law to Cromwell.)[10]

Deane (admiral), a tradesman's assistant.[11]

Colonel Goffe had been apprenticed to a drysalter.[12]

---

[1] When referring to this book in the list that follows, I shall simply put the letter B and the number of the page.

[2] When referring to this book I shall put the letter W with the number of the page.

[3] B, p. 155.   [4] B, p. 155 and W, p. 108.   [5] W, p. 108.

[6] B, p. 155, and W, p. 158.   [7] B, p. 155.

[8] B, p. 155, and W, p. 122.   [9] W, p. 122.

[10] B, p. 156, and W, p. 125.   [11] B, p. 156, and W, p. 121.

[12] B, p. 156, and W, p. 123.

Major-General Whalley had been apprentice to a woollen draper.[1]

Berkstead (a lieutenant of the Tower), had been a pedlar or hawker of small wares,[2] and, Winstanley declares, a shopkeeper in the Strand.[3]

Tichbourne or *Tichburn* (another lieutenant of the Tower) had been a linen-draper of London.[4]

Colonel Harvey was a silk mercer.[5]

Colonel Rowe was also a silk mercer.[6]

Colonel Wenn was also a silk mercer;[7] Winstanley declares he was a bankrupt one.[8]

Salway had been a grocer's assistant.[9]

Bond (of the Council) had been a draper.[10]

Cawley or *Crawley* (also of the Council) had been a brewer.[11]

Berners, John (also of the Council), had been a servant.[12]

Cornelius Holland (also of the Council) had been a servant;[13] Winstanley says "a servant of Sir Henry Vane's household."[14]

Packe (held office of trust) was a woollen draper.[15]

Pury (held office of trust) was a weaver.[16]

Pemble (held office of trust) was a tailor.[17]

Barebone (member of and most active in Barebone's Parliament) was a leather merchant in Fleet Street.[18]

Colonel Berry was a woodmonger.[19]

Colonel Cooper was a haberdasher.[20]

Major Rolfe was a shoemaker.[21]

---

[1] B, p. 156, and W, p. 108.   [2] B, p. 156–157.   [3] W, p. 114.
[4] B, p. 156–157, and W, p. 129.   [5] B, p. 157, and W, p. 129.
[6] B, p. 157, and W, p. 120.   [7] B, p. 157.
[8] W, p. 130.   [9] B, p. 157.
[10] B, p. 157.   [11] B, p. 157, and W, p. 138.
[12] B, p. 157.   [13] B, p. 157.
[14] W, p. 124.   [15] B, p. 158.
[16] B, p. 158.   [17] B, p. 158.
[18] B, p. 158.   [19] B, p. 158.
[20] B, p. 159.   [21] B, p. 159.

Colonel Fox was a tinker.[1]

Colonel Hewson was a cobbler.[2]

Allen, Francis (became Treasurer of War), was a goldsmith of Fleet Street.[3]

Clement, Gregory (a member of the Bloody Parliament), was a merchant.[4]

Andrews, Thomas, was a linen-draper in Cheapside.[5]

Scot, Thomas (a member of the Bloody Parliament), was a brewer's clerk.[6]

Captain Peter Temple was a linen-draper.[7]

Lieutenant-Colonel Daniel Axtell (Captain of the Guard at the King's trial) was the keeper of a country " peddling shop in Bedfordshire." [8]

Colonel Thomas Harrison was the son of a butcher at Newcastle.[9]

While among those who, though not so important as the foregoing, nevertheless came to prominence on the Puritan side in the Grand Rebellion, I might mention: *John Blakeston,* a shopkeeper in Newcastle,[10] *Vincent Potter,* whose origin was so mean that it is unknown,[11] *Thomas Wait,* who is in the same case,[12] and *Thomas Horton,* also in the same case.[13]

There was, besides, another and perhaps even less savoury element among the leaders of the Parliamentary party. I refer to those who, like Essex and Williams, opposed the King from some personal pique. It had often been the King's duty, as well as Strafford's and Laud's, during the eleven years' personal government, to call not only humble but also powerful men to order for crimes against the people or the State. I have spoken exhaustively enough of this element in Charles's opposition, in

---

[1] B, p. 159.   [2] B, p. 159, and W, p. 123.   [3] W, p. 126.
[4] W, p. 129.   [5] W, p. 131.
[6] W, p. 137.   [7] W, p. 141.
[8] W, p. 147.   [9] W, p. 107.
[10] W, p. 117.   [11] W, p. 139.
[12] W, p. 142.   [13] W, p. 131.

the preceding chapter. Still, there are one or two instances of flagrant and base vindictiveness which are worthy of particular mention here. *Dr. Turner* is a case in point. He was prominent among the so-called patriots and was reckoned with such men as St. John, Lord Saye and Sele, Sir Arthur Haslerigg and Sir Dudley Diggis. And how do you suppose that he came to join their ranks? He had been a place-hunting physician who for many years had haunted Charles's court in the hopes of being patronised, but whom the King had resolutely ignored owing to his "deficient veracity!" Another name that occurs to me is that of *Humphrey Edwards*, to whom the King had denied preferment owing to Edwards's total unworthiness. While the case of the disreputable alien, *Dr. Daurislaus*, who ultimately drew up the charge against the King and became ambassador to the Commonwealth in Holland, is scandalous enough. He was a low Dutch schoolmaster who, owing to some misdemeanour, had been forced to flee his country. He took refuge in England and settled down as a historical lecturer in Cambridge. The King was forced to interfere with his work at the University and wisely suspended him for a while; after which he was "hardly restored to his place"; and from that time forward, this criminal refugee who had no character and no nationality, became one of the rats concerned in compassing Charles's doom. It is always with the utmost satisfaction that I read and re-read the circumstances of his murder at the hands of English Royalists in his native country, after his appointment as English ambassador by the Commonwealth.

Thus, I think I have said enough to provide an adequate picture of the type of mind and body which was opposed to Charles in the last great struggle in which taste, tradition and quality were confronted with the savage hordes of vulgarity, trade and quantity in England—in the first place, the overwhelming multitude from the shop, the furnace, the office and the factory; secondly, the upstart and grasping landed gentry; thirdly, the men who in high places and in low had found Charles's patriarchal government too unfavourable to their criminal schemes.

Now, very early after the outbreak of the Grand Rebellion, all these elements joined in one determined and, I feel sure, partly unconscious, cry for Puritanism, Puritanism, Puritanism! Every time the peacemakers arranged negotiations for peace between the King and the so-called popular party, the greatest of the latter's demands was invariably that Puritanism should be established in England; and Charles's reiterated and determined refusal to accept this as a condition of peace was, as frequently, the major cause of the fruitless conclusion of all the pourparlers. But, I also have not the slightest doubt that, whereas the resolute cry for Puritanism, as the religion of business, of commerce and of manufacture (as we understand these things to-day), was very probably largely unconscious, in so far as its metaphysical aspect was concerned; it must certainly have been *conscious* in a large number of the multitude, who were quite shrewd and cunning enough to see how similar at least the morality of the new creed was to that of the rising trade and commerce associated in our minds with the economic school of *laissez-faire*.

Certain it is, that as soon as the rebel party were able, they began the work of imposing Puritanism by Act of Parliament upon the nation, and in this work of depressing, bleeding, besotting, uglifying, debilitating and disheartening the Englishman, so as to render him a slave fit for the office, the counter, the factory, the mine or the stoke-hole, the religious and the more practical business aims became so inextricably involved, that it is impossible to tell how much was unconscious and how much was conscious in this amazing act of religious creation of the seventeenth century.

At all events, the fact remains, that whether the metamorphosis of the Englishman was effected consciously or unconsciously under the cloak of religion, it was a feat that was ultimately accomplished: and the meek herd which it reared for the capitalistic traders of the eighteenth and nineteenth centuries, make it impossible to regard Puritanism as anything else than the great religious creation of the western world to meet the requirements of business profit and greed, under the rule of a " free," " democratic " parliament.

Now let us see how the metamorphosis was contrived, bearing in mind all the time that it was a matter of turning a spirited, beauty-loving, life-loving and vigorous population into a multitude which was just the reverse of all these things.

The first thing that the Puritan party conscientiously set about doing was to make the Englishman miserable. This is always the most efficacious means of depressing spirit, of destroying the awful contrast between characterless labour and well-spent leisure, and of preventing a drudge from feeling that life might be spent more healthily and happily.

Already in 1642 they were strong enough in Parliament to interfere with popular sports and pastimes in England, and the Sabbath, which, as Charles I had pointed out, was the only day on which the labouring man could enjoy himself, and preserve his spirit from desolation, was made as gloomy and as wretched as possible. Not only was all amusement forbidden, but the Church services themselves were made so insufferably tedious and colourless, and sermons were made to last such a preposterous length of time, that Sunday became what it was required to be by these employers of slaves—the most dreaded day in the week.

A certain well-known German philosopher has said: " It was a master stroke of *English* instinct to hallow and begloom Sunday to such an extent that the Englishman unconsciously hankers for his work and week-day again "; for, if you are going to rear a nation of slaves, this is the attitude you must force them to take towards the only day of recreation they are allowed. In that way they begin to regard their work, however appalling, with less resentment and less loathing.

Puritan preachers vied with each other, as to who would preach the longest sermons and say the longest prayers, and if any of the less attentive among their congregations should fall asleep during the former orations, which sometimes lasted over two hours, they were suspected of the grossest impiety.

The Puritans who, fortunately for England, crossed the Atlantic, were terrible in their Sabbath tyranny. Short prayers and short sermons were considered irreligious in New England, and it was not unusual for these to last one hour and three hours respectively. A tithing-man bearing a sort of whisk, would keep an eye on the congregations during Sunday service, brusquely wake all those who fell asleep, and allow no deserters. In winter the congregation shivered in an icy-cold atmosphere; in summer they stewed in glaring unshaded heat, " and they sat upon most uncomfortable, narrow, uncushioned seats at all seasons." [1]

Indeed it was not unusual in winter for the communion bread to freeze quite hard and to rattle " sadly in the plates." [2] But not only was all activity restrained on the Sabbath—the most natural and most ordinary acts of social life were punished with the utmost severity. In New London in 1670, a pair of lovers, John Lewis and Sarah Chapman, were accused of sitting together on the Lord's day under an apple-tree in Goodman Chapman's orchard [3] and were brought to trial for this offence. In 1656 Captain Kemble was set for two hours in the public stocks for his " lewd and unseemly behaviour "—that is to say, for kissing his wife " publicquely" upon the threshold of his house, after having been absent from her on a journey for many years. [4] And an English sea-captain was soundly whipped for kissing his wife in the street of a New England town on Sunday.

[1] *The Sabbath in Puritan New England*, by Alice Morse Earle, p. 81.
[2] *Ibid.*, p. 84.
[3] Alice Morse Earle, op. cit., p. 246.   [4] *Ibid.*, p. 247.

In Scotland, as Buckle has shown, matters were just as bad, and Sunday in North Britain in the seventeenth century was made a perfect hell on earth.[1] "It was a sin to go from one town to another on Sunday, however pressing the business might be. It was a sin to visit your friend on Sunday. It was likewise sinful either to have your garden watered or your beard shaved." [2]

In England, as soon as these maniacs had the power, they too, as I have shown, did everything they could to make the Sabbath a day hated and feared by all. For, to make depression perfect, it was not only needful to make Sunday service compulsory and tedious, it was also necessary to suppress everything in the nature of enlivening or inspiriting pastimes, upon the only day when the poor labouring classes could indulge in recreation.

In addition to the measures passed in 1642, an Act was passed on April 6, 1644, "*For the better observation of the Lord's Day*," in which we read—

"That no person or persons whatsoever shall, without reasonable cause for the same, travel, carry burthens, or do any worldly labours, or work whatsoever, upon that day, or any part thereof; upon pain that every one travelling contrary to the meaning of this Ordinance, shall forfeit, for every offence, ten shillings of lawful money; and that every person carrying any burthen, or doing any worldly labour or work, contrary to the meaning hereof, shall forfeit five shillings of like money for every such offence."

And in the section dealing with pastimes and amusements, we read—

"And let it be further ordained, that no person or persons shall hereafter upon the Lord's-day use, exercise, keep, maintain, or be present, at any wrestlings, shooting, bowling, ringing of bells for pleasure or pastime, masque, Wake, otherwise called Fasts, Church-Ale, dancing, games, sport or pastime whatsoever; upon pain, that every person

[1] See *History of Civilisation in England,* Vol. III, pp. 203 *et seq.*
[2] *Ibid.,* p. 260.

so offending, being above the age of fourteen years, shall lose, and forfeit five shillings for every such offence.[1]

"And because the prophanation of the Lord's Day hath been heretofore greatly occasioned by Maypoles (a heathenish vanity, generally abused to superstition and wickedness) the Lords and Commons do further order and ordain, that all and singular maypoles, that are, or shall be erected, shall be taken down and removed by the constables, Brusholders, Tythingmen, petty constables and churchwardens of the parish."[2]

Even the great festival of Christmas was condemned by these determined advocates of depression and low spirits, and, under the Commonwealth, attempts were made to suppress the celebration of this Church anniversary and to regard even the mince-pie as idolatrous.[3] "In place of the merry chimes," says Mr. W. Andrews, "which formerly welcomed Christmas from every church steeple in the land, the crier passed along the silent streets of the town ringing his harsh-sounding bell, and proclaiming in a monotonous voice, ' No Christmas! no Christmas! '"[4]

In some parts of the country, such as Canterbury, for instance, the people were so indignant that riots actually took place; but what the armed resistance of a great king had failed to do, could not very well be accomplished by isolated and sporadic risings on the part of his subjects.

In Scotland, W. Andrews tells us, the attempts to sup-

---

[1] The fine for allowing children to commit any of these sins was 12 pence for every offence.

[2] *A Collection of Acts and Ordinances of General Use, made in the Parliament from 1640 to 1656*, by Henry Scobell, fol. 68. "The New Haven code of laws ordered that 'profanation of the Lord's Day should be punished by fine, imprisonment or corporal punishment ; and if proudly, and with a high hand against the authority of God—*with death*."—Alice Morse Earle, op. cit., p. 248.

[3] See *The English Housewife in the Seventeenth and Eighteenth Centuries*, by Rose M. Bradley (1912), p. 79. "The Puritans did their best to put a stop to feasting and junketing. Christmas Day was not to be observed and the mince-pie was looked upon by the fanatics as idolatrous."

[4] *Bygone England*, p. 240.

press Christmas were more successful. And, as a proof of the inconsiderate brutality of these Puritanical fanatics, not only did the members of Parliament sit to transact business on Christmas Day, but, in order to show their utter contempt of the occasion, " the Reformers enjoined that their wives and servants were to spin in the open sight of the peope upon Yule Day, and that the farm labourers were to yoke their ploughs." [1]

And thus the power of the Puritans fell like a blight upon the land, killing good-cheer, healthy spirits and sport. Traill even goes so far as to say that " many sports which as sports they did not condemn, have ceased to exist, because the Puritans condemned their use on Sundays, the only day on which working people could practise them regularly." [2]

The pleasures and diversions of the stage constituted another of the vestiges of Merrie England which was also severely suppressed by these vulgar fanatics. On October 22, 1647, they passed an Act for suppressing stage-plays and interludes, and in it we read that " all person and persons so offending [acting in plays or interludes] to commit to any common Gaol or Prison, there to remain until the next general sessions of the Peace, holden within the said City of London, or Liberties thereof, and places aforesaid, or sufficient security entered for his or their appearance at the said Sessions, there to be punished as Rogues, according to Law." [3]

And according to another Act passed in 1647, " For the utter suppression of stage plays and Interludes," the spectator was to be fined five shillings for being present at a play, the money " to be levied by the Churchwardens of the said Parish "; while the money received at the doors of theatres was to be forfeited and given over once more to the Churchwardens!

But they went further. On May 2, 1648, in an absurd

---

[1] *Bygone England*, pp. 238, 242-243.
[2] *Social England*, Vol. IV, p. 167.
[3] Scobell, op. cit., fol. 135.

and savage Act passed, " For punishing Blasphemies and Heresies," they literally undertook to establish a credo by inhuman threat and punishment.

After enumerating all the beliefs concerning the Trinity, the Manhood of Christ, etc., this measure proceeds. as follows, " that all and such persons as shall maintain and publish by preaching, teaching, printing or writing that ' the Bodies of men shall not rise again after they are dead,' or that ' there is no day of Judgment after death ' [shall be] committed to prison without Bail or Mainprise, until the next Gaol delivery be holden for that place or County, and the Witnesses likewise shall be bound over by the said Justices unto the said Gaol delivery to give in their evidence; and at the said Gaol delivery the party shall be indicted for feloniously publishing and maintaining such Errour, and in case the indictment be found and the Party upon his Triall shall not abjure his said Errour and defence and maintenance of the same, he shall suffer the pains of death, as in case of Felony without benefit of Clergy." [1] This was not merely a brutal enforcement of superstition; it was a savage insistence upon dullness and stupidity.

Similar punishment was threatened if any one should " deny that St. Paul's Epistle to the Corinthians, or any other of the Canonical works of the Old or New Testament is the Word of God "; and prison was also the penalty for those who dared to say that " all men shall be saved," or " that man is bound to believe no more than by his reason he can comprehend," or " that the observation of the Lord's Day as it is enjoyned by the Ordinances and Laws of this Realm, is not according, or is contrary, to the word of God." [2]

Everything was done, too, to associate high spirit and proud daring with sin and the devil. Cotton Mather, that ranting, raving divine of Nonconformity, in a book entitled *Batteries upon the Kingdom of the Devil*, associated all vital and spirited things with Hell and Satan.

---

[1] Scobell, op. cit., fol. 149.   [2] *Ibid.*, fol. 149.

He was never tired of saying, "When Satan fills the Hearts of Men he makes them rush upon such hardy ventures as they must be utterly and for ever spoiled with"; or, "The Devil will make sinners venturesome when once he becomes a Commander of them"; [1] or "The Devil is a proud spirit; it was his pride that was his fall at first; and when he would give us a fall, he does first by Pride give us a lift." [2]   All excellent doctrines on which to rear slaves and not men, and quite typical of the gospel most Puritan divines were preaching at the time.

And here, perhaps, it might be as well to refer briefly to the chapter and text of the seventeenth-century Nonconformist's Scriptural warrant for his fiercely negative attitude towards life.   The fact that he defended himself and his position by an appeal to the Scriptures is plain and incontrovertible; but can it be said that Christianity is wholly on the Puritan's side?

To those whose bodies and general physical inferiority lead them to question the beauty and value of life on this earth; to those who are predestined by their physiques to take up a hostile or doubtful attitude towards the joys and the hardships of life—to such men, in fact, as I have described on pages 177 to 180 of this chapter—there are certainly several features about Christianity which will seem to substantiate and justify their position, more particularly if they rely entirely upon the Scriptures and divorce themselves wholly from the traditions of the Holy Catholic Church whose pagan elements tended rather to mitigate the sternly negative creed of primitive Christianity than to accentuate it.

We know the famous equation: The World = The Flesh = The Devil.   Now, to all men who are physically biassed in favour of such a chain of consequences, there is much in the Scriptures which will appear to sanctify their point of view.

In the first place, take the repeated references in the Bible to the baseness of this world and of this life, and the

[1] p. 16.   [2] p. 27.

glory of the world and the life to come. There is a peculiarly hostile spirit manifested against this earth and this world in many a Bible passage, and in the First Epistle of John we actually read the definite command: "Love not the world, neither the things that are in the world. If any man love the world, the love of the Father is not in him. For all that is in the world, the lust of the flesh and the lust of the eyes, and the pride of life, is not of the Father, but is of the world." [1]

The body and the flesh, too, come in for a good deal of hostile and even rancorous criticism, and for those who were prepared to revile them to the honour of the Spirit, there was ample support in the gospels and epistles of the New Testament.

In Romans we read: "Flesh is death; Spirit is life and peace. The body is dead because of sin; but the Spirit is life because of righteousness. If ye live after the flesh, ye shall die: but if ye through the Spirit do mortify the deeds of the body, ye shall live." [2] And even those whose *minds* were prepossessed in favour of carnal things are rebuked and cautioned. "For to be carnally minded *is* death: but to be spiritually minded is life and peace. Because the carnal mind *is* enmity against God: for it is not subject to the law of God, neither indeed can be. So then they that are in the flesh cannot please God." [3]

Such sentiments not only seem to cast a slur upon the natural functions and joys of the body, they also actually separate these functions and joys from all community with God; so that the fundamental instincts of life seem to lie under a ban, and to be covered with shame and disgrace. Thus *true* life involves the paradox of hostility to life, and St. Paul in his Epistle to the Galatians actually confirms this supposed eternal hostility. He says, "For the flesh lusteth against the Spirit and the Spirit against the flesh." [4]

He dares to go even further; he undertakes to enumerate the things with which he necessarily associates the

[1] 1 John ii. 15, 16.   [2] Rom. viii. 6, 10, 13.
[3] Rom. viii. 6-8.   [4] Gal. v. 17.

flesh. He says: "Now the works of the flesh are manifest, which are these: Adultery, fornication, uncleanness, lasciviousness, idolatry, witchcraft, hatred, variance, emulations, wrath, strife, seditions, heresies, envyings, murders, drunkenness, revellings, and such like." [1]

There is no mention here of the healthy and restrained joys and wonders of the flesh; no hint that only hogs must regard the flesh in this way. Indeed, if you had but the New Testament as your guide in matters of sexuality, you might reasonably be excused if you regarded all things connected with the functions of procreation as the most unpardonable sinfulness. St. Paul actually exhorted the Corinthians to cleanse themselves from all filthiness of the flesh;[2] in the first Epistle of Peter we are told of the "filth of the flesh,"[3] and we are also informed by St. Paul that to become Christ's we must crucify "the flesh with the affections and lusts."[4]

To deny, to revile, and to despise the body, would, according to these texts, seem to be the only road to salvation—a course utterly strange to him who is sufficiently master of his appetites to rejoice in his body and to enjoy it, without making, as the saying is, "a beast of himself."

"Walk in the Spirit," says St. Paul, "and ye shall not fulfil the lusts of the flesh"[5]; "they which are the children of the flesh, these are not the children of God,"[6] while St. John emphatically declares: "It is the spirit that quickeneth: the flesh profiteth nothing."[7]

But the very needs of the body and men's concern about it, receive a severe blow even from the Founder of Christianity Himself. Christ, in His famous Sermon on the Mount, said: "Therefore I say unto you, Take no thought for your life, what ye shall eat, or what ye shall drink: nor yet for your body, what ye shall put on."[8]

---

[1] Gal. v. 19–21.
[2] 2 Cor. vii. 1.
[3] 1 Pet. iii. 21.
[4] Gal. v. 24.
[5] Gal. v. 16.
[6] Rom. ix. 8.
[7] John vi. 63.
[8] Matt. vi. 25.

A DEFENCE OF ARISTOCRACY

Now it may be perfectly true that all this negativism towards the world, the body and the flesh, does not actually constitute the kernel of true Christianity, and it certainly never constituted the basis of the doctrine of the Holy Catholic Church; but, on the other hand, it must not be forgotten that with this negativism to be found and quoted as authority by men who were predisposed to question the value, beauty and joy of life and the body, it was only natural that the Puritans should regard their standpoint and their attitude as more than amply confirmed and supported by the texts of holy Scripture.

I have attempted to describe the kind of men they were,[1] and, if my description be at all true to reality, just ask yourself whether, in the few passages I have selected from the Scriptures, these men were not able to find more than the adequate foundation and justification which they most needed for their campaign against beauty, the body and its joys! Even if we admit that they exaggerated, distorted—nay, burlesqued—the teachings of Christ and His Apostles, we are still forced to acknowledge that at least the elements of their extreme attitude were undoubtedly to be sought and found in Christianity itself.

And if to-day we find it an almost universal tendency to exalt the soul at the expense of the body; if we find the modern world getting into trouble and confusion over its management of questions of sex, of healthy breeding, of healthy living and healthy thinking; if we find nervousness, insanity and general debility increasing so much that movements such as that of the Eugenists seem to be necessary and proper—it is impossible, and it would be unfair, not to point to precisely that element in Christianity which, though exaggerated beyond all reason by the Puritans, yet plainly means hostility and doubt in regard to the deeds, the joys, the beauties and the inestimable virtues of the body.

For all healthy peoples, all permanent peoples have always held that nothing on earth can justify a botched

[1] See pp. 177 to 180.

body, an ugly body, or foul breath. They have also regarded all the lusts of the flesh as legitimate if not sacred. But this exaltation of the soul, besides under-mining our joy and faith in the body, introduces an insidious plea for, and a dangerous sanctification of, botchedness. It says practically, since the body does not matter; since to be separated from the body is to be freed from sin,[1] why trouble about this earthly shell, why fret concerning this inheritance of hell? Is it botched?—then to be sure it contains a fine soul! Is it bungled and ugly?—then remember it encloses an immortal spirit! Is it repulsive, is its breath foul?—then think that this is but an earthly ailing![2] And so on!—All excellent excuses and pretexts for those whom the Old Testament ventured to call the unclean; but dangerous and insidious doctrines for a nation that would last and would be permanent and glorious.

Now there can be no doubt that the Puritans fastened on this particular aspect of Christianity with as much obstinacy as enthusiasm. And everything which was redolent of the world and the flesh—everything, in fact, that was fundamental in life, was to them anathema. Consistently with this attitude, therefore, they attacked beauty and good healthy living, because both lured and led back

---

[1] Rom. vi. 7.

[2] As an instance, of how universally this view is now accepted, at least in England, see how the very mob, which contains some of the healthiest elements of the nation, sings, enjoys and whole-heartedly approves of such Puritanical sentiments as we find in the chorus of some of the most popular music-hall songs of the last decade of the nineteenth century. To refer to a single example let me quote the lines of the popular music-hall chorus in the love-song, Sweet Marie—

> " Come to me, sweet Marie,
> Come to me, sweet Marie, .
> Not because your face is fair, love, to see.
> But your soul so pure and sweet
> Makes my happiness complete,
> Makes me falter at your feet,
>   Sweet Marie."

to the world, the flesh and the devil, and both opened the highway to the joys and the wonders of the body.

Not only was the beauty of the human body, however, the butt of their bitter hostility—every kind of beauty fell under the same ban. Wherever the Parliamentary rebels could do so, they destroyed the art-treasures and glories of English homes and churches, and as early as May 1644 an Act of Parliament was passed by these vandals to destroy all beauty in churches and to remove all organs. As M. B. Synge declares, "to the Puritan, beauty was a curse."[1]

That vile pamphleteer and murderer of Laud, William Prynne, spoke as follows concerning human beauty, and in his words the whole of the poisonous creed which sets bodily charm at naught and exalts that inward beauty of the soul, which can justify even a foul and botched body, comes vividly to light.

"Man's perfect Beautie . . . consists . . . in the inward Endowments, Ornaments, Trappings, Vertues, and the Graces of the Minde and Soule, in which the Excellency, Essence and Happinesse of men consist: This is the only Comelinesse, and Beautie, which makes us Amiable, Beautifull, and Resplendent in the sight of God, of Men and Angels: this is the only culture, and Beauty which the Lord respects."[2]

And again—

"A Studious, Curious, Inordinate, and eager Affection of Beautie, . . . must needes be sinfull and Abominable: yea farre worse than Drunkennesse, and excesse of Wine . . . because it proceeds most commonly, from an Adulterous, unchast, and lustfull Heart, or Meretricious, and Whorish affection."[3]

One can but marvel at the unscrupulousness of these monsters. But, again, let me recall how tragically all this prepared the way for this age, for *our* age.

[1] *A Short History of Social Life in England*, p. 207.
[2] *The Unlovelinesse of Lovelocks* (1628), p. 51.
[3] Op. cit., pp. 55–56.

"Those who have continent and chaste affections," Prynne continues, "as they deeme this corporall and out-side Beautie a needlesse and superfluous thing: so they are farre from seeking, or affecting it: that like that chast and beautiful Pagan, they would rather obscure and neglect, and quite deface their naturall Beauties, by inflict-ing wounds and scarres upon their faces, to make them more deformed, for feare least others should be infatuated and insnared with them." [1]

"Infatuated and snared" to what? To life, of course, to flourishing, healthy life, which is always associated with beauty; to the joy of life and in life, to a multiplication of joyful life!

The relationship between beauty and the stimulation of the sex-instinct was a thing not unknown to these filthy-minded Puritans; hence their loathing of this "outside Beauty," as Prynne chose to call it.

They also made more direct attacks upon the sex instinct itself; for in their suppression of sports and of the May-pole in particular, they were largely actuated by the feeling that all jollification which brought young men and girls together, *must* lead to the most horrible of all sins—the stimulation and promotion of sexual interest. We have only to recall the words of Charles I's "*Declaration to his Subjects concerning lawful Sports to be used on Sundays.*"[2] In it he said, "under the pretence of taking away abuses," certain festivals had been forbidden. We know what these Puritans regarded as "abuses." Anything was an abuse which, taking place round the Maypole, led to young lusty men and sun-warmed maidens falling into each other's arms before they had passed before the parson and the registrar.

But in order to make assurance doubly sure, they deter-mined to put an end to all spontaneous love—or as they in their bitterness said: *fornication*, by Act of Parliament. On May 10, 1650, any sexual intercourse outside marriage was made punishable by three months' imprisonment for

[1] Op. cit., p. 57.   [2] Quoted on p. 130.

both the man and the woman! We can imagine what this meant for the English man and maiden of those days! Now, of course, after two centuries of Puritan tradition, it is not hard to find men and women who are so depressed, so deteriorated, spiritually and sexually, that they can be content, nay, happy, as lifelong spinsters and bachelors. Vitality is now at such a low ebb, that though we still talk glibly of restraining our passions, and of controlling our instincts—as if they were still something quite as difficult to command as our *alimentary* appetite—there is not much hardship involved to the average English maid or man in holding a check upon his sex nowadays. He does it very well; so well, indeed, that it is a mere euphemism to speak of control. If a wet squib were able to speak, we should all laugh if it boasted of exercising control when it would not go off.

But in those days things were different, vitality was greater, and this law was an absurdity.

If the Puritans had so reconstructed the whole of society as to make early marriages possible for everybody, there would have been no stupidity, no brutality, and not necessarily any negativism in this law. But to allow the *status quo* to persist, and then to pass this surface sanctimonious legislation was a piece of sheer barbarism.

In many villages in France, as also in England, I have myself observed how beneficently the stern morals of a small and limited community solve this sex problem for themselves. Prostitution is absolutely unknown in such places, because non-promiscuous sexual intercourse between couples is tolerated, long before marriage is a possible consideration. The public opinion of the community, however, is powerful enough to keep the man to his bargain, and the few irresponsible men who always must appear, are ostracised. It is not unusual, for instance, in some parts of Picardy, for a bride-mother to stand before Monsieur le Maire at her marriage ceremony, with her two children, four and two years old— standing behind and witnessing the whole affair. This is not immoral; it is eminently practical and proper, and where this occurs the evils of prostitution are unknown.[1]

But what are the pre-requisites to such a scheme of sexual morality? The pre-requisites are two things that the Puritan tradesman did his best to destroy: a small village community where public opinion counts for something, and where, alone, public opinion *can* exercise discipline; and a stable population, which is not constantly tossed from one place to another, here to-day and a hundred miles away to-morrow. In the large towns created by the sort of industry and commerce which owe their growth to Puritanism, such a code of sexual morality is quite impossible. In such places public opinion is too vast and too heterogeneous to be concentrated on one particular point or quarter, and the population is too fluid for ostracism to be any hardship. Prostitution, therefore, is almost a foregone conclusion in such communities; unless you can so depress the vigour and vitality of the race as to exterminate the fundamental instinct of life. But even in spite of coming within measurable distance of this goal, the English race has already been deteriorated without prostitution having necessarily been abolished.

The object of the Puritans was to attempt to depress the fundamental instinct of life by *atrophy*. As I have

---

[1] Where this sort of thing goes on in England, as it does in Devonshire, Norfolk, Suffolk, and many other counties, there are always a host of idiotic puritanical and, unfortunately, wealthy old spinsters who do their utmost to interfere with it ; little dreaming in their stupid and unthinking brains that they are thus abetting and promoting prostitution. I once heard a certain fat and fatuous old maid boast that she had done her utmost in Devonshire to put a stop to what she called this " horrible immorality "; and Mr. F. E. Green in his stimulating book, *The Tyranny of the Countryside*, gives two examples of the same foolishness which are worth quoting. " I know of one lady," he says, " who has given orders to her steward that no girl who ' has got into trouble ' shall be allowed cottage room on her estate. . . . In quite a different county a pathetic appeal was made to me by a cowman who had been given notice to quit because his eldest unmarried daughter, aged nineteen, was *enceinte*. He had pleaded in vain to be allowed to remain, as his wife was about to give birth to another child," pp. 31–32.

already shown, they have indeed partly succeeded; but the condition of society to-day shows that their efforts have only given rise to the most wretched of all compromises, in which we find Prostitution with all its horrors and ill-health—for no form of prostitution can be worse than that which occurs under Puritanical conditions—abetting and promoting the general decline in vitality initiated by the Puritan's depressing and life-sapping creed, their unhealthy industrial occupations, and the bad city conditions to which the latter gave rise.

From the first, too, the wretched bawd was punished by them with terrible severity. By the Act of May 10, 1650, in which, as I have already shown, all sexual intercourse, away from the marriage bed, was punished by three months imprisonment, the bawd's penalty was fixed at being placed in the pillory, being branded with a red-hot iron on the forehead with the letter B, and being detained for three years in a House of Correction or in prison. A second conviction was punished by death.[1]

Not satisfied with these measures, however, three months later, on August 9, 1650, an Act was passed whereby any one condoning "fornication," or even thinking it right and proper, was made liable to six months imprisonment. Nor was this all; for in its savage ferocity this same Act ordained that any one who, having once been found guilty of this crime—of merely thinking that fornication was right—was convicted a second time, should be sentenced to banishment (which meant life-long slavery), and, failing his appearance at the port of embarkation—to death![2]

These legislative acts speak for themselves, and that is why I have preferred to quote them, often *in extenso*, rather than to enter into a more detailed history of the Puritans themselves. Unscrupulously, resolutely, fiercely, they set to work to damp, to eradicate, and, if possible, to kill the spirit of Merrie England. It is as if a vivid picture of the England of to-day had lain like a distant

[1] Scobell, op. cit., p. 121. [2] *Ibid.*, pp. 124–125.

mirage before their eyes, and they had sought by what means, by what artifices, they could help that mirage to become a reality. They saw it in all its ugliness, all its squalor, and all its hopeless drudgery, and every one of the manifestations of beauty, health and good taste about them in their day, seemed only like so many obstacles strewn in the path of its ultimate realisation.

So much, then, for their tamperings with the spirit and the sexual instinct of the nation—and I have purposely coupled these two things together, seeing that, as I have already said, there is strong interaction between them;— it now remains to discuss their tamperings with the body of the nation.

If a body can be directly depressed by drugs, or by poor diet, or by unhealthy living, there is no further need for spiritual means for accomplishing this end. For, where the bowel acts slowly, where digestion is retarded, and where the nerves are jaded—the very river or stream of the spirit is already poisoned at its source.

The story I am now going to tell is as strange as any that has ever been told inside the pages of what purports to be a serious work; but though apparently accident and design will often be seen to unite with wonderful preci- sion, in bringing about the desired unravelment, I submit that there is no such thing as accident or chance in the whole affair.

It was a question of altering the Englishman's body. What mattered it then that some drugs fell into the Puritans' hands, just as Manna had fallen on to the shoulders of the Israelites in the desert—fortuitously, gratuitously, unsolicitedly, just as if the God of Puritans had felt the urgent need of His people, and shed these drugs upon them? The fact that a thing falls into your hands by chance, does not force you to swallow it. Though innovations appear thick and fast about you, you are not compelled to adopt them. Taste discriminates and selects. If, therefore, certain new forms of diet appeared just at that psychological moment when it was

to the taste of Puritans to adopt them, surely the Puritans'
are to blame, and not the chance appearance of the new
forms of diet themselves. And this becomes all the more
apparent when we remember that, as Buckle points out,
they were able on occasion to study the effects of diet upon
the so-called " low lusts of the flesh." [1]

But of this anon.

The first direct attack that the Puritans made upon the
dietetic habits of the Englishman, consisted in an attempt
at suppressing the consumption of the wholesome alcoholic
beverages. And we know what the Puritans meant when
they attacked " drink." They did not necessarily mean
" drunkenness " as we see it to-day, at our street corners
and in our slums—for that sort of drunkenness literally
did not exist in those days. They meant, once more, that
conviviality, that good cheer, and those high spirits, to
which a good, wholesome and well brewed fermented
liquor gives rise. In Cotton Mather's *Batteries upon the
Kingdom of the Devil*, and in William Prynne's *Healthe
and Sicknesse*, there are fulminations enough against the
drinking of alcoholic beverages; and what was the reply
of the people of the day to these lucubrations? As Prynne
himself points out,[2] they replied that what the Puritans
called " drunkenness," was " hospitality, good fellowship,
courtesie, entertainment, joviality, mirth, generosity,
liberality, open-house keeping, etc." Of course, inasmuch
as some will always go too far—even if it be only in
playing an innocent game of bowls—cases of drunkenness
were not uncommon; but the after effects of such occasional excesses in those days were not in the least harmful;
because what was absorbed was good, and—in so far as
the ale was concerned—actually excellent nourishment,
and an energy- and spirit-giving drink.

And this brings me to the question of the national drink

---

[1] See p. 260, Vol. III, *The History of Civilisation in England* : " To
check the lusts of the flesh, they [the Puritans] furthermore took into
account the cookery, the choice of meats, and the number of dishes."

[2] *Healthe and Sicknesse* (edit. 1628), p. 5.

of England during the Middle Ages and up to the first half of the seventeenth century: this, as in glorious ancient Egypt, was simply barley-wine—or, in less high-flown language, ale, brewed from fermented barley.[1]

Athenæus's account of the ale of the Egyptians is very instructive for our purpose. He says it was very strong, and had so exhilarating an effect upon those who drunk it, that they danced and sang and committed all kinds of exuberant extravagances. And in this judgment he is confirmed by Aristotle.[2]

Diodorus also affirms that the Egyptian ale was scarcely inferior to the juice of the grape.[3] And this drink, like old English ale, was drunk by the peasants in all parts of the country.

Now, it is important to note that in all things relating to Egypt, we are concerned always with the taste of a people whose one passion was permanence. Indeed, so highly did they reverence permanence in dynastic, as well as vital matters, that Diodorus tells us, they despised gymnasia and refused to use them, because they believed that the kind of physical strength cultivated in such places, was less permanent than that gained in the ordinary pursuits of a healthy life.[4] Such a people as this, apart from the other proofs we have of their great wisdom and taste in art and government, would never have selected for their national drink a beverage which might have proved deleterious or unwholesome in the long run to their race. And the fact that the Egyptians existed for so many thousands of years as a highly civilised, proud and art-loving nation, is in itself the most convincing proof that can be found of the beneficial value of their national beverage.

And there is no reason to doubt Athenæus's word con-

---

[1] Diodorus, Book I, 34. Herodotus, Book II, 77.
[2] See *The Manners and Customs of the Ancient Egyptians*, by Wilkinson, Vol. I, p. 396.
[3] Book I, 34.
[4] Book I, 81. See also Herodotus, Book II, 91.

cerning the exhilarating effect of their ale upon them. Whoever has taken a good draught of the nearest approach our countryside now enjoys, to this old drink of ancient Egypt and Merrie England, will not doubt for one instant that it is absolutely true. Without a trace of the evil effects which come of drinking modern bitter beer or stout, this mild brown ale of the English agricultural village, which, remember, is not to be compared in quality with the liquor that the ancient Egyptian or the Englishman of the sixteenth century was in the habit of drinking, is still one of the most perfectly exhilarating and nourishing drinks one can obtain.

But apart from the testimony of so great a people and culture as those of Egypt, and apart from our own experience, we have the evidence of centuries of experience in England, and the support of public and scientific opinion, which are both in favour of the old ale that vanished when the Puritans triumphed.

In the folk-lore, the legend, and the poetry of England, the old ale of our forefathers—that which was brewed from barley malt alone—has been too well praised, and its sterling qualities too often enumerated, for me to attempt to do it adequate justice in a mere portion of an essay like the present. With its value as a body-building and health-maintaining liquor, tested on the battlefields of Great Britain and the Continent, and found in no way lacking, the evidence of our fighting peasantry alone would be sufficient to hallow it in our estimation as a national institution, and I could not attempt to vie with men like John Taylor of old, and John Bickerdayle of more recent times, in demonstrating its merits beyond all shadow of a doubt.

Nevertheless, to the reader who is not acquainted with all the facts that have been collected and adduced in its favour, perhaps a selection of these, briefly stated, will not prove unwelcome, and may even constitute an indispensable part of my argument.

From the earliest times to about the middle of the

seventeenth century, then, the staple drink of these islands, for the peasant as for the Sovereign, was the liquor produced by fermented barley mixed with pure water. The most valuable and principal ingredient in this beverage was the substance which chemists call *maltose*, or sugar of malt. Now this maltose, besides being acknowledged as the finest food for producing physical energy and heat, also enjoys the privilege of being a promoter rather than a retarder of the digestive process, as well as a potent and invigorating appetiser.[1] This is very important, because more than half the trouble which is occasioned by the Puritan substitutes for this drink, will, as I shall show, be seen to concentrate around the question of retarding digestion, and thereby lowering spirit and vitality.[2]

The ale of our forefathers contained at least eight per cent. of this maltose, and thus constituted a truly nourishing beverage.[3] Indeed there was an old proverb, current among the people of the sixteenth and seventeenth centuries in England which ran—

> " Wine is but a single broth
> But Ale is meat and drink and cloth."

This was the ale which the monk as well as the housewife had brewed for ages, which was drunk at Church-Ales, Bride-Ales, Scot-Ales, Wakes, and Feasts of Dedication, and the proceeds on the sale of which had often contributed to no small extent to the building of the

---

[1] *Food and the Principles of Dietetics*, by Robert Hutchison, M.D., p. 369.

[2] To the reader who would like to enter more deeply into the medical aspect of the question, let me recommend, for a start, pp. 91 *et seq.* in Mr. Hackwood's book on the *Inns, Ales and Drinking Customs of Old England*, and the whole of Chapter XV of Mr. Bickerdayle's book, *The Curiosities of Ale and Beer*.

[3] Even of our modern beer, which is as different from the ale of Merrie England as chalk is from cheese, Dr. Hutchison is still able to say : " The large quantity of carbohydrate matter in malt liquors renders them the most truly nourishing of alcoholic drinks " (op. cit., p. 370) ; so we may judge of the superiority in this respect of the purer and older brand.

neighbouring church or cathedral. As. Bickerdayle says: " These simple, hearty festivals of old in which our ancestors so much delighted, served to light up the dull round of the recurring seasons, and to mark with a red letter the day in the calendar appropriate to their celebration. It was these that gained for our country in mediæval times the name of ' Merrie England.' " [1]

If we remember the words of Athenæus concerning the exhilarating effects of this same malt-liquor upon the ancient Egyptians, we can imagine the cheerfulness, merriment and high spirits which must have characterised these picturesque country festivals of old, and we begin to understand how darkly, in later times, the cold and resentful Puritans must have stood, some distance away, watching the whole scene with bitter disapproval, and longing for the day of their power to come, when they would be able to crush out all this sinfulness for ever.

This was the ale which was drunk in the morning at breakfast, by peasant, lord and king. Even Queen Elizabeth's breakfast seems frequently to have consisted of little else but ale and bread,[2] and the very children in the nursery were not exempt from its use in a weakened form.[3] According to Mr. Hackwood, Good Queen Bess enjoyed a *quart* of this liquor at her early morning meal, and she is said to have called it " an excellent wash ";[4] while it

---

[1] *The Curiosities of Ale and Beer*, p. 232.

[2] Op. cit., p. 275.

[3] See Traill's *Social England*, Vol. IV, p. 670 : " Water was scarcely ever drunk, even by children, who drank small beer from their earliest years." See also John Locke, *Some Thoughts concerning Education* (edit. 1693), p. 16. After recommending good dry bread as a substantial portion of a child's daily food, the old philosopher says : " If any one think this too hard and sparing Diet for a Child, let them know, that a Child will never starve, nor want nourishment, who besides Flesh once a Day . . . may have good Bread and Beer as often as he has a Stomach." And later on he says, speaking of the Child : " His Drink should be only small Beer."

[4] *Inns, Ales and Drinking Customs of Old England*, p. 91.

was a common thing for Tudor ladies to have a gallon of ale for a nightcap as well.[1]

Together with the excellent bread of the period, no better meal could be imagined, and a continuous supply of this staple national beverage was as important to our ancestors as a continuous supply of water is to us now. It is for this reason that the Statute Book of olden times is full of references to this precious national asset.[2]

The value of this drink as a health-giver, to the poor particularly—who, thanks to its qualities, were often able to tide over a period of scant food without suffering any evil effects—cannot be overrated. "There exist, sad to relate," says Bickerdayle, "persons who, with the notion of promoting temperance, would rob us of our beer. Many of these individuals may act with good motives, but they are weak, misguided bodies who, if they but devoted their energies to promoting ale-drinking as opposed to spirit [and bitter beer] drinking, would be doing useful service to the State, for malt liquors are the true temperance drinks of the working classes."[3]

John Taylor, an old writer on ale, and an enthusiast whom nothing could repress, was another who noticed the inspiriting quality of the old English beverage. Writing in the middle of the seventeenth century, he saw precisely what the Puritans and Athenæus saw in old ale, but, far from complaining, he gloried in it. He knew it would "set a Bashfull Suitor a wooing,"[4] and in a long poem of over thirty verses he says—

---

[1] *Inns, Ales and Drinking Customs of Old England*, p. 91.

[2] See Hackwood, op. cit., p. 81 : "It was incumbent upon the brewers in old time to keep up an adequate supply of good ale, just as we nowadays insist upon a proper supply of pure water ; the former, however, was regarded more as a question of food supply, while the latter is mainly a hygienic precaution. The brewers were not allowed to cause any inconvenience by a sudden reduction of their output, on the plea, perhaps, that the State-regulated prices were unremunerative to them, or on any other excuse whatever."

[3] Op. cit., p. 14.   [4] *Drink and Welcome*, p. 5.

A DEFENCE OF ARISTOCRACY

"The Dick to his Dearling, full boldly does speak,
Though before (silly fellow) his courage did quaile,
He gives her the smouch, with his hand in his pouch,
If he meet by the way with a Pot of good Ale." [1]

Apart from its health-giving properties it was this quality of a spirit-tonic that made the ale of ancient Egypt and of Merrie England such a formidable national possession. And if the English peasant in arms was so proverbially feared by our continental neighbours under the Plantagenets and the Lancasters, and even by his fellow countrymen in times of peasant uprisings, it is impossible to dissociate this fact completely from his daily beverage and food, which, at one time, was the best that art and experience could contrive for rearing stamina and courage.

However, as this is not a book on dietetics, but simply a critical examination of the principle of aristocracy, to those readers who still doubt my word concerning this ale of old England, I can but tender this advice: let them look into the matter for themselves. It is sufficiently important to repay investigation. And they will find that no praise, however immoderate, that some have lavished upon it, is too great, for the merits of our old English drink.

At all events, though, I must point out, that my case neither stands nor falls with the claim that ale is the best possible drink of all. It simply relies on the fact that the substitutes which, owing to the Puritans, soon took the place of ale, were not a hundredth part as good as ale, and can, indeed, be shown to have been positively deleterious.

This point I should like to emphasise. For it is so easy to twist my argument into a panegyric on ale, when it is really only an attempt at showing the unquestionable superiority of our old national drink over all the substitutes which the Puritans helped to introduce.

I think, mark you, that the case for ale, as being the best possible drink, is an exceedingly good one; but, as I say, it is not essential to my argument.

[1] *Ale Ale-Vated into the Ale-Titude* (1651), verse 23.

With their vehement cry against drink, then; with their severe legislation against drunkenness, and particularly with their suppression of those feasts and public celebrations at which ale was drunk, the Puritans, as soon as they had acquired sufficient power, waged a war to the death against old English ale.

Too vulgar to see that you cannot have all the advantages of ale without, here and there, feeling some of its disadvantages; too stupid to see that the occasional drunkenness of the few was the inevitable reverse of a medal which was, nevertheless, worth keeping—more particularly as the evil effects of drunkenness in those days were practically nil—they inveighed against drink *per se*, and hated the spirit, the good cheer and the sexual stimulus which it engendered.

On August 9, 1650, in an Act, part of which I have already quoted, they made it a criminal offence even to " condone drunkenness " or even to " think drunkenness right and proper," and the punishment for these crimes of " condoning " and " thinking " were, for the first offence, six months' imprisonment, and for the second, banishment (which meant life-long slavery). Should the criminal, however, who had condoned drunkenness, or thought it right and proper, fail to repair to the port of embarkation in order to be shipped away as a slave, sold by his own fellow countrymen, he was to be put to death.[1]

The ferocious brutality of these Puritans was something incredible; and if there was one thing on earth that could possibly outreach or exceed it, it was, as in the case of the Low Churchman and Puritan of to-day, their absolutely unparalleled stupidity.

The greatest blow, however, which the Parliamentary party levelled against the old national beverage of England, was their tax on ale. To increase the price of the staple drink of the lower classes, and thus to render its consumption more difficult, was not only contrary to all precedent—for, as we have seen, the monarchs of the past

---

[1] Scobell, op. cit., pp. 124–125.

213

had always taken the most scrupulous care to guarantee a plentiful supply of it at the lowest possible rate to the working classes—but it was an indirect tax on labour itself, an absolutely unheard-of measure before that time, and a tax whose incidence fell on the poorest people with a thousand times more weight than upon the capitalists and the landowners.

In addition to that it opened the flood-gates to all the filthy substitutes for good old ale which, as chance would have it, happened to be waiting on the threshold of English social life for just such an opportunity as this.

And, seeing that, as I have already shown, trade supervision for the benefit of the consumer—the people—had been overthrown with the monarchy of Charles I, adulteration and the making of inferior beer soon arose to rob the people still further of the benefits of their proper standard beverage.

The greatest and most deleterious of the adulterants immediately put into more general use was hops. For years brewers had tried to palm off malt liquor adulterated with hops as true ale, and as often as they had done so, they had been severely punished by their rulers. For there was not only a strong prejudice against hops, which was entirely justified, but also a sound suspicion that hop-ale was *not* ale.

As Hackwood says: " Till the Revolutionary period of the seventeenth century, Englishmen had been content to drink malt liquor. It may be said that through the centuries till then, ale had been the wine of the country, the national beverage, all-sufficient for the taste and temperament of the Englishman. On the outbreak of the Civil War, in 1643, Parliament, with a view to increasing the national revenue, imposed Excise duties on ale. . . . The imposition of these duties, in that they eventually tended to alter the drinking habits of the people, will be found to be epoch-making and far-reaching in its effects." [1]

It is not easy to say exactly when hops were first intro-

[1] Op. cit., p. 124.

duced into England; but public attention was certainly called to them as early as the fifteenth century, for the common people and their sovereigns disliked 'the weed from the very beginning; while even as late as 1659, we gather from the evidence of an old play, that ale was still generally made without hops, especially in the country districts where the taste of the people was healthiest.[1]

Bickerdayle tells us that in the first year of Richard III's reign, a petition was presented to Lord Mayor Billesdon, by the Brewers' Company, showing "that whereas by the sotill and crafty means of foreyns dwelling without the franchises . . . a deceivable and unwholsome fete in bringing of ale within the said citie nowe of late is founde and practised, that is to say, in occupying and puttying of hoppes and other things in the said ale of old type used . . . to the great deceite and hurt of the King's liege people. . . . Pleas it therefore your saide good Lordshyppe to forbid the putting into ale of any hops, herbs, or any other like thing, but onely licour,[2] malte and yeste."[3]

The petition was granted and a penalty of 6s. 8d. was laid on every barrel of ale so brewed contrary to the ancient use.

Again, in the twelfth year of Henry VII's reign, John Barowe, and twelve years later Robert Dodworth, were prosecuted for using hops in the making of ale; while in the tenth year of Henry VIII, William Shepherd, servant to Philip Cooper, was similarly prosecuted. Henry VIII disliked the hop exceedingly, "and enjoined the Royal brewer of Eltham that he put neither hops nor brimstone into the ale";[4] while in 1542 Andrew Boorde, in his *Dyetary*, wrote as follows : "Bere is made of malt, hoppes and water; it is the naturall drynke for a Dutch-Man, and nowe of late dayes it is moche used in England to the detryment of many Englysshe people; specyally it kylleth

[1] Bickerdayle, op. cit., pp. 72-73.
[2] Water.　　　　　[3] Op. cit., p. 68.
[4] Op. cit., p. 71.

them which be troubled with the colyke, and stone, and the strangulation." [1]

Thus both popular and learned prejudice seem to have been vigorous and emphatic against the use of hops, and the outcry was general. The English believed, says Bickerdayle, "that they were like to be poisoned by the new-fangled drink which was not in their eyes to be compared to the sweet and thick, but honest and unsophisticated English ale." [2]

As a matter of fact the prejudice lasted until late in the seventeenth century, and had it not been for the policy of *laissez-faire* in matters of trade, which was inaugurated by the Puritans, and which put an end to all state protection of the consumer, and state supervision of trade, there is every reason to suppose that it would have lasted until this day.

In any case the liquor containing hops was not supposed to be called ale at all, but beer, and it is against this so-called "beer" that John Taylor, as late as the middle of the seventeenth century, inveighs so bitterly in his long poem on ale—

"To the Church and Religion it is a good friend,
    Or else our Forefathers their wisdome did faile,
That at every mile, next to the Church stile,
    Set a consecrate house to a Pot of good Ale.

"But now as they say, *Beer* beares it away ;
    The more is the pity, if Right might prevaile :
For with this same Beer, came up Heresie here ;
    The old Catholique Drink is a Pot of good Ale.

"This Beer's but an upstart from Dutchland here come,
    Whose Credit with us sometimes is but small :
For in the records of the Empire of Rome,
    The old Catholique Drink is a Pot of good Ale.

"And in very deed, the Hop's but a weed,
    Brought o'er against Law, and here set to sale :
Would the Law were renew'd, and no more beer brew'd,
    But all good men betake them to a Pot of good Ale." [3]

[1] Chapter X, paragraph *Beere*.　　[2] Op. cit., p. 70.
[3] *Ale Ale-Vated into the Ale-Titude* (1651), verses 26–29.

In the last pages of the book, John Taylor gives a number of medical reasons, in keeping with the knowledge of the time, why ale is superior to beer, and he very often lights upon what I believe to be a great truth. For instance, he says: " You shall never know or heare of a usuall drinker of Ale to bee troubled with Hippocondra, with Hippocondryacall obstructions or convulsions, nor are they vexed (as others are) with severall paines of sundry sorts of Gowts." [1]

While in his book *Drinke and Welcome*, he says—when writing in the middle of the seventeenth century, mark you!—" Beere is but an Upstart and a foreigner or Alien. . . . Nor would it differ from Ale in anything, but only that an aspiring Amaritudinous Hop comes crawling lamely in and makes a Bitter difference between them." [2]

As a matter of fact, it was a sound instinct that prompted the people of England to be suspicious of the hop; for, not only was the ale perfect without it, and simply adulterated by its addition, but also the properties of the adulterant itself were very far from desirable.

Hops, however, possess two qualities which, consciously or unconsciously, the Puritans must have thought very precious. Besides being a means of altering, adulterating and reducing the inspiriting ale of the past, hops constitute a soporific and an anaphrodisiac.

All the pharmacopæas mention it as an inducer of sleep, and most of them speak of its anaphrodisiac powers. As we read in the *National Standard Dispensatory*: " Hops may be used with benefit in the treatment of priapism and seminal emissions." [3] Yes! priapism and seminal emissions! We know how the Puritans were disposed to such things! How can the general use of hops in ale after the triumph of the Puritans in the seventeenth century any longer be regarded as an accident! As I say, choice is no accident. Hops fell into their hands like the Manna

[1] *Ale Ale-Vated into the Ale-Titude*, pp. 15–16.
[2] See p. 11. [3] See p. 799.

of the Israelites. Instead of rejecting them as previous generations had done, they accepted them. Such things are *not* accidents.

Brunton, however, mentions one more property of hops, which is important for my argument. He says: "Chief among the soluble ingredients of hops is tannic acid."[1] And we know that the effect of tannic acid is to retard digestion—that is to say, to depress, to lower spirits, to render lethargic, melancholy, humble and dull, in addition to leading to all kinds of serious physical disorders. Even if all the evil effects of hops were, however, very slight, their use as an ingredient in the old ale of England would still have to be deplored, seeing that this ale was in itself so good and wholesome a beverage that it could only be marred and not improved by the addition of any constituents foreign to its original nature.[2]

But by far the most extraordinary coincidence of this period of our history is that, precisely at the hour when Puritans were inveighing against drink and the merriment it engendered, at the very moment when by taxation, hostile legislation, and their indifference to adulteration, they were doing their utmost to abolish the good old ale of England, and almost compelling the working classes to cast about them to contrive other substitutes, two insidious drugs were knocking at the door of social England for admittance—two drugs which were of use to neither man

---

[1] *Text-book of Pharmacology: Therapeutics and Materia Medica,* p. 1031.

[2] In recent years, of course, the evils of beer-adulteration have attained such large proportions that it is now no longer a matter of objecting merely to the introduction of hops, but to that of all sorts of inexpensive and common substitutes, even more injurious than hops themselves, among which *quassia chips* easily take the first rank. This evil is, indeed, so far-reaching and serious that the very hop-growers themselves have organised a movement to resist it, and at the time of writing I have before me a number of leaflets and pamphlets, given me by a prominent promoter of this movement, in which the deleterious effects of the substitutes for that which in itself was originally nothing but an adulterant, are analysed and exposed.

nor beast, and which, in my opinion, have largely contributed to the physical impoverishment of the working classes of England. I refer to tea and coffee.

Sound scientific opinion is so unanimously agreed as to the harmfulness of these two vegetable poisons, that it might, perhaps, be sufficient for me simply to refer the reader to Dr. Haig's *Uric Acid*, Dr. Tebb's *Tea and the Effects of Tea-drinking*, Dr. Robert Hutchison's *Food and the Principles of Dietetics*, Dr. T. Lauder Brunton's *Pharmacology*, etc., where he would find more than I could tell him concerning the deleterious influences of these beverages. I will, however, enter briefly into the nature of these alleged deleterious influences, in order that there may be no doubt as to their general relation to the grand movement that was on foot.

Tea and coffee reached this island at about the same time, and began to claim the attention of ever wider and wider circles from the middle of the seventeenth century onward. Tea may have preceded coffee by a few years; but, at any rate, the difference was slight, and previous to 1630, neither of these beverages [1] was known to more than a very select minority in England.

In any case it is certain that the first coffee-house was opened in London three years after the murder of Charles I, and the others which speedily followed soon proved themselves to be redoubtable rivals to the old ale-vending tavern.[2]

With nothing to prevent the spread and general consumption of these non-alcoholic drinks, and with everything to encourage their adoption by the poorest majority in the land,[3] it did not take long for them to become almost

[1] Mr. W. Andrews, in *Bygone England*, fixes the date of the introduction of coffee into England at the year 1641 (see p. 149).

[2] See Hackwood, op. cit., p. 358 : "A rival to the tavern, in the shape of a public-house vending a non-alcoholic beverage, came in appropriately enough when England was under Republican government As a pamphleteer of the Restoration put it : 'Coffee and Commonwealth came in together.' "

[3] It should be borne in mind that, at least so far as tea was

the staple drinks of the people, and when to-day, in one of the gilt and marble tea and coffee emporiums of London, we see two undersized, pale and unhealthy-looking people of different sexes, simpering sickeningly at each other over their pap and poison—their white, adulterated bread, their boricised milk, and their tea—we know to what period of our history we owe the establishment in the land of the custom which makes it possible for two such specimens of botched humanity to imagine that they are partaking of *food* under such conditions.

Examine two such people more closely, however, and you will find that they are the most typical products of the diet that lies before them. Both suffer from indigestion, the girl more particularly; both have no fire, no light in their eyes; both are depressed, physically and spiritually; each has the swollen knuckles of the rheumatic invalid, neither of them has over much vitality, or sexual vigour. They will probably sit side by side day after day for years, sipping their poison and munching their pap, and be able to wait continently for marriage without either a pang or a pain. The girl laughs, and her long teeth, denuded of their gums at the fangs, by the heat and the tannin of her favourite drink, shine like the keys of an old cottage piano. He returns the smile, and all along the edge of his inflamed red gums you notice the filthy discharge characteristic of pyorrhœa,[1] which is a gouty malady of the teeth. No wonder such charms can be resisted for many a year! Puritanism can find nothing to criticise here. There is little that lures to life, and to a multiplication of life, in such ghastly people. Even a maypole would not make these people attractive. They are pecu-

---

concerned, it was impossible at first, owing to its prohibitive price per lb., for the poorer classes to touch it ; and they had to confine themselves to badly adulterated ale and to coffee. By the end of the eighteenth century, however, tea itself was sufficiently accessible to all ; for 23,717,882 lbs. were consumed in one year by a population numbering 16,794,000 (*i.e.* 1·41 lbs. per head).

[1] Pyorrhœa alveolaris.

liarly adapted to their drab, ugly city; to its harsh noises, its bad air, and its nervous ceaseless bustle.

A pretty waitress trips up to them. She is anæmic, but there is vitality in her. The sun of love has not yet reached her, and like all beautiful things that need the sun, she has grown pale from the lack of her natural element. The panel doctor prescribes iron; she herself has a shrewd notion that the doctor has misunderstood her malady. But so much about her has been misunderstood since she was a girl of thirteen, that she is beginning to doubt everything and to follow the main stream listlessly, patiently and with resignation.

The man belonging to the sickly couple looks up. He and his companion have finished their white adulterated bread and pressed tongue, and in his face one can see a faint burlesque of the determined look which might have fastened on the face of an old Roman bent on enjoying a banquet to the full. Gravely and portentously he orders two pieces of cake, and without a suggestion of surprise or wonderment—for this damnable farce is as common-place as the misty, murky atmosphere outside—the pretty waitress intersects the tables to the counter in order to carry out his order.

No matter whether it is tea or coffee they have had, the effects are much the same. The principal ingredients of both are the alkaloid *caffeine*, which is a whip to the brain and to the nerves, and which might be regarded as the most corroborative drug possible for the neurotic, hypertrophied and hypersensitive soul of the average modern townsman; and *tannic acid*, the tendency of which, says Dr. Tebb, "is greatly to impair digestion" and to give "rise to palpitation of the heart, headache, flatulence, loss of appetite, constipation and other symptoms." [1]

An ordinary infusion of tea is said to contain about three or four per cent. of caffeine, and ten to twelve per cent. of tannin; and according to Dr. Hutchison an

[1] Op. cit., p. 10.

ordinary cup of coffee contains about as much of the two drugs as an ordinary cup of tea.[1]

The retarding influence of tea and coffee on peptic digestion has been established by many scientists, among whom Fraser, Roberts, Ogata and Shulz-Schulzenstein may be mentioned. While Dr. Brunton, speaking of the effects of *tannic acid*, says, " even from small doses, there is a dryness of the fæces and lessened peristalsis." [2]

The importance of this effect of the tannin element in tea and coffee cannot be exaggerated, when we remember to what it leads in the matter of loss of spirit, fire, vigour, eagerness and general tone. While, among the subsidiary effects of caffeine, we should not forget its influence in increasing rather than diminishing tissue waste,[3] and its action as a depressor and paralyser once its stimulus to the nerves and brain have become exhausted." [4]

Among other authorities who have deprecated the use of tea are Sir Andrew Clarke, who thought that it was " a great and powerful disturber of the nervous system," and Sir B. W. Richardson, whose opinion is that " the alkaloid [theine] exercises a special influence on the nervous system, which when carried to a considerable extent, is temporarily at least, if not permanently, injurious." [5]

Now when it is remembered that at the present moment 255,270,472 lbs. of tea are used per annum in the United Kingdom, and that it has been calculated that the poor in London spend at least one-eighth of their income in buying this drug, it is difficult to realise the full importance of the revolution in so far as it undoubtedly affected this question of dietetics.

For again I should like to point out that even if it could be proved that tea and coffee are not nearly so harmful as I claim, the fact that with adulterated ale they ultimately became the masses' substitutes for the old ale of England,

[1] Op. cit., p. 324.   [2] Op. cit., p. 1032.
[3] Hutchison, op. cit., p. 333.
[4] Brunton, op. cit., p. 871 ; Dr. Tebb, op. cit., p. 19.
[5] Dr. Tebb, op. cit., p. 19.

which was at once a tonic and a food, would alone be sufficient to make us deplore their general adoption. For, in addition to their other shortcomings, as Dr. Hutchison points out, they are " in no sense foods." [1]

Nor can it be said that there were no cries of protest raised against their establishment as the staple beverages of the people.

From the seventeenth century down to our own time, an unceasing murmur of disapproval can be discerned beneath the general and indolent acquiescence of the majority, and it cannot even be urged that this disapproval has tended to diminish through the centuries. On the contrary, if science in her infancy once tentatively ventured to condemn the use of tea and coffee, she now does so with all the unhesitating emphasis that her increased knowledge allows.

One of the earliest objectors was Dr. Simon Pauli, who, writing in 1665, felt it incumbent upon him to warn Europeans against the abuse of tea. He declared that it was " moderately heating, bitter, drying and astringent"; [2] and the German physician Dr. Cohausen and the Dutchman Boerhave were of the same opinion, the latter emphasising the evil effects of tea on the nerves.

In 1673 the people themselves presented a petition to Parliament in which they prayed that tea and coffee might be prohibited, as their use interfered with the consumption of barley, malt and wheat, the native products of the country. " The petitioners," says Hackwood, " boldly asserted that the ' laborious people ' who constituted the majority of the population, required to drink ' good strong beer and ale,' which greatly refreshed their bodies after

---

[1] Op. cit., p. 334 (see also Dr. Tebb, op. cit., p. 19). " Poor people meet the craving for natural food by taking large quantities of tea. A strong craving for it is engendered which leads to the taking of tea at almost every meal, greatly to the injury of health. Poor women in the factory and cotton districts become actual sufferers from this cause, they are rendered anæmic, nervous, hysterical and physically feeble."

[2] Dr. Tebb, op. cit., p. 12.

223

their hard labours; and that the pot of ale or flagon of strong beer with which they refreshed themselves every morning and every evening, did them no great prejudice, hindered not their work, nor took away their senses, and while it cost them little money, it greatly promoted the consumption of home-grown grain."

William Cobbett, too, whom I have so often quoted in these pages, was very hostile to tea and coffee, and in 1829 in an address to young men wrote as follows: "Let me beseech you to resolve to free yourselves from the slavery of the tea and coffee and other slop-kettle, if, unhappily, you have been bred up in such slavery. Experience has taught me that these slops are injurious to health."[1] And again: "You are weak; you have delicate health; you are 'bilious!' Why, my good fellow, it is the very slops that make you weak and bilious! And, indeed, the *poverty*, the real poverty, that they and their concomitants bring on you, greatly assists, in more ways than one, in producing your delicate health."[2]

Dr. Simon Pauli was also strongly opposed to coffee, for the strange reason that he firmly alleged that it produced sterility. Of course, as a drug which, like tea, depressed the whole system, coffee must to some extent impair sexual potency; it is, however, doubtful whether it can, like hops, be regarded as a direct anaphrodisiac. At all events, however, Dr. Pauli's view is curiously confirmed by an extraordinary pamphlet which appeared in 1674. For even if we suppose that this pamphlet was meant only as a mere joke, surely the thought of connecting impaired

---

[1] *Advice to Young Men*, Letter 1, par. 31.

[2] *Ibid.*, Letter 1, par. 32. See also *Rural Rides*, Vol. I, p. 30, where, speaking of certain perambulatory impostors, Cobbett says: "They vend *tea, drugs* and *religious tracts*. The first to bring the body into a debilitated state ; the second to finish the corporeal part of the business ; and the third to prepare the spirit for its separation from the clay ! Never was a system so well calculated as the present to degrade, debase and enslave a people." See also *Rural Rides*, Vol. II, p. 272 : "If I had a village at my command, not a tea-kettle should sing in that village."

sexual potency with coffee can be no accident, and popular opinion and rumour based on popular experience, must to some extent have supported it, otherwise this pamphlet would have had very little point. It is called *The Women's Petition Against Coffee*,[1] and after much that I could not think of quoting, we read—

"The dull Lubbers want a *Spur* now, rather than a Bridle : being so far found doing any works of supererogation that we find them not capable of performing those Devoirs which their *Duty*, and our Expectations Exact. . . . The Occasion of which Insufferable *Disaster*, after a serious Enquiry, and Discussion of the Point by the Learned of the Faculty, we can Attribute to nothing more than the Excessive use of that Newfangled, Abominable, Heathenish Liquor called Coffee, which rifling Nature of her Choicest Treasures, and Drying up the Radical Moisture, has so Eunucht our Husbands, and Crippled our more kind Gallants, that they are become as Impotent, as Age, and as unfruitful as those *Desarts* whence that unhappy Berry is said to be brought. . . .[2] Wherefore the *Premises* considered, and to the end that our just *Rights* may be restored, and all the Ancient Priviledges of our *Sex* preserved inviolable; That our Husbands may give us some other *Testimonies* of their being Men, besides their Beards and wearing of empty *Pantaloons*. . . . But returning to the good old strengthening Liquors of our Forefathers; that Nature's *Exchequer* may once again be replenisht, and a Race of lusty Hero's begot, able by their achievements, to equal the Glories of our Ancestors."[3]

---

[1] By a Well-Willer. "Representing to Publick Consideration the Grand Inconvenience accruing to their sex from the Excessive Use of that Drying, Enfeebling Liquor."

[2] Page 2 of Pamphlet.

[3] Page 6 of Pamphlet. On page 5 of this pamphlet there is also shown some hostility to the weed tobacco. I do not intend to burden this essay any further by an examination of the effects of this drug ; certain it is, however, that tobacco, by paralysing the motor nerves of involuntary muscles and the secreting nerves of glands, does act as a powerful anaphrodisiac. Now it is well known that James I

Thus, at some length, I have stated the case for the old ale of England and against the innovations tea and coffee. And I have done this, not in the spirit of a diet-reformer, but rather with the view of showing how thoroughly and how perfectly both chance and design combined in the seventeenth century to render the most earnest religious desires and beliefs of the Puritanical faction capable of realisation in England.

As I pointed out at the beginning of this chapter, all deep religious movements have their hygiene and diet as well as their morality, and in this respect the religion of uncontrolled trade and commerce, which I suggest is Puritanism, is no exception to the rule. The desired end was achieved. The object of the Puritans was to convert England from a garden into a slum, from a land of spirited, healthy, vigorous, happy and beauty-loving agriculturists, herdsmen and shepherds into a land of unhealthy towns-men, hard manufacturers, docile and sickly factory hands and mill hands, and a sweated proletariat, indifferent alike to beauty as to all the other charms of full and flourishing life. And everything conspired to produce this result: the defeat of Charles I in the field of rebellion, the triumph of the trade Puritanical party and the advocates of a "Free" Parliament, the hostility of the Puritans to beauty, sex, life, high spirits and cheerfulness, and finally, the reforms they and their legislation brought about in the food and drink of the people.

For, as I have already shown, they also considered the question of solid food in its relation to the lusts of the body, and sought to reduce these as far as possible by dietetic means. Mrs. Cromwell, who was in a position to set an example to all the housewives of England, was a confirmed advocate of "pious plainness." "She ate," says M. B. Synge,[1] "marrow puddings for breakfast, and

---

and Charles I both hated tobacco smoke, and thoroughly disapproved of the habit of pipe smoking. James I even wrote a book against it ; but the Commonwealth men were, on the other hand, much addicted to it.

[1] *A Short History of Social Life in England*, p. 218.

fed her husband on sausages of hog's liver. . When she suspected general discontent in her household she was heard to remark: 'The Kingdom of God is not meat and drink, but righteousness and peace' "—precisely the root doctrine of her husband's party!

Another writer, speaking of Mrs. Cromwell's household, says: "The food is described as ordinary and vulgar, and no such dainties as *quelquechoses* were suffered. Scotch collops of veal was an almost constant dish, varied by a leg of mutton, a pig collared like brawn, or liver puddings. Mrs. Cromwell's usual drink was *Pumado*, which reads like a glorified edition of toast and water." [1]

Next to the physical and spiritual transformation of the Englishman, however, by far the worst results of the Puritanical Revolution consisted in the spread of the spirit of greed and gain in the nation, through the triumph of trade, and all the consequent evils of the prevalence of such a spirit—that is to say, (1) the increase of the shop-keeper or the middle-man class, (2) the opportunity and temptation to adulterate the vital nourishment of the people,[2] and (3) harshness towards the unprotected proletariat.

Taking these consequences in the order in which I have stated them, it must be obvious that any increase in the shopkeeper or middle-man class must be bad for three reasons: (*a*) owing to the undesirability of the type of man who is content and happy to spend his life unproductively in buying at one price and selling at another; (*b*) owing to the fact that the middle-man always separates

---

[1] *The English Housewife in the Seventeenth and Eighteenth Centuries*, by Rose M. Bradley, p. 150.

[2] In order to avoid burdening this chapter unduly, I have deliberately shunned any elaborate treatment of one of the most important items in the general charge I bring against the Puritan innovations. But there can be no doubt that an exceedingly good case could be brought against them, on the subject of adulterations alone ; for their régime of *laissez-faire* in trade morality certainly tolerated all kinds of abuses in food adulteration which must also have had a seriously deleterious effect upon the health and spirit of the people.

the purchaser from the producer and thus prevents everything in the shape of human intercourse, of healthy
criticism, of thanks, of gratitude or of an effort to please
between them; and (c) because the middle-man delays the
encounter between the product and the purchaser, and
therefore, by introducing the quality of staleness, gives
rise not only to ill-health directly, but also indirectly,
through the temptation to use adulterants which prevent
or disguise staleness.[1]   And all these three reasons are
independent of the greatest reason of all, namely, that
shops and shopkeeping make huge, unwieldy town populations possible and even plausible, and thus lead to all
the miseries with which we cannot help associating a
monstrous " wen " like London.

In regard to reason (c), that which constitutes its most
regrettable feature is the permanent lack of freshness which
characterises everything that the town man eats or drinks.
Those who have picked fruit from the trees on which
they grow, those who know what it is to drink fresh milk,
eat fresh eggs and pull up fresh lettuces for their evening
meal, must realise what it means to lead a life in which
all one's food is soiled, bruised, finger-marked, dog-eared,
tarnished! through having passed through the hands of
so many middle-men or shopkeepers before it reaches one's
table.   And yet how many millions of Englishmen lead
such lives, and without a murmur!

In regard to reason (b), William Cobbett has so many
interesting things to say that, at the risk of fatiguing the
reader, I feel I must quote him in full.

Writing on Sunday, October 22, 1826, Cobbett said:
" Does not every one see, in a minute, how this exchang-
ing of fairs and markets for shops creates *idlers and
traffickers;* creates those locusts called middle-men who
create nothing, who add to the value of nothing, who

[1] To refer again to ale, there seems to be no doubt that the whole
value of the hop, apart from its bitter flavour, consisted in the fact that
it preserved the malt liquor, thus proving a desirable ingredient to the
middle-man or shopkeeper.   See Bickerdayle, op. cit., p. 80.

improve nothing, but who live in idleness, and who live well, too, out of the labour of the producer and the consumer? The fair and the market—those wise institutions of our forefathers, and with regard to the management of which they were so scrupulously careful—the fair and the market bring the producer and the consumer in contact with each other. Whatever is gained is, at any rate, gained by one or the other of these. The fair and the market bring them together, and enable them to act for their mutual interest and convenience. The shop and the trafficker keeps them apart; the shop hides from both producer and consumer the real state of matters. The fair and the market lay everything open: going to either, you see the state of things at once; and the transactions are fair and just, not disfigured, too, by falsehood, and by those attempts at deception which disgrace traffickings in general.

" Very wise, too, and very just, were the laws against *forestalling* and *regrating*.[1] They were laws to prevent the producer and consumer from being cheated by the trafficker. There are whole bodies of men, indeed a very large part of the community, who live in idleness in this country in consequence of the whole current of the laws now running in favour of the trafficking monopoly. It has been a great object with all wise governments, in all ages, from the days of Moses to the present day, to confine trafficking, mere trafficking, to as few hands as possible. It seems to be the main objects of this government to give all possible encouragement to traffickers of every description, and to make them swarm like the lice of Egypt. . . . Till *excises*[2] and *loan-mongering*,[3] these vermin were never heard of in England. They seem to have been

---

[1] These laws were regarded, of course, as interferences with trade, and were soon abolished after the introduction of the *laissez-faire* policy of the Trade-puritanical party.

[2] The invention of the Puritans.

[3] The invention of statesmen of the second half of the seventeenth century under the government of the usurper William III.

hatched by that fraudulent system, as maggots are bred by putrid meat, or as flounders come in the livers of rotten sheep. The base vermin do not pretend to work : all they talk about is dealing; and the government, in place of making laws that would put them in the stocks, or cause them to be whipped at the cart's tail, really seem anxious to encourage them and to increase their numbers. . . ." [1]

But, alas! the fair and the market are as good as dead. Like the agricultural life upon which they rested as popular institutions, they were swept away by the triumph of trade and industry, and no one so much as questioned whether it were right or even desirable to abandon either.

The monstrous ulcers which are pompously and euphemistically called the hearts of the Empire grew swollen and inflamed to bursting-point under the new system, backed as it was by religion and the sword; so that even one hundred years ago one of the greatest and deepest men Europe has ever produced did not consider it an absurdity to say that the English were a nation of shopkeepers.

And now, when we look back on this terrible trans-formation; when we see the youth and flower of England's proletariat and lower middle class marching daily to their mill, to their factory, to their mine, to their suffocating stokeholds, to their stools in stuffy offices, to their shops where they stand like mere selling, virtueless intermediaries between the producer and the buyer, or their horrible benches in a telephone exchange; when we examine their pale and haggard faces, their listless eyes and their emaciated bodies, not even pretending to offer any spirited resistance to the ghastly dehumanising and devitalising nature of their labours; when, moreover, we watch the sweated pauper at his work, and inspect the environment in which he lives—the filthy grey slum, its crowded inmates, the bad air, the poor, adulterated and insufficient food and the racking labour—we cannot help being staggered by the amazing brutality of the whole scheme

[1] *Rural Rides* (edit. J. M. Dent), Vol. II, pp. 195–196.

of modern life, with loathsome, conscience-salving charity as its leaven, and by the inhuman cruelty of those who laid its most powerful and most solid foundation-stones.

Instinctively we cry with Cobbett, " My God! is there no spirit left in England? " [1] But when we remember how the metamorphosis of the Englishman was accomplished, what need is there for such a question? We know that there can be but very little spirit left in England.

Are there, however, any grounds for accusing the triumphant Puritan-parliamentary party of inhuman cruelty, as I suggest above? Were they brutal? Were they inhuman?

The difficulty in replying to such questions is not so much to collect evidence as to compress it, and to give its essence.

That the Puritan-parliamentary party were cruel and inhuman no historian ever seems to doubt. But even admitting that no deep religious transformation of a people can ever be accomplished without a cruel disregard of the type which it is proposed should be stamped out, and that, therefore, the very first accusation I have brought against the Puritan party in this essay—namely, that of having deliberately imposed the religion, hygiene and diet of commerce and trade upon their fellows in order to rear the necessary slaves for uncontrolled capitalistic industrialism—involved the accusation of cruelty, there is still a vast mass of other and independent evidence of their cruelty, as manifested in their activities as ordinary soldiers, rulers, prison-warders, judges.

To take only two instances from the Grand Rebellion —selected from the impartial and authoritative narrative of Professor S. R. Gardiner—who but a company of bloodthirsty and callous ruffians would in the fifth decade of the seventeenth century have put a gentleman of the stamp of Colonel Reade on the rack day after day, in the hope of wringing from him the secret of his master

---

[1] *Rural Rides*, Vol. II, p. 264.

Charles I's Irish schemes?[1] Who but a pack of cowardly blackguards would have behaved as Captain Swanley and his subordinates did in 1644 on the coast of Pembrokeshire? After capturing a vessel laden with troops from Ireland, these ferocious savages actually "tied the Irishmen back to back and flung them into the sea to drown!" And, as Gardiner observes: "Not a voice was raised in Parliament or in the City in reprobation of this barbarous cruelty."[2]

But perhaps the reader has read the trial of Strafford and the trial of Laud; and here, apart from all other evidence, has satisfied himself of the brutality of the Puritan party. Indeed, history teems with incidents which confirm my contention, and in concentrating upon the great Commonwealth leader alone, Oliver Cromwell, whose example must have exercised a powerful influence over his contemporaries, ample proof of my charge will be found.

Charles I, the most tasteful and, perhaps, the most patriarchal monarch that England has ever seen, was lying in London under sentence of death. Whatever Cromwell and his colleagues may have thought of him, at least the signing of the unfortunate King's death warrant should have been a solemn and awful affair. These men, it is true, did not know the nature of the crime they were committing, they did not in the least understand the great character of their victim or the value of the things for which he stood; but even if he had been the most disreputable criminal, the signing of his death warrant was certainly not a thing about which a joke could decently have been made or enjoyed. And yet what was Cromwell's behaviour at this solemn moment?

Like an idiotic school-boy he "ragged" and "rotted" his colleagues, and, after having affixed his damnable name to the warrant for Charles's murder, turned to Henry

---

[1] *History of the Great Civil War*, Vol. I, pp. 112–113.
[2] Op. cit., Vol. I, p. 337.

Martin, who was sitting at his side, and with his pen jokingly smeared Martin's face with ink! [1]

This is a small matter, you may think—so, perhaps, it is; but it is significant enough for my purpose. It sufficiently proves Cromwell to have been a man utterly devoid either of good taste or good feeling.

But now let me turn to charges which you may possibly consider more serious and more substantial. It is not generally known that in the seventeenth century Englishmen sold their own flesh and blood into the most cruel form of slavery—that form which compels a man to be transported to some distant land away from all his friends and relatives, to toil in tropical heat under the lash of a strange and frequently cruel taskmaster, and to die a victim to an inhuman tradesman who can turn human blood into gold. It is estimated that for some years after the triumph of the Puritans thousands were thus deported to Virginia and Maryland, and Cromwell was himself chiefly responsible for the enslavement of the majority of these thousands. In addition to the Scots taken on the field of Dunbar, the Royalist prisoners of the battle of Worcester and the leaders in the insurrection of Penruddock, Lingard tells us that Cromwell shipped thousands of Irish boys, girls and women to New England, into hopeless slavery, in his ferocious efforts to stamp out Catholicism in Ireland.[2]

All the tortures endured by the victims of the Inquisition pale before the lives of excruciating physical and mental suffering endured by these thousands of exiles, driven in herds on shipboard by Cromwell and his assistant butchers, and wrenched from all that they loved and cared for, in order to languish in bondage abroad.

The horrors of the negro slave trade were ghastly

---

[1] *Lives of the Archbishops of Canterbury*, by Dr. W. F. Hook, Vol. XI, p. 406.

[2] *History of England*, Vol. VIII, p. 357. For the measures taken by Cromwell to exterminate the Catholic population of Ireland, or to expatriate it, see pp. 356–357 and note.

enough. But what were they compared with the inhuman
and hideous brutality of this enslavement by one race of
its own kinsmen?

And you must not suppose that the negroes suffered
any more cruelly than did their white fellows in bondage.
Read E. J. McCormac's *White Servitude in Maryland*,
and see for yourself the brutalities of which these Puritans
in New England were capable. See especially the case of
William Drake,[1] who in September 1674 suffered such
excruciating tortures as a white slave that, as one reads
the story, it is difficult to credit one's eyes or the veracity
of the historian.

He who is simple-minded, innocent and stupid enough
to imagine that these unfortunate Irish Catholics suffered
the lash only for their indolence or for their inattention
to their labours had better give up thinking about these
matters altogether, and devote himself heart and soul to
the task that modern Fate in the twentieth century has
allotted him. But to one like myself, who has lived with
Low Churchmen and Nonconformists, and who has had
glimpses into their savage hatreds and their brutal potentialities, kept in check only by law and not by the humanity
or nobility of their natures, such a notion is quite absurd.
As one who has written so much about Nietzsche the
Ante-Christ, and who has been engaged for so long in
propagating his doctrines, I know what little chance of
quarter, of justice, or even of common or garden mercy,
I might expect if ever I got into their power, away from
the protection of the law.

Perhaps to some, though not to me, Cromwell's
massacres in Ireland will seem more terrible even than
his expatriations. The fact that, after taking Drogheda,
he gave up the inhabitants to a general slaughter, which
lasted for three days,[2] may strike one or two readers as

[1] On page 64 of the book mentioned above.

[2] In the words of a subaltern in Cromwell's own forces, the atrocities perpetrated at the massacre of Drogheda were terrible. Women
were ruthlessly murdered and their jewels torn from their necks and

more horrible and unpardonable than the brutality of his systematic enslavement of the Irish population.

As a matter of fact, whether this be so or not does not signify. The important point, and the one which is the real characteristic of all these atrocities, is the inhuman disregard of the unprotected and the helpless once they had come into the power of the conquerors. For this is precisely the characteristic of the whole of the modern scheme of life.

The revolting cruelties of our early factory and mining life, the appalling brutality of our treatment of children in industry, the callous barbarity of the apprentice traffic (once so scandalous in England), the hideous ill-treatment of the little chimney-sweeps, and the hard unconcern with which even the modern world allows thousands and thousands of the proletariat to be dehumanised and sickened by besotting and hopeless labours — all these things, with which no monarch, however benign, however patriarchal, can now interfere, I regard as merely part and parcel with the original brutality of the true ancestors of the modern world, the Puritan and Free Parliamentary party, whose power, whose principles and whose life-despising morality have been paramount in England ever since the last upholder of good taste and popular liberty was overthrown and murdered by them in the fatal fifth decade of the seventeenth century.

And when I look around me to-day, and perceive the harsh, ugly, unhealthy, vulgar, nervous and spiritless life of modern times; when I see the seething discontent in all grades of society, and especially in the women of north-western Europe, it seems to me by no means extravagant or even fantastic to suppose that at this present moment we are witnessing the final unfolding of the bloom, the finest flower and the most perfect product of that religion of gain and greed, of trade and

---

fingers, and little children were taken up by Cromwell's soldiers as bucklers of defence " to keep themselves from being shot or brained." See Lingard, op. cit., Vol. VIII, p. 635.

so-called liberty, of *uncontrolled* capitalism and unscrupulous exploitation; of the contempt of beauty, health,
vigour, sexuality and high spirits, whereof the hygiene,
the diet, the moral principles and the whole outlook on
the world are to be sought and found in the general
attitude of Prynne, Vane, Cromwell, Essex, Pym, Fairfax,
Harrison, Hewson, Waller and the rest of odd names and
natures which constituted seventeenth-century Puritanism.

CHAPTER VI

"The chief propelling power of democracy in England was misery."
J. HOLLAND ROSE, *The Rise of Democracy*, p. 19.

I FEEL that it is now time to restate my thesis, and that I shall be able to do so the more intelligibly for having written all that has gone before.

In the first place, however, I should like to direct attention to one or two popular points of view connected with my subject which, plausible as they may seem, are yet, in my opinion, based upon error.

With the test of success growing ever more and more final (for, according to most people nowadays, it is sufficiently crucial and decisive to be applied to anything and everything), there is a growing tendency among thinkers of the present day to repudiate any old institution whose dignity has been debased or overthrown by the *incompetence* of those in whose charge it happened to be found in the moment of its weakness.

As an example, take the institution of wealth and property.

There can be no doubt or question that wealth and property can be, and often prove, sacred and divinely beneficent powers. Once the lofty duties associated inevitably with wealth and property are fully comprehended by their owner, nothing is more sublime than the dual

237

A DEFENCE OF ARISTOCRACY

combination of a wise administrator and his possessions.[1]
But there can also be no doubt or question that for many
hundreds of years, here in England, and particularly
latterly, the divine dignity of wealth, the holy duties of
property, have again and again been wantonly violated
and desecrated by generation after generation of plutocrats who have made no effort to rise to the full beauty
and majesty of the position which wealth and property
ought invariably to involve. Thus in many quarters the
good name of wealth has been besmirched and sullied
beyond recognition, and has unfortunately given the
envious many a vile pretext for wagging their viperish
tongues.

That these things have happened nobody in his senses
would deny. The only doubt I entertain, however, is
whether most people put the proper construction upon the
fact.

Admitting that for many years now wealth and property
have been abused in England, save by a few select
individuals, who, nevertheless, have not been numerous
enough to give the direct lie to the others, how ought
this circumstance to be interpreted?

Unfortunately, there is a tendency all too general and
quite as absurd as it is artificial to lay the whole blame
of this abuse not on the unworthy individuals themselves,
but, if you please, on the shoulders of the institution of
wealth and property as such, as who should say that the
plough *must* be wrong if the furrow be crooked.

The Socialists bring a strong case against the abuses
of wealth; but I maintain that they bring no case whatever against wealth or property itself. And why they
should direct all their attacks against the institution of
power in property, when all the time this is obviously as

[1] The ancient Egyptians apparently held this view of wealth. An
Egyptian writer living 3,800 B.C. said : "If thou art rich after having
been needy, harden not thy heart because of thy elevation. Thou hast
become a steward of the good things belonging to the gods." Quoted
by Lecky, *Democracy and Liberty*, Vol. I, p. 328.

innocent as it is sacred, despite its pollution by many of its holders, is a question to which I have never yet heard them give a satisfactory reply.

Charles I would have said, just as Cobbett said long after him, " there is nothing wrong either in great wealth or in extensive property,[1] provided that it be wisely administered."

That is the whole point. Human nature, in casting her creatures, moulds many a one who is worthy of great possessions, and also many a one who is as unfit to use power in any form beneficently as a barbarous Fuegian. And where wealth and property are uncontrolled, as they always are in countries where *laissez-faire*, or something approaching to it, is the economical doctrine, both are sure to acquire a bad name through the villainy of the number of those who are unfit to possess them.

To attack wealth and property in themselves—to attack capitalism in fact—is, however, as shallow as it is specious. For these things have existed since the world began, and in their essence they are no more wrong than superior beauty or superior vocal powers. That which has ceased to exist, though, and whose collapse was the most fatal blow ever levelled at wealth and property, is that direction, guidance and control from above, which either a king of taste, a party of tasteful aristocrats, or a conclave of sages in taste, are able to provide, and which prevent the edge of power from being pressed too heavily and unscrupulously by the tasteless and vulgar among the opulent against the skins of their inferiors and subordinates.

The socialist attack upon wealth, then, is shallow and superficial. But so, too, is the democrat's attack on aristocracy, and for precisely the same reasons.

It is admitted that the aristocracies of Europe have on the whole wantonly blemished the sacred principle of aristocracy. It is also, however, a sign of the crassest and most unprecedented stupidity to repudiate the principle of aristocracy on that account; and it is more particularly

---

[1] See *Rural Rides* (edit. Dent), Vol. II, p. 7.

stupid to do so in England where we have only to think of such great men as Elizabeth's chief adviser Cecil, Charles's chief adviser Strafford, and the noble Earl of Shaftesbury of the nineteenth century—to mention only a few—in order to have before our eyes the very acme and quintessence of what the aristocrat should and can be.

And this brings me to my thesis, which I shall now restate before proceeding any further.

I take it that life, the process of living, is a matter of constantly choosing and rejecting. All life could be summed up in the two words *select* and *reject*. Healthy and permanent life chooses correctly—that is to say, selects the right, the healthy, the sound thing, whether it be a doctrine or a form of diet. Unhealthy and transient life chooses wrongly—that is to say, it selects the wrong, the unhealthy, the unsound thing in doctrine as in diet.

Now, most of the animals that we find about us to-day, creatures which are but the reduced and decimated representatives of the vast fauna which once inhabited our globe, have all survived as species only because they descend in a direct line from an uninterrupted chain of ancestors, all of whom chose the correct or proper thing in habit as in diet.

And, if these species continue to exist, it will be simply because, by means of their instincts (which are merely their spontaneous faculties of selecting and rejecting inherited from their discerning ancestors), they continue the process of life which is to choose and to thrust aside in the proper healthy and sound manner, just as their ancestors did.

As Bergson has shown so conclusively, however, Man, in acquiring his power over an infinitely greater range of adaptations than any animal has ever been able to achieve, has depended very largely upon his *intellect*, upon his rationalising faculty; and this has been developed at the cost of his instincts which, I repeat, constituted the transmitted bodily record of his ancestors' healthy selectings and rejectings.

We must imagine Man, therefore, as a creature cut

adrift from a large mass of incorporated ancestral selectings and rejectings, which must have been right, healthy
and sound, and we must see him as dependent very largely
upon his own wisdom for guidance in that continued
process of selecting and rejecting of which his life was still
bound to consist, after he had lost the direction of his
primeval instincts.

Admitting all this as being quite obvious, what is the
conclusion to which we are driven? As I pointed out in
the first chapter, we must conclude that this choosing and
rejecting in matters of doctrine and diet cannot be the
matter of a mere whim or mere passing caprice, neither
can it be a "matter of opinion"; it is a matter of life and
death. For the survival of man *as* man depends entirely
upon his life being carried on correctly.

The old and shallow English belief that every man has
a right to his own opinion, assumes that the individual conscience, whether it be that of a crossing-sweeper or of a
Chancellor of the Exchequer, is an adequate tribunal
before which any problem, however profound or intricate,
may be taken and solved.

But if life is a matter of choosing and selecting correctly,
there must be one opinion on these matters that is right,
and another that is wrong. Therefore to grant every one
the right to his opinion must in a large number of cases
involve not only anarchy but also a condonation of suicide;
for some men's opinions on vital questions, by being
erroneous, must lead to death—that is to say, to a cessa-
tion of man as *man*. It may, in addition, involve a condonation of murder; for those who hold and act upon
wrong opinions will not only cease to exist as men either
in their own or a subsequent generation; but they may
stand in the way of others' existing.

Very well, then, Taste, which is the power of discerning
right from wrong in matters of doctrine, diet, behaviour,
shape, form, constitution, size, height, colour, sound and
general appearance, is the greatest power of life; it is a
power leading to permanence of life in those who possess

it and who can exercise it. The absence of taste, or bad taste as it is sometimes called in these same matters, is a defect involving death, it is a defect leading to sickness or transiency in life in those who suffer from it.

Thus, the only man who could logically demand the right for the dictates of the absence of taste to be heard and obeyed would be the confirmed pessimist. The tenets of bad taste ought to be his guiding code of morals, because they are the certain road to death. On the other hand, the optimist who, on the stupid plea that every one has a right to his own opinion, unconsciously voiced the views of bad taste, would thereby defeat his own ends and prove himself a shallow fool into the bargain.

Having arrived at this conclusion, which slams the door in the face of anarchy (every one has a right to his own taste), and in the face of democracy (the taste of the majority is right), the question next arising is : Who is in possession of the touchstone of permanent life and of healthy life which I call taste? Who can choose correctly? Who is able to discriminate between the right and the wrong thing in doctrine, diet, behaviour, shape, form, constitution, size, height, colour, sound and appearance?

The complicated conditions arising out of a state of civilisation render it all the more important to arrive at some definite decision upon this point, seeing that there are many hidden and secret paths, and many broad and conspicuous highways too, in a state of civilisation, which, though they do not appear to the ordinary mind, for the first score of miles or so, to lead to Nemesis, do ultimately lead to a death which is apparent to the presbyopic sage.

The business of consciously choosing, therefore, has grown to be one of the most profound and subtle concerns of the activity of life; for, not every lethal draught is labelled *Poison*, nor has every one of life's elixirs been withdrawn from the ban put upon it by the man of no taste.

We have seen how things fared when the staggering insolence of the Puritan mind induced the most impossible Nonconformist sect in England to assume the lead in matters of choosing and discarding in this country. We have seen how many things they rejected and despised, that permanent and flourishing life demands and insists upon having, and we have seen how many things they selected and embraced which lead only to Nemesis and destruction.

I have not suggested, and do not wish to suggest, that, in thus choosing the wrong things, the Puritans *consciously aimed* at compassing their own or their fellows' degeneration and destruction. I submit only that while they thought they were but gratifying their own legitimate impulses and choosing the right things, they actually chose the wrong; and it was because they lacked taste, or, as the saying goes, because they had *bad taste*, that matters turned out as they did.

To take only one fact out of hundreds: if it be true, as medical men assure us it is, that, after three generations, born and bred cockneys become sterile, and that it is " the despised yokel who rejuvenates our cities, who recruits our army and who mans our ships of war," [1] then it is obvious that the kind of mind that chose the conditions in which the cockney is born and bred, or that laid the foundations of their existence, was one which had no taste, or had, as people say, *bad* taste.

It is often said when great changes or reforms come over a nation, that " the blind force of some abstract and inexorable economic law has made itself felt." This is simply nineteenth-century superior bunkum.

The whole truth of the matter is that when great changes or reforms have come over a nation, a certain portion of that nation—often the more powerful portion—has deliberately chosen and established those great changes or reforms in the teeth of an opposition which would have chosen otherwise. As I have shown in the case of the

[1] F. E. Green, op. cit., p. 15.

Puritanical reforms, you may, if you like, retrospectively superimpose a semblance of economic law on all that occurred in the seventeenth century, and thus disport yourself as a profound economist after the fact. But if, like myself, you are tired of this most fastidious kind of futility; you will see in the events of the first half of the seventeenth century, nothing more than a conflict of two tastes—one good, one bad, one vital, one deadly, one beautiful, one ugly—and the ultimate overthrow of the type which represented good taste.

For, there are millions of so-called economical laws, and any single group of them would be able to prevail, provided precisely that party in the State prevailed which in its taste happened to favour the direction or workings of that particular group.

To return, then, to my leading question: Who is in possession of this touchstone of what is favourable to permanent and healthy life, which I call taste? Who is able to choose correctly? Who can discriminate between the right and the wrong thing in doctrine, diet, behaviour, shape, form, constitution, size, height, colour, sound and appearance?

In answering this question I shall not reach up into the skies or out into the air for any new-fangled principle that has neither precedent nor warrant in fact. I shall rely simply upon the collected experience history gives us, and upon our knowledge of men and things.

For this, in short, is what I claim: I claim that among all the variations shown by all animals and all men, two are perfectly distinct, recognisable and constant, and might constitute the headings of a broad double classification of the fauna and of the men on this globe for all time. I claim that some animals and some men, thanks to a fortuitous and rare concatenation of happy circumstances, are born the examples of flourishing life—life in its maximum of beauty, health, vigour, will and sagacity within the species; and that others are born the examples of mediocre or impoverished life—life in its average or in its minimum of beauty, health, vigour, will and sagacity within the species.

This is a fact to be observed by all who live, breathe and think among living things; it is a fact that requires no demonstration because it is the experience of all.

Maximums, like minimums, are for some reason rarer occurrences than the mediocre or medium lives; but if we think of life at its best we instinctively call to our minds an individual who possessed or who possesses a maximum of beauty, health, vigour, will and sagacity; and if we think of it at its worst, we likewise remember or picture an individual who possessed or who possesses a minimum of beauty, health, vigour, will and sagacity. As examples more or less perfect of the first class taken at random, let me suggest the Frenchmen who were the second and third Dukes of Guise, the Englishman Strafford, the Corsican Napoleon, the Englishman Lord Stratford de Redcliffe, the German Goethe. As examples more or less perfect of the second class, also taken at random, let me suggest the Frenchman Calvin, the German Luther, the Englishman Cromwell, and the ancient Greek Socrates.

Now, if we can speak of "flourishing life" at all, how have we acquired our concept of such a phenomenon? Life is not a vast abstract and indefinite creature standing like a wire-puller and a monitor in the background of a group of living creatures. Only in poetical language do we speak of Life as something distinct from and independent of vital organisms.

We only know life, therefore, from the examples of living creatures we have seen, or of which we have heard. Life is a factor in the world process with which we are acquainted only through the living. All our notions about it are derived, not from our abstract poetical image of Life, but from creatures that have actually existed.

If, then, we speak of "flourishing life," we mean So-and-so who was an example of it—not a disembodied ideal created in the fervid imagination of a dreamer. In fact, So-and-so who was or is an example of flourishing life is the only canon and criterion we have of this kind of life; we have absolutely no other canon or criterion. And the same applies to the other kind, to impoverished and mediocre life.

This being so, the voice of flourishing life is not a voice descending from the clouds or any other part of the heavens; it is a perfectly definite sound emitted by those who are responsible for our being in possession of a concept of flourishing life at all. Just as the voice of mediocre, impoverished or degenerate life is a thoroughly definite sound which we expect to hear rising respectively from a crowd of ordinary people, from a party of decadents, or from a lazaretto.

Seeing, however, that our quest is to discover the needs, the desires, the likes and dislikes of flourishing life— because as optimists we desire permanence—whither shall we turn for an enumeration of these things? No scientific investigator, however wise, or however profound, can pretend to propound the taste of flourishing life by merely taking thought; no assembly of ordinary or mediocre people will ever be able to discover it by simply deliberating; because, as I have pointed out, it is not an abstract thing which can be imagined or formulated by an effort of the intellect—however great—it is a perfectly definite thing like gold, which you either have, or have not.

The only source to which we can turn, then, for the needs, the desires, the likes and dislikes of flourishing life, is the example of flourishing life himself. What he wants, flourishing life wants; what he selects, flourishing life selects; what he reviles, flourishing life reviles. His voice utters the taste of flourishing life; it is the canon and criterion of all that leads to permanence and resistance in life—it *is* Taste.

It may differ slightly in outward form in different times and climes—nay, it must so differ; but that it will remain constant if the same conditions persist is also obvious.

The taste of flourishing life, like our concept of it, is something the possession of which implies the possession of an example of flourishing life in our midst.· It is only then that life speaks healthily on matters of doctrine, diet, etc. And, as health in these matters means permanence and power, one of the first preoccupations of all great peoples should be to have, and to hearken unto, those who are examples of this maximum of life, and to take care that such are born.

For, as I have pointed out above, by far the greater majority of mankind are either simply ordinary, in which case their selectings and rejectings will be uncertain, mistaken, and often dangerously wrong; or they are decadent, in which case their selectings and rejectings are sure to be erroneous, and therefore prove deadly; or they are sick and degenerate, in which case their selectings and rejectings are *the* recipe *par excellence* for death.

The true aristocracy, then, the only genuinely best men on earth, are the examples of flourishing life whose likes and dislikes—whose discernment, in fact, is our canon of taste. The concern about living and lasting as a great power, as a great people, or as a great culture, is not only inextricably bound up with them, it is a futile, impossible, impertinent and hopeless venture without them.

And the healthy peoples of the past knew at least this fact. It was always their endeavour and their greatness to make the voice of flourishing life as generally and as universally accepted as possible. They were aware of the rarity of examples of flourishing life, so deeply aware, indeed, that all great religions may be regarded only as sacerdotal attempts at perpetuating and preserving the important utterances concerning taste of a few great men. They knew that one man who was an example of flourishing life, or many men who were examples of it, could not convert a whole nation into similar men; but they realised that he or they could impose their taste, their canon upon them, and thus make a people participators in their priceless and inestimable privileges.

Such an imposition of taste is, then, the greatest act of altruism that can be imagined; for it may save a whole nation from destruction for thousands of years; and their obedience is simply the soundest form of egoism possible; for, without it they may perish.

This, then, is the principle of sound aristocracy. *It is the principle of life.* Only he who is a pessimist can declare that it is wrong. For there are no two opinions about it; it is not a matter over which every upstart thinker can have his standpoint. He who is an optimist and who denies it is simply wrong.

But this principle of sound government is responsible not only for the healthy life and welfare of a people, not only for its survival and permanence, but also for its Culture and its Art. Because Art and Culture without direction from above, without a grand scheme of life providing the artist with the terms for his *interpretation of life*—such art is mere make-believe, mere affected fooling. For the architect, the sculptor, the painter, the poet, the musician and the actor are essentially dependants—dependants upon the superior man who is the artist-legislator. They themselves do not represent the will behind a great social organisation; they merely illustrate it and interpret it. That is why their function becomes meaningless and erratic, and their aims become anarchical, unless there be that in their life and in their nation which gives their art a meaning, a deep necessity and an inspiration. Hence the muddle in Art to-day! Hence its anarchy and its pointlessness! The chief artist, the artist-legislator being non-existent, his followers no longer have that momentum, that direction and guidance which their function requires for its healthy vitality.

Now, in the light of this basic principle of aristocracy, what precisely does democracy mean?

Most of us are familiar with the kind of argument which is usually levelled against democracy. I am not concerned, however, with the common and stereotyped attack which can be made upon the democratic position. When I read Sir Henry S. Maine's *Popular Government* and Lecky's *Democracy and Liberty*—works I would earnestly advise every one to study—I was amazed at the mass of subordinate, and to my mind entirely subsidiary reasons which the author of the latter work especially urges against democracy, and I was also deeply impressed by the sobriety of tone in which these reasons are marshalled and discussed. This work having been accomplished so well by others, however, I should only be performing a piece of superfluous duplication were I to restate all the cogent reasoning set forth by them.[1] While, therefore, I cannot help regarding Lecky's wonderful summing up of the usual case against democracy as very helpful to my position, and to the position of all those who, like myself, stand for an aristocratic order of society, and while I cannot help agreeing with much that Sir Henry Maine advances on the same side; I yet feel that the strongest and most formidable attack on the democratic position is left entirely out of our reckoning if we do not understand and are not told that *democracy must mean death*.

Although this conclusion arises quite naturally from the reasoning of the preceding pages, let me briefly restate the stages by which it is reached.

I have attempted to establish the following propositions—

(1) That life is a process of choosing and discarding in matters of doctrine and diet, etc.

(2) That to choose rightly in these matters for humanity means the permanence and the resistance of man as man, of a power as a power, of beauty as beauty.

(3) That to choose wrongly, or to discard wrongly, means the ultimate evanescence of man as man, or of a race as a race, or of a people as a people.

(4) That flourishing life, with its needs, is not an abstract entity which can be realised by meditation, or by

---

[1] The point that distinguishes the two volumes of Lecky's *Democracy and Liberty* more, perhaps, than anything else, seems to me to be the numerous adumbrations occurring throughout the work, of abuses and acts of corruption in the domain of politics which have taken place since the volumes were written in the years 1893–1895.

taking thought; but that it is something with which we become acquainted only through those rare possessors of it who are born from time to time amongst us, and who, for the lack of a better name, we may call the " lucky strokes of nature."

(5) That these possessors of flourishing life, or " lucky strokes of nature," are the only individuals of the human species who can exercise taste in discriminating between right and wrong in matters of diet, doctrine, etc., because flourishing life never becomes articulate about its likes and dislikes, save through them.

(6) That although one of these " lucky strokes of nature " cannot by an effort of will make all men like unto himself; he can, by imposing his taste upon his fellows, help them to share, for their own good, in the inestimable benefits of his judgment.

Now, what is the position of modern democracy? What indeed did the democrat claim even in the time of the Puritan rebellion?

While admitting that life is a matter of selecting and rejecting, the democrat has claimed all along, and in direct contradiction of historical facts, that not a few, but *all* men are endowed with the gift of selecting and rejecting correctly in matters of diet, doctrine, etc. ·

Forgetting Nature's irregularity, her comparatively few really lucky strokes, and her relatively infrequent absolute failures; forgetting, too, the total inability of man to become acquainted with the demands of flourishing life, save through its examples themselves, he, the democrat, literally overlooked, *discarded*, in fact, the question of Taste.

With those examples of flourishing life which are bound to occur, even in democratic days (though perhaps a little less frequently at such than at other times), he therefore proceeds to mass together all those examples of impoverished and mediocre vitality, who cannot open their mouths without expressing the taste of impoverished and mediocre life, and whose taste, accordingly, leads inevitably to impoverishment and mediocrity in life. The wrong thing is chosen and discarded in doctrine; the wrong things are selected and rejected in diet; however slow the process may be, the cumulative result must in the end be disastrous; and what happens? What cannot help happening? What indeed has happened under our very eyes?

Death begins to threaten all the power, all the health, all the institutions and all the prestige which were once built up by the tasteful founders of the nation.

Death begins to assail the nation's virtues, its character, its beauty, its world-ambition, its resistance, its stability, its courage and its very people. Death under the cover of insidious and almost imperceptible decay begins like a hidden vandal to undermine the great structure of a noble nation, and to level everything of value, of grandeur and of grace to the dust.

It cannot be helped! Nothing can stop it! It is a perfectly natural process. No mortal creation, however hardy, can bear for long the deadly course of selecting and rejecting the *wrong* thing in diet, doctrine, etc. And yet the very principle of democracy forces this lethal process upon all nations who adopt it.

The greater and nobler the edifice, of course, the longer it will take for the corrosive to destroy it. But, that its doom is inevitable, no one who has given the matter mature consideration can doubt for one moment.

Democracy forgets the vital element *Taste*. I say it forgets it; but it never actually takes it into account at all. It has no experience of the Taste which alone can discriminate between the right and the wrong thing; how could it make a place for it in the scheme of life?

Democracy, therefore, means death. It means inviting Life's adversary to the Council-board. It means admitting into the deliberations concerning life one, or rather many, who can be right about life only by a fluke, only by the merest accident, and who could no more be expected to voice the likes and dislikes of healthy permanent life, than a kangaroo could be expected to go foraging for pheasants.

And even if the whole of England rose up and with one voice cried out, " You are holding up an impossible scheme of things to replace that which, however bad, is at least possible and practicable! "

I should reply: "This may be a comment upon our present hopeless condition; it may be a true description of our degenerate state; it may possibly be a fact that the only practicable political means left open to us are those which lead inevitably to Nemesis; but that has nothing whatever to do with my contention. The fact that you no longer see any practicable method of installing " the lucky strokes of nature " in power does not in the least prove that democracy is not death! Often in a chase the last loophole left for a stag or a hare is the merciful precipice which shatters it to death. Do not let *us*, however, give *our* precipice euphemistic names which may make our death less noble even if thereby it become less painful. Do not let us call it the " liberty of man," the " freedom of Parliament," the " apotheosis of man's independence "!

Look about you to-day! See the confusion and chaos that reign over all questions of doctrine, diet, hygiene, behaviour, the relations of man to man, and above all of sex to sex; and ask yourself whether everything does not already bear the indelible stamp of having been left too long without the discriminating guidance of taste. Where traditional usages are breaking down, what is rising to take their place? Where old institutions are losing their power, where are the substitutes offered by the present age?

Whatever beauty we possess—the beauty of the warrior —marine and territorial—and his accoutrements, the beauty of royal ceremony and apparel, the beauty of our homes, of our churches, of our art, of our great inheritance, of our pride as a nation—derives all its power and all its depth not from the present, but from the past. The present is productive, it is even prolific, in innovations, complications and duplications; but it does not produce beauty—we are grateful if it produces things that are not positively ugly.

Thus, however weighty and forcible may be the arguments which Mr. Lecky or Sir Henry S. Maine bring against democracy, however imposing may be the mass of detail with which the former has adorned his indictment, the most powerful and most fundamental criticism of democracy still remains out of all reckoning, if notice is not taken of the profound truth that, since democracy includes the voice—and a majority of the voices—of mediocre or impoverished life, it is bound by slow or rapid steps to lead to Nemesis and to death.

You cannot with impunity drown the voice of flourishing life in your councils; you cannot go unpunished if Taste be outshouted at your governing board; you cannot hope to be permanent, or to attain to even relative permanence, in your power and prestige, if the very touchstone of that which is sound in choosing and discarding be excluded from your deliberations, or as good as excluded, by being hopelessly overwhelmed.

I have been at some pains in the preceding chapters of this book to show how far astray mankind has wandered in England, owing to the lack of the element Taste in our midst. I have enumerated a few of the hundreds of innovations and novelties that have been allowed to establish themselves in our society without provoking even a question, much less a protest, among the members of the governing body. I have also shown that while in Charles I we had at least some one who understood a number of the essential elements of true rulership, and primarily Taste, he was grossly and absurdly mistaken by his contemporaries, and was brutally supplanted by men who not only lacked the faintest notion of what true rulership meant, but, as I have tried to show, are also entirely responsible for our present muddle and madness to-day.

And, after all that I have said, how foolish does the popular belief appear which would have it that there is an obscure and natural law prevailing in this universe that nations should rise and fall, flourish and decline, despite all the efforts on the part of man to hold them upright. The very disparity between the duration of Egypt and Greece as civilised powers, or between the cultures of China and Europe, shows how eccentric this law must be, if it be a fact at all. Without the interfering action of a *vis major*, however, quite independent of the *inner* vitality and power of the civilisation itself and of its people, who can tell how long Egypt or China or ancient Peru might have lasted as examples of permanence for the whole world to witness? [1]

And when I contemplate this wonderful and stupendous Empire of Great Britain, and think of the noble blood and effort that have been spent in building it; when I realise its fabulous powers for good or evil, its almost unprecedented influence for virtue and quality, in the world, its vastness and its amazing organisation, I shudder to hear the modern cynic speak with calm resignation about a certain law of nations, according to which all this marvellous structure must vanish and be forgotten. I hate to listen to the sad but certainly unagitated tones with which the cultured Britisher sometimes acknowledges the fact that his country is standing at the cross roads, and that the heads of the foremost horses show a decided twist in the direction of the highway to ruin.

Knowing of the existence of no such obscure law relating to the rise and decline of nations—*for nations, unlike individuals, can regenerate their strength and their youth* [2]—I know only one thing, and that is, as I have said, that taste is a power of life, leading to permanence

[1] For an interesting discussion on the causes of national decline, and for a learned refutation of the old " moral " reasons of former historians, let me refer the reader to Gobineau's *l'Inégalité des Races Humaines,* Otto Sieck's *Geschichte des Untergangs der Antiken Welt,* and Reibmayr's *Inzucht und Vermischung.*

[2] See Otto Sieck's argument ending : " *Es ist also falsch, dass die gleichen Gesetze für Individuen und ganze Nationen gelten,*" op. cit., pp. 261–262.

in those who possess it, whereas the absence of taste is as certain to lead to death as any poison, slow or gradual, that the ingenuity of man ever concocted.

I know, therefore, that if this vast creation, the British Empire, be really in danger, if it be truly decadent and degenerate, it is possible to rescue it; its salvation is a conceivable thing; its preservation an act within our reach and within our power. And he who does not feel that there is something worth saving here, and something worth fighting for—whether he be a Scotsman, Welshman, Canadian, Australian or Irishman—is unworthy of being placed in the presence of anything great or noble created by the hands of man. I do not suggest, mark you, that the patriot's notion of preserving the British Empire should necessarily consist in becoming its wholehearted advocate alone. On the contrary, there are times when one's greatest friend would deem it an act of friendship to assail one. But all I wish to imply is that to any one —be he British or Colonial—there must appear to be something in this great realm that is worth perpetuating and guarding from ruin. And no friendship, no patriotism, could be more radical and fundamental than that which recognised that Taste, alone, the guidance and direction of flourishing life, alone, can be of service and of value here; and that nothing which thwarts and delays the prevalence of that one quality in our midst can be looked upon with patience, not to speak of equanimity. If England had never in her history produced men of taste; if her national records contained no instances of genuine ruler-spirits; if, as some would have us believe, there is something inveterately perverse about the Anglo-Saxon which renders all hope of his permanence as a world-power merely a wild and feverish dream, it would indeed be a hopeless outlook, and we should have no other alternative but to acquiesce with as good grace as possible in a doom as ignoble and inglorious as our past has been great. But I have myself, in this small book, been able to refer to a goodly number of such spirits;

nay, in the very worst period of England's history I have
been able to point to a whole number of them, and it
would be simply a piece of gratuitous injustice to assume
that such spirits will not or cannot occur again, or that,
if England's powers are suffering from momentary ex-
haustion, that these cannot be revived and regenerated
by a proper and judicious selection and encouragement of
her best and noblest qualities.

The above, then, is my thesis. It now only remains
for me to attempt to outline the manner in which the
principles it involves can be made practicable. But though
this will constitute the burden of the ensuing chapters, I
shall straightway reply to certain obvious objections to
my standpoint which occur to my mind as I write, and
shall conclude this chapter with one or two considerations
relating especially to the decline of manners and morals
under the modern Democracy of Uncontrolled Trade and
Commerce—considerations which I think all the more
worth stating, seeing that they are of a kind not usually
recorded in attacks upon the democratic position, and are
not, therefore, to be found in the ordinary anti-democratic
book or pamphlet of the day.

Turning to the obvious objections first, let me reply
to the opponent who very naturally inquires where and
when do I find the historical warrant for my thesis.

I find it in great historical individuals, and in groups
of individuals, who may be said to be, and who were
undoubtedly, examples of flourishing life.

Read the canon of the Brahmans—the Book of Manu;
read the canon of the Jews—the Books of Moses; read
the canon of the Mahommedans—the Koran! [1] In each
of these books, if you study them with care and understanding, you will see but the record of a few men's or
of one man's taste in diet, doctrine, behaviour, etc. And

[1] It is interesting to note, in reference to the facts adduced in
Chap. V. of this book, that the Koran forbids the drinking of coffee to
the faithful.

whatever permanence or power you may ascribe to the obedient followers of these books you will realise is due ultimately only to the elaborate direction and guidance of one man or of many men of taste, in the matter of selecting and rejecting.

In the case of the Jews and of the Mahommedans, for instance, we are concerned with two men, Moses and Mahommed, who were undoubtedly maximums of flourishing life; in the case of the Brahmans, we are concerned with an aristocratic group or body of examples of flourishing life, of whose traditional laws and customs the Book of Manu is but a codification.

As further examples of groups, or bodies of examples, of flourishing life whose rule made for the permanence, power and prosperity of their peoples, I would also refer to the semi-religious and semi-temporal aristocracies of ancient Egypt, whose culture endured for so many thousands of years, and of ancient Peru, whose culture, founded and maintained by the Incas, is, with Egyptian culture, one of the most amazing examples of aristocratic wisdom, foresight, clemency, practicality and art that the world has ever seen.

Neither will it be possible for you to divorce the circumstances of China's extraordinary permanence from the fact that, in Confucius, his great predecessors and his equally great followers, the Chinese people had men of taste, as I understand them, who once and for all laid down the basis of healthy and permanent life for the whole nation. While even if you inquire into the undoubtedly healthy regimen of the devout Catholic, with all his fast days and lenten abstinence (which were simply a religious insistence on periodical intervals of vegetarian or non-stimulating diet), and his festivals (which were likewise only the religious sanction granted for occasional fits of dionysian indulgence), you will be surveying merely the canonised taste of some of the greatest specimens of flourishing life that arose during the Middle Ages.[1]

[1] Among the rocks on which Catholicism foundered we cannot

A DEFENCE OF ARISTOCRACY

That the nations of antiquity fell only after they had ceased to hearken to the voice of flourishing life is a fact which must have struck many a historian or reader of history. We have only to think of the many exhortations, open or covert, on the part of the Jewish prophets, such as Jeremiah, for instance, or on the part of the Greek reactionaries, such as Aristophanes and Thucydides, or on the part of the Roman writers, such as Cicero [1] or Livy,[2] in which the keynote, tacit or expressed, is always fidelity to the nation's best traditions and to the customs and virtues of its forefathers (based, of course, upon the dictates of flourishing life), in order to realise how essential and how vital these virtues and customs of forefathers must have seemed. While in China the extreme reverence paid to ancestors, alone, is merely a socio-religious custom guarding against a too dangerous departure from the tradition of flourishing life.

It is even perfectly safe to prophesy, in the case of a race like the Chinese, that any material departure from the customs of their ancestors (which rely upon the original pronouncements of flourishing life) instigated by bad European taste is sure to lead to decadence and death; and unless the Chinese have the wisdom to use the science and culture of Europe merely as weapons with which to fight the European, without letting either that science or culture enter too deeply into their social and spiritual life, they are almost sure to be landed upon the highway to ruin. For if they really become democratic; if they not

---

include a lack of men of taste in its organisation, for from this lack it did not suffer. The primary reason I should give for its failure is the fact that its doctrine was paradoxical from the start, and contained an inward conflict ; and, secondly, that it attempted the task of the cosmopolitisation of the world without reckoning with the anarchical and barbarian people of the north of Europe, who were still insufficiently cultured to understand or appreciate any rule or order superior to that which they themselves had evolved.

[1] We have only to recall Cicero's constant reiteration of the expression " *mos majorum.*"

[2] See *History*, Book V, Chapters 51–54.

only pretend to play at Parliaments, but actually allow free parliaments to become the *summum bonum* of their existence, they will certainly land in disaster, owing to that strong element of ordinary or impoverished life which will enter into the administration of their public and social affairs.

In the ruin and downfall of the Peruvian civilisation built up by the Incas, it is true we have an instance of another kind of disaster—a disaster which cannot well be traced to any flaw in the inner harmony and wisdom of the civilisation itself; but here I think we have a right to speak of a *vis major* which cannot well be foreseen or forestalled by any precept of taste. Flourishing life may choose and discard the right thing in every particular, but it cannot help the earthquake which within a measurable space of time is preparing to swallow it and its order up; neither can it be so omniscient as to foretell and forestall an overwhelming invasion from a people that seems to have risen out of an ocean which hitherto had appeared to be endless.

Another opponent may ask, "Who instals these men of taste in power? Who 'elects' them to their position of trust and influence?"

Looking back upon history, I find that no such act of installation or election ever actually takes place, save as a surface movement. What really happens, what has always happened—save in degenerate times—is that those among humanity who were examples of flourishing life have always asserted and established their superior claims themselves. And in communities in which the proper values prevail concerning greatness, nobility, taste, beauty, power, sagacity and health, they find themselves as naturally raised to power by their own efforts as a frog rises to the water's surface by the movements of its agile limbs.

True, it is difficult to point to a great religion or to a great nation that has originated from the single-handed efforts of one man; but what usually occurs is this, that just as one fool makes many, so does one maximum of life prove a loadstone to all his equals and his approximations. Thus, while we find that a galaxy of men of power seem quite spontaneously to have clustered round the Founder of the Christian religion, we also see a group of the most able warriors spring as if by magic round the person of the great Napoleon.

It is this element in men of flourishing life which helps them to assert and establish their claims—this element of discrimination and attraction by which they choose and draw to them men who are like themselves and who can but strengthen their holy cause.

But for any such assertion and establishment of higher claims to be possible, the pre-requisite is that the community in which the attempt is made should, in the first place, be susceptible by education and general outlook to the charm and beauty of the values of flourishing life.

In a community where the wrong, the decadent, the degenerate and the impoverished values prevail concerning the qualities greatness, beauty, bravery, nobility, power, sagacity and death, it is obvious that the claims of superior life will not even be heard or understood, much less, therefore, appreciated.[1]

The very first step, therefore, to the assertion and establishment of superior claims in our midst is that we should be steeped in the values which make a recognition of such superiority a possible achievement. It is for this reason that all chance of a regeneration and a rejuvenation of a decadent society is such a hopeless matter; because although many may be born who could effect the necessary reforms, the fibre of the people is not precisely drawn to that degree of tension which would cause it to respond and vibrate in unison with its potential saviours. And

---

[1] As a matter of fact, in England and Western Europe of the twentieth century, all values are not only such as to make the rearing of great men improbable, but also of a nature which make the recognition and utilisation of greatness well-nigh impossible, even when it does appear.

a saviour, however willing, would be unable to effect anything if the people among whom destiny placed him were totally unable to respond to his personal appeal or react to the stimulus of his body and his spirit.

All preparation for salvation, all first steps to reform, in a decadent society should, therefore, consist in so shaping the body of the people, and so tightening the strings of their heart, that when the examples of flourishing life come to draw their bow, as it were, across the instrument by means of which, alone, they can assert their superiority, this instrument may respond with warmth to their touch, and not groan and screech discordantly until they are disheartened.

This may sound poetical, fanciful and, maybe, grandiloquent language wherewith to express an essential principle of practical politics. But let no one suppose that it is any the less reliable for that reason. He who declared that what we needed was a "transvaluation of values" hit the nail on the head in this matter. For unless the spirit of England be chastened and purified by a great disaster or by a tremendous awakening brought on by a vast trouble of some sort,[1] nothing but a "transvaluation of values," nothing, that is to say, but an attempt to make those values prevail which will render the people able and willing to recognise the claims of superior life, can ever make the people disposed to allow saviours to rise in their midst, or to appreciate them when they attempt to rise.

And this is what so many people overlook when they face the question of the revival of aristocracy. They

---

[1] It is curious to note that Bolingbroke held an almost similar view. He does not speak of a "transvaluation of values" as an alternative to a great disaster; but he certainly recognises the value of a disciplinary disaster or disciplinary stroke of fortune when a nation is decadent. He says: "It seems to me, upon the whole matter, that to save or redeem a nation under such circumstances from perdition, nothing less is necessary than some great, some extraordinary conjuncture of ill-fortune, or of good, which may *purge*, yet *so as by fire*."—*The Idea of a Patriot King*, pp. 64–65.

forget, in the first place, that examples of flourishing life assert their own superior claims; but, secondly, that, in order that this assertion may be effective, the proper spirit and the proper outlook must reign in the world, so that these superior claims may be met by some response.

Thus all those who to-day are anxious to revive an aristocracy of taste and discrimination which alone would be able to elevate us, and save Western civilisation from ending its momentary downward course in the pit of ruin and oblivion, will strive to find out first which are the values favourable to the recognition of superior life when it appears, and then, if they differ from existing values, to transvalue the latter with all possible speed and determination.[1]

It may be objected by some that, while it is easy to talk glibly of transvaluing values, the task is not so simple as it may seem—nay, is it either practicable or possible? Even when values have been transvalued, would it be such a simple matter to impose them upon a whole people?

I would not contend for a moment that this task of transvaluing values is *simple*, any more than is the task of imposing them upon a whole people; but that the feat is a practicable and perfectly possible one is proved not only by ancient but also by quite recent practice.

To avoid dwelling once more on the stupendous trans-valuation of values inaugurated by the Puritans, think only of the amazing unanimity of opinion concerning certain fundamental and essentially modern questions that reigns to-day in England! Consider the almost universal

---

[1] At the present moment it cannot even be urged by the indolent that this is an inquiry and a duty too fantastic to be undertaken. It cannot even be said that it is a task too colossal to be faced by one generation ; for, however inadequately the detail of the work may have been accomplished, and however much there may remain of this detail to be done, the modern world has in Nietzsche's stupendously courageous inquiry into the broad question of sick and healthy values, an outline of its task, and a signpost as to the direction that it should pursue, which it can ignore only at its own hurt and peril.

acceptance of the subsidiary values of modern uncontrolled capitalistic commerce and industry, with their unabashed and almost truculent worship of material wealth, speed, so-called " Progress," mechanical contrivances of all sorts, tasteless comfort, vulgar pleasures and shallow versatile learning! Question the non-analytic masses— whether of Belgrave Square, Shoreditch or Kensington (they are all " masses " to-day)—and ponder over the extraordinary agreement between them—sometimes, as we have seen, contrary to their own best interests—with regard to all questions of taste, of hope, of pleasure, of leisure, of industry and the like; and ask yourself whether something on a grand scale in the nature of a transvaluation of values has not already occurred, even since the time when men so different from each other as Byron and Cobbett · contemplated with the gravest alarm the innovations that, in the early years of last century, threatened completely to transform the face of England!

So far from its being impracticable or impossible, there is, as a matter of fact, nothing less difficult of accomplishment in the whole sphere of government than precisely this task of swaying, modifying and rendering uniform the opinions of those who expect their cue, their lead, their example to come from their leaders, and who often accept it cheerfully and unhesitatingly even when those leaders are but half fitted — or worse still — for their responsible position.

" But," continues my opponent, " if you admit this factor of recognition on the part of the masses of the people, you yield up your whole case to me; for that is the democratic principle, that people should be ruled only by their own consent."

I deny this imputation most emphatically, because I see no relation whatsoever between what I have said and the principle of democracy.

The assent which the people give · to the claims of superior life in my case has nothing whatever in common with that rational exercise of judgment which a democratic people are called upon to make in considering the *pros* and *cons* of a certain measure, a certain policy, or a certain doctrine.

The people who, as I say, respond to the claims of superior life do not need to *understand* or to *judge* the examples of flourishing life; nor could they do so if they tried, for this would imply an equal modicum of understanding on the part of the masses to that possessed by their superiors themselves, which it would be obviously absurd to expect. The people, however, do not say "we want these men because we understand them," but "we want them because we feel they understand us." They do not say "we want them because we judge them rightly," but "we want them because we feel they judge us rightly." It is the attitude of the child to its mother. The child can and does adore its mother without in the least understanding the principles or virtues of true motherhood. It assents to its mother as a mother, because it sees that its mother understands its needs, its likes and its dislikes, its foibles and its powers.

In the same way a people can assent to the rule or leadership of certain individuals without in the least understanding the *rationale* of their deeds and policy, without having attempted to enter into the *pros* and *cons* of their principles and measures; and seeing that, according to my hypothesis, the people would be unqualified to attempt such acts of judgment, the fact that, like children, they are simply able to feel and respond to those who understand and judge them correctly saves them from all necessity of appealing to that faculty of rationally weighing *pros* and *cons*, and of giving practised consideration to deep principles and policies, which is indeed presupposed by a democracy, and without the assumption of which even the abstract idea of democracy would be absurd.

Thus while the people, in my case, respond as a child does to its mother, because it feels itself understood, in a democracy it asserts its will because it claims that it *understands*—obviously a very different matter! In a proper aristocracy the people assent to the nature of their rulers without being called upon in the least to perform any mental gymnastics which, however well educated they may be, they are totally unfitted by tradition, upbringing and bodily gifts to perform; in a democracy they are drawn into the confidence of the elected active administrators, they share their troubles, their anxieties and responsibilities. They are actually invited to criticise, modify, arrest and even initiate certain acts of policy. In an absolute democracy they really govern.

Clearly, then, I yield no point to the democrats when I agree that the first pre-requisite to a beneficent aristocrat's rule is the sympathetic response of the people whom he would guide and govern. The oldest principles of Royalty and Aristocracy always regarded this tacit assent of the masses as one of the proudest tributes to their beauty and perfection; but this has absolutely nothing to do with the idea of absolute or even representative democracy.[1]

The assent I speak of is the kind given by and expected from the people of China. For many hundreds of years now the Chinese have been expected to assent to their ruler's rule; but this act of assent has never presupposed any more considerable exercise of judgment than that which can clearly be included in the act of realising that you are being understood and cared for as your body and your spirit require.

I trust that the difference is now obvious. The new element introduced by the idea of democracy is this: the

---

[1] According to Traill, even the Earl of Strafford seems to have considered the assent of the people as an essential warrant of good rule. Traill says: "Wentworth identified the happiness of the people with the vindication and establishment of the power of the Crown." And, speaking of his attitude to the assent of the people, Traill says: "It seems to me that he prized this assent and reckoned on securing it; only he refused to admit that the assent of an elective assembly—or at least of such an assembly as his own experience had familiarised him with—was equally necessary or equally possible to be secured by the governor."—*Lord Strafford*, p. 60.

people, instead of assenting to a manner of life, a scheme of life, designed and maintained by their superiors, and of which they only feel the working, are invited to consider whether they approve of their leaders doing this or that, whether they agree to their leaders engaging upon *this* or *that* course, whether the solution their leaders have given of a certain problem is the right one—all matters of principle, ratiocination, deep learning, leisured meditation and, above all, taste! They are conjured to think about the profoundest questions, the weightiest of state issues is not withdrawn from their deliberations, and their veto is final.

I beg to press upon the reader's notice that there are a host of stupid and utterly unwarrantable assumptions in this position, with which I should scorn to have any connection. When, therefore, I speak of the assent of the governed, let my opponents not think for a moment that I am either so confused or so utterly abandoned in so far as sound doctrine is concerned as to mean anything so ridiculous and so preposterously untenable as the democratic idea of the people's part in politics.

" But," my adversary will cry, " if you acknowledge that the assent of the people is necessary even to good aristocratic rule, then you commit yourself to granting the masses the right of rebellion when that rule is not good! "

Certainly! I admit it! And, as I pointed out in the first chapter of this book, in admitting the necessary correlative of popular assent, which is popular dissent, or rebellion, I agree not only with the deepest thinkers of China, but also with the deepest thinkers of Europe.[1]

Rebellion is the only means to which a subject people can turn, in order to rid themselves of tasteless rulers, once the caste to whose guidance they originally assented, has from some cause or other, degenerated; there is no other means. But the fact that before such rebellions have taken place—as in the case of the French Revolution, for in-

[1] See p. 14, Chapter I.

stance—tasteless oppression has, as a rule, grown so terrible as to be literally insufferable, shows with what docility and patience a mass of men will wait with unflagging hope for a salutary change, before they reluctantly avail themselves of the extreme and violent measure, naturally so loathsome to that portion of mankind which only asks to be left in peace, security and contentment, while it performs its daily round of duty, love and recreation.[1]

Let it be pointed out, *en passant*, however, that modern democracy is robbed, hopelessly and irretrievably, of this final and extreme cure of misrule. The hydra-headed administration of a modern democratic state, however bad and corrupt it may be, defies the salutary shears of any rebellion. As in the case of the limited liability company, of which it is the true parent and prototype, no one in a democratic government is responsible when anything goes wrong; and, unless the people choose to lop off their own heads, it is impossible for them to make an expiatory offering for any of the crimes and errors of what is ostensibly their own administration.

The cause of this appalling dilemma is to be traced, in the first place, to the average Englishman's misunderstanding of the essentials of real rulership. No child, however priggish and precocious, would be so foolish as to regard itself as wholly self-supporting and self-guiding, if, owing to their misdeeds, it had to throw over its parents. It might abandon its father and mother; but its one object thenceforward would be either to attach itself to some other adult who could beneficently undertake the respon-

[1] The Puritan Rebellion was an instance of another kind. Here we had oppression—certainly! but it was the sort of oppression that good taste will always exercise over the absence of taste, that good health will always exercise over the absence of health. And, in this instance, as I have shown, it was not the people rebelling against their rulers, but a vulgar, mercenary and influential portion of the rulers rebelling against the more tasteful portion, and with cries of ".Liberty" and " A Free Parliament," luring, by subterfuge, many of the ignorant masses over to their side.

sibility of ruling it, or readily to acquiesce in the claim of any beneficent adult who came forward with the offer to rule it.

On the same principle a popular rebellion in China, previous to the importation of shallow English and European doctrines, meant simply a change of rulers—*not* a usurpation of the duties of ruling on the part of the masses.

Englishmen and Europeans generally, on the other hand, seem completely to have misunderstood the true nature of ruling; and as often as their rulers have failed in their duties, they appear to have considered the occasion a sufficient excuse for perpetrating that grossest of all errors—the usurpation of the seat of rule by non-rulers.

A most puerile and, at the same time, senseless *non sequitur* is involved in this error; for, although the demise or suppression of a great ruler caste may be an extremely staggering event, it nevertheless possesses none of those magic or miraculous powers which can convert a man into a creature which he is not, or which can endow with superior qualities a whole body of mediocre and ordinary men who, hitherto, have led mediocre and ordinary lives.

If all the engineers in Christendom were to become defunct to-morrow, none but the veriest dolt of a layman would believe that he thereby automatically became an engineer; and yet the equivalent of this act of impudence and stupidity is one which has been perpetrated again and again in the field of practical politics.

The supreme difficulties of ruling, the terribly profound problems it involves, the great native gifts it requires, and the enormous number of human sympathies it calls into play, have only seldom been appreciated in Europe, and that is why non-imaginative and non-meditative classes cease to recognise their limitations, once their values become such that they do not favour the rise of true rulers in their midst.

Continuing to raise objections, my opponent may exclaim: " If it is, as you say, that certain exceptional, well-favoured individuals establish the taste for their fellows for whole centuries, what need is there of the further exercise of taste once this initial promulgation of the law has been accomplished? "

It is obvious that if we were in a world without seasons, and in a universe in which change were not a constant factor with which man is obliged to reckon, a single proclamation of the law in matters of choosing and discarding would certainly suffice for all eternity; hence the natural but hopeless attempt on the part of the common people of all countries in which change is very slow, to try at all cost to preserve and maintain the *status quo*, once they feel themselves in possession of valuable utterances concerning taste; for they instinctively realise that these can continue to apply only so long as the *status quo* persists. As examples of such peoples, behold China and all Mahommedan countries!

But we are in a world in which change has to be faced as a condition of existence, and although some of the utterances of taste will last as valuable truths until the crack of doom, others will require modification, adaptation and readjustment; while all innovations and novelties will exact fresh efforts and judgments of taste, not included in the original promulgation of the law.

In all great civilisations, then, into which change is constantly entering in the form of a host of isolated and often obscure innovations, a continued exercise of taste, subsequent to the original promulgation of the law, is an essential pre-requisite of healthy and permanent life; and it was for this continued exercise of taste that the priests of ancient Egypt provided when they selected, educated and initiated those who were going to replace them in office under the man-god the Pharaoh, and that the Chinese provided when they selected, educated and initiated the candidates for those walks of life which lead to the mandarinate.

So much for the first crop of obvious objections, which

seemed quite naturally to spring from the clear statement of my thesis; now it will be my endeavour to discuss with more detail the subject contained in the title to this chapter.

To many readers, probably, there will seem little need to enter into the details of the question. They may think, and perhaps rightly too, that if my thesis be correct—then, since we are now living under a Democracy of uncontrolled Trade and Commerce, in which men of taste are far outnumbered by men of no taste, the necessary consequence must be a decline, not only in art and culture, but also in the manners and morals of the mass of the population. This is perfectly true. If my thesis be correct, this must inevitably be the consequence of our present state. Such readers will point to many signs of the times which show conclusively not only that manners and morals are declining, but also that they continue to do so more and more every year.

There is a *laisser-aller* in conversation, behaviour and dress, the treatment of women by men and *vice versâ*, the performances at music-halls and musical comedies, which, while suggesting an increase in licence, is still covert, cowardly and brutal, and has nothing of the nature of a healthy return to paganism in its constitution. Newspapers are becoming cruder without showing any more mastery or art in regard to questions of sex. Side by side with this, there is among the barbarian section of the nation a tightening rather than a relaxing of the strings of Puritanism, and the negative attitude towards life and humanity is consequently increasing in such quarters.

With regard to manners, it must be obvious to all who move and travel in big cities, that these are at their lowest ebb. Motors hoot peremptorily at anybody and everybody; their chauffeurs, forgetting that the highway belongs first to the pedestrian and secondly to the vehicle, insist upon your making way for them at all costs, charge at you like at an enemy, sometimes compelling you to run at the risk of considerable danger to your person. And the meek way in which the pedestrian, as a rule, repeatedly submits to this treatment is sufficiently revelatory. The meaning of this blustering importance on the part of the new-fangled vehicle, is that it is now the symbol either of opulence, or at least of fair means; and that these are now the highest values recognised either by the leaders or the loafers of a big urban population. The driver of a car, whether he be the owner or the paid servant, feels he is intimately linked up with the most powerful force in the nation—money; his impudence is the impudence of the occupant of a place of power and possession, which does not necessarily impart any culture or taste to him who occupies it.

And who are these meek people who wait for whole minutes by the road-side, who advance, retreat, venture a few steps and recoil, plunge and stagger, to the hoot of the new car? They are ordinary pedestrians, who may be jealous of wealth, who may covet it, who may even despise it temporarily for the same reason as the fox called the grapes green; but who, by every one of their movements, acknowledge, nay, proclaim to the world that in their heart of hearts they are convinced that mere material wealth and the comfort it brings are the highest things on earth. Resent as they may the importunity of all the affluence which they behold, they are still worshippers at its shrine, and think that there is indeed some holy right, some sacred privilege behind this blatant, ostentatious and tyrannical " Clear-the-road ! " " Clear-the-road ! " implied by the motor-hoot which they have neither the spirit nor the necessary " outlook " to resist or scorn. Not one of them knows the real sacredness of wealth, the real virtues of opulence; not one of them has a notion of its true dignity, its possible holy powers. They know only that it brings comfort, motor-cars, theatres, week-ends away from the smoky " wen," and fine, sleek clothes. Hence, though they may envy those who possess it, they have no notion of the contempt or even the anger which rises up in the breast of the man of taste when he sees the powers of wealth thus reduced to a mere purchasing power over amusements, good dinners, comfortable surroundings and speedy conveyance!

None but a spiritless and wholly subjected people, completely convinced of the superlative value of money as a purchasing power of this nature, would ever have tolerated the advent of the motor-car. With its cloud of dust and puff of scornful stinks as it turns its back on you, with its insolent command of " Clear! " as it ploughs through the human crowd in front of it, with its tasteless and inconsiderate treatment of the rural village and its children [1]— it is a fitting symbol of the arrogant contempt which mere wealth may well feel for the mass of foolish and spiritless sheep, which have allowed it, uncontrolled by taste or good feeling, to become paramount in their midst.

Some such considerations will naturally occur to the mind of the thoughtful reader, and he will feel that these and many others that could be mentioned tend to confirm my contention concerning the present decline of morals and manners. He may also have heard of the overbearing rudeness of the sporting " gentry," or of private parks which, not so very long ago, were, by the courtesy of their owners, kept open to the public, until the gross and inconsiderate behaviour of picnicking parties and touring cyclists forced these generously disposed owners to close their gates against all strangers. He may think of the increasing disrespect with which young people treat their elders, inside and outside the home. He may himself be able to testify to the decline in the dignity and good tone of Parliamentary debates. He may have observed a growing lack of reserve in dress and speech in all ranks of life. He may be aware of a certain pronounced deterioration in

[1] A fact from Mr. F. E. Green's book sheds a curious light on this aspect of the question. He speaks of a notice-board he saw by a roadside hedge near Greywell, Hants, which proclaimed the following message : " Please drive cautiously. Hound puppies are at walk in Greywell village." As the author remarks : " Hound puppies, mark you ; not village children ! "—*The Tyranny of the Countryside*, p. 180.

the kind of literature which now satisfies the needs even of the so-called educated classes.

Above all, he may have noticed a decline in the beauty both of his fellows and of their surroundings; for taste enters into the smallest matters, and when the ordinary mind rules, all kinds of ugly beliefs, things, structures and pastimes are allowed to find a place in society which they could not otherwise have found, while beautiful things meet with no special favour [1] and are thought of no special value, save when they become the hall-marks of opulence and power, and thus minister to the general desire for ostentatious display. This explains the love of beautiful and expensive old furniture, plate and pictures, on the part of those who are often the most vulgar people in a democratic age.

These are some of the features of modern life which almost every one can see for himself. But it is not of these aspects of the decline in manners and morals that I here intend to speak. I have referred to them briefly and lightly because it struck me that if I omitted all mention of them the reader might imagine that I paid them no heed at all. This is not the case. As a matter of fact I am fully aware of the minor symptoms of the decline; but, in the conclusion of this chapter, I wished more particularly to refer to two or three broader and deeper factors in the general scheme of modern vulgarity, which are perhaps not so obvious, and not so generally discussed as are the instances of the motor-hoot, etc., which I have just touched upon.

Foremost among these broader and deeper factors are the causes which, in my estimation, are leading to the gradual *passing of the gentleman*. All the world over,

[1] In his *Theory of the State* (Authorised Translation, Clarendon Press), p. 483, Bluntschli says that in a democracy " there is more difficulty than in other constitutions to induce the State to attend to the loftier interests of art and science. A democratic nation must have reached a very high stage of civilisation when it seeks to satisfy needs of which the ordinary intelligence cannot appreciate the value or the importance to the national welfare."

where flourishing and powerful societies have been formed and maintained, the notion of the gentleman has appeared in some form or other as a national ideal. Nobody reading Confucius, for instance, or the Li-Ki—which is the Chinese Book of Ceremonies—can doubt for one instant that the idea of the gentleman was and still is a very definite thing in China; nor could such a reader doubt that the Chinese gentleman, even of two thousand years ago, would have been able perfectly to understand every movement and every scruple of his fellow in rank in England of the twentieth century.

There was also the gentleman of ancient Egypt, the gentleman of Athens, and the gentleman of Rome.

All huge and powerful administrations have to rely very largely upon the trust which they can place in a number of high responsible officials who, in moments of great temptation or great trial, will stand honestly and bravely at their posts. All stable family life, too, depends upon the existence of a number of such men, who need not necessarily be State servants, but who, engaged in other walks of life, reveal a similar reliability.

The very existence of a large administration, or of a large nation of citizens, is impossible without such men. And all societies which have started out with the idea of lasting, growing and standing upright, have always instinctively developed the high ideal of the gentleman—the man who can be trusted at all times and all places, the man who is sincere, the man who is staunch and constant in matters of principle, *the man who never sacrifices the greater to the less*, and the man who is sufficiently self-reliant to be able to consider others.

It is obvious that the gentleman class, or the body of men who possess the above qualities, falls naturally into various orders; but by far the highest order, is that consisting of those men who, without being necessarily examples of flourishing life, are yet so square and strong in body and soul, that their honour can be subjected to the greatest strain without snapping.

DECLINE OF MANNERS AND MORALS

Now it is upon such men alone, that a great nation relies for the preservation and maintenance of its best traditions, for the filling of its most responsible civil offices, and for the high duty of inspiring trust in the mind of the public.

If England has shown any stability at all, it is owing to the fact that as a nation she has reared crop after crop of such men, and that these men have been sent to all corners of the globe, from Barhein in the Persian Gulf, to Kingston in the Island of Jamaica, to represent her and to teach the gentleman's idea of decent living to the world.

Once this class begins to decline, England will be in sore straits; for even examples of flourishing life, when they appear, must find worthy and trusty servants to fill high places, otherwise the best supreme administration would be helpless.

But how do you suppose the virtues of the gentleman are reared? For you are too wise to believe that copy-book precepts can do any good, save as a mere confirmation of a deep bodily impulse. You are surely too experienced to suppose that the leopard can change his spots, or that a negro can beget a white child? Then how do you suppose that a strong virtue—a virtue which, like a powerful iron girder, nothing human can snap—is cultivated and produced in a family, in a line of human beings, even in an animal?

On this question Aristotle spoke words of the deepest wisdom. He declared that all virtue was habit, habituation, custom. "The virtues," he says, "we get by first performing single acts . . . by doing just actions, we come to be just; by doing the actions of self-mastery, we come to be perfected in self-mastery; and by doing brave actions, brave." [1]

And then he proceeds: "And to the truth of this, testimony is borne by what takes place in communities; because the law-givers make the individual members good men by habituation, and this is the intention certainly of every law-

[1] See Chapter I, Book II, *Ethics* (Chase's translation).

275

giver, and all who do it not fail of their intent; but herein consists the difference between a good Constitution and a bad." [1]

A gentleman in body and soul, then, is a creature whose very tissues are habituated to act in an honourable way. For many generations, then, his people must have acted in an honourable way. In order that the first and strongest impulse in his body may be an honourable impulse, such impulses must constantly have been favoured at the cost of other impulses by his ancestors, until the voice of the others is weak and the roar of the honourable impulse fills his being with a noise that drowns all other voices.

And this brings me to the subject of conscience, on which, at the risk of digressing, I must say a passing word. What is conscience? The Christian religion rightly says: " It is the voice of God in one's body." But what does this phrase mean precisely? Who knows what the voice of God can be? The voice of God, in the Christian sense, is obviously the voice of the giver of Christian moral law. To whom does the Christian think he owes his moral law? To God! Very well, then, his conscience must mean to him the voice of God!

But men who have left Christianity, who repudiate Christ, the Holy Ghost and the Gospels, still possess a conscience. Let them deny it as much as they like, we all know they have a conscience. What, precisely, is that conscience? Let us put the question in a different form. Who is the law-giver whose voice speaks in their breasts when they do a deed which makes them hear a sort of whispered protest in their hearts?

Think a minute on the lines of Aristotle's concept of virtue! Your greatest law-giver, the creator of your conscience, is obviously your line of ancestors. It is they who have implanted those impulses in your body which they, by their habits and customs, cultivated and produced. Very well, then, say you do a deed which your ancestors did a thousand times before you, what happens? A warm

[1] See Chapter I, Book II, *Ethics* (Chase's translation).

murmur of approval fills your heart. All the tissues of your body are familiar with the deed, they rejoice in the chance you have given them of venting a power long stored up by generations of practice. In other words, your ancestors have said : " You are right; you did this deed as we have done it; we approve."

Now reverse the process; do something that is in conflict with your traditions; indulge in any habit of life out of keeping with your best traditions; be for a moment untrue to your ancestors! What happens? Immediately the voice of your progenitors says : " You are wrong, you did this deed as we have never done it, or you did this deed which we have never done; we disapprove! "

Thus the diversity of men's sensitiveness where conscience is concerned, is accounted for by the diversity of their ancestry. Some men, for instance, can indulge in sexual perversity without being weighed down by moral indignation, while others feel suicidal after the first act of the kind. In the first case, sexual perversity may be suspected in the ancestry, because obviously the voice of ancestral protest is not strong; in the second case sexual purity may be suspected in the ancestry, because the voice of disapproval is obviously loud and severe. The same holds good in regard to little acts of deception, little thefts, little lies. In one case no moral indignation is produced by these deeds, in another case severe and bitter moral heart-burn is generated by any one of them.

Conscience, then, to the non-Christian, is simply the voice of his ancestors in his breast; and he should remember that he has it in his power to weaken or strengthen that voice for his offspring and for *their* offspring. For, just as virtues may be reared, so, as Aristotle points out, they may be destroyed at will.

With this side-light upon the meaning of conscience, we are now in a position to face the problem of the gentleman from the inside.

I have said that his most typical virtues are : that he can be trusted at all times and in all places, that he is sincere, that he is staunch and constant in matters of principle, that he never sacrifices the greater to the less, and that he is sufficiently self-reliant and strong to be able to consider others.[1]

Now what is the kind of ancestral and present environment that can rear such virtues and implant them with the strength of iron girders in a character? It is obviously an environment which is above all the petty deceits, all the subterfuges, tricks, expedients and wiles, which are inseparable from a sordid struggle for existence.

Behold the jungle!

In the jungle the only animal that does not require to tread softly, to avoid crackling leaves and creaking branches, the only animal that can dispense with deceit and with *make-believe*, and who can come and go as he likes and trumpet forth the truth honestly to the world without either compromise or caution, is that animal whose power and strength are above the ordinary attacks of his neighbours, and whose food springs from the soil about him, without his having to lie in ambush for it to appear and be waylaid. All other animals must practise deceit, subterfuge, falsehood, ruse, craft and a great variety of attitudes. All other animals must be histrions of no mean attainments; they must know how to crouch, how to crawl, how to cringe, how to dissimulate, and *how to pretend*. Nature condones all these accomplishments in those of her creatures which are caught in the cruel wheel of the

---

[1] To those to whom the last point is not obvious let me offer a little explanation in this footnote, so that I may avoid breaking up the discussion once more by subsidiary considerations. It must be clear to all that a baby, an invalid, a blind man, or anybody who is weak with any physical defect, must be selfish and cannot consider others. Weakness must cry out: "All for myself!" otherwise it cannot exist. The moment a baby or an invalid began to consider the feelings of those around it more than its own it would endanger its own existence. Strength, on the other hand, is able to consider others, because its own existence is already secure. The professed unselfishness of weak people, therefore, is mere cant, mere lip-service, beneath contempt. The only valuable altruism in the world is a strong self-reliant man's consideration for others.

struggle for existence. If she did not condone these accomplishments, either they would never get a meal, or they would always be providing meals with their own bodies to those who were stronger than they. The elephant alone can afford to be honest, *is* honest. The elephant alone can practise sincerity, staunchness and constancy to principle; he alone can let others live.

If all this can be applied to human society, there is a grave moral to be drawn from the application. The trend of human society, at least in modern Europe, is to draw ever greater and greater numbers and kinds of people into the vortex of the struggle for existence. And, under a Democracy of uncontrolled Trade and Commerce, there is a danger that all orders of society will ultimately be drawn into the struggle. The class that once stood immune from this struggle—the mammoth men, the men of leisure and secure power—are gradually ceasing to be the most revered and most admired members of the community; or, worse still, they are gradually ceasing to be bred. With great wealth as the highest value, people are ceasing to consider how it is acquired, and all are being tempted to take up that occupation by means of which it can be acquired with the greatest possible speed. Whether all the traditionally leisured families were capable of all the gentlemanly virtues or not, is not necessarily the point at issue. But one thing, in any case, is quite certain, and that is that among them, alone, were these virtues to be sought if they were to be found at all.

For it is pure romanticism to suppose that you can have the virtue without the soil from which it springs. You cannot have your cake and eat it. You may long in vain for the virtues which belong to the animal that stands aloof from the jungle struggle, if you actually participate in that struggle. And to suppose that mere precept and education will cultivate these virtues in you, if you do not possess, or have not practised them for generations, is to suppose that the leopard can by a course of training change his spots in a single generation.

A DEFENCE OF ARISTOCRACY

To-day, as we know, even the traditionally leisured class is being drawn, *has* been drawn, into the field of struggle. The very soil which alone is favourable to the growth of sincerity and staunchness and constancy to principle, is therefore no longer being tilled or cultivated. The influence of the principle of unrestricted competition (the modern form of that *bellum omnium contra omnes* which Hobbes rightly regarded as the condition of chaos preceding order), has reduced everything, even the power of being an influence for good or evil, to a struggle for existence, and as a result—unpleasant as the fact may seem—we are now undoubtedly witnessing the *passing of the gentleman*.

Everybody is now one or the other of those lower inmates of the jungle. Everybody now must at some time or other in his life be a " histrion of no mean attainments "; everybody must be wily, crafty, full of resource in subterfuge, pretence, deceit and dissimulation.[1] Sincerity, staunchness and constancy to a principle are dying out. It grows every day more and more difficult to find a man whom one can trust wholly and thoroughly. If things get worse and the *passing of the gentleman* is complete, we shall be able to trust no one.

We all know that this is so; we realise it every day of

---

[1] The notion that rigid honesty and uprightness are essential attributes of *the* gentleman, seems to have been lost many years ago in England. This is probably owing to the fact that by no means the best trading and commercial conditions have prevailed for so long in this country. For instance, it was possible for that old ass Macaulay, writing in the *Edinburgh Review* in December 1831, to say of Charles I : " It would be absurd to deny that he was a scholar and a gentleman. . . . But he was false, imperious, obstinate," etc. This unwarrantable association by Macaulay of falsity with gentlemanliness never seems to have affected that writer's reputation in the least, because it did not strike the educated Englishman, even of that age, that the two were hopelessly incompatible. Charles I was either a gentleman, or he was false—he could not be both But in a country in which uncontrolled trade and commerce prevail, the title " gentleman " evidently deteriorates just as surely as the genuine article itself does ; hence, Macaulay, Puritan as he was, was able to betray the Puritan's notion of a gentleman.

our lives. But what we do not realise keenly perhaps, is that with the *passing of the gentleman* we must renounce all hope of holding a great nation like England upright.

I do not mean this as a bitter attack on tradesmen and men of commerce; these men have their uses and their merits like all parts of a great organisation. All I wish to emphasise is the fact that it would be just as ridiculous to expect grapes to grow in Iceland as to expect the soil created by trading and commercial conditions to rear the virtues of the gentleman. And when trading and commercial conditions will have become almost general, when the world will have been turned into a huge office with a factory adjoining, the very conditions upon which gentlemanly virtues depend for their growth and their stability will have long ceased to exist.

The man immersed in the struggle for life, and the man who emerges from it successfully, are not therefore necessarily despicable or the reverse. All I maintain about them is that they never can, and never ought to, be placed in any high position where absolute sincerity and absolute staunchness and constancy to principle are the only safeguards that a people can have against their betraying their trust. They are not essentially wrong men, they are simply wrong men for the places in question—the high offices of a nation, the high positions of trust which all great administrations have to fill, and all posts in which magnanimity, sincerity and absolute rigidity of principle are pre-requisites.

I have referred to the relatively insignificant amount of peculation, corruption and malversation that was allowed or even overlooked during the time that Charles I and Strafford held the reins of government; but see what a change came over England when the Puritans and tradesmen triumphed! Even Needham, the Government historian, admits that three-quarters of the adherents of the Parliamentary party were worldlings, interested and not disinterested partisans, and as Dr. Cunningham declares:

A DEFENCE OF ARISTOCRACY

"The Long Parliament attained an unfortunate notoriety for the worst forms of political corruption."[1]

The tragic feature connected with a democracy of uncontrolled Trade and Commerce is that it creates precisely the environment which is most poisonously unfavourable to the healthy growth and multiplication of the gentleman.

The next most important factor in the decline of morals and manners is the deleterious influence which an almost full share in the direction of foreign and even home affairs of State has upon the masses in a democratic country.

Since the publication of Machiavelli's *Prince*, opinion in Europe has been hopelessly divided upon one important point in connection with politics. This point is the relation of political to private morality.

Machiavelli says definitely that political and private morality are different things. He tells the ruler outright that "he need never hesitate to incur the reproach of those vices, without which his authority can hardly be preserved,"[2] and that in certain circumstances a lie, an act of cruelty, of fraud, of deliberate subterfuge, of breach of faith, is often necessary and statesmanlike,[3]—nay, that it is often the only powerful weapon a ruler is in a position to wield, and that such an act cannot and must not be judged from the standard of private morals. He says that for a prince or a statesman to act in his po t ca capacity always according to the moral standard of his iprlvate life, would often mean the absolute ruin and Nemesis of the State he was ruling. He even goes so far as to say that though it may be useful for the ruler to *appear* to be acting always according to the moral precepts of private life, it would frequently be to his injury actually to do so.[4]

---

[1] *The Growth of Industry and Commerce*, Vol. II, p. 182.

[2] See *The Prince* (translated by Ninian H. Thomson, M.A., 1898), pp. 111–112.

[3] *Ibid.*, pp. 111, 119, 126, 127, 138.

[4] *Ibid.*, p. 128. "It is not essential, then, that a Prince should have all the good qualities which I have enumerated above, but it is most

Against this view we find a curious and motley throng, and *for* it, three of the wisest men the world has ever seen.

First among the opponents of Machiavelli are the Jesuits. This is strange, especially when one remembers their doctrine of the end justifying the means. Their opposition to Machiavelli, however, is perhaps best understood and esteemed at its proper worth when we realise their position. The Jesuits, admirable and profound as they are in their organisation, would have been the first to see that the sanction of super-morality in the State would be tantamount to endowing the secular body with powers with which they would find it difficult if not impossible to cope. In their struggle against all states on behalf of the Church, with the view of subjecting the former to the latter, it is comprehensible enough that they could ill abide the independence which Machiavelli claimed and recommended. We cannot, therefore, help but take their objections to the great Florentine secretary *cum grano salis*.

Again in the case of the Huguenots, fighting against the Crown of France, we are justified in suspecting motives which must have been far from purely moral. Their opposition to the Machiavellian doctrine was, to say the least, an interested one. If Machiavelli lent strength to their enemies, this was reason enough for condemning him.

Professor Villari mentions Giovanni Bodino, the author of the work *De Republica*, and Tommaso Campanella, a philosopher and Dominican Friar, as being also opposed to Machiavelli in doctrine; but by far the most interesting of the group of anti-Machiavellians are surely Frederick the Great of Prussia and Metternich.

The former, who throughout his reign at least acted as one of the most devoted followers of Machiavelli, actually wrote a book, *Réfutation du Prince de Machiavel*, in which

---

essential that he should seem to have them ; I will venture even to affirm that if he has and invariably practises them all, they are hurtful, whereas the appearance of having them is useful."

he attacked the doctrines of *The Prince* one by one with great vigour. How is this to be explained? As in the case of Metternich, this opposition can be understood only as an example all too common in countries like Germany and England, of the manner in which practice and theory often conflict in the life of one man. The clear logical intellect of the Southerner is not often guilty of such muddle-headedness; but the Northerner is frequently able to express the most sincere hatred of a principle in the abstract, though he pursues it with the utmost energy and resolution in his everyday life.

Thus Frederick the Great, despite his sudden and unwarrantable attack on Maria Theresa, his conquest of Silesia, and his treaties of alliance so often broken without qualm or scruple, is able to work himself up into a fit of righteous indignation over the man who gives rulers the formulæ of these sometimes necessary state crimes.[1]

Macaulay, being one of a similar northern stamp of mind, and overlooking the innumerable occasions when England has acted and triumphed entirely on Machiavellian lines, also works himself into a passion over the "immorality" of the Florentine; and with a sublime Puritanical stupidity, condemns the doctrine of *The Prince* with scorn. But what are we to expect from a writer who is so confused in his thought as to be able to say of one and the same man that he was a "gentleman" but "false"!

And now, who are the people on the other side—the people who were lucid enough to realise that political morality and private morality are two different things, and

---

[1] Frederick the Great's attitude in regard to Machiavelli's *Prince* is also open to another interpretation. We may, for instance, agree with Voltaire, who, in speaking of his great friend's book against Machiavelli, said : "*Il a craché dans le pot pour en dégouter les autres.*" But, in any case, in order to mitigate the severity of the above censure, it should be remembered that Frederick was only twenty-seven when he wrote his *Anti-Machiavel,* and that so young a man is frequently guilty of an idealism which, fortunately, is often wont to leave him with maturity.

who were honest enough to face the fact without any canting circumlocution?

Among the earlier monarchs who are of this group we may mention Charles V of Germany, Henry III and Henry IV of France, and Queen Christina of Sweden. But among the men who really count, among the spirits who rise to the pinnacles of human greatness, we find Lord Bacon of Verulam, Richelieu and Napoleon, all of whom believed and defended Machiavelli's doctrine.

This should be sufficient for us. To all who believe, not in metaphysical discussion or the mere bandying of words, but in men; it ought to be enough that Napoleon and Richelieu held the view which Machiavelli upholds in *The Prince*—the view that political deeds are not bound by any morality which governs private conduct. But, in truth, to all such people who are profound enough to make men and not disquisitions the measure of their choice in doctrine, Machiavelli's contention will seem the merest platitude. For what, at bottom, does it really mean? It means simply, in reference to *internal politics*, that the morals for the child cannot constrain or trammel the parent; and in reference to *external politics*, that the morals which rule the conduct of each individual member of the herd to his neighbour, cannot constrain or trammel the leader of the herd in his position of defender or assailant facing a hostile or strange herd.

You will say, perhaps, that this is obvious? You will point to a thousand instances in European and American and Asiatic history, in which this principle is exemplified, proved and justified. You will show how again and again, if the statesmen of England, or Germany, or America, had acted along the lines of merely private morality (*i. e.* morality within the herd), they would have belittled, impoverished and humiliated their country. Very true! But you must remember that there are hundreds and thousands of fools, including Macaulay, with motives far purer than those of the old Jesuits or the old Huguenots, and with minds a million times more confused than that of Frederick the Great, who declare that this is wrong and that political and private morality may and can be reconciled without danger.

Let them say?—Certainly!—I merely thought it would be well to call attention to the fact that Machiavelli's doctrine — however obvious — has been attacked and opposed, because certain points in the argument which follows would be missed if this fact were not borne in mind.

Taking it for granted, then, that political deeds and promises and contracts cannot and must not be judged from the standpoint of private morality, what is the further conclusion to which we are driven?

An orderly state is one in which the intra-herd morality is strictly and peacefully observed by all citizens. Indeed an ideal state would be one in which the intra-herd morality had actually become instinctive in all those classes of citizens who are the better and the happier for having rigid and inexorable rules of conduct prescribed and laid down for them.

The honest, hardworking citizen, then, must regard his morality as the only morality. His private morality must, in his opinion, be that which, dictated by God and His angels, is right for all time. His simple faith in its efficacy, his simple trust that the practice of it—however hard on occasion and however unrewarded it may go for some time—will ultimately be repaid, must never be shaken, lest the foundation of the nation's virtue be undermined.

Very well, then, a mind more subtle, a creature more cultured, a product of civilisation standing more firmly, more intellectually, more consciously on his legs than the simple citizen, will be required for that practice of the two moralities—the private and the political—without either of these suffering corruption from being placed side by side with the other in the same mind.

Not only the exoteric aspect of morality, but also its esoteric aspect, will have to be known to a man who, without running any risk of impairing his private morality, is called upon to practise the other for purposes of State.

The " gentleman " I have just described above, whose virtues of sincerity and steadfastness are as rigid in him as iron girders, can afford, for his country's good, to tinker with strategy, ruse, craft, deception and dissimulation, out- side the herd, without any fear of upsetting his private morals. His effort in political morality is intellectual, conscious; neither his heart nor his spirit is involved, save in so far as his aim is a patriotic one.[1] But even the gentle- man can prove at times too simple in his private virtue to be a match for foreign diplomatists, as history has sometimes shown.

That margin, however, which is permissible to one who stands firmly upon a solid bedrock of private morality, would be a dangerous concession to make to the simple citizen, whose constant struggle for existence forces him often enough to trespass against his private morality at the cost of his liberty if he be found out, and at the cost of his sleep if he merely fear lest he be found out.

For the private citizen to realise that there are two moralities, one which is intra-herd and the other which is inter-herd, would very quickly put an end to all virtue whatsoever; for his private morality, already in a weak position, would then be utterly routed. It could not bear the proximity of another morality at its side, which con- tradicted many of its most treasured tenets; the one would either corrupt the other completely or a wretched com- promise would be contrived which was neither fish nor fowl, neither virtue nor vice.

---

[1] Captain F. Brinkley, in his *History of Japan* (Vol. II, p. 198), gives an interesting instance in support of this contention, in which he shows how the Japanese "gentleman" was capable of practising the two moralities and keeping them separate. " It may be broadly stated," he says, " that moral principles received no respect whatever from framers of political plots or planners of *ruses de guerre*. Yet the *Taiko*, who stands conspicuous among Japan's great leaders for improbity in the choice of means to a public or military end, desired to commit suicide rather than survive the ignominy of failure to fulfil a pledge."

For the private citizen to *practise* two moralities, however, would be even more fatal. For not only is his private virtue insufficiently rooted in him, owing to the struggle for existence; but he is also quite unable to act either intellectually or consciously enough, in the realm of morality, to preserve his private morality quite unimpaired during the experiment.

But this practice of two moralities is essentially the task which a democratic state imposes upon its simple citizens. And for this reason alone, from the standpoint of intra-herd morality, democracy must be regarded as profoundly, insidiously, dangerously immoral. However slight may be the share which the people of a democracy are called upon to take in the administration of, say, foreign affairs; however much the secret diplomacy may be conducted by the elected officials themselves; ultimately, if not immediately, the morality of the inter-herd attitude must become apparent to the multitude; their will must be exercised one way or the other as a sanction or a veto upon the negotiations; and it is then that the poison will enter their unresisting and feeble spirits.

The fact that democracy means the imposition of the practice of two moralities, often so incompatible, as that of politics and of private life upon the multitude, is one of the most immoral aspects of the democratic state; and when this state in addition is one of uncontrolled commerce and industry, in which unrestricted competition (Hobbes's *bellum omnium contra omnes*) is the prevailing rule, then the situation becomes absolutely hopeless. For unrestricted competition already introduces elements of inter-herd morality into the herd, and whatever participation in political morality the multitude may enjoy besides simply increases the forces of dissolution which are already reducing and destroying the fibre of intra-herd morality on which the prosperity of all great nations must repose.

The replies to this are obvious, and the ardent democrat may advance two, either of which I shall show to be equally deplorable.

DECLINE OF MANNERS AND MORALS

Democrat A. denies that Democracy is immoral, because he believes that it is possible for the multitude to govern their State strictly along the lines of private morality, without any danger accruing to the nation. He likes England's strength and would love to preserve it; but forgetting that he cannot have it both ways, imagines that this great nation, constructed upon the most skilful practice of inter-herd morality, can be run by the morality which rules in his own back parlour.

This man is obviously beneath notice. He does not understand history or politics; not to speak of the very springs of his own actions. Let him ask himself how many states would ever have lasted more than three generations if their inter-herd negotiations had been governed by intra-herd principles. Let him ask himself why the Jesuits, profound as they were, detested and loathed Machiavelli. Does he suppose the Jesuits would have troubled themselves about the doctrines of this Florentine secretary if they had not perceived that in these doctrines there lay an inexhaustible fund of strength which might be drawn upon by any secular power with which they might some day find themselves in conflict?

Let such a man dwell for a moment upon the sentiment of the proverb, " Blood is thicker than water "; and then let him ask himself honestly whether those same scruples which animate him when he feels himself one of a body of men, all from the same home, can hold any sway over him when he is forced to face strangers and foreigners, and to safeguard the interest and the security of that same home against them.

But Democrat A.'s contention will find many to support it, and any weakness or humility that may enter into our negotiations with foreign powers will be due to the preponderance of men like Democrat A. in the nation and in the government. In fact signs are not wanting which show conclusively that Democrat A.'s view is growing extremely common in England; and the more the franchise is extended, the commoner it will become. For it is only natural that the more stubborn and the more moral among the simple citizens should refuse to believe that their right to vote must involve, immediately or ultimately, the practice of a kind of morality, the tenets of which they would loathe from the bottom of their hearts.

Democrat B. declares, with a lump in his throat and a tear in his mild cerulean eye, that all the individuals constituting mankind form a brotherhood, and that if it is impossible to be strong and overwhelming as a nation without differentiating between intra-herd and inter-herd morality, then the sooner inter-herd morality is swept away the better, and this is precisely what democracy, with its inclusion of the voice of the multitude, aims at doing.

Democrat B. is more logical than Democrat A. He sees that inter-herd negotiations, to be strong, cannot be governed by the same morality as intra-herd negotiations; but, like the honest, simple citizen that he is, he feels himself unable to abandon the morality of private life and prefers to see the power, the will to power, the preservation of power in his nation go to the deuce, rather than that he should be called upon to have a share in that inter-herd morality which he scarcely understands and emphatically detests.

This is an attitude which is also becoming more and more general, and all those who share Democrat B.'s outlook are likely in the future to be very hostile towards any high-handed or powerful act of inter-herd morality which the government in power may find it necessary to perform. In a nation that wishes to remain great and mighty, democrats of the stamp of B. are likely to prove a very dangerous weakening influence, because the only way of propitiating them involves the relinquishing of all that inter-herd licence in morality which is frequently the only weapon with which a state can hold its own.

Behind Democrats A. and B. there is a vast crowd of the ignorant, of the licentious, of the lax and of the dissolute, who can see in the principles of inter-herd morality simply a sanction for their own anti-social designs against their neighbours within the herd; and to these .the invitation received from a democratic government to confound political with private morality, can have only the most utterly dissipating and demoralising effects.

Thus we find modern democracy confronted with the following dilemma: either inter-herd morality must be sacrificed, in which case the nation's relation to other powers is bound to be weakened; or inter-herd morality is to be preserved, in which case the multitude who are invited to share in the government are bound to taste the forbidden fruit of a morality strange to intra-herd principles, and to lose their rigidity and their virtue in consequence.[1]

The escape from this dilemma is, as a rule, as we see to-day, merely an utterly despicable compromise which only adds one more factor to the many already at work corroding the foundations of the Empire.

The last important phase in the decline of morals and manners in a Democracy of uncontrolled Trade and Commerce—or at least the last to which I shall refer for my particular case[2]—is the demoralising influence which is exercised by the materialistic principle of numbers, by the

[1] For some interesting examples taken both from French and English history of the difficulties involved in the conduct of foreign affairs under a democracy, see Chapter XV in J. Holland Rose's valuable little book, *The Rise of Democracy*. The chapter concludes with these words : "If the United Kingdom is to recover its rightful influence in the world, it will not be merely by vast armaments, but by the use of different methods in foreign affairs from those which must necessarily prevail in our domestic concerns. An electorate which is largely inexperienced may, possibly for several decades, enthrone the principle of flux in our home politics, but that same electorate will assuredly learn by bitter experience that unless our foreign policy is firm and continuous, we shall remain without an ally, and be condemned possibly to an unequal struggle even for the maintenance of our present possessions."

[2] I should like to remind the reader that I take it for granted that he is familiar with the usual arguments brought against democracy in the works of men like Lecky and Sir Henry Maine, and even in the works of democrats like Mill and Bentham, with most of which usual arguments I heartily concur.

conscious power of being able to override and refute any principle, truth or judgment, however profound and however sacred, by the mere accumulation of voices against it.

At the basis of all democracies is the scheme of life which makes a majority omnipotent. And with a majority, the greatest wisdom, the profoundest insight and the most far-sighted judgment simply fight in vain.

There can be no definite right or wrong, no absolute [1] standard of good or evil, and no sacredness in superior wisdom, superior insight, superior foresight, or superior judgment, in a land where a mere majority can make all these things utterly null and void; and in such a land the intrinsic value of a principle, of a precept, or of a proposition, will be certain to be eclipsed by the extrinsic value which the favour of a mere majority can put upon its opposite, its contradiction or its refutation.

But, apart from the fatal effects of this fact alone, what are likely to be the consequences to the majority themselves of the exercise of this shallow and senseless power? It is obvious that a certain contempt of sound judgment, as such, and of taste and penetration, as such, will be bound to grow in such communities. For can these qualities do anything against numbers? In a country in which the constitution provides the means for outvoting a god, what can be thought of that wisdom, judgment and discrimination which in some human beings can attain almost the divine?

There are causes enough in all conscience, which are at work to-day, compassing the doom of the workingman's intelligence, but this principle of the omnipotence of majorities is surely the most potent of all. The best of the ancients would have laughed at the materialistic notion that the mere body-weight behind a measure or a policy, or a judgment, was sufficient to sanctify—nay, justify that measure, policy or judgment. But to-day, with absolute gravity and earnestness, with imperturbable calm and

---

[1] To the thoughtful optimist flourishing life is the test of the absolute in all doctrine.

conviction, we leave our moral judgments, our intellectual discoveries and conclusions, our hard-thought-out plans and policies to take care of themselves, and all we do is to weigh bodies. The scales descend on the left, the bodies shouting "nay" have it—and the wisdom even of a Solomon is cast carelessly on the dust-heap. A god himself could not contend with any hope of success with this essentially materialistic method of differentiating right from wrong in doctrine and policy by the measure of the butcher's scales; but think of the besotting effect of the method upon those whose bodies only are weighed and whose judgment is ignored, whose capacity for judgment is ignored! Think of the bottomless stupidity of their laughter when their mere "arm-in-arm-together" opposition can outweigh the utterance of a practised, tried, discriminating and tasteful thinker! What respect can they have for God or man, for wisdom or meditation, for beauty or real power, when this weighing of meat, this literal reckoning of carcasses, of bones, flesh and blood, becomes the sole criterion, the one and only test of superior divination, selection and rejection!

And the demoralising influence of this immoral creed of majorities, is the one which is most powerful to-day, not only in governments but wherever you turn and find men opposed to one another; so much so, indeed, that the masses are losing all the instinct, which they once possessed, of distinguishing intuitively between that which is superior and that which is inferior to them, save in mere numbers; so much so, that the masses are rapidly being turned into merely movable herds of cattle, a sufficient number of which it is necessary to drive bleating into one's pen, before one can dare to utter any truth, any warning or any prophecy, however deep, however sound and however urgent; so much so, that our only hope, our only trust can be that the masses themselves will one day halt, and, sick of being herded into the scales or into the pens of party and propaganda, and tired of bleating to order, will cry aloud for that saviour, that leader of men, that powerful ruler-spirit and creator of national order, who, though caring nothing for their bleating, will yet understand their needs better than they can possibly under- stand them themselves, and treat them as something a little higher, a little nobler and a little more precious than mere meat for the scales.[1]

[1] As Bluntschli says, in *The Theory of the State* (authorised translation, Clarendon Press), p. 194 : "'The real interests of the proletariat proper demand Patrons rather than representatives, which it cannot find in its own ranks. The higher the position and influence of the 'patron' the more effective would be the defence of the rights of the proletariat."

CHAPTER VII

THE ARISTOCRAT AS AN ACHIEVEMENT

"That kingdom where Sudras [common, low people] are very numerous, which is infested by atheists and destitute of twice-born inhabitants [aristocrats] soon entirely perishes."—*Laws of Manu*, VIII, 22.

IN the statement of my thesis I defined the aristocrat broadly as the example of flourishing life among men. Let me now be quite plain as to what I mean by *flourishing life*. I have said that it was that manifestation of human nature possessing a maximum of beauty, health, vigour, will and spirit. Of course, I meant, *within a particular race;* for that is an essential condition of such powers constituting the best in a given community.

What, then, does flourishing life mean within a particular race? It means that example of life in which the race's view of beauty, health, vigour, will and spirit appear in a maximum degree of development. It means that example of life on which the whole of a particular race can look with the approbation of proud spectators saying: "This is our highest achievement in instinct, virtue, beauty and will!"

And with this I come to the kernel of the question; for *the aristocrat is an achievement*. He is not the mere foam on the surface of a society; he is a society's top-wave.

But an achievement implies design, endeavour, the patient exercise and garnering of virtuous, volitional, and bodily accomplishments. An achievement involves effort. This, however, is precisely what constitutes the aristocrat. He is the outcome of effort. He is the product of long, untiring endeavour. As a being in possession of highly developed instincts and virtues, he is essentially a work of human art, and as such he naturally prizes himself, and is naturally prized by others.

Let me, however, define my terms. What are instinct, virtue, beauty and will? These are words used and mis-used with a looseness which can lend only to the worst confusion. They, nevertheless, stand for very definite ideas, and to every strong race, or even people, they are, and always have been, very definite ideas.

Instinct in man is the knowledge of certain things, or the inclination or ability to practise certain more or less complex actions, prior to experience. It is either racial experience, racial memory, or it is an inevitable tendency arising out of a certain correlation of bodily parts; and, after experience has been acquired, *while it is being acquired*, instinct remains a predisposition, a bias, in favour of a certain mode of action, a certain course of conduct.

An instinct may remain dormant, it may not find a favourable environment for its expression; but it cannot be created by environment; it cannot be generated by something outside man; because it is essentially something in him, something embedded in the very heart of his ganglia and muscles, and something, therefore, as unalter-able as a leopard's spots.

As Theognis of Megara said: "To beget and rear a man is easier than to implant a good soul in his body. No one has yet known how to do this; no one has yet been able to change an imbecile into a sage, or a bad man into a good one." [1]

No historian has told us, no historian knows, the very beginning of races. The most that historians know is that a certain number of races are to hand, *or were to hand at a certain date*, and that some have flourished, some have never risen above a certain low level, some have survived in more or less modified forms to this day, and some have become totally extinct.

[1] *Fragments*, 429–431. The words "bad" and "good" here mean nothing more than "plebeian" and "noble" respectively.

THE ARISTOCRAT AS AN ACHIEVEMENT

The inception of a particular race with definite instincts is a thing which is mysteriously buried in the darkness of prehistoric antiquity. All we know is, that whereas some of the races of this world step into history fully equipped with the instincts calculated to make them attain to a state of high civilisation—others in circumstances equally favourable, but without these instincts, enjoy a much less dignified and much less noble fate, and remain for ever in barbarity, or at least at a very low level of culture.

With Gobineau, therefore, we are forced to conclude that there is inequality between the races of man, and that barbarity, far from being a primitive state, or an infantile state of historical humanity in general, is rather the inevitable and permanent state of certain races with instincts incompatible with any other condition, while civilisation is the inevitable and certain creation of races with other instincts.[1] To take an instance: it is not only extremely doubtful, but well-nigh thoroughly improbable, that the Fuegians of whom Darwin speaks,[2] would ever have created the civilisation of the Incas, even if they had lived in their circumstances; while it is also thoroughly improbable that the ancient Peruvians would have developed the low and degraded social organisations of the Fuegians, even if they had been in circumstances ten times as unfavourable as they.

Darwin says, glibly: "The perfect equality among the individuals composing the Fuegian tribes must for a long time retard their civilisation."[3] Gobineau would reply: "Their civilisation is as it is, and will remain as it is, as the result of conditions which sink much more deeply into their lives, than that which appeared to Darwin to be a mere convention of their social life. The equality that Darwin read as the obstacle to their advancement, was but the surface manifestation of an obstacle far greater and far more formidable, which resided in the very hearts of their bodies."

[1] See Chapter V, of Vol. I, *Essai sur l'Inégalité des Races Humaines.*
[2] *Journal of Researches*, Chapter X. [3] Op. cit., p. 228.

A DEFENCE OF ARISTOCRACY

This is not the occasion to examine all Gobineau's support of his claim concerning the inequality of human races; suffice it to say that he utterly, and in my opinion, successfully, routs those who would sentimentally contend that all mankind is equal, and that the difference between the negro and the Caucasian is simply the difference between youth and maturity.

Civilisation, then, outside a cultured nation, must always mean a transfusion of blood?

Gobineau does not hesitate to draw this inevitable conclusion from his arguments.[1] He says, practically, you cannot turn the Fuegian into a man capable of a high state of civilisation, save by destroying his innate instincts *by cross-breeding him with a superior race.*

The interesting converse of this contention, however, is, that you cannot re-convert a civilised man into a brute, save by cross-breeding him with an inferior race; and it is this contention of Gobineau's which makes his work so intensely valuable to the historian as well as to the sociologist whose gaze is directed towards the future of his nation.

For it is this contention which all races of antiquity unconsciously grasped and acted upon. And it was only when the jealous idea of race came to be undermined by democratic influences such as wealth, or the idea of the equality of mankind, that the highly civilised peoples of antiquity declined.

---

[1] Op. cit., Vol. I, p. 62 : "En adoptant comme justes les conclusions qui précédent, deux affirmations deviennent de plus en plus évidentes : c'est, d'abord, que la plupart des races humaines sont inaptes à se civiliser jamais, à moins qu'elles ne se mélangent ; c'est en suite, que non seulement ces races ne possèdent pas le ressort intérieur declaré nécessaire pour les pousser en avant sur l'échelle du perfectionnement, mais encore que tout agent extérieur est impuissant a féconder leur stérilité organique, bien que cet agent puisse être d'ailleurs très énergique." See also Reibmayr, *Inzucht und Vermischung,* p. 71 : "Just as inbreeding serves the purpose of creating the ganglia of civilisation, so cross-breeding serves the purpose of spreading and handing on the same."

THE ARISTOCRAT AS AN ACHIEVEMENT

As Reibmayr has so ably shown,[1] it was in islands (Crete), peninsulas (Greece, Italy), or in naturally enclosed lands (Mesopotamia, Egypt, Peru), where inbreeding and the consequent preservation of a particular type, were best ensured, that culture attained to its highest degree of beauty and permanence, and it was only when these civilisations began to lose their isolation and independence, that degeneration set in with that most potent destroyer of instinct, indiscriminate cross-breeding.

Indeed, Reibmayr goes so far as to declare that all culture depends for its production upon the close inbreeding of a particular leading stock, and that without such close inbreeding within a superior class or group, man would never have been able to raise himself out of his original condition of barbarism.[2] Like Bluntschli, Nietzsche and many others, Reibmayr maintains, simply what history proves, that every elevation of the type man, every culture and civilisation, has always been the work of a small leading caste of inbred aristocrats at the head of a community; "but," he says, "it is more difficult for an exogamic than for an endogamic people to rear a leading caste possessed of pronounced characters, and that is why such peoples are never able to play a prominent part in the history of human civilisation, so long as they remain faithful to the custom of exogamy. In the struggle for supremacy they almost invariably have to give way to those communities who are strictly endogamic, and with whom the rearing of a leading caste is a perfectly natural phenomenon."[3]

In every race that has achieved anything in this world, there has always been a feeling, conscious or unconscious, among its leaders, that they and their followers were the chosen people and that they must wrap themselves jealously in the mantle of their own natures and eschew the foreigner, lest they lose their most precious possession. This marvellous insight on the part of the people of

---

[1] *Die Entwicklungsgeschichte des Talentes und Genies*, Vol. I, p. 9.
[2] *Ibid.*, p. 6.   [3] *Inzucht und Vermischung*, p. 73.

antiquity, seems almost incredible in its wisdom—more particularly now that we are able to look upon it, and whole-heartedly to uphold it, with the knowledge of the fact that science entirely confirms the prejudice of these ancient peoples. Yet it is impossible to think of a great nation that did not share this belief in ancient times.

Herodotus tells us that the Egyptians despised the foreigner; [1] he also says: "The Egyptians are averse to adopt Greek customs, or, in a word, those of any other nation. This feeling is almost universal among them." [2] Elsewhere he writes: "The Egyptians call by the name of barbarians all such as speak a language different from their own." [3] While in Genesis we find the following confirmation of this view: "And he [Joseph] washed his face, and went out, and refrained himself, and said, Set on bread. And they set on for him by himself, and for them by themselves, and for the Egyptians, which did eat with him, by themselves: because the Egyptians might not eat bread with the Hebrews; for that is an abomination unto the Egyptians." [4]

Like the Jews, who probably derived the idea from them, the Egyptians believed they were "a chosen people"; they were the only men whom the gods really cherished. They alone, in fact, were *men* (romet); all other peoples were Asiatics, Niggers or Lybians, but not men. [5] Strangers were forbidden to enter the country, and for the exigencies of trade, certain definite places were allotted. The Greeks, for instance, who traded with the Egyptians, were confined to the town of Naucratis. [6] A stone pillar, hailing from the time of Userteseen III (*circa* 1630 B.C.) has been found, bearing a written warning to all strangers, not to cross the frontiers of Egypt, and we are told by Herodotus that the Ionian and Carian troops of Psammatichus (*circa* 664 B.C.) were the first foreigners

---

[1] Book II, 41 and 79. [2] *Ibid.*, 91.
[3] *Ibid.*, 158. [4] Gen. xliii. 32.
[5] Reibmayr, *Inzucht und Vermischung*, p. 160.
[6] Wilkinson, op. cit., Vol. I, p. 328.

to be allowed to settle in the country, and even these were given a special place a little below Bubastis, called the camp.[1] In short, as Wilkinson tells us, the Egyptians treated foreigners "with distrust and contempt,"[2] and, like the Chinese, tolerated rather than liked their appearance even on the frontier.

And the Jews, in the same way, despised the alien, and were forbidden to intermarry with him. We read in Deuteronomy: " When the Lord thy God shall deliver them [the Hittites, the Girgashites, the Amorites, the Canaanites, the Perizzites, the Hivites and Jebusites] before thee; thou shalt smite them and utterly destroy them; thou shalt make no covenant with them, nor show mercy unto them. Neither shalt thou make marriages with them; thy daughter thou shalt not give unto his son, nor his daughter shalt thou take unto thy son."[3]

And why?

" For they will turn away thy son from following me [that is, destroy his particular kind of social instinct— the Jewish kind] that they may serve other gods: so will the anger of the Lord be kindled against you, and destroy thee suddenly."[4]

Here is the essence of ancient wisdom with regard to the preservation of a valuable type, by means of inbreeding. And why did the type wish to preserve itself? Because of its pride in itself. Because of its consciousness of its peculiar virtues.

The chapter continues: " For thou *art* an holy people unto the Lord God: the Lord thy God hath chosen thee to be a special people unto himself, above all the people that *are* upon the face of the earth. The Lord did not set his love upon you, nor choose you, because ye were

---

[1] Book II, 154. This statement is not so wrong as it seems, for there are reasons for believing that the Jews were allowed to settle in Egypt only when a kindred race (the Hyksos) was putting sovereigns on the throne.

[2] Op. cit., Vol. I, p. 35.

[3] Deut. vii. 2–3. See also Joshua xxiii. 12–13 ; 1 Kings xi. 2.

[4] Deut. vii. 4.

more in number than any people; for ye were the fewest of all people : But because the Lord God loved you, and because he would keep the oath which he had sworn unto your fathers," etc.[1]

Now hear how the prophet Ezra bewails the terrible fact that this pride of his race has fallen, and that his co-religionists have condescended to mix with the foreigner!

"Now when these things were done, the princes came to me, saying, The people of Israel, and the priests, and the Levites, have not separated themselves from the people of the lands, doing according to their abominations, even of the Canaanites, the Hittites, the Perizzites, the Jebusites, the Ammonites, the Moabites, the Egyptians and the Amorites. For they have taken of their daughters for themselves, and for their sons : so that the holy seed have mingled themselves with the people of those lands : yea, the hand of the princes and rulers hath been chief in this trespass. And when I heard this thing, I rent my garment and my mantle, and plucked off the hair of my head and of my beard, and sat down astonied." [2]

To this extent were the best of the Jews unconsciously certain of the fact that races are a matter of instinct, and that races are destroyed by the extinction of those particular instincts constituting their identity through indiscriminate cross-breeding.

The Greeks, too, in their healthiest period, were just as hostile to the foreigner, and to the base-born man, as the proudest of the Egyptians or Jews.

"Both metropolitans and colonists," says Grote, "styled themselves Hellenes, and were recognised as such by each other : all glorying in the name as the prominent symbol of fraternity—all describing non-Hellenic men or cities by a word which·involves associations of repugnance. Our term barbarian, borrowed from this latter word, does not express the same idea : for the Greeks spoke thus indiscriminately of the extra-Hellenic world

---

[1] Deut. vii. 6–8.
[2] Ezra ix. 1, 2, 3, etc. See also Neh. xiii. 23–31.

with all its inhabitants, whatever might be their degree of civilisation. The rulers and people of Egyptian Thebes with their ancient and gigantic monuments, the wealthy Tyrians and Carthaginians, the phil-Hellene Arganthonius of Tartessus, and the well-disciplined patricians of Rome (to the indignation of old Cato) were all comprised in it. At first it seemed to have expressed more of repugnance than of contempt, and repugnance especially towards the sound of a foreign language." [1]

As Grote shows, in this passage, the matter of the degree of civilisation attained by a foreign people, was not considered by the Greek of antiquity. But neither was it considered by the Jews; for the Jews could scarcely have regarded themselves as more highly civilised than the Egyptians. This is sufficient to show us that this race-feeling was not asserted only in relation to the member of an inferior or savage nation; it was the attitude of a proud people, conscious of their physical and spiritual possessions, towards all the rest of the world. And it is this fact which makes it so astounding. Nothing but the sound, though unconscious, " hitting of the nail on the head," by the men of taste among the Egyptians, the Jews and the Greeks, would ever have led a whole race thus " blindly," so to speak, to conduct themselves as if they knew all that the science of historians and anthropologists now lays down as the *rationale* of all this race prejudice and race-exclusiveness.

It is impossible to explain this healthy profundity on the part of these people of antiquity, save by some such hypothesis as the one I have suggested in my thesis. For only the voice of healthy, flourishing life could, without conscious science or experiment, have lighted intuitively upon just precisely that measure of preservation for a race, which is involved in this prejudice against the foreigner.

All the disabilities imposed upon the metics in Athens; all the contempt shown to freedmen and slaves, are only

[1] *History of Greece,* Vol. II, p. 162.

other expressions of the same feeling. For the ever-present danger to such societies as those of Athens and Rome, must have been the vast number of aliens from all climes and races who gradually found a footing as something more than despised slaves in the heart of these communities.

Theognis, the poet of Megara, had witnessed changes enough in his native city in the sixth century B.C. to cause him the gravest alarm. He saw what no other man perhaps then saw, that the gradual encroachment of the metic and the plebeian upon the higher classes through the steady rise in the dignity of mere wealth, was the greatest danger threatening his people. And the phenomena which were later to make their appearance in Athens, were watched by him with the most serious qualms in his own city.

Addressing his friend Cyrnus, he says: "We, Cyrnus, go in search of rams, asses and horses of a good breed so that they may give us progeny like unto themselves. But the man of good birth [literally 'the good man'] does not decline the daughter of a churl or ruffian [literally 'a bad man'] provided she brings him wealth. Neither is there any woman who would not consent to become the wife of a churl or ruffian if he be rich, or who would not prefer the wealthy before the honest man. Riches are all that people consider, the man of birth finds a wife in the house of the churl, the churl in the house of the man of birth. Wealth mixes races. Do not therefore be astonished, Polypædes, that our fellow-citizens' blood is degenerate, seeing that the bad and the good are mixing."[1]

The point that is important here, is not only the evidence that this passage provides of Theognis's knowledge of the levelling or mixing influences that the power of wealth exercises over a community consisting of different races; but that he deplored it because he was aware of the disintegrating effects of cross-breeding upon the instincts of a particular type.

[1] *Fragments*, 183–192.

THE ARISTOCRAT AS AN ACHIEVEMENT

Elsewhere he says: "Never is a slave's head erect; but always bowed, and the neck bent. For neither from the bramble spring roses or hyacinths, nor ever from a bond-woman a noble child."[1]

Indeed, so conscious was he of the importance of purity of stock that he was suspicious even of the exile—even, that is to say, of the man who, though born and bred a Greek, had spent some time away from his native soil. Addressing his friend Cyrnus once more, he says: "Do not ever embrace the exile in the hope of gaining anything! When he returns home he is no longer the same man."[2]

Reibmayr would have it that it is a natural instinct in a race not to mix its blood with that of any other.[3] But if this theory is true I have some difficulty in understanding why the lawgivers of all races seem to have been so particular about forbidding *mésalliances* with the foreigner to all their fellow-countrymen. No other instinct requires thus to be ratified by law. An explanation which seems to me much more likely is that, in accordance with my thesis, only those supremely happy or lucky strokes of nature within a certain race, with their taste perfectly attuned to every matter of selection and rejection, intuitively selected the right attitude here, and sought to impress it upon the rest of their race. For any law on the matter would surely be superfluous if there actually did exist an instinct in man which made all but the women of his own race creatures both loathsome and repulsive to him.

In any case, no law seems to have been more easily broken or ignored, more particularly in cities like Athens and Rome, where the constant presence and contact of metics and slaves of foreign origin offered all sorts of opportunities to the Hellenes and the Romans to step

---

[1] *Fragments*, 535–538.   [2] *Ibid.*, 429–431.
[3] *Inzucht und Vermischung.* Chapter: "Ursachen der Inzucht beim Menschen."

aside from the proud path of an exclusive and self-conscious race.

We know how wealthy many of the metics were in Athens, and we also know how some of their number, as well as numerous freedmen, were ultimately included in the franchise by Cleisthenes in the fifth century B.C. After this first step in the direction of absolute democracy pressed upon the community by the steady rise in the dignity of mere wealth, how could the old race feeling any longer assert itself? It was still strong, of course; but it had been assailed in a manner which rendered it almost impossible for it ever to recover its former vigour. The words of Theognis about Megara in the sixth century now applied to Athens in the fifth: " Our fellow-citizens' blood is degenerate, seeing that the bad and the good are mixing."

In the fourth century we find Aristotle saying with perfect gravity, " Slaves have sometimes the bodies of freemen, sometimes the souls " [1]—the feeling of aversion is vanishing—and about the year 325 B.C. the proud sense of race was so near extinction that Alexander was able seriously to contemplate, and to establish the precedent of, a fusion of Greeks and Asiatics. At Sura, the King himself married Statira, the daughter of Darius; his bosom friend Hephæstion took her sister, and a large number of Macedonian officers wedded the daughters of Persian noblemen. Of the rank and file of the Macedonians, 10,000 are said to have followed the example of their leader and his officers and taken Asiatic wives, and all those who did so were munificently rewarded by Alexander.

Long before this happened, however, Greece had fallen into a state of steady decline, and the art, alone, of the Hellenistic period shows clearly enough how the sympathies of the ancient Hellenes, how their sense of the beautiful in man and their range of subjects fit for art had long since begun to include the " barbarian " and his attributes.

[1] *Politics*, Chapter V, 1,254*b*.

THE ARISTOCRAT AS AN ACHIEVEMENT

The same observations apply to the Romans. To the early patricians, the plebeians—a class which included foreign settlers and manumitted slaves of plebeian residents—were not merely a despised class, they were regarded as profane men. To admit them to any share of privilege was tantamount to flinging scorn at the ancestral gods. Roman jurisprudence proscribed the marriage of a citizen with a metic or foreigner, and, in the days of freedom and virtue, a senator would have thought it beneath him to match his daughter even with a king. As late as the last half-century B.C. Mark Antony's fame was sullied by his union with an Egyptian wife—despite the fact that she was the descendant of a long line of kings; while in A.D. 79 it was popular opinion and censure that compelled the Emperor Titus to part with his great love, the Jewess Berenice.

Not quite three centuries later—to show how long this feeling survived, at least in certain exalted quarters—Constantine is found cautioning his son against mingling his blood with that of the princes of the north, "of the nations without faith or fame," who were ambitious of forming matrimonial alliances with the descendants of the Cæsars. "The aged monarch," says Gibbon, "in his instructions to his son, reveals the secret maxims of policy and pride, and suggests the most decent reasons for refusing these insolent and unreasonable demands. Every animal, says the discreet Emperor, is prompted by nature to seek a mate among the animals of his own species; and the human species is divided into various tribes by the distinction of language, religion and manners. *A just regard to the purity of descent preserves the harmony of public and private life; but the mixture of foreign blood is the fruitful source of disorder and discord.*"[1]

But by the time that Constantine ascended the throne the Romans had long ceased to be Romans—just as the Greeks had long ceased to be Hellenes in the Hellenistic

---

[1] *Decline and Fall* (Methuen, 1898), Vol. VI, Chapter 53, p. 86. [The italics are mine.—A. M. L.]

age. Their blood had been mingled with that of the foreigner for so many generations that, as Gobineau very rightly points out, it is absurd to speak of the " decline and fall " either of the Athenians or the Romans; because the men of the decline were no longer either Athenians or Romans. They were a hotch-potch of humanity, possessing only an infinitesimally small remnant of the blood, and therefore of the instincts, of the original founders of the two great cities. Those who know the history of Athens, if only from the time of Cleisthenes, will not question this view. While in so far as Rome is concerned, the two excellent chapters on " The Extirpation of the Best " and on " Slaves and Clients," in Otto Sieck's *History of the Downfall of the Ancient World*,[1] are evidence enough in support of Gobineau's standpoint.

Sieck says: " If we assumed that, in the year 400 B.C., four-fifths of the free population in the states of the classical world consisted of the descendants of manumitted slaves, far from overstating the actual facts, we should be making a very moderate computation." [2]

Now, says Gobineau, if this be so, it is no longer with the original Greeks or Romans that we have to deal when we concern ourselves with the decline of these two nations, but with a people who would have been utterly and hopelessly incapable of maintaining, much less of founding, such states as Athens and Rome. We have to deal with a pot-pourri of lethargic Asiatic, African, Jewish and other alien instincts, which did not, and could not, have any influence in the original construction of these national organisms, or they would never have come into being as the powerful and highly civilised creations which we know them to have been.[3]

[1] *Geschichte des Untergangs der Antiken Welt* (1895), Chapters III and IV., Vol. I.

[2] Op. cit., pp. 297–298. See also his remarks upon the degenerate sort of Eastern slave who had the greatest chance of obtaining freedom in the Roman world.

[3] Op. cit., Vol. I, p. 24 : " En montrant comment l'essence d'une

THE ARISTOCRAT AS AN ACHIEVEMENT

I have gone—all too briefly, I fear—into these questions in order to show two things: (1) The store which, in their profound wisdom, the great cultured nations of antiquity unconsciously set by instinct, and (2) how the gradual break-up of old civilisations seems always to have been strangely synchronous with laxity in matters of race pride and of prejudice towards the foreigner. I cannot attempt to go into the details of the second contention nearly as adequately and fully as such men as Gobineau, Reibmayr and Otto Sieck have done; but, basing my contention wholly upon their conclusions, I believe it to be well founded.

Let me now try to show what part instinct plays in the life of a nation, in order that we may esteem at its proper worth the depth of insight and intuitive good taste which has always led all great nations, or their leaders, to regard the foreigner and his blood with suspicion.

I have said that during the lifetime of men—while, that is to say, they are acquiring experience—instinct may be defined as a predisposition, a bias in favour of a certain mode of action, a certain course of conduct.

I will now go further—and in doing so proceed to make myself clear concerning the question of will—by adding to this definition of instinct the following clause: that instinct, as a hereditary bias to act, to select or to reject in a particular way, constitutes the peculiar *will* of a people. To their particular instincts and will, whether slowly and arduously acquired or implanted in them from their very birth as a race, they will owe their foundation as a great nation; to their instincts and will they owe

---

nation s'altère graduellement, je déplace la responsabilité de la décadence ; je la rends, en quelque sorte, moins honteuse ; car elle ne pèse plus sur le fils, mais sur les neveux, puis sur les cousins, puis sur des alliés de moins en moins proches ; et lorsque je fait toucher au doigt que les grands peuples, au moment de leur morts, n'ont qu'une bien faible, bien impondérable partie du sang des fondateurs dont ils ont hérité, j'ai suffisament expliqué comment il se peut faire que les civilisations finissent, puisqu'elles ne restent pas dans les mêmes mains."

their triumphs, their glories, the fruits of their culture, the possession of virtues whereof they may be justly proud, and whatever beauty they may have achieved in their own bodies or in their material creations.

It was this half-realised, half-conscious thought that made the nations of antiquity, or at least their leaders, so jealously proud of the attributes of their blood. It constituted their will. Other blood might be as highly ennobled, as highly cultivated as theirs; other instincts might prove as triumphant and as eminently admirable as theirs; but inasmuch as they were different, inasmuch as they led to a different will, a different course of determined conduct in other nations, these nations must be eschewed as breeding mates, lest a conflict of wills, a neutralisation of wills, a mutual destruction of instinct which is the basis of all will, should lead to the decline of will, to the disintegration of will—that is, to instinctive weakness and the paralysis of all endeavour, all purposeful, resolute and unswerving action in the spirit of the original founder, in the spirit of the great national ancestors.

Thus even the blood of a king was scorned by the early Roman patrician seeking a mate for his daughter; not because a kingly man was scorned, but because a king must of necessity have been a foreigner, a member—however great—of a strange people, and therefore a creature whose instincts, whose will would probably be in conflict with the instincts and will of the Roman. Thus, too, Mark Antony is scorned, not because he chose a low-born lady—Cleopatra was the daughter of a long line of kings—but because Cleopatra was Egyptian, and must be possessed of instincts and a will strange and possibly poisonous to the instincts and will of the Roman. The same remarks apply to the Jewish prejudice towards the Egyptian, and to the Greek prejudice towards the Persian. It manifested itself by an inability to sink race-pride and race-prejudice beneath a rational recognition of superior, or at least equal, claims to culture and refinement in another nation.

THE ARISTOCRAT AS AN ACHIEVEMENT

At the risk, now, of breaking into the general argument, I must attempt to show the relation of instincts to will, and thus clear up the matter of volition, at least from the aristocratic standpoint.

To be quite plain, let us suppose with Reibmayr that all men's instincts may be classified under the three heads: (A) The self-preservative, (B) the reproductive and (C) the social.[1] However much these may be subdivided, however differently they may be coloured, however disproportionately their respective strengths may be combined in the same individual, the peculiar adjustment of (A) (B) (C) will always constitute the character of that individual.

(A) may be paramount and all-powerful, and (B) and (C) may be subservient; (B) may be all-powerful, and (A) and (C) may be subservient; or (C) may be all-powerful, and (A) and (B) may be subservient. But whatever the ultimate adjustment of the three instincts and their subdivisions (the virtues) may turn out to be in the individual, that adjustment will constitute the characteristic keynote of his character and his direction. Whichever instinct obtains the mastery over the others, that instinct will thereafter determine the actions of the whole man, and constitute his will.

A man may be born with all his three instincts almost equally powerful. Life soon gives him opportunities enough of realising their conflicting claims in his breast; and unless one of his instincts, by constant struggles with the other two, attains to mastery, his conduct will always occasion him the most appalling and staggering difficulties.

Let us take a hypothetical case: H—— W—— is a man of thirty with a great life-work before him in the legislature, and the abilities to meet the demands which this life-work will make upon his talents and his energy.

---

[1] *Die Entwicklungsgeschichte des Talents und Genies* (Munich, 1908), Vol. I, p. 242. *Der Erhaltungstrieb, der Geschechtstrieb und der Soziale oder Geselligskeitstrieb.*

He is not securely established in life yet, and his position is still precarious. He meets a woman who charms him so completely that the question of marriage confronts him for the first time in his life with all the terrible force and persuasiveness of a passionate desire.

What is the conflict here? His self-preservative instinct (A) is hostile to an immediate match, because marriage always means a great material sacrifice, and, as his position is still uncertain, it can ill-endure any great strain of this nature upon it. His social instinct (C) is hostile to an immediate match, because his life-work requires all the concentrated attention he can give it, and marriage is likely to divert this attention from its principal object. His reproductive instinct (B) is eloquent, urgent, pressing and importunate, and is prepared to put up a good fight.

It is a clear issue, and, all these instincts being equal, the odds are two to one against his marrying the girl.

But if for many generations the reproductive or sexual instinct has been indulged in his family, it will probably be very powerful, and, like Mark Antony, he may abandon everything for the woman—that is to say, his *will* will reside in the guiding force of his paramount reproductive instinct. If his self-preservative instincts have for many generations been indulged by his family, it will likewise probably be very powerful, and, like Cecil Rhodes, or any other great magnate of mere self-aggrandisement, he will be capable of acting indifferently to women's charms, and will cast the girl aside. His *will* will reside in the guiding force of his paramount self-preservative instinct. If, finally, his social instincts have for many generations been indulged by his family, it will probably be very powerful, and, like Alexander, Cæsar, Charles I and Napoleon (who were never influenced by women), he will be able to divorce himself absolutely from the power of sex, if he should think it necessary, and will only take the woman when he sees that his union with her will serve a purpose very often (though not always necessarily) independent of the mere desire of gratifying his sexual instinct.

I have given this example not so much to prove as to illustrate broadly the relationship of instinct to will. But it will easily be seen that illustrations could be multiplied *ad libitum.*[1]

You have only to think of the subdivisions of the three instincts, and of the numerous virtues to which they can give force and resolution, in order to realise that the will of a man may reside in a whole string of virtues or vices which are either desirable or undesirable, and that the various adjustments of these virtues, backed by the strength of their generating instincts, constitute the varieties of races and of individuals.

We would define will, then, as the guiding force generated by one or two of the instincts. *Strong will* is, therefore, always the sign of a strong leading instinct, bidding the individual pursue such and such a direction or purpose and no other; and weak will is the absence of a strong leading instinct, and the consequent ignorance of any direction or purpose whatsoever.

Now, how do the voluntarist's and determinist's positions stand in the light of this view of will?

The whole discussion about free will and determinism could only have arisen in a weak and sickly age; for, as a matter of fact, they both stand for precisely the same thing, and, as ideas, arise from a similar state of decadence and disease.

To the strong there is no such thing as free will; for free will implies an alternative, and the strong man has no alternative. His ruling instinct leaves him no alternative, allows him no hesitation or vacillation. Strength

---

[1] It should always be borne in mind, however, that the very conflict between the three fundamental instincts in man is very often the primary cause of there being strength in him at all; for it is after a struggle between them that the conquering one, through the exceptional effort it has made, establishes its permanent supremacy by having far outreached the others in power.

of will is the absence of free will. If to the weak man strong will appears to have an alternative, it is a total misapprehension on his part.

To the strong there is also no such thing as determinism as the determinists understand it. Environment and circumambient conditions determine nothing in the man of strong will. To him the only thing that counts, the only thing he hears is his inner voice, the voice of his ruling instinct. The most environment can do is to provide this ruling instinct with an anvil on which to beat out its owner's destiny, and beneath the racket and din of its titanic action all the voices of stimuli from outside, all the determining suggestions and hints from environment, sink into an insignificant and inaudible whisper, not even heard, much less heeded, therefore, by the strong man. That is why the passion of a strong man may be permanent, that is why the actions of a strong man may be consistent; because they depend upon an inner constitution of things which cannot change, and not upon environment which can and does change. If the strong man is acquainted with determinism at all, it is a *determinism from within*, a voice from his own breast; but this is not the determinism of the determinists.[1]

Who, then, has free will—or appears to have it? Obviously the man who, to himself, even more than to others, seems to have an alternative. His inner voice, the voice of his ruling instinct, even if he have one, is so weak, so small in volume, so low in tone that all the

---

[1] Hence the strong man is not, as a rule, susceptible to sudden conversions, sudden changes of opinion, or of his scheme of life. And that is why he is often called wicked by the weak man. For the weaker man knows from experience that he, personally, has been altered or modified by advice, by good counsel, by a word or a text, and he thinks that if the strong man were not "wicked" or "perverse," he also could be altered in this way. The strong man, on the other hand, never calls the weak man "wicked," because, knowing perfectly well that his own deeds are inevitable, he imagines that the weak man's deeds are also inevitable. Consequently he scoffs at, laughs at, or pities the weak man, but does not condemn him from any moral standpoint.

voices from his surroundings dare to measure themselves against it. His mind's ear, far from being deafened by the sound of his own inner voice, is able to listen with respectful and interested attention to the stimuli from outside; it is able to draw comparisons between the volume of sound within and without, and to itself it seems able even to elect to follow the more persuasive and more alluring sound. From this apparent ability which the weak man has of electing one voice or the other—the one in his heart or the one outside—he gets to believe that he has free will; but as his inner voice is generally far weaker than that coming to him from his environment, the determinists are perfectly right in telling him that *he* has not decided the course of his action. That is why the passion of a weak man, if he appear to have any, is never permanent, that is why the actions of a weak man are never consistent; because they depend upon environmental stimuli which change, and not upon an inner constitution of things which does not change.

Determinism from without, then, is characteristic of the weak man's action. But because he is not abashed at the voice from outside daring to measure itself against his inner voice, he imagines he exercises what he calls free will—the solace and the illusion of the degenerate!

Thus the doctrine of free will and that of determinism are essentially the same, and the controversy about them could only have arisen, and could only have been fought with vehemence and misunderstanding, in a thoroughly weak age.

Having explained precisely what I mean by the two terms instinct and will, it now remains for me to make myself equally clear concerning the terms virtue and beauty.

A virtue is essentially an off-shoot, a minor manifestation of one of the dominating instincts. Being essentially a wilful adaptation of the instincts to the conditions and needs of a given environment, it is capable of being modified, of being trained, of being acquired, schooled, perfected, deteriorated and provoked.

For instance, a man is born with a good eye—a powerful, observant, keen and altogether excellent eye. If he be born in a warrior nation of primitive people, prompted by his self-preservative and social instinct, his eye is almost certain to make him develop all the virtues of a good marksman—the certainty of aim, patience in watching for a quarry, self-control over muscles and emotions, and self-reliance and courage *vis à vis* the foe or the beast of prey. Prompted by his reproductive instinct, he will develop the virtues of the fastidious and exacting connoisseur in selecting his mate among women. He will notice things other men fail to notice. He will admire grace of limb and body, and desire and take grace of limb and body.

If he be born in a peaceful, highly cultivated nation like the early Egyptians, prompted by his self-preservative and social instinct, his eye is almost certain to make him develop all the virtues of the good artistic craftsman—the certainty of expression and of judgment of form of the good painter, decorator or sculptor; the patient industry of the expressor who has his hardest critic constantly by him in his own organ of sight, the self-control over muscles and emotions characteristic of him who sets himself a definite task and desires to accomplish it single-handed, and the self-reliance of one who can trust his own ability.

Thus a virtue, though it can be strengthened hereditarily through generations of men who steadily practise it, is much more a personal acquisition than an instinct; it is often a thing that a man watches grow and become perfect in himself during his own lifetime, and as such is a far more conscious possession than the instinct. A man can be extremely proud of virtues which he knows he has strengthened or even acquired during his own lifetime, without ever feeling the slightest pride concerning their root, the strong instinct which has forced these virtues to the fore, or forced him to bring them to perfection.

THE ARISTOCRAT AS AN ACHIEVEMENT

It is for his virtues' sake that man has always dreamt of immortality and longed for it, not for his instincts' sake. These virtues, these possessions, which he is *conscious* of having tempered and perfected under training and under self-training, guided by a strong desire he does not understand, make him feel very naturally proud, and reluctant to part with them or to lose them. It is so much wilful endeavour, wilful self-control, hard toil gone to waste, apparently irrevocably lost! Thus the virtuous man always proudly repudiates the concept of irrevocable, irretrievable annihilation, and, if he is positive to this world and loves it, he hopes and longs for an eternal recurrence, as the Egyptians did; and if he is negative to this world and despises it, he longs for a Beyond away from this world and utterly different from it.

What, then, in the light of these observations, is beauty? Beauty is essentially that regularity, symmetry and grace of feature and figure which is gradually acquired by a stock pursuing for generations a regular, symmetrical existence, under the guidance of the particular values of their race. As these particular values give rise to particular virtues, so the faces and bodies of a people come to be stamped with the character associated with the virtues most general among them. And a certain association, often unconscious, of the two—virtue and physiognomy—always grows up within the race, so that the most beautiful person is always he who, in his face and figure, stands for the highest product of the virtues most prized by the community. In a vigorous, healthy race the idea of ugliness is always clearly associated with a degenerate face or figure, or with the face and figure of the foreigner and stranger. The foreigner or stranger, though beautiful perhaps to his own people, stands for a regularity, an order of virtues and their basic instincts which is unknown, strange or unfamiliar—therefore he is ugly. The moment a race begins to think another race beautiful, its faith in its own instincts and virtues and the type they produce is beginning to decline.

A. DEFENCE OF ARISTOCRACY

We are now in a better position for appreciating the profound wisdom of the ancient prejudice and the prejudice of all stronger races against race-mixture.

For what does mixture do? It can do but one thing: *it breaks the will.*

Every race has its own special adjustment and development of the instincts, its own notion of virtue, its own standard of will-power and its own concept of beauty.

What happens, then, when two races mix?

Obviously, two voices instead of one now speak in each man's breast. When confronted by two alternatives, instead of being able to point to " this " or " that " without hesitation, each man now vacillates, temporises, doubts, stammers, ponders, and is overcome by a paroxysm of perplexity.[1] When coming upon two directions, instead of stepping deliberately and composedly into one of them, each man now stumbles, falters, wonders, staggers, and often falls.

As a matter of fact the promptings of two totally different and often hostile sets of ancestors are now heard in his conscience.[2] He becomes unreliable, unsteady, uncertain. Not only can he not be trusted to choose the correct course of conduct for his neighbour's or employer's interests, he can scarcely be trusted to choose the correct course of conduct for himself. As Reibmayr says : " The root of a national character resides in the mass of the people, and in the individual peculiarities fixed and become hereditary in it through generations. That is why inbred people have character, and why half-castes or hybrids are notoriously characterless." [3]

---

[1] The old Egyptian word for indecision actually took this condition into account, and implied that these wisest of people knew perfectly well what was wrong with the man who hesitates. Their term for what we understand by doubt and lack of decision was " *hèt-snaou,*" which means " that which has two hearts." See Letourneau, *l'Évolution de l'Éducation*, p. 308.

[2] See pp. 276–277 of Chapter VI in *this* book.

[3] *Inzucht und Vermischung*, p. 37.

The unreliability of the half-caste is well known both in India and America, and the proclivity these people often show to practise the lowest and most spiritless forms of crime is evidence of their lack of will and character. Manu condemned inter-class *mésalliances* because they "caused a mixture of the castes among men, thence follows sin, which cuts up even the roots and causes the destruction of everything. . . . But that kingdom in which such bastards, sullying the purity of the castes, are born, perishes quickly, together with its inhabitants." [1]

It is now—that is to say, at times of promiscuous crossbreeding—that the voice from outside begins to be heeded; it is now that external stimuli can decide an issue; it is now that environment has, as it were, a chance of determining a course of conduct. Nothing is certain, nothing stands on solid ground—the very breeze about him makes a man twist and turn like a weathercock. It is for this reason that the ancient customs and institutions of a people begin to totter and to crumble away after a general mixture of blood. It is for this reason that the social life degenerates and breaks up. Hence the profound wisdom of Constantine's observation that "the mixture of foreign blood is the fruitful source of disorder and discord." [2]

All the virtues strung like beads upon these fundamental instincts of one race in a man's body are at variance with those belonging to the other race. Chaos is necessarily the result, and a state of absolute weakness supervenes. The instincts of the man are confused and his will is, therefore, broken; his modicum of bodily strength, though it is the same as it was before, or only slightly increased, has now twenty instead of ten virtues amongst which to divide itself up, and consequently the vigour of his virtues, their power, declines. He is perhaps more versatile, more catholic, more ready to lend an ear to every sound; but he is no longer what he was, he can no longer do what he did, he has become weak, faithless and infirm of purpose. Like

---

[1] *Laws of Manu*, Chapter VIII, 353, and Chapter IX, 61.
[2] See p. 307 of this chapter.

the Lombards whom Gibbon mentions,[1] he may be terri-
fied by the sight of his ancestors, he may look with awe
upon their feats and their features; but he is incapable of
doing as they did, or of looking as they looked. Often he
is incapable even of carrying on the work they bequeathed
to him.

In his face you notice strange features, unlike those of
either of his ancestral races; he is, racially speaking,
"ugly," and is very often so from every other point of
view.

Multiply the mixtures, and all the evils enumerated
above become a thousand times more acute, until all
character vanishes, all will disintegrates, and all virtue
disappears.

It is for this reason that, in democratic times—in times,
that is to say, when much is said about the equality of all
men, and the "brotherhood of the human species," and
when much is done, too, which is in keeping with these
doctrines, when everybody marries, and can marry anybody, and there is no distinction among peoples or classes,
it is for this reason, I say, that in such times, the will of
communities gradually declines,[2] the character of communities slowly goes to pieces,[3] and ugliness in face and

---

[1] *The Decline and Fall*, Vol. V, Chapter 45, p. 27.

[2] See Gobineau, op. cit., p. 89: "Plus une race se maintient pure,
moins sa base sociale est attaquée, parceque la logique de la race demeure
la même."

[3] The chief characteristic of weakness, which is to be wholly at the
mercy of external determinants, also shows itself in the form of an
increase of vanity and a decrease of pride in democratic times. For
vanity is simply the self-esteem of the modest man who depends for his
opinion of himself upon the opinion that others have of him—whose
opinion of himself, that is to say, is suggested to him by his environment, and who, in order to make this environmental opinion a good
one, is always trying to seduce the world to a good opinion of him by
every manner of artifice, trick and exertion. The proud man, however,
whose self-esteem arises from an inner knowledge of his value, and who
is, therefore, independent of environmental opinion, tends to become
extinct in democratic times. On the increase of vanity nowadays see
remarks by Arthur Ponsonby, op. cit., p. 124.

figure and in the homes of men, steadily becomes an ever more common and every-day occurrence.

It is these evils which the racial pride and arrogant self-esteem of all great races intuitively sought to guard against and to avoid, by means of their unanimous and vigorous distrust and contempt of the foreigner, the stranger, or the " barbarian." Just as the man, conscious of having reared a virtue in himself by the sedulous and painstaking exercise of certain principles, has a just pride in his achievement which safeguards him against a *mésalliance* which would too obviously imperil the transmission of that virtue to his family; [1] so, as we have seen, the nation which is conscious of having reared something worth keeping in instinct, virtue, will and beauty, cultivates and nourishes a bitter, implacable and determined feeling of distrust and contempt of the foreigner, whoever he may be, queen or king, noble or sage, god or magician.

But, you will object, inbreeding cannot go on for ever. In time sterility supervenes, blood is impoverished, constitutions become enfeebled and stature declines. All this is perfectly true, though extreme.

The reproductive powers which consist simply of a periodical amputation from the body of forces which are unamenable to the will—that is to say, which the will is not sufficiently powerful to organise and to use for its own purposes—would naturally tend to decline when, through inbreeding, the will is driven up to its maximum of organising power, and when every degree of energy the individual body possesses can be given a task, a purpose, an accomplishment, within the individual himself and not outside him in the form of a bud or offshoot of himself, with which his will was unable to cope.

The very rise of the reproductive powers, when an inbred race is mixed, shows through the coincident drop in

[1] That is why, in periods where there is little will and little virtue abroad, *mésalliances* of the most *outré* nature are consummated with such wantonness and levity.

will power, explained in detail above, how deeply the two are interdependent.[1]

Thus vigorous and rich reproductive powers can always be associated with a low order of will-power, and *vice versâ*.

Nevertheless, before that point is reached when, although the constitution and blood are not impoverished, inbreeding has so cultivated the will as to make its organising power sufficiently perfect to preclude all possibility of generative amputations from the soma taking place, the practice of inbreeding can last a very long while, and has been known to last a very long while, in such nations, for instance, as the ancient Hindus, the ancient Egyptians, and even among certain divisions of the ancient Hellenes.

Admitting, however, that if the inbred race is to survive, sterility must be corrected, even though constitutional decline is still a very long way off, the question next arises, what are the ultimate risks of a judicious mixture?

"The principal effects of cross-breeding," says Reibmayr, "are the maintenance of constitutional vigour and the modification of character. It keeps the blood and the nervous system sound and active, and checks the production of extreme characters. In its effects, it is thus exactly the reverse of inbreeding, the operation of which is to fix and petrify characters, to favour the rearing of extreme idiosyncrasies, and in the long run to enfeeble constitutional and sexual vigour."[2]

Thus, when that extremity is reached when an inbred race is threatened with extinction through sterility, cross-breeding, while giving fresh life to its constitution, undermines the character. This is the worst possible consequence of the most extreme case. But, what indeed could be worse? To lose your character is to lose your iden-

---

[1] As far as I know this is the first time that this explanation of the sterility of highly inbred races has been advanced. The first to suggest that reproduction was a sign of a certain impotence of will was, however, Friedrich Nietzsche.

[2] *Inzucht und Vermischung*, pp. 70–71.

tity; it is practically to cease to be. It is to take leave of everything that makes you yourself.

Of course, the larger the number of the original endogamic community, the longer will it take for inbreeding to show its evil effects. For instance in Sparta, which was famous in antiquity owing to its capacity for permanence, it took from six hundred to eight hundred years (*i. e.* twenty to thirty generations) to reduce a ruling caste which once consisted of from eight to nine thousand families, to a class consisting of only a few hundred families. But nowhere was inbreeding more severe than in the nobility of Sparta.

Increase the number of the families in your endogamic community and you naturally postpone the evil day of reckoning, when all this rearing and cultivating of special characters to a maximum degree must be paid for. Exercise severe selective principles among them, principles as severe if possible as some of Natures own, and you will postpone the evil day still longer.

Sooner or later, however, if your community is to survive, you must contemplate a cross of some kind with a neighbouring people.

It is, however, quite ridiculous to suppose that, for the purposes of the rejuvenation of stock, that cross must be effected with a people as remote and as different as possible from the inbred community in question.

It was this ridiculous error in cross-breeding that proved so fatal to the communities of antiquity, and which ultimately swamped their original identity completely out of existence.

The Asiatic, Jewish and Northern barbarian slaves, as Otto Sieck has so well shown,[1] who ultimately mixed their blood with the Roman, had very little in common with the Roman people—so little, indeed, that where character modification took place at all it was rather a process of cancelling out until nil remained, than of merely introducing conflicting tendencies which might be reconciled,

[1] Op. cit., Chapter " Sklaven and Klienten."

or of which some might become supreme. And even where the Asiatic character prevailed, as it sometimes did, in its indolence, apathy and spirituality, it was scarcely of a type to take over and continue the strenuous far-reaching and utilitarian work of the original Romans.

But, although every sort of cross while rejuvenating stock must to some extent implant two voices in a man's breast and thus, up to a certain point, destroy character, it is not necessary, if the conflict be not too great, that this destruction should be permanent.

A certain period of disturbed equilibrium must be overcome, as in Egypt after the Hyksos invasion, but once the effects of the mixture have been felt and its benefits to the body fully enjoyed, *another process begins to operate* which is most important for the future welfare and power of the original race: the process of attaining once again to harmony or to regularity of character by a reconciliation of the conflicting elements in each man's breast, or by the subordination of a part of them to a set of virtues, or to an instinct which gains supremacy.

If the characteristics of the two stocks are not too far asunder, this is possible and often beneficial. For, just as a man's instincts, as I have shown, by struggling together drive the potentially powerful one to its highest point of vigour, so, in a crossed breed, after a period of doubt, weakness and decharacterisation, a struggle may ensue between the voices of the two sets of ancestors in each man's breast, which may prove the most potent spur to the supremacy of the race's strongest and best potentialities. This, of course, would be possible only if a period of severe inbreeding followed upon a period of cross-breeding. It would be quite impossible if, as we find men doing nowadays, cross-breeding were carried on promiscuously and habitually with anybody and everybody without let or hindrance.

The ancient Egyptians, for instance, suffering no doubt from the evil effects of a too lengthy period of inbreeding, were overcome and conquered by the Shepherd Kings.

What happened? After a period of from four hundred to six hundred years, during which the Shepherd Kings ruled supreme in Egypt, and cross-breeding was practised between the two races, especially in the upper classes, without restraint,[1] the more highly cultured race showed itself pre-potent, as it always does, recovered from the shock to its character, absorbed the best from the Hyksos, successfully drove them out, and rose from the experience a refreshed and greater people; for now they had added the warrior spirit of their late invaders to their former character.

Thus, it is possible, when two races blend, for their respective characters, after a struggle, to arrive at some sort of harmony, and to grow, if anything, stronger in the process of attaining to this harmony than they were before. A judicious cross, therefore, while it will be sure to render character unstable for a while, need not do so permanently. The only thing that destroys character permanently is the general, continual, indiscriminate, inter-class, international and inter-racial cross-breeding that is the rule and custom to-day, and which always becomes the rule and custom in democratic times.

The mixture of race in the ancient Greeks, for instance, though it never ultimately attained to any successful harmony—for the Aryan and the Pelasgian were apparently too hostile ever to come to a settlement in the breast of the ancient Hellenes in so short a time—produced some very great people while the struggle between the two characters lasted; and without the insidiously destructive action of the freedman and metic element, which was continually rising up into the ruling caste like mud from the bottom of a pool, there is no telling to what heights the Greeks might have attained if the two original races in their breasts had arrived at some adjustment.

The English, again, offer an example of a people who, up to the time of Elizabeth, were very fortunate indeed in

---

[1] The conquerors, being a less cultivated race than the Egyptians, were proud to mix with the latter; and powerful enough to override popular prejudice against such unions.

their crosses; for, in almost every case, save for their inter-marriage with the Celts of their western and northern provinces, their crosses have been with closely allied races who could not introduce a very disturbing or degenerating element into their characters.

Thus while an occasional cross, if consummated with a people whose will and whose virtues have a direction not too extremely hostile to their own, may prove the salvation of a too highly inbred race, nothing could be more fatal to the character of a people than the constant, indiscriminate and tasteless cross-breeding which we find comes into fashion—nay is almost *de rigueur*—in democratic times. But whereas the nations of antiquity did not consciously know this, and were blissfully unaware of the dangers they ran by promiscuous cross-breeding, save that they knew how their noblest ancestors had for some reason or other—to them probably unknown—forbidden it; we of the twentieth century know these things. We know what constitutes character, and we know how character is destroyed, and we can offer no excuse if we persist in errors the consequences of which we can gauge and foresee.

Even the Emperor Constantine seems to have been sufficiently modern to have known that although crossing was bad, not all crossing was to be deprecated; for, while we find him forbidding his son to marry a daughter of one of the foreign princes of the north " without fame or faith," he made an exception in the case of Bertha, daughter of Hugo, the King of Italy. And why did he make this exception? Because he esteemed the fidelity and valour of the Franks, and because Hugo was, more-over, a lineal descendant of the great Charlemagne.[1]

Reibmayr is quite clear on this point. He says : " The crossing of varieties which are closely allied in bodily and spiritual characteristics always produces the best results, and is always the best means of keeping a race viable and pro-lific and of checking the effects of severe inbreeding. Whereas the experiments of animal breeders show that great

[1] See Gibbon, *Decline and Fall*, Vol. VI, Chapter 53, pp. 87–88.

disparity of race and character in cross-breeding only leads to the formation of discordant, vacillating natures; in fact, to characterlessness. That is why, as every one knows, all caste-bastards—more particularly those that issue from the union of castes very distant from each other in the matter of character—have notoriously a bad name." [1]

Now, it is obvious that in all endogamic peoples, whether of a mixed or pure race, who are so keenly conscious of differences and distinctions, and who are so very much alive to that which separates them from other peoples that they endeavour unceasingly to maintain their particular traits like treasure-trove, a very quick perception of differences within their own community must be a perfectly natural possession. Where great stress is laid upon the existence of any particular quality, and where such a quality is jealously preserved, it stands to reason that the different degrees of its purity or intensity within the confines of a people will be speedily recognised and appreciated by all members of the social body.

Indeed, so keen will this recognition and appreciation be, that a sort of natural differentiation of man from man and of woman from woman will grow up almost unconsciously among them and give rise gradually to orders of rank, wheresoever that order of rank is not in the first place established in bi-racial peoples by the relation of conqueror to conquered.

And it also stands to reason that according as the intensity or purity of race-will, race-virtue, race-instinct, race-beauty and race-vigour is either great or small in a certain individual, so he will stand either high or low in the order of rank. And if he stand high, he will be valued not only because he is fair to look upon, not only because he can be relied upon as a standard of the race's virtue and instinct, and not only because he is something strong to cling to, but also, and sometimes chiefly, because he is a great achievement. It is felt, it is known, it is understood, that in order to produce him, many generations must have

1 *Inzucht und Vermischung*, p. 50.

garnered and accumulated untold treasure in virtue, volition, vigour and beauty. It is realised that such intensity and purity in a people's particular character is not attained without an effort, a prolonged and sometimes patient struggle in silent and unostentatious paths, and that therefore, such a man is to a very great extent a feat, a prize, an *achievement* par excellence.

All grace, all beauty, all strength, all *ease*, has a past, a long, arduous past, and it is because of this past, in addition to the practical value of the qualities above-mentioned, that a race who knows what these things cost and how difficult they are to obtain, prizes and values those of its members who belong by nature to the first order of rank.

Gradually, therefore, in all tasteful peoples who are self-conscious about their virtues, a social ladder is formed in which the "lucky strokes of nature," the examples of "flourishing life" inevitably stand at the top, to direct, to lead, and to show by means of living examples to what heights in virtue, beauty and will the type man can scale if he choose.

And among these various grades or strata of people within a community, very much the same feeling naturally develops in their relations with each other, as obtains between the whole social body and the stranger or foreigner.

Knowing their beauty and their virtues to have been acquired with great pains and with generations of effort, each division in the order of rank, proud and jealous of its achievements, is naturally loth to part with them or to have them undermined or destroyed by *mésalliances*.

Within an endogamic people you now find whole divisions which practise on a small scale what the whole race is practising on a large scale. Castes are formed and their virtues and particular characteristics are as jealously guarded against those of other castes, as the racial instinct is guarded against the stranger and foreigner. Matrimonial lapses, *mésalliances*, are strictly prohibited and severely punished. It is realised that the preservation, even of virtues, depends upon careful inbreeding, *or upon the most scrupulous care in selection, if cross-breeding becomes a necessity.* Down below, at the foot of the ladder, a hotch-potch of outcasts eke out a humble and despised existence. They are either foreigners, the fruit of crosses with the foreigner, or the issue of flagrant breaches of the matrimonial laws between the castes. It is generally understood that they cannot be trusted, it is understood that they cannot be used in any high office, it is believed that the god of the race himself has condemned them to their insignificant existence.

An aristocrat, overcome by momentary lust, who takes one of the women of this lowest order to his bed, commits the most heinous of crimes and will certainly go to hell. A man of this lowest order who, meeting a daughter of the aristocrat, succeeds in luring her to his bed, is instantly killed on being found out.

It is felt that there is something worth preserving and worth treasuring in this society, and the present keepers of the Bank of England could not be more vigilant, nor the present laws against thieving more severe, than are the guardians and laws of such a society.

I am, however, not concerned with the whole society in this essay; I am concerned only with those that stand first in the order of rank. And to speak of these highest blooms of a nation's virtue, beauty and will, as the true aristocrats, as the only aristocrats, and as the creatures who, every time that a high culture has developed in the history of the world, have been responsible for that culture, is not a mere romantic fiction; it is not a fantastic creation of the imagination : it is one of the most solid historical facts and truths we possess.

Whether we turn to the sacerdotal aristocracy of Egypt, the Incas of Peru, the Brāhmans of India, the Jews of the desert, the Eupatrids of Attic Greece, the Patricians of Rome, or the German nobility of the Middle Ages, we are concerned in each case with the best that a particular people were able to achieve in the rearing of flourishing specimens;

and the story of these people's high culture is the story of the aristocratic influence they underwent.

In each case, too, the class was a hereditary one, or at least, its strongest prejudice was in favour of the hereditary principle; though, as we shall see, fresh blood from other castes was courted, if not coveted on occasion, by the wisest among the aristocracies mentioned. We know that the Egyptian priests, the Incas of Peru, the Brahmans and the Jewish priesthood were, within certain well-defined limits, hereditary orders, while as to the others, their very names, as Bluntschli points out, testify to their hereditary character.[1]

To deal with the Egyptians first, Herodotus tells us that the aristocratic sacerdotal order which directed, guided and watched over them with such paternal care, was a hereditary order,[2] and despite the doubt that has been cast upon this statement of the great historian, there is probably a good deal of truth in it.

Endogamic and proud of their race as the Egyptians were, we do not require to be told that the feeling of distinction, of exclusion and separateness was most probably extended from an inter-herd to an intra-herd application; for, as we have seen above, it is the acquisition and consciousness of particular virtues, produced at great cost, that make men feel their distance from other men, and make them anxious to preserve themselves from all those influences which, in a matrimonial union, might undermine their stock.

---

[1] See *The Theory of the State* (3rd Edition, Authorised Trans., Clarendon Press), p. 121: "The old nobility (Adel) whom we find in Europe in the earliest records, was everywhere a hereditary class, and, as a rule, absorbed the chief functions of the two highest castes. Language generally bears witness to its hereditary character : the Athenian *Eupatridae* and Roman *Patricii* are so called from their descent from noble fathers, while the German Adalinge derive their name from the family (Adal) from which they drew their blood. . . . The Lucumones of Etruria and the knights of the Gauls were a hereditary nobility."

[2] Book II, 37.

Moreover, the Egyptians were among the few people who were so keenly aware of the danger of inter-caste or inter-class marriages that, like the Incas, they tolerated the marriage of brothers and sisters in order to be quite sure that the qualities not only of the individual caste, but also of the individual family might be preserved. We can form but an inadequate idea to-day, of the health and excellence of bodily constitution that was required for such marriages to have been as regular as they were in Egypt for centuries, without causing grave physical degeneration. We are all too ill nowadays to risk a marriage even between first cousins—not to speak of brother and sister. But, if you recollect that such close consanguineous marriages are deprecated to-day only because they multiply the chances of handing on to the offspring a hereditary family taint, which here, in the marriage of brother and sister or of first cousins, forms a double instead of a single stream; you will be able to realise the great advantages secured through such marriages by people who were healthy enough to consummate them. What a multiplication of virtue, will, beauty and vigour! Not only the advice of the Eugenist and moralist, but also the whole prejudice of modern democratic and liberal mankind, is, however opposed nowadays to this exclusiveness and sense of distance and distinction in the mating of couples; and, as Gobineau says, the whole object of modern science as of modern popular opinion is to show that the story of a race which did and could perpetuate itself by intra-herd and intra-family unions alone, is a dangerous and inadmissible fiction.[1]

---

[1] Op. cit., p. xviii. "Il fut un temps, et il n'est pas loin, où les préjugés contre les mariages consanguins étaient devenus tels qu'il fut question de leur donner la consécration de la loi. Épouser une cousine Germaine équivalait à frapper à l'avance tous ses enfants de surdité et d'autres affections héréditaires. Personne ne semblait réflechir que les générations qui ont precédé la nôtre, fort adonnées aux mariages consanguins, n'ont rien connu des conséquences morbides qu'on prétend leur attribuer ; que les Seleucides, les Ptolémés, les Incas, époux de leurs sœurs, étaient, les uns et les autres, de très bonne santé et d'intelligence

There can be no doubt, however, that the Egyptians were such a race, and their very gods set them the best example in this respect. The brothers Osiris and Set married their sisters Isis and Nephthys; while, as for the Egyptian Kings, close consanguineous marriages were not only quite *de rigueur* in their families from the earliest times, but the custom actually lasted as late as the Roman period, and is said to be common, among the people, even at the present day, in the form of first-cousin matches.[1]

Thus we find that Ptolemy II married his daughter and then his sister; Ptolemy IV married his sister; Ptolemy VI and VII (two brothers) married, one after the other, the same sister; Ptolemy VIII married, one after the other, his two sisters; and Ptolemy XII and XIII married, one after the other, their putative sister Cleopatra.

To raise doubts concerning the hereditary character of the highest castes in such a nation, as some historians have done, seems to me to be somewhat gratuitous, not to say absurd. Nevertheless, knowing the profound wisdom of the Egyptians, it is probable that whenever and wherever the evil results of close inbreeding—sterility, for example—began to show signs of appearing, they not only tolerated but encouraged inter-caste unions.

The two highest castes, for example, were the sacerdotal and the military; it was from either of these two

---

fort acceptable, sans parler de leur beauté, généralement hors ligne. Des faits si concluants, si irréfutable, ne pouvaient convaincre personne, parcequ'on prétendait utiliser, bon gré mal gré, les fantaisies d'un libéralisme, qui, n'aimant pas l'exclusivité capitale, était contraire à toute pureté de sang, et l'on voulait autant que possible célébrer l'union du nègre et du blanc d'où provient le mulâtre. Ce qu'il fallait démontrer dangereux, inadmissible, c'était une race qui ne s'unissait et ne se perpétuait qu'avec elle-même."

[1] See Reibmayr, *Inzucht und Vermischung*, p. 165. "It is quite certain that in the whole realm of Egypt, and throughout all its historical periods, the closest inbreeding was regarded as something perfectly natural and self-understood ; just as the marriage of first cousins is regarded by modern Egyptians as the most obvious step, commended equally by nature as by reason."

castes that the King was chosen; and we are told that it was not uncommon for a priest to marry a daughter of the military caste and for a warrior to take his wife from the sacerdotal caste.[1] While, as I shall show later, fresh blood was even allowed to rise up from the very lowest classes, in cases where exceptional ability was shown.

We may conclude, therefore, that despite anything that has been said to the contrary, Herodotus was probably right in his claim that the castes were hereditary, and that therefore the highest caste, the sacerdotal aristocracy, were, within reasonable limits, a hereditary caste. As to their ruler qualities, I shall speak later; but as to their beauty, as Reibmayr says, to judge from the monuments, it must have been of a very high order.[2]

My insistence in the matter of the beauty of the true aristocrat will strike many of my readers as strange. But, as a matter of fact, it is only strange in modern ears, Foolishly, recklessly and, as I think, at great national peril, we have allowed the Christian doctrine of the soul to mislead us and corrupt us on this point; but the healthy truth nevertheless remains, that there can be no good spiritual qualities without beautiful bodily qualities. Be suspicious of everybody who holds another view, and remember that the ugly, the botched, the repulsive, the foul of breath, have *reasons* for adhering to this doctrine that "a beautiful soul can justify and redeem a foul body"; for without it the last passport they possess for admittance into decent fragrant society is lost. Think of the men who have created things worth having in their lives; think of Kephrën in the Fourth Dynasty of Egypt, think of Pericles, of Alexander, of Cæsar, of Mahommed, of Cæsar Borgia, of Napoleon, of Goethe; recall the reputed beauty of the ancient Incas, the reputed beauty of the gods—and you have a gallery of the most beautiful beings that the mind of any artist could conceive. Now

[1] The marriage of the legislator Joseph and the priest's daughter Asenath is an example of this.
[2] *Inzucht und Vermischung*, p. 171.

think of the men who have created or established things that all good taste must deplore—things of which the whole world will one day regret ever to have heard— Socrates, Luther and Cromwell, and you have three of the ugliest beasts that have ever blighted a sunny day.

The prejudice of the ancients, as we know, and shall also see, was entirely in favour of the theory of the concord of bodily and spiritual beauty, and one has only to think of the Greek phrase καλὸς κ' ἀγαθός,[1] so frequently applied in cases where in English phraseology we should use the word "good" alone, in order to realise how deeply the two ideas must have been welded together in the hearts, at least, of the ancient Hellenes.[2]

But, to return to the question under consideration, the classical instance, of course, in regard to the exclusiveness of the caste system is afforded by the society of the ancient Hindus.

The aristocratic Brahman was perfectly self-conscious of all his virtues, and in the Law Book of Manu, we get an ingenuous proof of the pride of this great caste, and the jealousy with which they preserved their purity.

"Of created things," we read in Manu, "the most excellent are said to be those which are animated; of the animated those which subsist by intelligence; of the intelligent, mankind, and of men, the Brahmanas.

"A Brahmana, coming into existence, is born as the highest on earth, the lord of all created beings, for the protection of the treasury of the law.

"He sanctifies any company which he may enter."[3]

People who feel like this about their order are not playing a part; they are too deeply conscious of the sacred-

---

[1] This phrase seems originally to have been applied to the *nobles* or *gentlemen* : Lat. *optimates*, like the old French *prudhommes*, German *gute Männer*; but later, as in Aristophanes, it meant a perfect man, a man as he should be (see Liddell and Scott).

[2] See on this point a few notes on pp. 11 and 12 of this book.

[3] Chapter I, 96, 99, 105, *The Laws of Manu* (translated by G. Buhler), 1886.

ness of their privileges. They know the kind of fibre and stamina required for a knowledge of the greatest things, and they are aware that not only they themselves, but even knowledge itself is abased, when the right to possess it is given into the hands of those who have not either this fibre or stamina.

"Sacred learning approached a Brahmana and said to him : 'I am thy treasure, preserve me, deliver me not to a scorner; so preserved I shall become supremely strong!

"'But deliver me, as to the keeper of thy treasure, to a Brahmana whom thou shalt know to be pure, of subdued senses, chaste and attentive.

"'Even in times of dire distress a teacher of the Veda should rather die with his knowledge than sow it in barren soil.' "[1]

The best light thrown on the relative importance of the four ancient Hindu castes, seems to me to consist of verses on names.

"Let the first part of a Brahmana's name denote something auspicious; a Kshatriya's be connected with power; and a Vaisya's with wealth; but a Sudra's express something contemptible.

"The second part of the Brahmana's name shall be a word implying protection; of a Vaisya's a term expressive of thriving; and of a Sudra's an expression denoting service."[2]

And how see how the pride and self-preservative instinct of this ancient people led them to ensure for all time the purity and excellence of their aristocratic stock—

"By practising handicrafts, by pecuniary transactions, by begetting children on Sudra females only, by trading in cows, horses, and carriages, by the pursuit of agriculture and by taking service under a king.

"By low marriages, by omitting the performance of secret rites, by neglecting the study of the Veda, and

[1] Chapter II, 113, 114, 115.   [2] Ibid., 31, 32.

by irreverence towards Brahmanas, great families sink low."[1]

And listen to this—

"A Brahmana who takes a Sudra wife to his bed, will after death sink into hell, if he begets a child by her, he will lose the rank of a Brahmana.

"The manes and the gods will not eat the offering of that man who performs the rites in honour of the gods, of the manes, and of guests, chiefly with a Sudra wife's assistance, and such a man will not go to heaven.

"For him who drinks the moisture of a Sudra's lips, who is tainted by her breath, and who begets a son on her, no expiation is prescribed."[2]

Not only the health but the beauty of the Brahman must be preserved, therefore he is recommended most urgently to select a beautiful woman,[3] and to avoid her who "has black hair on her body," or who is "subject to hemorrhoids, or phthisis, or weakness of digestion, or epilepsy, or white and black leprosy."[4] Neither must he marry a girl with a "redundant member," nor "one who is sickly."[5]

Although he must not insult the maimed, the botched, and the inferior, he must be brought up to avoid them. He must understand, and rightly too, that a certain stigma attaches to disease and ill-health, which nothing can remove. Thus the sick and the bungled themselves learn to know their proper place on earth and their proper worth, and are not encouraged as they are to-day to push themselves insolently to the fore, and regard themselves as the equals of the sound and the healthy, simply because of the pernicious doctrine of the redeeming soul.

A Brahmana must "not insult those who have redundant limbs or are deficient in limbs . . . not those who have no beauty or wealth, nor those who are of low birth; but he must carefully avoid their company. Thus he

[1] Chapter III, 63, 64.   [2] Ibid., 17–19.
[3] Ibid., 60–62.   [4] Ibid., 7.   [5] Ibid., 8.

must avoid: eunuchs,[1] one afflicted with a skin disease,[2] a physician,[3] those who subsist by shopkeeping,[4] a man with deformed nails or black teeth,[5] one suffering from consumption,[6] one whose only or first wife is a Sudra female,[7] a one-eyed man,[8] a drunkard,[9] him who is afflicted with a disease,[10] an epileptic man,[11] one who suffers from scrofulous swellings of the glands,[12] one afflicted with leprosy,[13] a madman,[14] a blind man,[15] the club-footed man.[16]

This valuation of the diseased, the misshapen, the bungled and the botched, is more merciful and more practical than the methods of isolation, segregation and sterilisation proposed by the Eugenists; because, if the fact of bungledom and disease is bravely faced by the sound and the sick alike, so that they may each feel they are a class apart that must never mix, all compulsory pre-nuptial separations and prohibitions from the quarter of the Eugenist's surgery become superfluous. What is cruel, what is inhuman, is to rear people in the sentimental and quasi-merciful belief that there is nothing degrading and " unclean " (the good Old Testament adjective applied to disease) in disease and bungledom, but that a beautiful soul justifies everything; and then, when the world has got into such a state of physical degeneration through this doctrine, to suggest the organisation of a pre-nuptial check on all unions contemplated under the influence of this belief, without making any attempt to alter values. But this is just the sort of cruelty which becomes indispensable after too long a spell of sentimental nonsense.

Thus we see that everything possible was done to preserve the Brahman, the superior caste of the Hindus, from

[1] Chapter III, 150.
[2] Ibid., 151.
[3] Ibid., 152.
[4] Ibid., 152.
[5] Ibid., 153.
[6] Ibid., 154.
[7] Ibid., 155.
[8] Ibid., 155.
[9] Ibid., 159.
[10] Ibid., 159.
[11] Ibid., 161.
[12] Ibid., 161.
[13] Ibid., 161.
[14] Ibid., 151.
[15] Ibid., 161.
[16] Ibid., 165.

degeneration by cross-breeding either with a lower caste, a diseased or bungled stock, or an ugly family. But the people, of whose laws the Book of Manu is but a codification, were a wise people, and they knew perfectly well that a loophole of escape must be left open to the highest, in order that, if they liked, they might help to regenerate their stock by marrying outside their caste, when inbreeding threatened to produce sterility. And, in Chapter X, all those laws and regulations are to be found dealing with the issue of such mixed marriages and with the number of generations the progeny has to wait, before it is included in the highest caste. For instance: " If a female of the caste sprung from a Brahmana and a Sudra female bear children to one of the highest rank, the inferior tribe attains the highest caste with the seventh generation." [1]

Inbreeding with the occasional alternative of refreshers from the other castes, this—as in all other wisely administered aristocratic states—was the rule among the Hindus.

Turning now to the Jews, we find much the same system, on a less complicated scale. But in this case we are particularly fortunate in being able actually to trace the rise of their aristocracy to a single family—an authentic instance of a rule which probably holds good for the origin of all aristocracies. [2]

In Apocryphal and Rabbinical literature, Levi, the third son of Jacob and Leah, is represented as a person of great piety, a visionary who foresaw the glory of his family, and to whom Jacob, his father, entrusted the secret writings of the ancients, in order to keep them in his family for all time. At the time of Israel's entrance into Egypt, we are told that this Levi had three sons, Gershon, Kohath and Merari; [3] but, when we reach the date of the exodus which, according to the Bible, is 430 years later, [4] these had grown into a numerous tribe.

Now about eighty years before the departure of the Jews from Egypt, " there went a man of the house of

[1] Chapter X, 64.
[2] See also p. 330.
[3] Gen. xliv. 11.
[4] Exod. xii. 41.

Levi, and took to wife a daughter of Levi." [1] .This man was Amram, and his wife was Jochebed, his father's sister.[2] "And the woman conceived, and bare a son : and when she saw him that he was a goodly child, she hid him three months." [3]

This child, brought up by an Egyptian princess and consequently learned in the science of Egypt, became the man Moses, who ultimately, as we know, led the Israelites out of Egypt.

Whatever distinction the house or tribe of Levi might have enjoyed previous to the exodus from Egypt, it is obvious that once two such members of it as Moses and his elder brother Aaron had appeared, its destiny as a leading caste was assured. And, indeed, we find that very soon after the people of Israel had entered the wilderness, and Moses had given them their laws and had built them their tabernacle, Aaron and his sons are chosen for the priest's office.[4] A little later the office is made a hereditary privilege of the whole family when God commanded Moses, concerning his brother and his nephews as follows—

"And thou shalt bring Aaron and his sons unto the door of the tabernacle of the congregation, and wash them with water.

"And thou shalt put upon Aaron the holy garments, and anoint him and sanctify him; that he may minister unto me in the priest's office.

"And thou shalt bring his sons, and clothe them with coats :

"And thou shalt anoint them, as thou didst anoint their father, that they may minister unto me in the priest's office : for their anointing shall surely be an everlasting priesthood throughout the generations." [5]

What happens here is perfectly plain. In the presence of a people whom they had greatly benefited, and who had followed their leadership and had accepted their guidance without question, the heads of the tribe of Levi consecrate

---

[1] Exod. ii. 1.   [2] Exod. vi. 20.   [3] Exod. ii. 2.
[4] Exod. xxviii. 1, 3, 41.   [5] Exod. xl. 12–15.

their tribe the aristocrats, for all time, of the Jewish people. And in the face of all they had done, and promised still to do, it is not surprising that their dependents and followers in the desert acquiesced without a murmur in this self-appointed aristocracy.[1]

Simple and comprehensible as this story is, it must represent fairly accurately that which has always occurred when a true aristocracy has raised itself to power, particularly among nations in which the conquerors themselves do not constitute the acknowledged rulers of a subject people different in race from themselves. And it is such aristocracies, taking their strength from the approval and admiration of the people, which naturally have the greatest promise of permanence and power. It is significant, however, that the Israelites, coming from a land in which the highest caste was that of the priests, should have instituted a sacerdotal aristocracy themselves.

About fourteen months after the flight from Egypt, when Moses is commanded to number the people, in order to determine "all that are able to go forth to war in Israel," we find not only that Aaron's and Moses' branches, but that of the whole family of Levi, is now treated with special distinction.

"Even all they that were numbered were six hundred thousand and three thousand and five hundred and fifty.

---

[1] Joshua, the successor to Moses, also has an interesting history. The grandson of Elishama, who was the chief of the tribe of Ephraim, he was the descendant of that remarkable cross between the minister and legislator, Joseph, and Asenath, the daughter of an Egyptian priest. Thus he had the very best traditions in his veins, and probably some of the best blood both of Egypt and Israel. For it need not be supposed that Jacob's preference for his grandson Ephraim (who, by the by, received the rights of the firstborn from his grandfather, despite the fact that Manasseh was the elder), was based upon a mere whim. This incident alone shows how elastic the idea of the firstborn actually was, and how infinitely more probable it is that the firstborn was simply the pick of the brood, selected by one who could tell what men were, rather than the first in order of birth. For we have the case of Esau whom Isaac rejected most probably because certain of his deeds were distasteful to his parents (see p. 341).

"But the Levites after the tribe of their fathers were not numbered among them.

"For the Lord had spoken unto Moses, saying,

"Only thou shalt not number the tribe of Levi, neither take the sum of them among the children of Israel:

"But thou shalt appoint the Levites over the tabernacle of testimony, and over the vessels thereof, and over all things that belong to it: they shall bear the tabernacle, and all the vessels thereof; and they shall minister unto it, and shall encamp round about the tabernacle." [1]

And to show that this was no ordinary privilege, no trivial exaltation, but one which enjoyed the mark of the most solemn sanctity, Moses is told "the stranger that cometh nigh [to the tabernacle] shall be put to death." [2]

Previous to this self-exaltation of the sacerdotal aristocracy of the tribe of Levi, the leaders of the people, the priests of Israel, had been the firstborn. Thus Isaac is his own priest, Jacob is his own priest, and when a family divided, each man as he became the head of a family also became his own priest. A certain sanctity attached to the firstborn among the Israelites, and one of the reasons given in the law for this sanctity is that " he [the firstborn] is the beginning of his [the father's] strength." [3] And the Old Testament has many instances of the expression "firstborn" being used as an adjective meaning the highest, or the greatest, or the superlative of a certain order. [4]

In placing the firstborn at the head of affairs, it was thus thought that the best strength of the nation would be drawn into the governing body, and, all conditions being favourable, that is to say, when there was a strong desire for a male child, as there always was in Jewish families on the part of both parents, and when these parents married in their prime and had a strong desire,

[1] Num. i. 46–50.   [2] Num. i. 51 and iii. 6 *et seq.*
[3] Deut. xxi. 17.
[4] See Job xviii. 13 ; Isa. xiv. 30 ; Col. i. 15 (see note, p. 340).

one for the other—there is a good deal to be said for the plan; the firstborn in such circumstances, like the proverbial love-child, who is almost always a first child, must spring from the best of the parents' strength.

This idea of the " best," however, had to be overcome, before another " best " could be put up, and we, therefore, find Moses recording God as having said—

" And I, behold, I have taken the Levites from among the children of Israel instead of all the firstborn that openeth the matrix among the children of Israel: therefore the Levites shall be mine." [1]

" And the Lord spake unto Moses saying,

" Take the Levites instead of all the firstborn among the children of Israel, and the cattle of the Levites instead of their cattle; and the Levites shall be mine: I am the Lord." [2]

Like most aristocracies, this aristocracy of the Levites thus superseded an older aristocracy—that of the firstborn; but we shall see that the firstborn were not altogether excluded from the priesthood.

The next question that arises is: Was the Jewish aristocracy a select, inbreeding caste? Within the usual wise limits, I think we shall find that it was.

In the first place, as we have seen, its greatest members, Aaron and Moses, were the issue of a marriage which at the present day would be considered incestuous, and this fact alone gives us some idea of the closeness of the inbreeding practised by the tribes. Moses' mother was also in the position of his great-aunt—the sister of his grandfather—and it is impossible, when contemplating the will, the reputed beauty and the force of character of Moses, to ignore the circumstance of his origin.

It is true that, after the people of Israel had been long in the wilderness, it was thought expedient, if not imperative, to put an end to these closely inbred matches; [3]

---

[1] Num. iii. 12 and 41.
[2] Num. iii. 44, 45 ; see also Num. viii. 9–26.
[3] See Lev. xviii. and xx.

but the promulgation of these laws which form the basis of our own table of Kindred and Affinity " wherein whosoever are related are forbidden in Scripture and our Laws to marry together," could not have taken place until at least one hundred years after the marriage of Amram and his aunt Jochebed, when the evil effects of a too lengthy period of such close inbreeding may probably have been beginning to make themselves felt.

In any case, the promulgation of the ordinance concerning unlawful marriages does not forbid inbreeding within the tribe, and it is certain that the tribe of Levi must, with very few exceptions, have bred among themselves for many generations. They were, in any case, careful of avoiding women lacking in virtue, and they are told distinctly that their high priest, at least, should take to wife " a virgin of his own people." [1] The fact, however, that the circumstance of a priest's daughter being married to a stranger (*i. e.* a man not of the tribe of Levi) is mentioned specially as a condition precluding her from attending her father's board,[2] proves two things : first, that a certain loss of privilege was involved by a priest's or aristocrat's daughter marrying out of her people; and, secondly, that such marriages must have occurred, however seldom, otherwise this special reference to and provision for, them would have no point. We certainly know, from chapter xxxvi of the Book of Numbers, that, at least among the propertied members of the various tribes, the daughters were commanded by God to choose husbands in the tribes of their respective fathers, so we cannot be far wrong in assuming that inter-tribe marriages were rare in the ruling caste.

In addition to inbreeding, however, there were other

---

[1] Lev. xxi. 14.

[2] Lev. xxii. 12–13: " If the priest's daughter also be married unto a stranger, she may not eat of an offering of the holy things. But if the priest's daughter be a widow, or divorced, and have no child, and is returned unto her father's house, as in her youth, she shall eat of her father's meat ; but there shall no stranger eat thereof."

expedients resorted to for keeping the superior caste free
from degenerate, ugly, diseased or other undesirable
elements. And again in this case, as in that of the
Brahmans, although there is no question of insulting the
unfortunate examples of Nature's failures, they are declared
most distinctly to be undesirable, and to be deprived by
the mere fact of their botchedness of the privileges of
their high birth.

"And the Lord spake unto Moses, saying,

"Speak unto Aaron, saying, Whosoever he be of thy
seed in their generation that hath any blemish, let him
not approach to offer the bread of his God.

"For whatsoever man he be that hath a blemish, he
shall not approach: a blind man, or a lame, or he that
hath a flat nose, or anything superfluous,

"Or a man that is broken-footed, or broken-handed,

"Or crookbackt, or a dwarf, or that hath a blemish
in his eye, or be scurvy, or scabbed, or hath his stones
broken;

"No man that hath a blemish of the seed of Aaron
the priest shall come nigh to offer the offerings of the
Lord made by fire: he hath a blemish; he shall not come
nigh to offer the bread of his God . . .

". . . He shall not go in unto the vail, nor come
nigh unto the altar, because he hath a blemish; that he
profane not my sanctuaries: for I the Lord do sanctify
them." [1]

What could be wiser than this precaution! Bravely,
honestly, squarely, without any lachrymose sentimentality,
these people realised that a great nation, in order to last,
must have healthy bodies, and that a great aristocratic
order, above all, can be permanent and powerful only if
it casts a stigma upon physiological botchedness and
bungledom among its members—a stigma recognised by
all, and the apparent justice of which grew up in the
hearts of the people; so that it became a natural intuitive

[1] Lev. xxi. 16–23.

feeling to avoid those who had a blemish? For did not even Jehovah Himself acknowledge that if they approached His sanctuaries they would profane them?

Hard and unmerciful as this may seem at first sight, it is not nearly so hard and unmerciful as the measures to which modern Eugenists will soon have to resort in order to prevent the excessive multiplication of the ugly and the physiologically bungled and botched, reared through the fact that long centuries of the gospel of the soul have at last killed healthy man's natural inclination to avoid the imperfect, the foul of breath, the ugly and the deformed.

Fancy a God of Love declaring that a man with a flat nose could *profane* His sanctuaries! But if we understand what love is, and realise that the greatest love to humanity would leave no stone unturned to keep the human species healthy and beautiful, we perceive at once that only a God of Love could have held such a view. Because a God of Love must be truthful and straightforward with His people, and He cannot rock them by highfalutin fairy tales about the beauty of the soul into a slumbering neglect of the body—only to be forced to waken them brutally later on by means of a terrific nightmare in which threats of " segregation," " isolation " and "¡sterilisation " figure more prominently than anything e se.

But this by the way. What is important is to observe the caution with which this aristocracy of the people of Israel, like the Brahmans of India, set about the task of preserving their beauty and their virtues. As to a provision against the evils of too close breeding, which, as we have already seen, was made both by the Egyptians and the ancient Hindus, there can be no doubt that such a loophole of escape from the confines of the tribe did actually exist among the Levite aristocracy. We have seen how occasionally a daughter married out of her tribe —a liberty which must have had its counterpart in the men of the tribe—and how only for the high priest is it strictly stated that a wife should be found " of his own people." There can be no doubt that, among a patriarchal people like the ancient Jews, such loopholes of escape as existed according to the law were used only with the permission and at the discretion of the elders of the family; but the fact that, in the case of families who clearly required refreshing, such permission or abetment was given or proffered long before it was even solicited can scarcely be questioned for one moment.

When, in addition to this, it is remembered that fresh blood must in all probability have been poured steadily into the aristocracy by a modified and improved survival of the "firstborn" custom of old,[1] which made all the firstborn of the land the possession of the Lord and His priests, and which was never quite extinguished even after the triumph of the Levites, it will be seen that the priestly aristocracy possessed all the necessary checks against the evils of too close inbreeding, if they cared to use them.

I have already referred to the hereditary character of the Greek Eupatrids and of the Roman Patricians, and now I think I have collected enough data to sum up and draw general conclusions.

In the first place, we have seen that all nations of antiquity who attained to any culture, and who may be called the founders and creators of all this earth's civilisation, *and of all that is still best in it*, were undoubtedly opposed to the stranger and the foreigner, whatever his degree of refinement might be. Whether it was from a jealous self-consciousness of their own beauty and virtues in the mass of the people, or from the initiation of penetrating, discerning and tasteful leaders, it is difficult to

[1] From the number of names of priests in the Old Testament who were not descendants of Levi it is pretty certain that many of the firstborn of other tribes continued to be accepted into the priesthood, even after the substitution of the Levites for the firstborn sacerdotal body, referred to above. But whereas in former times they belonged to this body by right, after the exaltation of the Levites, it is probable that a more severe method of selection was exercised, and that only the very best were admitted.

determine; but in any case we find that among those people who—whether originally pure or mixed—had at least passed through a period of inbreeding sufficiently prolonged to have arrived at a harmonious working adjustment of their instincts there obtained a profound prejudice against the alien and against matrimonial unions with him. Sometimes this prejudice was linked up with a religious belief, sometimes it was not; but in any case there seems to have been a sort of half-conscious, semi-lucid notion among these peoples that instincts and valuable virtues, as the possession of cultured ganglia, can be destroyed only by a confusion of the ganglia by crossing—a conclusion that Gobineau draws in his book, *l'Inégalité des Races Humaines*, which I have sufficiently quoted.

We have also seen that within these endogamic peoples, provided the race were, to begin with, at all prone to a high state of civilisation, culture has risen to very high levels—and this in a comparatively short space of time; whereas in exogamic peoples, or in peoples like the Fuegians, who were not *younger* but *different* from the races capable of civilisation, a high culture was either not reached at all, or at least only approached at an extremely slow rate of progress.

The nature of instinct, will, beauty and virtue having been explained, it was shown how utterly the balance and strength of these possessions could be undermined by introducing into the same body which possessed them other instincts and other kinds of will, beauty or virtue; and thus the conclusions that Gobineau draws were made a little more comprehensible.

Attention has likewise been called to the fact that once endogamy and the development of a certain distinct culture had created a sharp distinction between a race and its neighbours, further distinctions within the race itself were bound to occur, owing to the long practice of particular virtues on the part of the different strata of the race— these strata all being created originally, as I have suggested, by a bodily differentiation which initiated the virtue.

A DEFENCE OF ARISTOCRACY

Once these distinctions arose, the various strata or classes would feel the same jealous love for their particular virtues and their accompanying bodily beauty, as the race, generally, felt for all those things which differentiated it from other races. And thus would arise the feeling of caste : the pride of the aristocrat, the pride of the warrior, the pride of the agriculturist and the pride of the artisan, with a corresponding disinclination to mix, unless it meant to rise.

Now all this is not a romantic dream. It is what actually has happened, and does happen, wherever a race attains to any high culture of which it can be proud, and whenever within the race a certain number of people acquire any virtues of which they can justly be proud.

It now remains for me to point out to what extent I differ from Gobineau and incline to Reibmayr's side.

Gobineau would like to prove that all crossing, all mixture, leads to degeneration; in fact, that crossing *is* degeneration.

Now I should be the last, after all I have said, to underrate the value of race. No one realises better than I do how intimately a strong character and long, uninterrupted tradition are related. But the history of peoples shows me, in the first place, that purity of race, even as far back as the earliest Egyptians, is a quality which can scarcely be posited with any certainty, not to speak of irrefutable proof; and also that in those cases where a definite cross has been made and has been followed by a renewed period of inbreeding, none of the evil results which Gobineau classes under degeneration have necessarily followed; owing, as I have pointed out, to the fortuitous triumph of one set of instincts and virtues over the other set (a triumph which sometimes occurs) and the consequent increased strength of the triumphant party, together with the enhanced bodily vigour gained from a cross after a too prolonged period of inbreeding.

But I should like to emphasise the fact that when I speak of a salutary cross in this sense, I do not mean that sort of mixing which goes on to-day in our age of democracy and of the belief in the supposed equality of all men, according to which all peoples marry all peoples, and all classes all classes, without any interval of inbreeding or of isolation, during which the result of the cross can work out its destiny in the hearts of a nation. The process to-day is not the crossing of two races or two classes, it is sheer confusion, complete chaos, and as such can lead, and does lead, only to the utter loss of all will, instinct, virtue and beauty, and therefore to the decline and evanescence of character. In an age like the present you may be certain that ideas of race-character and the transmission of acquired characteristics will be scouted, because nothing is done, nothing is coveted or desired, which could make either of these two ideas realities in our midst.

Let us, however, return to the original point. With Reibmayr, then, I believe not only that a cross need not necessarily lead to degeneration, even though I admit that it temporarily and sometimes permanently destroys character; but also that it is sometimes fruitful of the best possible results. It must not, however, be indiscriminate, nor must it be between peoples who are obviously poles asunder, and whose instincts could never arrive at a strong and creative readjustment, once they had come into conflict through mixture.

What applies to races or peoples applies equally well to classes within a race or castes within a people. It is absurd and romantic to suppose that any virtue or ability can remain the possession of a people if everybody in that people is allowed to marry anybody of whatever class. But it is equally absurd to suppose that a people can maintain its castes permanently at a given standard if inbreeding within each caste is to be an absolutely inviolable custom. And, as we have seen, all the great peoples of the past, the Egyptians, the Hindus and the Jews—and the world has seen no greater races than these since—understood this need and provided for it. The

Egyptians, despite their excessive bias in ·favour of in-breeding, not only allowed the highest castes to inter-marry, but made it possible, as we shall see, for exceptional ability among the lower classes to rise to the topmost pinnacle of the state, as the Chinese do. The Hindus did not even preclude Sudra blood from the highest caste, provided, after a number of generations, it showed itself by virtue and ability worthy of a Brahman's admiration; and the Jews, by their custom of the firstborn and his provisional right to the priesthood, ensured a constant flow of fresh and good blood from below into the aristocracy.

Thus, as we have seen, the matter which concerned these people, and which still concerns us, is not that an occasional cross between a higher and a lower caste should not be made, but that it should be, in the first place, absolutely necessary and judicious, and that the blood from the lower caste should be of the best. Again, the process which the laws and customs of these ancient races tried to prevent was not occasional refreshment from below, but constant indiscriminate *mésalliances* which are so destruc-tive of all virtue and of all character, and which bring about the decline of an aristocracy even more quickly than they compass the doom of a nation.

No discussion on the question of aristocracy would have been complete without this examination of the practice and prejudice of the founders of human culture in regard to the relationship of virtue, character, etc., to race and race-mixture. It is for this reason that I have gone into the question with what may seem to some unnecessary elaboration. This chapter, however, has not only given me an opportunity of stating my ·position definitely con-cerning such debatable terms as will, instinct, virtue and beauty—a task which in any case I should have had to perform as a digression in another chapter; but it has also allowed me to enter more deeply into the nature, the rear-ing, the production and the *cost* of the example of flourish-life who is but one of nature's lucky strokes among the highest caste of a nation, and to show to what an extent and with what justice such a creature, with all his acquired virtues, sharpened senses, widened intelligence, discerning vision and splendid traditions may be called an *achievement*, an arduous and creditable achievement on the part of those who have preceded him, of those who support him, and of those on whose shoulders he has been able to climb to the highest pinnacle of his people, to guide and direct them for their general weal.

CHAPTER VIII

THE ARISTOCRAT IN PRACTICE

"For my own part, I should consider it a misfortune if the hereditary element, of which it [the Upper Chamber in the English Legislature] is now mainly composed, were not still largely represented in it."—LECKY, *Democracy and Liberty*, Vol. I, p. 381.

THOSE who have read my thesis in Chapter VI with any sympathy, and who have likewise appreciated the principles laid down in the chapter immediately following, will hardly require to be told that the present aristocracy of England do not by any means represent what I understand by the best.

Such readers will also understand, without my requiring to go into any very elaborate analysis of the actual state of the classes in England, that those classes immediately below the aristocracy are now, on the whole, not a very favourable soil for the rearing of candidates for the aristocratic dignity, whenever and however the aristocratic body might require refreshment.

The occupation of buying and selling for profit, though it remain in certain families for many generations, is not in itself of a nature capable of rearing virtues and qualities or of establishing a tradition which can be valuable, when those who pursue that occupation and the kind of life that it now involves are able to raise themselves by wealth into influential circles; neither are the decharacterising and emasculating labours of the lowest classes that form the ultimate soil from which all ranks receive fresh recruits calculated to make even the most successful members of these lowest classes very desirable additions to any superior class, however effete. And it should be remembered that

352

the occupation of buying and selling for profit, and the decharacterising and emasculating labours of the lower classes are drawing ever greater and greater numbers of the nation under their influence.

Nevertheless, this book would have accomplished a very useless and futile purpose if it had been written merely to show that the plight of a true aristocracy in England was utterly hopeless.

In certain quarters of the Empire, in certain dignified occupations, and among certain distinguished, respectable or simply industrious people I believe that there are still to be found men and women of good tradition, possessed of will, virtue, beauty and sound instinct; nor do I think that the system of uncontrolled commerce or mechanical industry has nearly succeeded yet in making the numbers of such people so desperately or ridiculously small that their total may be considered a too insignificant factor with which to reckon.

The influence of uncontrolled commerce and of mechanical industry, coupled with that most baneful outcome of democracy which causes all unostentatious and concealed work to be shirked, *because it is beneath the free vote-possessing citizen whose lot in life it is to perform this work*,[1] are both decimating these last veterans of a better and more civilised state, and are thus steadily reducing virtue in our midst. But it is because I feel that this devastating work of the modern "system," coupled with democracy, has still not done its worst; it is because I believe that there is still a considerable amount of solid virtue and sound tradition in the country, that I am convinced of the hopefulness of any counter-movement that will enlist these better elements into its ranks.

Only thus, in any case, can that soil be formed upon which a healthy aristocracy can stand and act beneficently; only thus can that atmosphere be created which, as I

---

[1] This is only one of the many influences that are undermining all good service, all conscientious labour and—what is a little less obvious—all cleanliness and care in small matters.

pointed out in Chapter VI, is favourable to the self-assertion of the truly superior man.

Turning to the aristocrats themselves, I should be loath, in these days of the hypertrophy of the soul and of the intellect, to be confounded with those who are agitating for an aristocracy of brains or of the sages of science; and I trust that I have made it sufficiently obvious in the statement of my thesis that I stand for neither of these supposed desiderata. While as for the cry of "a government of business men," the reader will realise that I have replied sufficiently fully to that in my two chapters concerning the Stuarts and the Puritans.

Hostile as I am, therefore, to much which characterises the present House of Lords, and conscious as I feel of the incalculable distance which all too frequently separates the members of it from the true aristocrat who is the example of flourishing life, I cannot help recognising that it contains many of the elements of a sound aristocratic power, and would be able to disarm much criticism, if only the sense of duty at its back, if only its consciousness of the sacredness of power, could be regenerated in such a manner as to bring home to its members a deep conception of the terrific responsibility of their position, the magnitude of their powers for good or evil, and the high services compatible with their exceptional privileges.

Some of you in reading this book will contend that I have laid too many of the errors of England's social organisation at the door of a mistaken and undutiful aristocracy. You will say that a good many of the charges I bring against them cannot be upheld in view of the fact that the Lower House, the Commons, where the representatives of the people were assembled, always participated in the work of legislation. This objection would be sound enough, if it were actually a fact that the House of Commons had acted entirely or even preponderatingly as the representatives of the people, and had so influenced legislation as to make it the combined work of the masses and of the aristocracy.

But, unfortunately for the apologist of the English House of Lords, this, as we know, is not a fact.

It is indeed strange to see how the prophetic feeling of the noble Earl of Strafford concerning the new spirit of the Commons in the seventeenth century proved ultimately to be correct. Strafford refused to trust the government of England to Parliament, because he knew that the lawyers and country gentlemen who sat in it only partially represented the nation. He also knew that these country gentlemen " too often used the opportunities of their wealth to tyrannise over their poorer neighbours." He foresaw that the victory of the Parliamentary system would give the territorial aristocracy an opportunity of using the forms of the constitution " to fill their own pockets at the expense of the nation and to heap honours and rewards upon their own heads." [1]

How sound and true his feelings were! For it is since his death and that of his master that the power of Parliament has been most unquestioned and the liberties of the people most ignored. And, as Lecky has so ably shown in the work to which I have already referred, ever since the extension of the franchise through the three Reform Bills, the desire for equality has done so much more to animate the deliberations of the lower legislative assembly than the desire for liberty that the latter is still the neglected principle of government. For equality is naturally hostile to true liberty, and the much vaunted freedom of our national life has declined rather than

---

[1] Gardiner, *The Personal Government of Charles I*, Vol. I, pp. 168 and 281. See also Benjamin Disraeli's *Sybil* (Longmans, Green and Co., 1899), p. 35. " A spirit of rapacious covetousness, desecrating all the humanities of life, has been the besetting sin of England for the last century and a half, since the passing of the Reform Act the altar of Mammon has blazed with triple worship. To acquire, to accumulate, to plunder each other by virtue of philosophic phrases, to propose a Utopia to consist only of Wealth and Toil, this has been the breathless business of enfranchised England for the last twelve years, until we are startled from our voracious strife by the wail of intolerable serfage."

increased since the inclusion of the popular vote.[1]   But I have already shown conclusively enough how the inclusion of the popular vote could not possibly have improved anything or anybody.

To return, however, to the point under discussion, practically ever since the Revolution of 1688, and up to the time of the first Reform Bill, aristocratic influence in the Constitution had been paramount, though not absolute.   In the latter half of the eighteenth century it was possible for Paley to write that only one-half of the House of Commons was elected by the people—an understatement rather than an overstatement of fact—and that the other half consisted of the nominees of the governing classes.[2]   And this controlling power of the aristocracy over the House of Commons lasted well into the nineteenth century.

During the existence of the Irish Parliament matters were not very different, for in 1785, of the 300 members constituting that assembly scarcely a third were elected by the people.[3]

Mr. James Macintyre gives the following statement of the general plan of the parliamentary representation of England during the great revolutionary war, and down to the year 1832.[4]

---

[1] For Lecky's illuminating arguments on this point see *Democracy and Liberty*, Vol. I, Chapter III, pp. 212–215.

[2] Sir Thomas Erskine May, in his *Constitutional History of England* (Vol. I, pp. 332–333), says : "No abuse was more flagrant than the direct control of peers over the constitution of the Lower House. The Duke of Norfolk was represented by eleven members ; Lord Lonsdale by nine ; Lord Darlington by seven ; the Duke of Rutland, the Marquess of Buckingham and Lord Carrington, each by six.   Seats were held, in both Houses alike, by hereditary right."   This abuse was indeed flagrant ; but, if only it had recoiled to the honour and genuine prosperity of the people of England, no one would ever have dreamt of raising a voice against it.   For, if the aristocrats had really been worthy of their dignity, the fact that they nominated members to the Lower House would have proved an advantage rather than a disadvantage to the nation.

[3] *Political History of England*, Vol. X, by W. Hunt, p. 288.

[4] See *The Influence of Aristocracies on the Revolution of Nations*, p. 246.

"Members returned to Parliament, supposed to have been the representatives of the people of England, Wales, Scotland and Ireland . . , . 658

Returned as follows—

By 80 or 90 Peers for England and Wales 218	}	
By 20 to 25 Peers for Scotland . . 31	} 300	
By 32 to 36 Peers for Ireland . . 51		
By 90 Commoners for England and Wales 137	}	
By 14 Commoners for Scotland . . 14	} 187	
By 19 Commoners for Ireland . . 20		
By Government 16		

Total returned by denomination of individuals 487

Leaving returned by constituencies not altogether dependent upon patrons 171

Total 658

Thus it would hardly be fair to exonerate the aristocracy from the chief blame for any evils which might be traced to bad government, or to institutions and innovations allowed to establish themselves, between the years 1688 and 1832.[1] Indeed, if ever the English aristocracy had a chance of vindicating its right to rule, subsequently to the Grand Rebellion, it was in the eighteenth and early nineteenth centuries. But, as we have seen, is was precisely during that period, and particularly the latter part

[1] It is difficult to listen with patience to those who, while talking glibly of the great progress of England since the Revolution of 1688, abuse and revile the House of Lords. If *real* progress there has been, if we, as a people, have truly improved since the seventeenth century, and if this age, which is the outcome of the eighteenth and early nineteenth centuries, actually is an age to be admired, then, to the Lords, and to the Lords alone, who guided and directed the fate of present England throughout its period of incubation, so to speak, is certainly due all the credit of the supposed wondrous changes.

357

of it, as Holland Rose tells us, that " misery " proved to be " the chief propelling power of democracy."

It is not in the nature of a wise people to abandon or to resist their rulers, if they recognise that it is to their advantage to continue submissive and obedient. On the contrary, the natural inclination of the class which is immersed in the daily task and in the struggle for a competence which will enable it to enjoy its modest share of domestic comfort and pleasure, is to be enduring, long-suffering and patient, even under the harshest oppression, rather than to concern itself with matters which its best instincts tell it are beyond its highest powers.

It was with such a populace that the landed aristocracy of England had to deal for many a score of years, and yet, if we watch the gathering of the storm which, beginning in 1782, ultimately gave rise to the three Reform Bills of 1832, 1867 and 1885; if we contemplate the work of such agitators as Major Cartwright, Horne Tooke, William Cobbett, Henry Hunt, William Lovett, Henry Vincent, Hetherington, John Cleave, William Carpenter, etc., and if we remember the misery of the masses, the tyranny of such institutions as the press-gang, and the constant introduction of all kinds of interested and untried institutions in their midst, in addition to all the other abuses of which I have given a selection in Chapter II, we cannot help acknowledging that the aristocracy of England failed hopelessly in its task.

Everything was in its favour—the price of newspapers was prohibitive, a tax on paper checked the dangers of cheap knowledge, the orthodox Church was on its side, even the natural conservatism of the masses was a bulwark it knew how to use; and yet the whole movement of the people in England, from 1780 to 1911, can be said to have consisted of one long struggle to limit and restrict aristocratic power!

The Lords forgot that they could not have it both ways. They overlooked the fact that if they failed too long in protecting their charges—the people—these would find no other alternative than that of trying to protect themselves; and since at that time the masses did not know how impossible, how futile, and how dangerous such an undertaking would prove, since the people of the nineteenth century had not a notion of the stupendous difficulty of the task they had appointed themselves, the principle of aristocracy, which is the principle of life, was reviled and sacrificed, simply through the incompetence of its representatives, and not through any flaw or error in the principle itself.

For, let it be remembered, and well understood, that one of the most vehement, determined and unflinching opponents of the Reform Bill of 1832, and the leader of the opposition in the House of Lords to the Reform Bill of 1867 and the Ballot Act of 1872, was none other than the noble-minded, generous and hard-working protector of the people, their wives and children—the celebrated seventh Earl of Shaftesbury!

Why was this? To the average Englishman there will seem to be something incongruous, inconsistent and muddled in the atitude of this great Earl. Why stand in opposition to the so-called "rights of the people," if, at heart, you are in very truth a protector of the people?

As a matter of fact, there is nothing at all inconsistent about this attitude on the part of Shaftesbury. It was precisely because he knew himself able and ready to protect the people, and to guide and direct them, that he naturally resented the introduction of measures which not only would render him powerless to perform his beneficent functions, but would also transfer political power from those who, if they were made of the proper material, and were willing, could have wielded it for the general good, to those who, however much they tried, could not, under any circumstances whatever, wield it even for their own individual good.

For it is an empty and exploded illusion to suppose, as Bentham supposed, that "because each man sought his own happiness, the government of the majority would necessarily pursue the interests and the happiness of that majority." [1] A perusal of history for the last forty years, apart from the contention in my thesis, would be sufficient to disprove this supposition. And that is why, to the Earl of Shaftesbury, the word " democracy " was always, and rightly, a term of " reproach." [2]

Another protector of the people, a commoner, Mr. Michael Thomas Sadler, was also an uncompromising opponent of political freedom, and for exactly the same reasons; and, if we examine the names of those whom we find opposed to the social reforms patriarchally introduced by the Earl of Shaftesbury and Thomas Sadler, we shall not be surprised to find among them the very men who were most energetic in their advocacy of an extended franchise.

People like Gladstone and Cobden, who had not the faintest idea of what was meant by protecting the masses, or by genuine aristocratic rule, naturally opposed anything in the way of patriarchalism in order with clap-trap and tinselled oratory to introduce the absurd and hollow ideal of a self-ruled and self-guided nation!

And thus a whole century was wasted and squandered, and a whole Empire tricked and deluded. For, the real question, the burning question, the question that was shelved for over one hundred years, was, or ought to have been: " How could the rulers of the country be improved? " not " How could the common people be converted into rulers? "

But men like Gladstone, Cobden and even Bright, were too stupid to see this point, and men like Shaftesbury and Sadler were kept too busy by the wail of suffering arising all around them, to think of anything else than the redressing of evils, and the abolition of abuses as quickly as possible.

It is only now, after all the tumult and clamour of the

[1] See *The Rise of Democracy*, by J. Holland Rose, p. 34.
[2] See *The Seventh Earl of Shaftesbury, K.G.*, by Edwin Hodder, p. 14.

utterly futile and fruitless battle that has raged around the " vote," is over, that a few, here and there, are beginning to realise that, in spite of it all, it is still *rulers* that we want, and that not a thing has been done to meet this need, which was felt as early as 1780, and which will continue to be felt as long as men are men, and as long as some are born to lead, to direct, to choose and to guide, while others are born to follow, to enjoy simple and lowly forms of power, and to be happy in obeying those who understand them and those whom they feel they can trust.

I shall now discuss as briefly as possible those essential factors in the maintenance of an aristocracy which either are or are not to be found observed in the organisation of the aristocracy constituting our House of Lords, and I shall make various suggestions as to the lines along which reforms, if they are to be undertaken, should be made.

I have said that the present aristocracy of England do not by any means represent what I understand by the best : let us now attempt to discover why this is so, and by what means matters could be altered.

In the first place, let me state it as one of the most incontrovertible facts of science and human experience, that *there is extraordinarily little chance and accident in the production of great and exceptional men.* Reibmayr, in a work that has been very helpful to me,[1] maintains, and I think proves, the proposition that " the appearance of a talented man, or a man of genius, is not to be ascribed to any phenomenon akin to blind chance." The two volumes of his study constitute a most able and learned discussion of this question, and show the extent to which a *sound tradition* is necessary, if not to ensure, at least to render likely, the production of exceptional men—a conclusion to which the science of heredity is slowly but surely tending.

[1] *Die Entwicklungsgeschichte des Talentes und Genies,* Vol. I, p. 3 : " *Zweifellos ist das Erscheinen eines Talentes und Genies keinen blinden Zufall unterworfen.*"

A DEFENCE OF ARISTOCRACY

Now it can be laid down almost as a law concerning most European aristocracies, that they have always relied more or less indolently and ignorantly upon chance and accident, rather than upon wilful and deliberate design and intention in the rearing of their great examples.

And if we turn to the English aristocracy, in particular, we find this principle carried to an absurdly dangerous extreme.

The production of a creature who is to be an example of flourishing life, involves four essential conditions: (1) Race; (2) Long, healthy and cultured tradition; (3) Rigorous discipline in early life, and (4) An optimum of conditions away from the vortex of a sordid struggle for existence.

Number four is the only one of these conditions which can with any justice be said to have been fulfilled in the life of the average English aristocrat; but, although it is important and indispensable, it is not in itself sufficient.

It is foolhardy and ridiculous to suppose that greatness will continue to show itself, generation after generation, if the very first conditions for its production are persistently scouted and ignored. As Reibmayr says,[1] even a shepherd would hesitate to take as a sheepdog an animal that had not all the innate qualities and training of that particular class of canine creatures, and yet for the most difficult of all arts, the art of ruling men,[2] people are selected and reared, almost at random and with the most frivolous carelessness imaginable.

You will tell me that the English aristocracy does not represent a class that is selected at random, and reared with a careless indifference to its ultimate purpose. I shall show you that it does to a very large extent.

To begin with, take the question of the internal discipline of the body itself. What sort of an organisation have the aristocracy of England evolved, among themselves, whereby they can exercise some powers of censure,

---

[1] *Die Entwicklungsgeschichte des Talentes und Genies*, Vol. I, p. 143.
[2] "*Die schwierigste aller Künste, die Menschenbeherrschung.*"

selection, criticism, emulation, discipline and chastisement one upon the other? In view of the tremendous gravity of the issues at stake, in the face of the far-reaching consequences to their nation and even to the world at large, of their deliberations and judgments, what attempt have they made rigorously to exact a certain high standard of competence, efficiency and even ability, from the members constituting their body? You would have thought that their self-preservative instinct, alone—apart from any other consideration—would have prompted them to exercise some disciplinary powers over each other, in order that any weakness in their organisation might be discovered, checked and corrected by themselves, long before its consequences could be felt, or become known, by the general public. This is one of the many precautionary measures against decline and disorganisation which might have contributed to their permanence and greatness, but we find it utterly overlooked by them in their scheme of life.

Take the principle of primogeniture, for instance! If such an inner council of discipline, selection and criticism as I suggest, had ever existed within the body of the peerage, this very principle could have been made more elastic, less rigid and less inviolable. When it is a question of saving the prestige of a whole body of rulers, the elders of that body constituting its inner circle, might with the enormous majesty of their high functions, easily prevail upon one family, or even upon several families, to institute exceptions, to waive even a regular custom. For, although a sound tradition makes the likelihood of the appearance of hereditary characteristics very great, it does not ensure their appearance in the firstborn.[1] A selecting,

---

[1] As an instance of this, think of the case of Pitt. Whatever one may say about the elder Pitt's qualities—whether they were admirable or not—they certainly did not descend to his first, but to his second son ; and scores of similar instances could be given. Moses, Charles I and Richelieu, were all second sons, Napoleon and Nelson were both third sons, and Wellington was a fourth son.

wisely discerning inner council, therefore, would, after the style of Isaac and Jacob, sometimes have felt itself compelled, for the sake of the vigour of the exalted class to which it belonged, to waive the law of primogeniture in favour of a second, third, fourth or even fifth son. When great issues hang upon the breaking of an arbitrary and, in many respects, unjustifiable law, it is merely an ordinary act of commonplace mediocre judgment, to allow exceptions to that law, or to render it at least sufficiently elastic to enable men of wise judgment to decide when exceptions should be tolerated or even insisted upon.

And this is only one of the many possible ways in which such an inner council of discipline, selection and criticism might have acted for the general good, the general vitality, vigour and quality of the whole body of the peerage. Decline must be warded off; bad, inferior blood, must at all costs be kept out; a high standard must be maintained —surely the need of being vigilant here, of being drastic and hypercritical here, ought not to be overlooked! But it has been overlooked—nay, it has never even entered into the organisation of the British aristocracy!

And the fact that it was overlooked by previous aristocracies, constitutes one of the causes of their failure also. If with Professor Bury you trace the gradual transformation of the aristocracy of Athens into a *timocracy*, you will find that it was precisely because there was no attempt made to maintain such a standard as I mention—apart from property and birth—and no one to see that it was maintained, that the conversion of the aristocrat into a mere plutocrat was made so simple and so inevitable a process.[1] Because where birth and property alone constitute the qualifications for political power, and where no higher standard of fitness for rule is exacted, or striven after, mere wealth and property, by virtue of their being a much more tangible and more self-evident claim to power than mere birth, are bound in the end to establish their supremacy over the other qualifications. But mere wealth,

[1] *History of Greece* (edit. 1900), pp. 173–177.

as a standard, inasmuch as it allows the man of no birth and no tradition to press himself into the ruling body, is bound, as Bury shows,[1] to pave the way to democracy, and even *ochlocracy*, and is the surest foundation to all the evils and abuses incidental to such orders of society.

Again, if we watch the rise and fall of the aristocratic Fujiwara family in Japan during the Heian Epoch (from the end of the eighth to the middle of the twelfth centuries), we find that their decline, at the close of this epoch, was due to the fact that, in the zenith of their greatness, they had foolishly made their hereditary tenure of power independent of all qualifications to exercise it, with the consequence that, after a number of generations, during which they admittedly produced many geniuses, "they had ultimately ceased to possess any qualifications whatever." In this way, when their privileges were challenged and usurped by the rising military clans of the provinces, they were as powerless to defend them as the ancient patriarchal families had been to defend theirs, at the time when the Fujiwara themselves had been the usurpers.[2]

These military clans, however, whose highest types were the bushi or samurai, certainly did not follow the example of their predecessors in power, in so far as individual and co-operative discipline was concerned. On the contrary, as an aristocracy of warriors, their mutual supervision and chastening influence was of the severest order. We are told that a Japanese classic of the seventeenth century was able to lay down as a maxim that "it is impossible for an evil-hearted man to retain possession of a famous sword,"[3] and in every respect the *Bushi-Do*, or the way of the warrior, seems to have been a way which was the very reverse of smooth and easy-going.

Truthfulness and the most unfailing and unremitting

[1] *History of Greece* (edit. 1900), pp. 118 and 175.
[2] See *Japan, its History, Arts and Literature*, by Captain F. Brinkley, Vols. I and II, Chaps. VI and VII and I respectively.
[3] *Ibid.*, Vol. II, p. 150.

self-control[1] seem to have been expected from all who claimed the privilege of the bushi's or samurai's sword, and these virtues were practised with such persistence and steadfastness, that they gradually became the characteristics of manliness for the whole nation.

Captain Brinkley, speaking of the bushi's or samurai's morality, says: "This doctrine [of truthfulness 'for the sake of the spirit of uncompromising manliness'] gradually permeated society at large. In the seventeenth century, written security for a debt took the form not of the hypothecation of property, but of an avowal that failure to pay would be to forfeit the debtor's title of manhood."[2] To this extent are an aristocracy able, if they choose, to establish an ideal, and a lofty, practical course of conduct for a whole people![3]

The severity with which the virtues, the deeds and the beliefs of the ancient Brahmans were controlled and kept up to standard, by the religion with which their functions and privileges as aristocrats were connected, may be learned in the pages of Manu, and there can be no doubt that this severity afforded this Indian aristocracy a check against degeneration, without which it is difficult to conceive of any institution or body whatsover lasting very long after the death of its original founder.

In the same way the Holy Catholic Church has achieved relative permanence. For it is impossible to imagine that it could have lasted all this while, in spite of its many bad leaders, without a system which involved a rigorous discipline and control of the large body of its priesthood.

---

[1] Brinkley, op. cit., Vol. II, p. 183 : "The Bushi was essentially a stoic. He made self-control the ideal of his existence, and practised the courageous endurance of suffering so thoroughly that he could without hesitation inflict on his own body pain of the severest description.

[2] Op. cit., Vol. II, p. 200.

[3] See Aristotle, *Politics*, Book II, Chap. XI, 1,273*a*, *b* : "For what those who have the chief power regard as honourable will necessarily be the object which the citizens in general will aim at." A reflection for the leaders of modern society !

THE ARISTOCRAT IN PRACTICE

Venice, however, offers the most astounding example in Europe of a community governed by a well-disciplined and highly tasteful aristocracy. For, as Lecky observes: "It should not be forgotten that the most enduring aristocratic government that the modern world has known was that of Venice, the work of a landless and mercantile aristocracy."[1] And, I add, that in order for them to last as they did last, and to accomplish, in order and culture, what they were able to accomplish—not to speak of matters of honour, art and beauty generally—that aristocracy must, and we know it did, exercise the severest discipline upon the members of its own body. The Council of Ten, which formed the most powerful bulwark of the state, was just such an inner council as I have suggested once or twice above, and the control it exercised was essential to the health and vitality of the whole community. The punishments inflicted upon members of the aristocratic body, who failed to maintain the standard of their rank, seem sometimes to have been out of all proportion to their crimes; but, if we remember exactly what was at stake, if we think of the authority, the trust, the prestige, the rectitude, the lofty altruism, the presbyopic wisdom, and above all the taste, which were here indispensable and practically inviolable, we shall take a more reasonable view of these expiatory degradations which sometimes shattered the body and spirit of the aristocratic delinquent.[2]

Finally, to turn once more to a people often mentioned with reverence in these pages—that is to say, the ancient Egyptians; there can be no doubt that their sacerdotal

[1] *Democracy and Liberty*, Vol. I, p. 354.

[2] The terrible discipline exercised by the *Inquisitori del Doge defunto* in Venice, should also be remembered in this connection. "They were three in number," says Alethea Wiel, "and were to examine into the rule and administration of the late Doge, to see whether he had lived up to the promises made by him in his *Promissione*, and if in any case they found him wanting they would call upon his heirs to atone as far as possible for the shortcomings laid against him."—See *Venice*, by Alethea Wiel, p. 155. For a similar custom in Egypt, see Wilkinson, op. cit., Vol. III, pp. 453–454.

aristocracy was even more unremitting than the Brahmans' themselves in its self-discipline and its supervision of the members of its caste. They even taught and trained the Pharaoh himself, in all things connected with his duties. Wilkinson concludes his remarks upon their rule as follows : " The system and regulations of the Egyptian priests were framed with wisdom, and tended to the happiness as well as to the welfare of the people." [1]

Such results are not attained over a long period of time without the strictest and most untiring control being exercised over the elements constituting the aristocratic body; and, indeed, if we inquire into the matter, we find that the severest rules governed their mode of life, both as private and public men. They were austere in their outlook on life, abstemious in their habits, guarded and dignified in their behaviour; carefully avoiding all excesses, and paying the most scrupulous " *attention to the most trifling particulars of diet.*" [2] They were, moreover, extraordinarily careful of their bodies and of their raiment; observed the strictest rules of cleanliness, and their fasts, some of which lasted from seven to forty-two days, were a constant exercise in self-control and self-denial. For during these fasts, not only were certain foods forbidden, but all indulgence of the passions was absolutely prohibited. Nothing, in fact, was neglected, nothing forgotten, which tended not only to rear rulers, but to maintain them up to a given standard of excellence.

And now, if we look back upon the hundred and fifty years, or thereabouts, during which the aristocracy of England had the greatest opportunity for good and for power, of any aristocracy that has ever attempted to assert its sway over a people, do we see any approach to this element in the organisation of this body? We see nothing of the sort! We see rivalry, indeed, and bitter animosity and hatred, between different political groups; we see an assumption of virtuous indignation on the part of one

[1] Op. cit., Vol. I, p. 178.
[2] *Ibid.*, p. 179. [The italics are mine.—A. M. L.]

group when its political enemies in the other are guilty of any State or civil crime. But there is no sign of that internal machinery for discipline and for the vigorous maintenance of a certain standard, which is beyond party and beyond rivalry, and which has for its aim the preservation of a high level of rulership and a regard for the nation's prestige and welfare. For, truth to tell, if we could see a sign, in the British aristocracy, of this essential element in the organisation of any highest ruling caste that strives to be permanent, it would be hard to understand how the events of the nineteenth century ever came to pass, and still harder to realise the full significance of the Parliament Act of 1911.

It would seem to be a first principle, therefore, of all aristocratic government, that the aristocrats themselves should exercise some powers of selection, censure, criticism, emulation, discipline and chastisement over each other; and any aristocracy that aspired to be relatively permanent, would sooner or later find it absolutely necessary to evolve some such controlling power within its own body.

Only a deep, solemn and almost religious sense of the great and sacred things that were at stake for the nation at large and for the aristocracy itself, could, however, render such an inner council at all practicable, or compel those who came before it to accept its judgment with reverence and submission. The fact, however, that such powers have been exercised in the world before, and that kindred powers are still exercised within the central controlling bodies of all great armies and navies, shows conclusively that they are not only necessary but eminently practical.

The absence of any such feature from the aristocratic organisation of England, shows the happy-go-lucky, careless and foolhardy fashion, in which great possibilities, great expectations and almost fabulous potentialities for good, have been deliberately allowed to slip the grasp of the most favoured body of men in this kingdom for the last two centuries.

Now, to my next point! I contend that the rearing of our aristocracy has been a random process. How so?

This question brings me to the much disputed problem of heredity, which we shall now face; but before plunging into this labyrinth of controversy, let me first call attention to one of the hitherto neglected aspects of the question.

A very-valuable and interesting fact to grasp in this matter is, that the enormous stress which is at present laid upon the one problematic and debatable question of heredity in rulers, as affecting the destiny of nations or institutions, owes more than half its force and relevancy only to the chaotic and disintegrated nature of our social system.

When you find so much importance attached to the inheritance of particular human qualities by individuals in the position of power, you will probably be very wide indeed of the mark, if you do not also suspect an unstable and fluid condition of the laws and customs prevailing in that part of the world where this particular attitude towards hereditary political rule obtains.

For wherever laws and customs are not fluid, and are not in a state of very unstable equilibrium; where, moreover, a whole people are led, and have been led for generations, by one general aspiration and idea, and where customs and laws have endured so long and satisfactorily as to have reared almost instinctive co-operative and harmonious action in a nation, the mere accident of personality in the seat of power, though important, is by no means so vital a consideration in actual practice as it would seem to be at first sight.

All great social systems, all great hierarchies and cultures, based upon the solid bedrock of the inveterate habits and impulses of a people, have been able to survive temporary unfortunate lapses on the part of the law of heredity. If they could not have done so, they would have been unworthy of the name of a social system, a hierarchy or a culture, as we understand it. I do not mean to suggest

370

that a prolonged abuse of the seat of power is not a thing to be guarded against and an evil which might lead to the most serious consequences in the body even of the most stable nation. I am merely insisting upon the fact that a large amount of the excessive stress which is now laid upon the hereditary principle in the ruling caste, and upon the so-called dangerous pranks it may play with a nation's destinies, derives by far the greater part of its force from the circumstance that at the present day the liquid disintegrated state of our customs, institutions, ideals, aspirations and morals, actually does make the mere breath of personality a highly important and momentous consideration. At a time when the mere eloquence of a few Radical politicians can lead to the modification of our constitution, people naturally expect the roof to fall in at the slightest sign of vibration. When the smallest breeze can produce a dangerous wave, things are in such a state that the fierce force of a gale cannot be faced, much less weathered. Personality is all-powerful to-day because tradition has gone to pieces, and a general landslide of principles, values, customs, virtues and instincts has occurred, which has rendered all things the prey of any momentary and transient influence that may happen to arise. But wherever stability reigns in the customs and aspirations of a people, wherever virtues are firmly rooted, and it is possible to make some reasonable forecast of the nation's behaviour, not only for a week, a fortnight, or three weeks, but for three centuries ahead; whenever, in fact, the nation has in its heart the natural corrective for all tricks of heredity in the seat of power, upon the surface of such a people even a hurricane of temporary misrule could not produce more than a ripple, while slight gusts of abuse would pass by quite unobserved.

I would like to repeat that I do not underrate the importance, nay, the essential need of a high traditional standard in the seat of power—truth to tell, the whole of my book reveals the importance I attach to this need—but I merely point out that all the frantic stress now laid upon

this element in discussing the principle of hereditary rulership, is largely due to the fact that the modern historian,
like the modern man, sees life through the glasses of his
age, and cannot help magnifying the significance of the
mere personality of him who is at the head of a system;
because this age and its culture and organisation are so
feeble and so shaky as to render personality all important.
Place Napoleon in Egypt at the zenith of its life as a well-
ordered state, and his personality loses more than half of
the importance it had in disordered and disorganised
France immediately after the Revolution.

Thus all aristocracy may regard itself as hopelessly in-
secure and ephemeral, where the people over which it rules
are not led, guided and inspired by one general idea which
animates all their hopes and plans, colours all their deeds
and endeavours and kindles all their passions and desires;
where they are not governed by the same inviolable values
that permeate all their loves and hates, all their virtues and
vices, and all their domestic and public manners,[1] and
where there are no superior minds to give them what even
John Stuart Mill—of all people!—acknowledged they
could not discover or create for themselves, namely, " the
initiation of all wise or noble things."

For, as he says, they could never " rise above mediocrity " [2] except in so far as they " let themselves be guided
(which in their best times they have always done) by the

---

[1] See Aristotle, *Politics*, Book II, Chap. VII, 1,266b: " For it is
more important that the citizens should entertain a similarity of sentiments than an equality of circumstances." See also Lecky : " All real
progress, all sound national development, must grow out of a stable,
persistent national character, deeply influenced by custom and precedent
and old traditional reverence."—*Democracy and Liberty*, Vol. I, p. 127.

[2] This, of course, is Mill's own expression, and I need hardly say
that I heartily disapprove of it. For there is absolutely no need for
them " to rise above mediocrity." There is nothing disreputable in
mediocrity as such. Mediocrity simply wants to be preserved against
its own mistakes ; it does not want to rise above itself—the idea is
absurd and romantic ! All it requires is to have its lack of taste and
judgment supplemented from on high. In this sense what Mill says has
some meaning for me.

counsels and influence of a more highly gifted and instructed One or Few." [1]

I shall now attempt to deal with the question of heredity, and in all my observations upon it I will take for granted the conclusions drawn in Chapter VII; while here and there many statements left inadequately supported in that chapter will find scientific confirmation.

There is no doubt that the general consensus of opinion among all wise men and races, has always been that, although the offspring of the same parents can show huge divergences, and can differ as individuals sometimes to an enormous extent, from their progenitors as individuals, the total sum of qualities distributed among a single family of children will always be found to be stock qualities or family qualities, appearing in a lesser or greater degree of intensity in each individual child. By stock I mean the whole family with its main and collateral branches.

In the history of a family, the changing opportunities offered by its fluctuating fortunes, may occasionally blind us to this general resemblance, and seem to pick one out of the rest of a single generation or line, so as to make him appear utterly different from and unrelated to the rest; but if we look into the matter more closely, we shall find that it is more frequently a difference of degree rather than of kind which has caused the salient distinction, and often a difference of degree which is smaller than we might at first expect.

If we can recognise a general resemblance of features between the members of a whole stock—as we usually can —it is ridiculous to suppose that a correlated similarity of

---

[1] The paragraph continues : "The initiation of all wise or noble things comes and must come from individuals ; generally at first from some one individual. The honour and glory of the average man is that he is capable of following that initiative ; that he can respond internally to wise and noble things, and be led to them with his eyes open."— This from the democrat Mill ! (*On Liberty*, Chapter : "The Elements of Well-being ").

character and disposition is not also present. And for all practical purposes, we can state it as a law, that, *provided a family of children be sufficiently large, at least one if not two of the children will bear a strong individual resemblance to one of the parents, at least one if not two will be a fair blend of both parents, and the rest will be more or less simple or complex combinations of the general stock qualities.*

What has made the law of heredity so difficult to uphold and so apparently easy to refute, especially in respect to the families of geniuses, artists, high-born aristocrats and other great men, is that, as a rule, their families are so absurdly small that the necessary quantum of chances allowed for a fair series of possible combinations of parental and stock features to be born is never reached, with the all too frequent result that various combinations of the stock features alone appear, twice, thrice, or sometimes four times, and then no more children are born. With the law of primogeniture, especially among the aristocracy, this evil is intensified; for, apart from the fact that there is nothing in the law of heredity to guarantee that the first-born will necessarily be the child who will have most of the parental qualities, there is not necessarily any inducement to continue adding to the family for long after the first or perhaps the second son's birth.

Thus the Royal Psalmist, who said, " Happy is the man that hath his quiver full of them " [children], uttered a very much more profound truth than most people imagine. For, in the light of the desire to transmit a great tradition, a quiverful of children certainly provides a much better chance of achieving this end than one, two or three.[1]

This is a fact upon which sufficient stress is never laid in discussions upon heredity. Here in England we have got firmly fixed in our minds the two notions—primogeniture and heredity. Again and again, though not always of course, we have seen that heredity seems to fail, and we

[1] The very lavishness of Nature's provision in the matter of germ cells lends colour to this contention.

374

never trouble to inquire whether nature, or whether a foolish custom based upon an ignorant solution of the problem of inheritance, be at fault.

The sort of arguments usually advanced by those who question the general fact of heredity are of the following kind : They say that Marcus Aurelius, who was one of the greatest of the Roman Emperors, had a worthless and dissolute son, the notorious Commodus; that Napoleon—the great general, thinker, statesman and man of power—had an insignificant nincompoop like the Duke of Reichstadt for heir; that Goethe, one of the greatest geniuses the world has ever seen, had in August Goethe a son utterly unworthy of his father; or that Louis XIII, the weak tool of Richelieu, was the son of Henry IV, surnamed the Great.[1]

All these statements are very true; but, as arguments against the general fact of heredity, they are utterly ridiculous.

Apart from the fact that such cases as Hannibal, the worthy son of Hamilcar; Alexander, the worthy son of Philip of Macedon; Titus, the worthy son of Vespasian; and a host of others, including such modern men as Dumas Fils, the brilliant son of Alexandre Dumas; and John Stuart, the worthy son of James Mill; may be quoted against a list like the preceding one, the circumstance that should always be borne in mind when dealing with a law so complicated as that of heredity, is that these sons, Commodus, the Duke of Reichstadt and August Goethe, were the *only* legitimate sons of their respective fathers. Now it is known—everybody knows—that the happiest combination of two parents' qualities, or even the happiest replica of a single parent, does not necessarily appear first among the children of every family. As I said above, " it is necessary that a certain quantum of chances should be

[1] Sometimes they add to this list the son of Luther, who is said to have been violent and insubordinate. But surely this is the best proof of heredity one could have. Was not Luther himself a revolutionary, and violent and insubordinate towards the Church of Rome ?

allowed for a fair series of possible combinations " to be born. How then can a law, the working of which depends upon the various adjustments of three factors : the father's, the mother's and the stock's influences—be rightly judged by a family consisting of one? In any case it would be ridiculous to judge it by such a case, and to declare it refuted, because the solitary child happened to have the least significant of the stock's qualities, instead of the best of the parents' or *vice versâ*.

Do the people who advance such arguments as these bear in mind that if the families of Charles Darwin, the Earl of Chatham, Handel, Machiavelli, Cavour, Sebastian Bach, Disraeli, Rembrandt, Rubens, Wagner, Emily Brontë, Bacon, Boileau, William Pitt the younger, Moses, Cæsar Borgia, Charles I, Richelieu, Napoleon, Nelson, Wellington, Beethoven, Shakespeare and a host of others, had consisted only of one child, those eminent people whom I have just mentioned would never have been seen. Are these people aware, moreover, that if Darwin's father had been contented with three children, the great naturalist would never have been born; that if Wellington's and Rembrandt's fathers had been content with three sons, the victor of Waterloo and the painter of the Night Watch would never have been born; that if Edmund Nelson and Bonaparte's father had been content with two sons, neither Napoleon nor Nelson would ever have been born?—not to speak of Joseph, Boileau and Bacon who, if their fathers had been satisfied with five or more sons would also never have been heard of!

It is idle to question the general fact of heredity from the evidence of small families. For, the above instances ought to suffice to show us that the happiest combination of parental, or stock qualities, are by no means certain to appear in the first, or in the second, or even in the third born.

That is why, I repeat, the Royal Psalmist's maxim was deeper and truer than most people think; and, *in order to carry on a great tradition*, in order even to have an ordinary chance of so doing, a large family, which is also, by the by, the *healthiest and happiest family*, must be regarded as a necessity, as a duty, as a privilege.

I am fully aware of the vast number of eminent people who have been first or only sons: Velasquez, Hobbes, Bolingbroke, Hawke, Meredith, Matthew Arnold, Isaac Newton, Julius Cæsar, Alexander, Gibbon, Milton, Dr. Johnson, Shelley, Bismarck, Columbus, Heine, Goethe, Colbert, Corneille, Molière, Nietzsche, etc., etc. But, as I have already said (on p. 341), all the circumstances being favourable, a first son is likely, as the Jehovah of the Old Testament put it, to be the "beginning" of his parent's "strength." Nevertheless I have also shown how elastic this rule was made, both by Isaac and Jacob, who thus established a precedent for allowing the full force of the law of heredity to operate in the families of their people. Jacob's favourite, for instance, is not Reuben, his firstborn, but Joseph, who ultimately proved himself to be the most distinguished of the sons of Jacob.[1]

As I say, I am fully aware of the vast number of eminent men who have been first or only sons; and in view of the relatively small families reared by the majority of men, it is fortunate for mankind that the percentage of great men who are of the firstborn should be so large. This, however, is only one proof the more of the general reliability of the law of heredity; for it shows that there is at least a slight natural bias in favour of early happy combinations.

To allow the law the greatest possible number of chances of operating, however, remains the soundest principle in practice, and any custom[2] or social condition which

---

[1] This fact rather shows how competent Jacob must have been as a judge of men, and explains the wonderful submission which was shown when he deliberately placed Ephraim above Manasseh, although Manasseh was the elder (see Gen. xlviii).

[2] This reminds me of a passage in one of Darwin's letters to J. D. Hooker. Writing on January 25, 1862, Darwin said: "I have sometimes speculated on this subject; *primogeniture is dreadfully opposed to selection;* suppose the firstborn bull was necessarily made by each farmer

prevents *a good valuable stock* from doing this, is the creation of an error of taste and judgment, which, in the end, can only rarify and decimate good qualities in a people.

Save when it is thwarted, therefore, the law of heredity may be regarded as the most reliable for all practical purposes that could be found; and this view has generally been in agreement with the consensus of wise opinion on the subject in healthy times.

I have shown in sufficient detail what the ancients thought upon the question of heredity. It is evident from the elaborate precautions they took, both as races and castes, to preserve a type pure, once it had been attained, that experience must have told them that which science now generally takes for granted, viz.: "That the present is the child of the past, that our start in life is no haphazard affair, but is rigorously determined by our parentage and ancestry; that all kinds of inborn characteristics may be transmitted from generation to generation." [1]

" In short," as Professor Thomson concludes, " the fundamental importance of inheritance was long ago demonstrated up to the hilt." [2]

But behind the usual modern arguments against heredity there is an element far more profound and far more irresistible than mere foolishness. There is the fundamental dislike and distrust which all democrats feel towards all distinctions and differentiations between one man and another. Under the growing influence of democratic ideas; with the spread of the doctrine of universal human equality, a certain prejudice has grown up against the old and well-established habit of attaching importance to birth, to blood, and to pedigree in men. As Reibmayr says: " People nowadays attach more importance to the pedigrees of domestic animals than to the pedigrees of

---

the begetter of his stock ! "—*Life and Letters of* C. *Darwin,* Vol. II, p. 385.

[1] Professor Thomson, *Heredity*, p. 9.   [2] *Ibid.*

men." [1]   The democrat prefers to ascribe individual excellence or superiority to accident, to some inexplicable force which he likes to call "the madness of genius," [2] and to a spurious notion of individual effort (self-help)—as who should say the leopard *can* change his spots if he likes—rather than to the greatest of all determinants, high innate quality, lofty inborn potencies, good *blood* in fact.

There is something less humiliating to the low-minded man in thinking that inequality of environmental conditions rather than the fundamental inequality of man is a paramount factor here.   And when he is faced by such cases as Commodus, August Goethe, the Duke of Reichstadt and Louis XIII, he much prefers to think that there can be nothing really true about this boasted claim of superior stock, rather than to suppose that although the probabilities undoubtedly were all in favour of Henry IV of France, of Goethe, of Marcus Aurelius and of Napoleon having one, two, or even more superior men as sons, they either did not give the law of heredity a sufficient number of chances to hit the happy combination which they would have been quite justified in expecting, or else their mates were too great a disturbing influence.

And this brings me to another aspect of the modern prejudices against the heredity principle—an aspect upon which Th. Ribot rightly lays some stress, without, however, drawing my ultimate conclusions from it.

The appearance of the above-mentioned men—Louis XIII, August Goethe, Commodus and the Duke of Reichstadt, is susceptible to two explanations, or to a blend of the two.   Up to the present I have only suggested one—the likelihood of their having been unhappy combinations

---

[1] *Inzucht und Vermischung*, p. 82 (note).

[2] Lombroso's book, *The Man of Genius*, in which the author attempts to show that all genius is insanity or degeneration, was a masterpiece of democratic insolence.   But its tremendous success shows the eagerness and enthusiasm with which people were ready to receive a scientific consolation for being mediocre.   "We are mediocre, it is true," the middling people of a democratic age were able to say ; "but at least we are not mad."

of stock or parental qualities, which in itself is not a refutation, but simply another form of proof of the principle of heredity. But, as Ribot says, " the maternal heredity of Commodus, Louis XIII, August Goethe and the Duke of Reichstadt is clear," and explains a good deal.[1]

This factor, the choice of a mate, in the case of a man who has a valuable tradition to transmit, or in the case of every man for that matter, is a most important and most vital concern. How can we tell now to what extent *the mother*, and not merely an unfortunate shuffling of the stock's and the father's qualities, was responsible for Pericles' foolish sons Paxalos, Xantippos and Clinias; or for Aristippos's infamous son Lysimachus, or for Thucydides' poorly gifted offspring, Milesias and Stephanos? How can we tell that the mother was not behind the unworthy sons of Sophocles, Aristarchos and Themistocles? [2]

Nothing could be more far-reaching, more serious in its consequences than this matter of choosing a mate—more particularly when great issues depend upon it, as they generally do in royal lines, in aristocracies, and in all families in which there is something worth preserving, worth enhancing or intensifying.

Take the case of Dante, for instance. From his first wife, Dante's father, Alighiero, had a son Francesco, over whom the breath of centuries has passed in silence; but with his second wife, Donna Bella, he had Dante. I do not mean to suggest that in his second marriage Alighiero exercised more conscious discrimination than in his first; but certainly he must have exercised better taste unconsciously. Again, in the case of the Czar Alexei, his second wife must certainly have been selected with finer discrimination than his first, for, by the latter he had two sons, one delicate and the other weak-minded; while by the second he had Peter the Great. And the same observations apply both to Bacon's father and to Boileau's. We hear no mention of the three sons who were born to Bacon's father

[1] *l'Hérédité Psychologique* (Paris, 1882), p. 230.
[2] See Ribot, op. cit., 229–230.

by his first wife; but the second son of his second wife became Lord Verulam. Boileau's father had five sons from his first wife and from his second three,[1] the third of whom was Nicholas Boileau, the illustrious French poet and critic.[2]

These four cases are interesting as showing how the same father can have a son of great or of mediocre gifts, according to his choice of a wife; and when, as in the case of Boileau, we find all three children by the second wife showing some distinction, we realise that Boileau himself cannot be explained as a mere " sport " or " mutation."

When we think of the great issues depending upon a man's choice of a mate, it seems ridiculous that this matter should so frequently have been taken so lightly, and continues to be taken so lightly by some.

Take the case of Henry IV of France! What curse, what damnable evil genius, cast its fatal spell over this man in order that, after ridding himself of Marguerite de Valois, he should turn his eyes towards Marie de Medici? Who knows, who can reckon, the incalculable loss that was suffered not only by France but also by England, as the result of that accursed second match! Think of the situation!

France was being ruled wisely, ably, justly and beneficently; her most trusted servant under the King was the great Sully himself. Even if Henry IV had died as prematurely as he actually did, after having married a better wife than Marie de Medici, at least the chances were that his great example would have been ably followed during the regency, his sons would have been greater men, and the Revolution, comparatively so near, might never have occurred, might never have been provoked!

---

[1] The two elder brothers of Boileau were also very gifted. Gilles, who was for some time a court official, became a member of the French Academy, and Jacques was a learned priest.

[2] Händel was also a second son of a second marriage, his father, George Frederick Händel, having already had by his first wife, Anna Oettinger, six children of whom the world has never heard.

A DEFENCE OF ARISTOCRACY

In England, too, the great beneficent ruler Charles I would have been wedded to a better wife, a wife who would have had the untainted traditions of a great ruler in her veins, and who would not only have borne him better sons, but would also have abstained from certain frivolities and weaknesses which, although never disastrous or serious, often lent a disagreeable colour to the captious and bitter criticisms of his worst enemies. The Grand Rebellion might have taken place notwithstanding; for nothing can ward off the results of a hatred so secret, surreptitious and cowardly as that of the anarchist who places a bomb beneath a fine structure; but its reaction, guided by the sons of Charles I and of this hypothetical daughter of Henry IV, would at least have made the England of the eighteenth century a very different country from that England which was destined ultimately to give birth to the present age; with the consequence that, to-day, instead of having to execrate our rulers for the past century and a half, we might all be singing their praises, we might all be proud of our country on their account alone, and might place the matter of our total annual exports and imports a little lower in the hierarchy of our idols.

But as the accursed luck of England and France would have it, Henry IV was deeply indebted to the Medici family. He did not particularly care for Marie de Medici, or want her, although her portrait did not displease him.

But, in view of his huge indebtedness to the Florentine magnates, it was thought that it would be a reasonable, judicious, *expedient* marriage. In this way the commercial and banking profits of these Italian plutocrats became the price of the order and good government of both France and England, and Henry IV married a woman whom he never liked, with whom he was constantly quarrelling, and who was a thousand times uglier and less attractive than her portrait. And thus this weak, violent, intriguing, obstinate woman, arrogant and servile by turns, according to her fortunes, and possessing but one quality which

382

happened to be hereditary in her family—the love of letters and the fine arts—became the mother of France's royal children and the grand-dam of England's kings!

And this is but one example in a thousand. If it were possible to know the secret history of all European aristocracies, it would be simply one example in a million.

Listen to these words of Karl Pearson! "Looked at from the social standpoint we can see how exceptional families, by careful marriages, can within even a few generations obtain an exceptional stock, *and how directly this suggests assortive mating as a moral duty for the highly endowed.*[1] On the other hand, the exceptionally degenerate, isolated in the slums of our modern cities, can easily produce permanent stock also: a stock which no change of environment will permanently elevate, *and which nothing but mixture with better blood will improve.*[1] But this is an improvement of the bad by a social waste of the better."[2]

This is all obvious, self-evident, trite! Moses knew it, the ancient Egyptians knew it, the ancient Hindus knew it, the Greeks at their zenith knew it, and so did the Romans. But in our times we have to be told these things afresh, at the cost of tremendous pains and infinite patience, by a power called Science, which every day gets to look more and more like a gigantic unwieldy and inadequate substitute for the things that men, unguided by superior taste, are liable to forget.

Now, what is meant precisely by "assortive mating" from my point of view? It is obvious that if, as ought always to be the case, the object to be attained is the consolidation of character—the fixing or enhancing of a certain will, of distinct virtues and of a particular kind of beauty—assortive mating means simply the deliberate selection of mates who in their tradition, their aspirations and their class are as much like yourself as possible. Then

---

[1] [The italics are mine.—A. M. L.]
[2] *The Grammar of Science*, 2nd edition, 1900, p. 486.

all that you possess in will, virtue and beauty finds itself preserved, confirmed, accentuated, often multiplied, in your offspring.

The proud, tasteful man who is conscious of his possessions in instinct, will, virtue and beauty, who is aware how much of them he owes to his ancestors and how much to his own individual efforts and self-discipline, and who, therefore, wishes to preserve them and if possible to fix them, is intuitively disinclined, unless he be prevented by democratic or romantic notions, to marry some one who is not his like; because he feels that there his instincts, his virtues, his will and his beauty, instead of being preserved, will be diluted, thwarted, decimated, crossed!

If he can, he will, as far as possible, marry within his family; for it is there, as a rule, that he is most certain of finding his like. If he fails to find his mate in his own family, he will turn his attention to the select circle of his nearest friends; and if he fail again, he will at least try to keep within his class. For if a whole class has for many generations pursued the same aims and shared the same traditions, a man may often run just as good, and sometimes a better, chance of finding his like in his class than in his family.

In this way character is built up and fixed, and beauty is attained, and generations are produced even in the lower classes which, if not necessarily capable of ordering things themselves, are at least amenable to and fond of order.

I shall now suggest two reasons why the democrat and a democratic age are opposed to the kind of assortive mating described above.

(1) Concurrently with the decline of really superior men—of the specimens of flourishing life, as I call them —through the neglect of the principles which rear such men, there has also taken place a decline in that element of taste whereby ill-health and degeneracy are warded off and eliminated. And the inevitable consequence has been that both ill-health and degeneracy have seized a fast hold

upon the populations of modern civilised countries. In England, alone, for instance, the report of the Lunacy Commissioners for 1913 records the fact that insanity is on the increase; and, in view of the supposed marvellous strides of medical and surgical skill in this country, the continued high percentage of physiological botchedness and bungledom shows that disease is, if anything, increasing by leaps and bounds.

Together with this general sickness which, as I have already shown, is largely the outcome of democracy and democratic conditions, there has developed a concomitant and very natural dread of marrying one's like, and more particularly a relative. "The idea that the marriage of near kin," says Professor Thomson, "is a cause of degeneracy seems to be relatively modern."[1] Certainly it is modern! But it is obvious why it should be modern. Democracy finds itself in a vicious circle. It is sick for the want of proper guidance.[2] The only thing that rears character and produces specimens of flourishing life, however, is inbreeding; while that which causes the disintegration of will and character is persistent cross-breeding. *But*, inbreeding multiplies disease wherever it is present, and intensifies a taint. Ergo: the only kind of mating that sick democratic conditions allow—the choice of a mate as remotely different from yourself as possible—simply increases the democratic diseases, lack of character and weakness of will.

Mr. George Darwin has argued very powerfully in favour of the view that consanguineous marriages are not *in themselves* causes of degeneracy,[3] and Professor Thomson,

[1] Op. cit., p. 391.

[2] To those who may rightly point out that long before a democracy was established in England, this country had already been made sick for want of proper guidance, I reply, not only that their contention is perfectly correct, but also that they should remember how, in times when the rulers of a country—however aristocratic their *claims* may be—are not true aristocrats as defined in this book, the same conditions prevail as in a democracy, *i.e.* good taste is not the guiding power.

[3] See a paper read before the Statistical Society, March 16, 1875, on

c c

voicing almost the whole sentiment of antiquity on this point, says: "Biologically it seems certain that close inbreeding can go far without affecting physique, and that it is very useful in fixing character and developing prepotency." [1]

I have referred to the Incas and to the Egyptians; but Professor Thomson provides us with two modern instances —the Norfolk Islanders and the people of Batz on the lower Loire—among whom, he says, close inbreeding has not been followed by ill-effects. [2]

But he argues, just as the ancients would have argued: "It seems equally certain that, if there be any morbid idiosyncrasy, close inbreeding tends to perpetuate and augment this." [3]

All of which simply confirms some of my conclusions in Chapter VII.

Thus the natural prejudice of the democrat against the idea that there can be anything worth preserving pure by a marriage with his like, or with the closest approximation to his like, is seen to be simply the self-preservative bias of a sick man. It is, in fact, a symptom of sickness. And it is curious to note how this sick prejudice against a first or second cousin has grown into a general prejudice against one's like.

You hear people talking foolishly and romantically nowadays about the desirability of marrying one's complement, one's opposite, one's other extreme! A pseudo-scientific maxim is hawked about in the guise of wisdom, and people repeat mechanically that nature is always seeking to establish a steady level, hence the marriage of tall

---

"Marriages between First Cousins in England and their Effects," in which, on p. 172, the author concludes, "there is no evidence whatever of any ill results accruing to the offspring in consequence of the cousin-ship of their parents."

[1] Op. cit., p. 391.   [2] Op. cit., p. 391.

[3] *Ibid.* See also p. 392 : "It goes without saying that if there is a diseased stock, or rather a stock with an hereditary predisposition to disease to start with, then the evil results of inbreeding will soon be, evident." Of course bad, like good, qualities are intensified by endogamy !

with short, fat with lean, dark with fair, beautiful with ugly! All these are the ideas of sickness and of morbid self-contempt. There is no such thing as this search after a dead level in nature; the only dead level that is sought in the world to-day is that which the democrats themselves are trying to establish. If there really were this apparent levelling tendency in nature, whence would come the superbly magnificent feline race, with all its beauty, strength, grace, courage and agility, side by side with the race of the sloths, of the skunks, and of the toad and the tapeworm? Such ideas are all nonsense, and when you find them in scientific text-books, be quite sure that they have crept in there unawares, like microbes, from the mass of decaying democratic carrion outside.

And this brings me to the second reason why the democrat and a democratic age are necessarily opposed to the kind of assortive mating described above, in which it is sought to preserve, intensify or fix instincts, will, virtues and beauty.

(2) I have shown in Chapter VII what I mean by instinct, will, virtue and beauty. Now it must be obvious that if strong, desirable character, which is the sum of all these, is to be preserved, indiscriminate cross-breeding between nations and classes must not be allowed to go on persistently. But this is precisely what is allowed—nay, abetted—in democratic times, under the belief in the equality of all men.

What happens then? Instinct, will, virtue and beauty gradually decline, and ultimately disappear. Nobody is deeply, proudly, almost religiously conscious of possessing something or having acquired something during his lifetime which is worthy of preservation and perpetuation in his family line. Things are even worse than this. There is scarcely a man to-day who does not believe that it is his duty in mating to choose a creature utterly different from himself, so great is his inner and often unconscious self-contempt. Having no real pride either in his will, his instincts, his virtues or his beauty, he feels intuitively that his object must be to find a corrective—that is to say, something that will modify, transform, or conflict with his own nature. And the popular mind is gradually possessed by the idea that a man should select his opposite, his complement, his other extreme!

Confusion thus rapidly multiplies; everybody becomes a coil of petty conflicting motives, desires, likes and dislikes, prejudices and prepossessions, diluted vices and diluted virtues; and weakness, doubt, discontent and sorrow begin to take up their permanent headquarters in the hearts of men and women. Nobody knows what he wants, nobody has any fixed belief, nobody is capable of any permanent sentiment or passion, and nobody is capable of steadfastness or staunchness and constancy in matters of principle. For in order to have an aim, a conviction, a cheerful trustfulness in life, and permanent passion or sentiment and steadfastness or staunchness in matters of principle—virtues, instincts above all, and will are necessary and indispensable.

We must, therefore, take no notice of a violent prejudice against the idea of " blood " and of its preservation in modern times, even when the prejudice dons a scientific garb; because it is only a symptom of a state of degeneracy already becoming an intuitive guide to conduct.

It is known that persistent cross-breeding among the lower animals will make cultivated types ultimately return in looks and habits to the type of their original ancestors —Darwin's experiments with pigeons proved this. Now is it not perhaps possible that the present lack of culture, the present worship of Nature and of the immature, may have a similar cause? The prevalent bias in favour of pure unhandseled Nature, free from the hand of man, the prevalent bias in favour of all that is primitive, free and uncultured, might be the inevitable outcome of such a long mixture of men that in the very heart of big cities, nowadays, true barbarians are being produced whose only modern characteristic is the cowardice and weakness necessarily associated with the poor physique they derive from the nature of their conditions. At all events, the faces and tastes of the modern mob lend colour to the suggestion, although its truth is in no way essential to my argument.

To sum up, then, there are three reasons why the claim of distinction, and of the duty to maintain it, are hateful to the modern man—

(1) Because, with his belief in the equality of all men, he is suspicious and intolerant of all distinctions.

(2) Because he is sick, and can save himself only by seeking a mate different from himself.

(3) Because, having nothing to preserve,[1] and feeling that his characteristics require correcting rather than intensifying, he seeks his opposite rather than his like.

There remains one aspect of the question of heredity which now requires to be elucidated. I refer to what is called the transmission of characteristics acquired in a single generation, or in the lifetime of a single individual.

It would be more than presumptuous on my part to pretend in this book that I am able to make any dogmatic or categorical statement concerning a matter which, if modern scientists are to be believed, is so exceedingly problematic. But perhaps the little I have to say on the subject will not be without interest.

Proved, or not proved, the transmission of acquired characteristics is not nearly so important to the advocate of the hereditary principle in great families or great classes as is *that pre-disposition to acquire good characteristics* which finds its root in the inborn virtues and instincts of a good family or caste.

Nevertheless, since the cumulative result of the transmission of acquired characteristics would prove, in the

---

[1] It should be remembered that even if a man to-day have anything to preserve either in virtue, will, or beauty, the very values prevalent about him are so opposed to the idea of his preserving them in the proper way that when he comes to think about marrying the consciousness of their possession alone will frequently be an insufficient ground for his acting contrary to the strong prejudice of his age.

long run, enormous, it is a matter which must interest any one who is concerned about the improvement or the selection of stock.

Defining an acquired characteristic as a quality which has become the possession of one individual or one generation, alone, and the very latest and most recent feature of that individual or generation, it will readily be understood how easily such a possession will yield before the prepotency of earlier and more long-established qualities in the type, and what a small chance it has of contending with success against these for a place in the offspring of the individual.

Just as a highly cultured and inbred type with a long pedigree is prepotent when crossed with a less cultivated type, owing, apparently, to the strength garnered through long tradition,[1] so, too, it seems obvious that the older and more long-established qualities of a stock must be prepotent as against the more recently acquired qualities.

Example: A young man whose family has been in commerce for five generations may, owing to sudden extraordinary prosperity, find himself able to study art, or literature, or music, as an amateur, and even to attain to some proficiency in one of these pursuits. As an individual who has acquired this new feature during his lifetime, however, it is obviously very doubtful whether he will be able to transmit this newly acquired attribute to his offspring. The older tendencies, rooted more deeply in his ancestral line, will certainly stand a better chance of being transmitted.

This is simply common sense, and by experiments on yourself you can even gauge the different strengths of your acquired characteristics themselves.

Take, for instance, the gift of speech—everybody is born with that, for it is simply the potentiality of being able to express one's needs, one's emotions, one's feelings by articulations. A baby and a deaf child articulate. But

[1] For confirmation of this see Professor J. A. Thomson, op. cit., pp. 113–116 and 138.

as no *form* has yet been given to their articulations (and can never be given in the case of the deaf child), they are incomprehensible to their elders who have acquired a certain arbitrary form—say English, French, or German.

One of the baby's first acquired characteristics, therefore, will be the particular form given to his power of articulating, or to his powers of speech. And if he is English, that form will be the English form. If, later in life, however, that baby, now a youth of fourteen, learn French very well indeed, his power of speech will then have been given two forms.

Now, suppose he is exiled to Germany or to Sweden for the rest of his life, after his acquisition of French— which acquired form of speech will he be likely to lose first? Obviously the French form, because the other will have taken firmer root, and will have been in his possession for a much longer period of time.

What is true of the individual here, I imagine, is also true of the race. The more recent acquisitions, owing to their being less deeply and less firmly rooted in the ganglia of the body, are not nearly so readily or so easily retained as the older and more traditional qualities.

This fact, I believe, is the cause of a good deal of the doubt which has been cast upon the possibility of acquired characteristics being transmitted.

To argue from this fact, however, that acquired characteristics are not transmitted seems to me to be the height of unscientific and excessive caution. Naturally, the very circumstances of the case would render the slight modification caused by an acquired characteristic a very difficult feature to trace among all the stronger and older characteristics in the offspring. But to say that no transmission ever occurs, simply because frequently it is for all practical purposes invisible, or because, often, it actually does not occur, is surely ridiculous.

Moreover, when one sins here, by affirming the fact of the transmission of acquired characteristics, it should be remembered that one is doing so in excellent company.

Lamarck, Darwin, Spencer and many lesser biological lights also held this view.

What are the strongest arguments brought against the position of those who claim that acquired characteristics are transmitted?

They are most of them based on the most absurd and most hopelessly senseless experiments which could possibly be imagined—experiments which are a disgrace both to science and to the modern scientist alike.

Remember that you have in the average highly organised animal — whether a frog or a French poodle — a creature of a very superior grade of sensitiveness, of nervous energy, power and control. Any experiments made upon such a creature with the view of discovering the extent to which acquired characteristics are transmitted ought surely to have reckoned with this nervous system, which is a system of control and of memory as well as of communication.

When one remembers that the mere expectation of his meal by a dog will cause his gastric juices to flow as if food were in his mouth; and when, moreover, the intimate relationship of function to instinct, or organ to mental attitude, and of member to mental idiosyncrasy, is thoroughly grasped, it is obviously preposterous to question the nervous control of our highly organised animals—in short, it is unscientific to forget the spirit.

And yet the average naturalist, setting about the task of discovering whether acquired characteristics are transmitted, began by cutting off rats' tails, docking ears and generally mutilating unfortunate animals' bodies in every conceivable way, and then setting them to breed to see whether they would produce maimed offspring!

The veriest dolt could have told beforehand that such experiments were absolutely futile and inconclusive. Because that which results from a *vis major*, descending unexpectedly in the form of an outside, unknown cause upon an animal's body, can have no possible relation to the inner workings of that body, or to the causes which make it grow. To cut off a rat's tail does not even amount to removing the cause of the growth of the tail —unless the tail is its own cause; how, then, could the cutting off of the tail be transmitted as an acquired characteristic to the rat's offspring? The cause of the growth of the tail is still inextricably associated with the rat's whole life and growth, it is still part of its nature. Cutting the tail off has removed a manifestation of rat-nature, it has not necessarily modified rat-nature itself.

This is *not* the way animals lose their parts. An animal's body knows nothing about knives or about amputations. How could the repetition of its controlling nervous system in its offspring repeat an experiment it knows nothing at all about—save that a *vis major* appeared one day, and that thenceforward it had no tail?

Watch the way animals — tadpoles, for instance — gradually lose their parts, either tails or gills, or fins or what-not, and you will find that the process has nothing whatever to do with knives. But the way in which a tadpole loses its tail is understood by Nature, and on those lines Nature can work.

The correlation of will and instinct to part should not be overlooked, especially by naturalists. The correlation of will to part is intimate, it is certainly incomprehensible; some have declared that it is creative. But at all events any forcible extirpation of a part will not create another will in the individual which is capable of turning a tailed race into a tailless race.

The argument that acquired characteristics are not transmitted because mutilations are not transmitted is, therefore, as utterly insane as any argument possibly could be, and none but supinely mechanical minds could ever have dreamt of such experiments as a test of transmission.

The next argument is that no *mechanism* is known by which acquired characteristics can be transmitted. According to Weismann the germ-plasm is quite independent of the soma or body, and is unaffected by the latter's vicissitudes; or if it be claimed that it is affected by the latter's vicissitudes, "we cannot imagine how a modification might, as such, saturate from body to germ-cells." But, as Professor Lloyd Morgan says, "this does not exclude the possibility that it may actually do so";[1] but there is another objection—why should the process be a mechanism, as we understand that expression? Dr. George Ogilvie observes: "In a subject so involved in obscurity the present incomprehensibility of certain relations can hardly serve as an argument against their existence."[2] This is the only honest thing that science can say at present on the question—not, remember, because the transmission of acquired characteristics is not a possible and proven phenomenon, but because it is one of the democratic rules of modern science to take nothing for granted which cannot be made comprehensible by a diagram or a mechanism to every Tom, Dick and Harry.

The fact, however, that the only experiments which have shown the smallest measure of success have been carried out on the nerves and not on the muscles of animals proves that the nearer you get to that seat of control which consists of the instinct-saturated ganglia,[3] the more likely you are to make a deep-rooted and permanent impression upon the parent animal, and therefore upon the offspring. Because the ganglia know how to lose things or grow things. They are the storehouse of the race-memory. It is they who generalise from experience, and who organise and control accordingly. Touch them, through their members, the nerves, and you are very near the directing force of the whole animal.

In this way, in modifications of the ganglia, in modifica-

[1] See Professor J. A. Thomson, op. cit., p. 200.
[2] Ibid., p. 201.
[3] Ibid., p. 168 : "It is hard to find evidence of the power of the personal structure to react upon sexual elements that is not open to serious objections. That which appears most trustworthy lies almost wholly in the direction of nerve-changes, as shown by the inherited habits of tameness, pointing in dogs, and the results of Dr. Brown-Séquard's experiments on guinea-pigs."

tions of the will, it seems to me that a particular kind of training, especially when it becomes traditional in a line, must in the end show by its cumulative results, however imperceptible at first, marked changes in the aptitudes and proclivities of a race; and if it does, the theory of the perfectly isolated unaltered germ-plasm must be to a great extent sadly at fault. For is not all modification effected through the will, even in one's own lifetime? Is not training in itself but the habituation of the ganglia to certain processes, the giving of a particular direction to the will?

See the shifts to which scientists are driven who, in the face of all evidence to the contrary, still maintain that acquired characteristics are not transmissible, even in their cumulative results. Professors Mark Baldwin, Lloyd Morgan and H. F. Osborn suggest that "adaptive modifications may act as the fostering nurses of germinal variations in the same direction." [1]

What need is there of these roundabout explanations, depending upon chance for their existence, when we know that, though the process is often an invisible one in its initial stages, persistently acquired characteristics all of a like nature do in the end produce tangible results? Surely all culture, all rapid advance or decline in any direction, involves a process more reliable and more certain in its action than the mere chance production of germinal variations of a similar nature to the acquired characters. But, in any case, where is the advantage of substituting an accidental and unaccountable process here for an orderly and accountable one? As Reibmayr points out, "the speed with which the culture of a nation develops depends to a very great extent upon the transmissibility of acquired characters." [2] However much the course of evolution, which has no set plan, may have been determined by spontaneous mutations, surely it seems a little far-fetched to explain the course traversed by a developing culture

[1] Professor J. A. Thomson, op. cit., p. 243.
[2] *Inzucht und Vermischung*, p. 6.

which is founded in the taste of its leaders also to spontaneous mutations! Nor does the argument depending
upon spontaneous mutations stand on any sounder facts
than the argument for the transmission of acquired characteristics. All we know is that spontaneous mutations
occur—just as we know that certain cases of transmission
of acquired characteristics occur—we know nothing about
their mechanism!

Taking it all in all, the statements of the two Professors,
V. A. S. Walton and L. Doncaster, sum up the question
exceedingly well for the scientific school, and show how
great is the uncertainty still reigning in this department
of biology. The former says: "To sum up the main
argument, it must be said that there is some presumptive
evidence in favour of the inheritance of acquired characteristics, but that direct experiments have given positive
results of only the most meagre and inconclusive kinds." [1]

We know what these experiments have been, for the
most part; and is it not possible that even the best experiments have been carried out with too sanguine expectations? Seeing, as I said at the opening of the inquiry
on the subject, that all acquired characteristics are recent
and short-rooted, and therefore, that they must yield to
the older and more traditionally established characteristics
in the order of precedence, is it not obvious that any trace
of them in the first generation must be very faint, however
considerable and unmistakable their cumulative effect
may be?

Doncaster writes as follows: "The tendency of biological thought is towards a recognition of the unity of
the organism as a whole, including its germ-cells, and
especially where the organism adapts itself to change, it
seems possible that this adaptation is transmissible. The
belief that somatic changes could not be transmitted rests
largely on the idea that every character is determined by
a factor or determinant in the germ-cell, but it is clear
that any character is not developed directly from the

[1] *Heredity* (T. C. and E. C. Jack), p. 42.

germinal determinant, but by the relation existing between the determinant and its surroundings, viz. the body of the organism." [1]

This shows which way the wind is blowing in the world of science, and I have no doubt that, one day, biologists will return as resolutely to Darwin's and Spencer's belief in the transmission of acquired characteristics, as they turned against it under the influence of Weismann. But with good reason they will probably maintain, as I maintain, that it is absurd to expect the same conspicuous and unmistakable evidence of the transmission of acquired characteristics, as of the transmission of racial and long-established ones, because the former, being so recent and so lightly and shallowly rooted in the parent nature, can make but the faintest modification in the offspring, and can be detected probably only after a long series of generations, when their cumulative results begin to be substantial.

All people, then, who believe in the power of high culture over a race that is susceptible to high culture, must take for granted the cumulative effects of imperceptible transmissions of acquired characteristics, and must believe in the miracles that can be, and are, worked by long tradition.

For even if those biologists are right, who maintain that while there is no such thing as the transmission of persistent modifications, there is a tendency for germinal variations of a like nature to be preserved by them, *tradition* still remains the important factor; and, to keep that as unbroken as possible must be the chief aim of all educators and cultivators.

This reconciliation of the two hostile scientific camps in the one word *tradition*, [2] ought to be sufficient for the ordinary man. Both the believers and the disbelievers in the transmission of acquired characteristics, believe in

---

[1] *Heredity in the Light of Recent Research*, p. 97, note.
[2] See L. Doncaster, op. cit., p. 50.

the importance of unbroken tradition—and·this, after all, is sufficient for my purpose.

The Incas, the Brahmans, and the Egyptian aristocracy understood perfectly well how important tradition was, if virtue, will and beauty are to be reared in the body of a nation and kept there. Indiscriminate crossing between the castes, each of which *had its particular occupation*, was loathsome to the ancient Hindu. It was also loathsome to the Inca and to the Egyptian. Indeed, so far did the two latter nations go in trying to prevent a break in tradition, and in thus preserving virtues from degeneration, or dilution, that, in addition to casting a stigma upon half-caste people and doing all they could to avoid their multiplication, they even encouraged the retention of the same occupation in a family from generation to generation.[1]

Speaking of the Egyptians, Diodorus says: "For among these people only is the whole artisan class accustomed to take no part in any occupation . . . other than that which is prescribed to them by their laws and handed down to them by their ancestors."[2]

Wilkinson denies that this principle was insisted upon by law, and he says that it was merely customary, as it is in India and China, where the same trade or employment is followed in succession by father and son.[3]

It is sufficient for my purpose, however, to know that it was so general a practice as to be regarded almost as an unwritten law, and the fact that Diodorus took it to be compulsory, only supports this view. In any case, Dr. Henry Brugsch Bey supplies an interesting piece of evidence, showing the extremes to which the Egyptians sometimes went in observing the custom of hereditary

---

[1] A certain Inca, Terpac Jupangi, expressed himself as follows on this point : "Il faut que, parmi le peuple, chacun apprenne le métier de son père ; car ce n'est point au vulgaire à commander aux autres ; et c'est faire tort aux charges publiques que de l'employer."—Ch. Letourneau, *l'Évolution de l'Éducation*, p. 199. See also p. 304 of the same book for evidence of similar customs in Egypt.

[2] Book I, 74   [3] Op. cit., Vol. I, p. 157.

occupations. It relates to the pedigree of the architect Knum-ab-ra (490 B.C.), chief minister of works for the whole country. He was the twenty-fourth architect of his line; his remote ancestor Imhotep, who lived in the third dynasty, having been an architect of Southern and Northern Egypt and a high functionary under King Zasar.[1]

This, together with a healthy distinction between high and low, man and man, which is always felt in inbreeding classes, is the only way in which virtue, strength and will can be garnered and stored over generations, in order at any time to produce a crop of fine, conscientious and skilful artisans, or artists, or leaders of men. In itself the custom seems natural, obvious, I would almost say, inevitable enough; and provided it have just that amount of elasticity that can allow of exceptional men breaking themselves free from their family tradition, in order to attempt higher things—a possibility provided for in Egypt, China and India—and to allow of cross-breeding in cases of real effeteness, which are, at all events, rare when an inbred class is large, only good can be expected to come of it.

Thus alone can that culture be reared which is based upon solid virtue; for the bodily reward of any occupation, if it be noble and healthy, is the acquisition of certain virtues—dexterity, strength, self-control, self-reliance, patience, endurance, perseverance, regularity, reliability, not to mention again, will-power and beauty. And wherever an occupation is constantly changed, *either in a single lifetime or in the life of a family*, or wherever its nobility declines—as, for instance, when a man is asked, as he is nowadays, to turn a lever from left to right all his life—the stored up virtue of generations must gradually be dissipated until none remains. When such things

[1] *History of Egypt*, Vol. II, p. 309. The retention of certain professions and trades within a family in antiquity was not, however, restricted to ancient Peru and ancient Egypt. Hippocrates, for instance, was the seventeenth medical practitioner in his family.

happen not only the working classes, but the nation itself is in danger.[1]

For virtue, like will and beauty, is no accident. It is invariably the outcome of long traditional effort, it is always the achievement of a long line of people who have stored it, built it up, garnered it and laboured for it. Just as a falling object gathers momentum as it descends, and may attain an almost irresistible power if the descent be long enough, so if in a family line the will has been concerned long enough with the same occupations, problems and obstacles, the momentum it acquires in its descent may also prove well-nigh irresistible. It is, in fact, in matters of will and virtue, the only possible source of power; and though a man can add his own strength to it in his lifetime, if it is truly great in him, at least the major part of it is the work of his predecessors, i. e. the distance it has already covered. It is for this reason that traditional occupations are important, not only among an aristocracy, but among a people; because the people, who are the ultimate source of refreshment for an aristocracy, cannot supply that refreshment unless they too have acquired through traditional occupations the first prerequisites of aristocratic equipment—will and virtue. To point out that *this is precisely the reverse of the principles we see practised to-day* is a sufficient comment on our age.

Summing up now, on the question of the transmission of acquired characteristics, we see that, although the acquired characteristics of an individual, owing to the very recent nature of their citizenship in his body, make a much fainter impress upon, and are much more imperceptible in, his offspring than the older and more traditional characters of his race, they must be there in humanly imperceptible form, otherwise it is impossible to explain results which can only be ascribed to their cumulative

[1] See Aristotle, *Politics*, Book VIII, Chapter II, 1,337*b*: "Every work is to be esteemed mean, and every art and every discipline which renders the body, the mind, or the understanding of freemen unfit for the habit and practice of virtue."

effects in subsequent generations. Even if those are wrong, however, who ascribe these perceptible modifications—as, for instance, the gradual high culture of a people—to the cumulative effects of transmitted acquired characteristics, they and their opponents are at one on the matter of tradition, which is essential to both hypotheses, *i. e.* either to the hypothesis which postulates the cumulative result of acquired characteristics as a factor in modification (in addition, of course, to mutations); or to the hypothesis which postulates mutations alone, fostered by persistent modifications of the same nature, as the cause of all development or retrogression.

Thus unbroken tradition comes out of the discussion without a stain upon its character; and to-day, just as it was four thousand years ago in Egypt, we must conclude that it is the greatest force in the rearing of all virtue, will, beauty, or quality of any sort in the body of a nation, and especially among the members of an aristocracy.

Turning now to the English aristocracy represented in the House of Lords, how does the above examination of the question of heredity help us?

In speaking about the principles upon which a sound aristocracy should be based, the criticism recently levelled by the more rabid Radicals against the present House of Lords will not be found to be of much service, and might just as well be left out of our reckoning altogether. The war-cries of political parties, in the thick of a party struggle, are not as a rule reliable, even as sign-posts, for the purpose of the investigator. Nevertheless, there was one criticism which figured very prominently and very frequently above the rest, and that was the criticism of the hereditary principle. It is not implied here that any Radical who voiced this criticism understood its full political import or depth—otherwise he would probably have been less lavish in his repetition of it; nor is it suggested that the criticism itself was based upon a sound analysis of the question of heredity in general. As a war-cry, however, it certainly pointed to the kernel of the whole question of traditional rule and government, and no aristocracy now aiming at permanency can hope to arrive at a sound foundation for its order, unless it face this question, in the light of history and science. And the more it draws from the former, and the less it draws from the latter, the better.

The bitter hatred of the hereditary principle, however, has not found expression only in the mouths of Radical orators, or in the columns of Radical newspapers; it is to be found even in the pamphlets and books which purport to deal seriously with the question of aristocratic rule.

Such writers as John Hampden,[1] J. Morrison Davidson,[2] and Howard Evans,[3] lay it down as a fact that the hereditary principle must be bad; while in a compilation published in 1898, almost every writer shows himself hostile to the idea that the right of ruling should descend from generation to generation in the same family.[4]

After what we have said and seen on the matter of heredity, and even on the matter of the influence (I will not say the inheritance, as the point is still unsettled in many distinguished minds) of acquired qualities, it seems strange that there should be this bitter hostility on the part of many thinking men towards hereditary rulership.[5]

Is it not possible, however, that after inquiry we may find that this hereditary principle of the House of Lords, is merely in superficial appearance the cause of the trouble? No one, I believe, could speak more severely on the misrule of the English aristocracy than I have spoken in this book; and yet I absolutely decline to ascribe this misrule either to the evil effects of inbreeding or to

[1] *The Aristocracy of England.*
[2] *Book of Lords.*   [3] *Our Old Nobility.*
[4] *The House of Lords Question.* Edited by A. Reid.
[5] Even aristocrats themselves, or at least the more stupid ones, are beginning to feel that there may "be something in it." They are beginning to be converted unthinkingly to the Radical position, simply because its features have been voiced and urged so repeatedly of late.

the supposed unreliability of the hereditary principle. And all those who do account for it in this way, show themselves to be utterly shallow investigators into the problem.

I say that, whatever the misrule of the English aristocracy may have been, it is not the outcome of the evils resulting from inbreeding or from the alleged freaks of the hereditary principle : in the first place, because the first-named evils have literally not had the time to be brought about; and secondly, because it is ridiculous to call the House of Lords essentially a hereditary Chamber at all, even if the law of heredity, starting with good material, had been allowed its full modicum of chances by the peers. I would go even further, and declare most emphatically that if the hereditary principle had only had a chance of working on the foundations of good stock, there would to-day be absolutely no outcry against the House of Lords and its methods of rulership.

Let me enter briefly into the recent history of the House of Lords.

Not more than 29 temporal peers received Writs of Summons to the first Parliament of Henry VII; Henry VIII never summoned more than 51; and at the death of Queen Elizabeth this number had increased only to 59. James I created 62; Charles I 59;[1] Charles II 64; and James II 8.[2] Thus, at the end of the Stuart line, the peerage should have numbered 252, but during the Stuart reigns 99 peerages became extinct, so that at the Revolution of 1688 the peerage stood at

---

[1] J. Bernard Burke, in his *Anecdotes of the Aristocracy* (Vol. I, p. 105), speaking of Charles I's creations, says : "They were all selected from old and well-allied families."

[2] Lord Erskine, in *The Constitutional History of England* (Vol. I, p. 274), makes an interesting comment on the Stuart creations. He says : "As many of the peerages were sold by James I and Charles II it is surprising that the creations were not even more numerous." When we compare the twenty-two years of James's reign with the fifty-nine years of George III's reign, during which the number of creations amounted to 388, we realise the full significance of Lord Erskine's remark.

about 150. William III and Queen Anne increased this further to 168, and the first two kings of the House of Hanover continuing to make additions to the peerage, brought it in 1760 up to 174.

Then followed one of the worst reigns for political corruption and general jobbing in titles and peerages that England has ever seen. Places in Parliament were bought outright, men who held seats were bribed with money, knighthoods, baronetcies or peerages to give them to a certain party, and altogether from 1760 to 1820 no less than 388 creations were made.

One of the worst offenders in this indiscriminate augmentation of the hereditary lords was William Pitt the younger,[1] and there is no doubt that if the prestige of our aristocracy has considerably diminished in the last hundred years, and if, as men of wisdom, ruler power and ruler gifts, their credit is low, it is largely to Pitt that the country owes this unfortunate change. Referring to Pitt's creations, Green writes as follows—

"The whole character of the House of Lords was changed. Up to this time it had been a small assembly of great nobles, bound together by family or party ties into a distinct power in the state. From this time it became the stronghold of property, the representative of the great estates and great fortunes which the vast increase of English wealth was building up."[2]

Thus, upstart capitalists began to form a large percentage of the Upper Chamber, and there was often absolutely nothing in their past lives or in their achievements to show that this highly influential position in the legislature would be filled by them with ability or success.

---

[1] See Lecky's *History of England in the Eighteenth Century*, Vol. V, p. 275. Referring to Pitt's creations, he says: "He distributed peerages with a lavish and culpable profusion." And on p. 292: "No previous minister created peers so lavishly for the purpose of supporting his political influence, or affected so permanently and so injuriously the character of the House of Lords."

[2] *A Short History of the English People* (1891), p. 816.

Speaking of this class of peer, Lecky says: "They were nearly all men of strong Tory opinions promoted for political services, the vast majority of them were men of no real distinction, and they at once changed the political tendencies and greatly lowered the intellectual level of the assembly to which they were raised."[1]

Now even if inbreeding had had time to work its worst evils among the descendants of these peers, which it certainly had not, what in any case could have been expected from the progeny of such men? The law of heredity does not work miracles, it cannot turn sows' ears into silk purses; and if by 1820 there was already some outcry against the hereditary chamber, let us be quite satisfied that this outcry was not provoked by the degeneration through close intermarriage of these eighteenth-century creations—numbers of which were not yet fifty years old.

It is only stupidity and ignorance that can make a man ascribe all the misrule of the House of Lords in the latter half of the eighteenth and the first quarter of the nineteenth centuries, to the evils of close inbreeding and to the sad uncertainty of the hereditary principle. For, in the first place, close inbreeding would have to go on for a very long time indeed, far longer than the existence of the majority of the present peerage, before its evils could begin to show themselves; and, secondly, if you have bad material to start with, it is ridiculous to ascribe to the hereditary principle an evil which it has never been claimed that it can remove.

Considering that in 1860, a century after the accession of George III, no more than 98 of the odd 450 peers could claim an earlier creation than the reign of that monarch, it would be far more just, far more historically correct, and far more penetrating, to say that the incompetence and general lack of ruler ability (in *my* sense, not in the Radical sense) which characterise the House of Lords, were due to the method of selection rather than to the hereditary

---

[1] *History of England in the Eighteenth Century*, Vol. V, p. 293.

principle.[1] But selection is precisely what the Radicals are clamouring for! The very principle which has been pursued with such disastrous results ever since 1760, is that which the Radicals would fain put in the place of the supposed hereditary principle which not only has never had a fair chance of showing its true merits, but has also been the subordinate principle in the House for over one hundred years!

When you bear in mind that since the year 1760 over 600 new peers, i. e. more than nine-tenths of the whole House—and that since 1820, at least three-quarters of the total number of members of the House of Lords have been created; when, moreover, you recollect that there are twenty-six bishops and forty-four Irish and Scottish Peers —all selected, the hereditary character of the peerage begins to acquire a very insignificant character indeed; and if incompetence and misrule are noticeable in it, they must surely be traced to another source than to close inbreeding and the hereditary principle.

Let me quote the following figures from the Constitutional Year Book of 1913, to show the number of *additions* to the House of Lords made since 1830 alone—

Under Liberal Ministries			Under Conservative Ministries		
Earl Grey .	1830–1834	37	Sir Robert Peel	1834–1835	6
Viscount Melbourne	1835–1841	46	*Id.* . .	1841–1846	6
			Earl of Derby	1852	3
Lord John Russell	1846–1852 .	12	*Id.* . .	1858–1859	10
			Id. . .	1866–1868	7
Earl of Aberdeen	1853–1855	1	Mr. Disraeli .	1868	9
			Earl of Beaconsfield	1874–1880	29
Lord Palmerston	1855–1858	12			
Id. . .	1859–1865	15	Marquess of Salisbury	1885–1886	11

[1] Of course, as Lord Erskine points out (op. cit., p. 282), " this fact [the number 98 who can claim an earlier creation than the reign of George III] is an imperfect criterion of the antiquity of the peerage. When the possessor of an ancient dignity is promoted to a higher grade in the peerage, his lesser dignity becomes merged in the greater, but more recent, title."

THE ARISTOCRAT IN PRACTICE

UNDER LIBERAL MINISTRIES			UNDER CONSERVATIVE MINISTRIES		
Earl Russell .	1865–1866	8	Marquis of	1886–1892	38
Mr. Gladstone	1868–1874	39	Salisbury		
Id. . .	1880–1885	28	Id. . .	1895–1902	44
Id. . .	1886	8	Mr. Balfour .	1902–1905	18
Id. . .	1892–1894	11			
Earl of Rose-					
bery . .	1894–1895	5			
Sir H. C. Ban-	1905–1908	21			
nerman					
Mr. Asquith					
	1908–Dec. 1912	52			
Total created in 47 years		295	Total created in 34 years		181

This gives us a grand total of 476 creations in eighty-one years! In the face of these figures it is not only absurd, but literally dishonest to inveigh against the hereditary Chamber as if it consisted of a body of effete aristocrats, so closely inbred for centuries that all the evils of sterility, degeneracy and feebleness had now seized upon them. Neither is it sensible to say that in view of their misrule the law of heredity must have failed.

If the Lords have on the whole shown themselves unworthy of their high position in the State, and if from 1688 to 1832 they showed themselves unworthy of having all the power in their own hands, it is because the majority of them were not the right sort from the start. Commercial magnates, without any claim to distinction, apart from their wealth; borough-mongers, devoid of all public spirit and patriotism; and bribees of all descriptions—these are not the people who by their deeds can shake our faith in the value of aristocratic government. To set a jester on the throne is not to refute monarchy.

It is perfectly true, of course, that the hereditary principle, alone, cannot improve such stock; but that is not the fault of the principle. If it could, it would be less reliable than it is.

" A body so constantly changed and recruited from all

classes of society," says Lord Erskine, "loses much of its distinctive hereditary character. Peers sitting in Parliament by virtue of an hereditary right, share their privilege with so many who by personal pretensions have recently been placed beside them, that the hereditary principle becomes divested of exclusive power and invidious distinction." [1]

Not only, then, has the selective principle been far more active than the hereditary one in increasing the peerage, but also the very method of selection itself, has been so faulty, so foreign to any proper consideration of what true rulership means, that it was bound to fail, bound to be found out, and bound to drag the name of true aristocracy through the dust.[2]

But if there is little, for instance, in the successful banker, factory owner, ship-builder or general trade magnate to make one take for granted that he is fit to be one of the first rulers of a great nation, what on earth is there in the lawyer to make one think that he, too, after attaining to a certain high position in his profession, should necessarily be fit to govern?

The Earl of Strafford was suspicious enough of lawyers as legislators, and rightly too, I think. But what would he have said if he could have seen the following list of lawyers who between 1691 and 1912 have been elevated to the peerage? [3]

---

[1] *The Constitutional History of England*, Vol. I, p. 285.

[2] Mr. Luke Owen Pike, who, in his *Constitutional History of the House of Lords*, does not set up nearly so high a standard of aristocratic power as I do, is yet able to write as follows : "In one respect the House of Lords fails, and has always failed, to reflect the powers of the nation. The new men who have made their way into it have always been men of action rather than men of thought. . . . The robes of the judge, the wealth of the financier, the pomp and circumstance which attend the victorious general strike more deeply into the popular imagination than the untiring industry, the silent meditation, and the unseen flash of intellect, which brings into being things that the world has never seen before."

[3] This list, with three or four omissions and several additions, is taken from John Hampden's *The Aristocracy of England*, p. 302.

DATE	PRESENT TITLE	MAN ENNOBLED	LEGAL POST
1693	Earl of Guildford	Edward Nash .	Chancellor of Court of Augmentations
1695	Earl of Lisburn .	John Vaughan .	Lord Chief Justice Common Pleas, Ireland
1691	Earl of Stair . .	James Dalrymple	President of Court of · Session
1714	Earl of Aylesford .	Heneage 'Finch .	Attorney General
1784	Baron Alvanley .	Richard Pepper Arden	Ld. Ch. Just. Com. Pleas
1795	Visc. Avonmore .	Barry Yelverton .	Ld.Ch.Bn.of Exchequer, Ireland
1765	Marq. of Camden ·	John Pratt . .	Ld. Ch. Jus. Com. Pleas
1789	Earl of Clare . .	John Fitzgibbon .	Lord Chancellor
1793	Earl of Clonmell .	John Scott . .	Ld. Ch. Jus. King's Bench, Ireland
1767	Earl Cowper . .	William Cowper	Lord Chancellor
1799	Earl Eldon . .	John Scott . .	Ch. Jus. Com. Pleas
1782	Baron Grantley .	Fletcher Norton .	Ch. Jus. in Eyre
1783	Earl of Hardwick .	Philip Yorke . .	Ch. Jus. King's Bench
1776	Earl of Harrowby	Dudley Rider .	Ch. Jus. King's Bench
1788	Baron Kenyon .	Lloyd Kenyon .	Ch. Jus. King's Bench
1768	Baron Lifford . .·	James Hewitt .	Ld. Chancellor, Ireland
1765	Earl of Lovelace .	Peter King . .	Ld. Ch. Jus. Com. Pleas
1715	Earl of Macclesfield	Thomas Parker .	Lord Chief Justice of Queen's Bench
1776	Earl of Mansfield .	William Murray .	Lord Chief Justice ot King's Bench
1715	Visc. Middleton .	Allan Brodrick .	Ld. Chancellor, Ireland
1783	Earl of Roden . .	Robert Jocelyn .	Ld. Chancellor, Ireland
1780	Earl of Roslyn .	Alex. Wedderburn	Ch. Jus. Com. Pleas
1744	Lord Talbot . .	Charles Talbot .	Lord Chancellor
1778	Baron Thurlow .	Edward Thurlow	Lord Chancellor
1743	Baron Walsingham	Wil. Walsingham	Ch. Jus. Com. Pleas
1823	Earl of Abinger .	James Scarlet . .	Ld. Ch. Bn. of Exchequer
1830	Baron Brougham .	Henry Brougham	Lord Chancellor
1841	Baron Campbell .	John Campbell .	Lord Chancellor
1836	Baron Cottenham .	Charles C. Pepys	Lord Chancellor
1834	Baron Denman .	Thomas Denman	Ch. Jus. King's Bench
1802	Earl of Ellenborough	Edward Law . .	Ch. Jus. King's Bench
1806	Baron Erskine . .	Thomas Erskine .	Lord Chancellor
1824	Baron Gifford . .	Robert Gifford .	Ld. Ch. Jus. Com. Pleas

DATE	PRESENT TITLE	MAN ENNOBLED	LEGAL POST
1831	Visc. Guillemore .	Standish O'Grady	Lord Chief Justice, Exchequer, Ireland
1819	Earl of Haddington	Thos. Haddington	Lord Advocate, Scotland
1836	Baron Langdale .	Henry Bickersteth	Master of the Rolls
1802	Visc. Melville . .	Henry Dundas .	Ld. Chancellor, Scotland
1800	Earl of Norbury .	John Toler . .	Lord Justice Common Pleas, Ireland
1827	Baron Plunket . .	William Conyngham Plunket	Lord Chancellor, Ireland
1802	Baron Redesdale .	John Milford .	Ld. Chancellor, Ireland
1827	Baron Tenterden .	Charles Abbott .	Lord Chief Justice, King's Bench
1838	Marquis of Winchester	William Paulet .	Lord Chancellor
1829	Baron Wynford .	Wm. Draper Best	Ch. Jus. Com. Pleas
1885	Lord Monkswell .	Robert Collier .	Judge
1897	Lord Ludlow . .	H. Lopes . . .	Judge
1910	Lord Robson (Life Peer)	William Robson .	Attorney General
1910	Lord Mersey . .	John Bigham . .	Judge
1909	Lord Gorell . .	John Barnes . .	Judge
1885	Lord Ashbourne .	Edward Gibson .	Ld. Chancellor, Ireland
1895	Lord Rathmore .	David Plunket .	Lawyer
1911	Lord Haldane . .	Richard Haldane	Lawyer
1906	Lord Loreburn .	Robert Reid . .	Lord Chancellor
1905	Lord Atkinson (Life Peer)	John Atkinson .	Attorney General, Ireland
1912	Lord Moulton .	John Fletcher Moulton	Judge
1915	Lord Wrenbury .	Henry Buckley .	Judge

It is preposterous to inveigh against the principle of aristocracy itself, or against the principle of hereditary rulership, when the body of aristocrats in the country has been constantly swelled by selections of this sort; and the length of the lists could be doubled in the case of purely business men who have become peers.

With wealth or political influence as the chief qualifications, what could be expected of the men who forced themselves into the aristocratic ruling body? The only essential conditions of the aristocrat which they possessed were leisure and the best possible circumstances for rearing and maintaining an excellent physique. But to suppose that these conditions are sufficient is to misunderstand the whole question.

Nor need it be supposed that the creations from the ranks of capitalism after 1830 were, on the whole, any more judicious or far-sighted, or that they were made with a deeper understanding of true rulership than those made before that time.

Speaking of the bulk of them, Lecky says: "Great wealth, even though it be accompanied by no kind of real distinction, especially if it be united with a steady vote in the House of Commons, has been the strongest claim; and, next to wealth, great connections. Probably a large majority of those who have of late years risen to the peerage are men whose names conveyed no idea of any kind to the great body of the English people." [1]

In other words, the test of great material success has been the most general test employed in the selection of the peerage. But such a test would, in itself, have excluded some of the greatest men the world has ever seen!

How could any great institution survive such a process of recruitment for any length of time?

"The worst aspect of plutocracy," says Lecky, "is the social and political influence of dishonestly acquired wealth. While the worst fields of patronage and professional life have been greatly purified during the present century [nineteenth], the conditions of modern enterprise in the chief European countries, and still more in the United States, give much scope for kinds of speculation and financing which no honest man would pursue, and by which, in many conspicuous instances, colossal fortunes have been acquired. It is an evil omen for the future of a nation when men who have acquired such fortunes force their way into great social positions, and become the

[1] *Democracy and Liberty*, Vol. I, p. 354.

objects of admiration, adulation and imitation. One of the first duties, and one of the chief uses of courts and aristocracies is to guard the higher walks of society from this impure contact; and when courts and aristocracies betray their trust, and themselves bow before the golden idol, the period of their own downfall is not far distant." [1]

I would not suggest for one instant that the bulk of the peerages connected with trade are of the nature alluded to above; but that a few of them must be is unquestioned. My particular point, however, is that success in trade, like success at law, is absolutely no criterion of ruler quality or of taste; on the contrary, it is more often the proof of the reverse of these two possessions. An aristocracy recruited from successful men of this sort alone would require ages and ages of training and culture and careful discipline to approach even approximately close to "the best."

Take the following list of peers either connected with trade or created either directly or indirectly through success in trade—

The Duke of Leeds, the Earl of Craven, the Earl of Radnor, the Earl of Feversham, Lord Ashburton, Lord Carrington, Lord Overstone, Lord Wolverton, Lord Belper, Lord Rendel, Lord Sanderson, Lord Tweedmouth, Lord Winterstoke, Lord Pirrie, Lord Strathcona, Lord Blyth, Lord Mountstephen, Lord Masham, Lord Armstrong, Lord Brassey, Lord Wimborne, Lord Dewar, Lord Rothschild, Lord Avebury, Lord Revelstoke, Lord Holden, Lord Wandsworth, Lord Burton, Lord Hindlip, Lord Iveagh, Lord Ardilaun, Lord Pauncefote, Lord Glantawe, Lord Cowdray, Lord Furness, Lord Michelham, Lord Addington, Lord Aberconway, Lord Airedale, Lord Aldenham, Lord Allerton, Lord Ashton, Lord Devonport, Lord Hollenden, Lord Inchcape, Lord Merthyr, Lord Swaythling, Lord Whitburgh, Lord Biddulph, Lord Faber, Lord Emmott, Lord Hillingdon, Lord Inverclyde, Lord Joicey, Lord Peckover, Lord Pontypridd,

---

[1] *Democracy and Liberty*, Vol. I, p. 329.

Lord Rotherham, ·Lord Southwark, Lord Sumner and Lord Armitstead.

Sixty in all, most of them quite recent creations, and the list by no means complete! Of these sixty peers, twenty-one are connected with the banking business, five are connected with the wine and beer trades, four are connected with railways, three are connected with shipping, six are merchants, six are connected with iron, steel and engineering works, one was a tobacco magnate, and the remainder are either manufacturers, founders of big industries, or company directors.

Writing in 1881, Mr. T. Fielding, as a friend of the Upper Legislative Chamber, said: "I should say that fully one-half of the peerage is directly interested in trade." [1] *Now only about half-a-dozen of the peerages enumerated above were in existence in* 1881; so that we can fairly assume that the proportion. suggested by Mr. T. Fielding still holds good.

To the reader who has followed the arguments in this book at all closely no comment on the above facts will be necessary.

Just as a participator in a law-suit cannot at the same time be the judge or a member of the jury, so is it unreasonable to expect these men .of action, these people immersed in the activities of a particular department of life, to take such an intelligent, broad and general view of life as to enable them to rule a living concern like a great nation with wisdom and with understanding. And this objection to them is quite distinct from the fundamental objection arising out of my thesis, which consists of a flat denial. of the assumption that because they have been successful in the struggle for existence in present conditions, that they must necessarily be spokesmen of the taste and judgment of flourishing life.

Thus even if, at the start—say in 1688—the odd 150 peers had all been true aristocrats, which they were not,[2]

---

[1] See *The House of Lords*, p. 34.

[2] In *The Rise of Great Families* Burke makes an interesting comment

the mode of selecting recruits for the House of Lords from that time to this has been so utterly devoid of true insight that they would have struggled in vain against the overwhelming numbers of their inferiors in the Upper Chamber.

Nobody realises better than I do how great is the need of refreshing aristocratic stock from time to time; but while it is not necessary to do it nearly so often as it has been done in England, it is also most essential that only those members of the nation should be selected who show at least some ruler quality—who show some affinity, that is to say, to the aristocrat himself.

The ruling order in Rome, Venice, Bern and Nürnberg, as Freeman points out,[1] received new families within their pale; but they did so by their own act. Not the struggle for existence, but the patriarch Jacob, is the best judge of what constitutes a man *who knows*. The struggle for existence may force to the top a man who knows only how to fill his own pocket; but not one who necessarily knows things, knows how to discriminate good from bad, healthy from unhealthy, good taste from bad taste.

It is suicidal for any true aristocracy to allow its ranks to be filled by these forced plants, sprung from the artificial manure of modern conditions; it is even suicidal for them to allow their ranks to be filled at all at any time, save by their own choice and the exercise of their own discrimination.[2]

---

on the constitution of at least a portion of the peerage after the Grand Rebellion. He says (p. 42) : "The Civil War ruined many a Cavalier and transferred his lands to a rich merchant or a successful lawyer, and then the new proprietor was enabled to take a foremost place in his county, possibly to obtain its representation and in due course to reach the Upper House."

[1] *Comparative Politics*, p. 270.

[2] In fairness to the nobles in the House of Lords at the beginning of the eighteenth century, it should be noted here that they did show a strong dislike of the principle which made it possible for their ranks to be swelled inordinately by means of the Crown's unrestricted right to create peers, and in 1719 Stanhope and Sunderland accordingly recom-

THE ARISTOCRAT IN PRACTICE

Again, in this respect the aristocratic principle cannot be blamed for the incompetence or crude egotism of the English peerage. For what with the corruption of the Georgian epoch, and the need of rewarding political friends and assistants in the Victorian era, large contingents have been drafted up to the Lords, without that body having been allowed a word of 'choice in the matter, and without their having even been asked for advice.

"When a patriciate has risen," says Freeman, "it seems essential to its being that no new members can be admitted to the body except by its own act." [1]

Certainly it is essential. But this is one of the essential rules that has been broken again and again by our system in England.

Aristocracy means essentially power of the best—power of the best for good; because the true aristocrat can achieve permanence for his order and his inferiors only by being a power for good.

But power is not a possession which, once it is established, can last for ever, without nurture or repair. On the contrary, to endure it must be constantly vigilant, constantly on the alert, *continually seeking out its like in the nation and drawing it into its own body.* To give aristocratic power even relative permanence, therefore, it must be so organised as to be able to draw all the national manifestations of its like into its own body. Wherever men of profound ideas, men of thought, men of taste, men of good quality in the matter of living and appearance are to be found, there the vigilant eye of a powerful aristocracy should seek them out, and recognise in them the spawn, the reserve, the only refreshment of its strength. From their whole number, but the very smallest proportion

---

mended to the King the surrender of that right. The King eagerly accepted the proposal, but the Bills formed for the purpose of making it law all had to be dropped, and the last one was rejected by the Commons, under the leadership of Walpole, by a majority of 92.

[1] Op. cit., p. 270.

might ultimately be taken; at least, however, they would constitute the best aspirants for the position of the best that could be found. The mere fact that so many essentially great rulers, such as Pericles, Cæsar, Charles I, Napoleon, have shown fastidious taste in the very minutest concerns of daily life, and that so many artists, such as Diognetus, Lamachus, Leonardo da Vinci, Rubens, have shown ruler qualities of no small order, ought to have been sufficient to put mankind on the right scent here, and to prevent mere material success from being the sole criterion of excellence.

For in the end it is taste, it is proper ideas, it is healthy standpoints that conquer and prevail. And if men of taste, of proper ideas and of healthy standpoints are constantly overlooked, the power that overlooks them must decline, and must ultimately fall a victim to all powerful hostile elements, however bad and tasteless these may be.

As I said at the beginning of Chapter II of this book, walk through Arundel Castle or Goodwood on any afternoon in the summer; notice the pictures on the walls, especially when they are modern pictures—for these alone reveal the actual taste of their owner—notice the ornaments and the decorations, the books and the magazines, and then ask yourself whether the Duke of Norfolk or the Duke of Richmond and Gordon has that vigilant and discerning eye which can discover and appropriate aristocratic quality wherever it is to be found down below in the unennobled strata of the nation.[1]

Of course, neither of them has it. Neither of them has

[1] See *The Decline of Aristocracy*, by Arthur Ponsonby, p. 139 : "The old aristocracy were sometimes regarded as patrons of literature, but this is a function their successors have entirely abandoned. Theirs would be the last opinion to be consulted on literary matters. Any one must be struck in visiting an old·country house to see on the library shelves a full collection of eighteenth and˙early nineteenth century literature— Clarendon, Robertson, Gibbon, Scott, Byron, Bewick, Thackeray ; but on the table for the daily consumption of the present owners, magazines, vulgar weekly periodicals, and a few lending library novels."

a notion of what taste actually means, and how unlimited is the extent of its range.

And, being devoid of taste themselves, they are naturally unable even to supply the lack of this quality in their household by a careful selection made outside it. And they are, therefore, powerless.

Apart from their property, they are powerless. Devoid of taste, judgment and ideas, they have no other weapon than their wealth. But this weapon alone is naturally utterly inadequate to-day; for all capitalists can wield it with equal force, and perhaps with less scrupulosity than these noble gentlemen.

It is for this reason that the Lords were so helpless in 1911,[1] and for this reason, too, will they continue to be helpless.

For even if they were unable actually to enlist into their own ranks whatever elements of aristocratic spirit they might find in the nation, at least they ought to have got such elements into their service, exploited them or used them in some way—at all events in order to strengthen their position and to maintain it.

Wherever culture shows its head, wherever particular ability manifests itself, wherever there is seen a marked power to order, to select the right and reject the wrong, there the agents of the aristocracy or they themselves ought to be present to promote it, to help it, and thus to make it theirs.

Knowing the power of proper ideas; knowing that all that characterises our present condition is the creation of a certain set of ideas which might have been stifled, uprooted, cast aside and extirpated at the moment of their inception; and knowing that if another order is to be created, that order will likewise be the outcome of a new set of ideas, the vigilant eye of the aristocrat ought to be

---

[1] See *The Decline of Aristocracy*, p. 135 : " Even in fighting the battle to retain their ascendancy the nobility and aristocracy showed themselves as a body with very few individual exceptions poorly equipped intellectually, blind, and ill-informed."

constantly watching not only for men of right ideas, but, what is still more important, for men who by their physical constitution cannot help having right ideas.

At least they ought to try to understand such men, to *comprehend* them; for that is equivalent to *comprising* or *possessing* them. In this, however, their very self-preservative instinct has failed them. Not only have the aristocrats omitted to select the best from the nation for themselves, but they have also omitted to watch for it or to understand it.

No power, however well established, could have lasted under such circumstances. As Machiavelli says: " A Prince ought to show himself a patron of ability, and to honour the proficient in every art." [1] Why? Not because it is nice to do so; not because it is benevolent, or philanthropic, or generous to do so! Machiavelli was not a sentimentalist! But because it is good policy to do so; because it is expedient, sound, essential, indispensable to do so. Because men of ability and men proficient in art possess some of the most essential qualities of the aristocrat, and are the only kindred spirits to the aristocrats in the whole of a nation.

All this in later times they have omitted to do; for, ever since Samuel Johnson's terrible rebuke to one of their order, things have grown, if anything, worse than they were before.

It will be remembered that the Earl of Chesterfield had undertaken to assist Samuel Johnson in the production of his famous dictionary, and had appointed himself Johnson's literary patron. For many years, however— that is, while there still existed some element of doubt concerning the success of the enterprise—Johnson appealed to the nobleman in vain for assistance, and could not even obtain an audience from him when he called. Finally, however, when the dictionary appeared, the Earl of Chesterfield had the impudence to pose not only as its author's *impresario*, but also as his protector.

[1] *The Prince*, Chapter VII.

THE ARISTOCRAT IN PRACTICE

The words of Johnson's fine ironical rebuke are worth quoting, and I shall give them as a concrete example of that growing breach between aristocracy and culture, the first signs of which were visible in the eighteenth century—

"Seven years, my Lord, have now passed, since I waited in your outward rooms, and was repulsed from your door; during which time I have been pushing on my work through difficulties of which it is useless to complain, and have brought it, at last, to the verge of publication, without one act of assistance, one word of encouragement, or one smile of favour. Such treatment I did not expect, for I never had a Patron before. . . .

"Is not a Patron, my Lord, one who looks with unconcern on a man struggling for life in the water, and when he has reached the ground, encumbers him with help? The notice which you have been pleased to take of my labours, had it been early, had been kind; but it has been delayed till I am indifferent, and cannot enjoy it; till I am solitary, and cannot impart it; till I am known and do not want it. I hope it is no very cynical asperity, not to confess obligations where no benefit has been received, or to be unwilling that the Publick should consider me as owing that to a Patron, which Providence has enabled me to do for myself.

"Having carried on my work thus far with so little obligation to any favour of learning, I shall not be disappointed though I should conclude it, if less be possible, with less; for I have long awakened from that dream of hope, in which I once boasted myself with so much exaltation, my Lord,

"Your Lordship's most humble,
"most obedient servant,
"SAMUEL JOHNSON."[1]

This wonderful letter, written by a man of culture to a man of the Earl of Chesterfield's stamp—for the Earl

[1] Boswell's *Life of Johnson* (February 7, 1775).

419

of Chesterfield was not an upstart peer of Georgian creation—shows how matters stood even as early as the year 1775. And he who imagines that things have improved rather than deteriorated since that time is a fantastic dreamer. Even Disraeli was able to write in 1845: "There is no longer in fact an aristocracy in England, for the superiority of the animal man is an essential quality of aristocracy. But that it once existed, any collection of portraits from the sixteenth century will show." [1]

Now, to sum up this section of the chapter, I think I have shown with sufficient detail that: (1) An Aristocracy ought itself to select the new families it allows to become part of its exalted body, and it ought to do so with a very definite standard of what constitutes aristocratic ability. To omit to do this is to court disaster. The very failure of the aristocracy of England ought to be sufficient to prove that the kind of people that have as a rule been elevated to the peerage have not possessed the proper qualifications for the position. (2) An Aristocracy ought to be vigilant and alert, and ought to be able and eager to understand, to use and to possess all those elements of ability and of exceptional proficiency among the population in which taste, good judgment and a certain instinctive knowledge of good and evil are inherent. (3) An Aristocracy ought to be a patron of culture and of ideas—not only because there is charm in these things, but also because upon a right notion of culture alone, and upon right and proper ideas concerning humanity and the world, can a good natural administration be founded.

There remain now only two more points to be elucidated: the question of education and that of marriage.

Dealing with the question of education first, it must be obvious that if an aristocracy is aiming at permanence and at the best for the nation, the national system of education ought to be its most important weapon of

---

[1] *Sybil* (Longmans, Green & Co., 1899), p. 12.

selection. There is no better pretext for a national organisation which is able to bring all the elements of the nation under the vigilant eye of an aristocracy's agents than the pretext of education.

Under the plea of educating the people, you get the raw material of the whole nation under your eye, and you get them at a time when they are in the most malleable condition, when they have not yet become perfectly moulded to their inferior surroundings, and when, if you see promise in them, exceptional members of the community can be withdrawn from their environment and helped to better things.

This process of selection would naturally have to be conducted by men, not necessarily of scholastic learning, but by men fitted to judge men—and of these there should always be a plentiful supply not only among the aristocrats themselves, but among their immediate entourage and agents—and they should select only according to a certain standard.

The fact that the huge machinery of our Educational Department of Government has not yet been used as a selective system for the best purposes of State, shows how utterly careless and ignorant the rulers of this country have been of the true and most exalted uses of such a system.

For in so far as a great nation is concerned, it is not nearly so essential that everybody should reach the fifth or sixth standard in school as that those who are really able should be chosen out from among the rest.

The rest might be eliminated from the schools after passing the second standard, and good rather than harm would be the result. This was the system, of course, in Egypt, and it still remains the system in China, where not examinations alone, but the personal judgment of the teacher is the first and chief instrument of selection, and very often the first starting-point on a distinguished official career.

For such a judgment to be sound, however, and reliable,

not only must the teacher be a knower of men, but his tuition must be a personal affair, during which he can come into contact daily with his pupil and even with his pupil's relatives. This is precisely what happens in China. There is no class teaching in Chinese schools, only personal tuition; and according as to whether the teacher recognises possibilities or not in his pupil, so is he able distinctly to encourage or discourage any exalted ambition which the pupil himself or his parents may cherish for the career of the scholar.

Thus utterly hopeless cases are turned away at an early age, freed, before they have wasted years of their life in an occupation which could profit them nothing; while more promising cases are encouraged to ascend step by step to the highest position in the state—an accomplishment often witnessed in China, just as it was witnessed in ancient Egypt." [1]

By this means a huge educational organisation may serve as a most perfect means of selection in a nation; and when this selection is carried on under the guidance of a wise aristocracy, and for its high purposes, it naturally contributes very materially indeed, as it did in Egypt, and as it does in China, to the permanence of the ruling body. Incidentally it also serves as an economiser of national energy. For there are thousands of boys who are happier and more useful, learning their business, agricultural or industrial, at an early age, than sitting, long after they are able to profit from it, at a school table or desk, learning things in which they are not interested and which they forget as soon as they have left school. And a discerning eye could detect such boys and release them from their insufferable and unprofitable drudgery.

So much for the view which the aristocrat should take of national education. As to what he should do in the matter of educating his own offspring, this should be a matter chiefly of the training of the will, of disciplining the body and the mind, in the first place to exercise self-

[1] See Dr. Schmid, *Geschichte der Erziehung*, p. 173.

control and subsequently to control others. Education was conceived by the great Kant himself primarily as a matter of discipline and will-development,[1] and indeed, this should be its chief aim. The acquisition of knowledge, which is made the principal feature to-day, is purely secondary and subordinate. A man of will can learn anything he wishes to know. A man full of knowledge without will, although a common occurrence to-day, is fit only for the scrap heap, and the sooner he gets there the better.

The training of the young aristocrat, therefore, provided he be of the right sort, and a chip of the old block, should be extremely severe; much more severe than it is at present, and much more in the hands of his father than it is at present; for, how can a learned plebeian teach anything worth knowing beyond mere facts to a young aristocrat?

The whole of the present system of trusting almost entirely to strangers to guide and to rear the youth of the ruling classes under the plea of "educating" them is utterly misguided. A wise father is his son's best educator, and the finest men I have ever met have been their father's creations. Anything a wise father cannot teach a boy is simply not worth knowing; but when his father has taught him all he knows, and the boy has watched him and found him worth watching, he will have acquired a valuable basis upon which he himself can build. Happy the boys whose fathers understood the *child* as the *chela!*

Strangers can and do give you the raw material of knowledge, but your interpretation, co-ordination, arrangement and use of it depend upon what you are, what your father is, how much of his wisdom you have incorporated, and how he has trained your will. In the superior classes of society to-day, however, the relationship between child and parent is becoming ever more and more superficial and less and less intimate.[2]

[1] See *Ueber Pädagogik* (edit. Professor Willmann), p. 69.
[2] See Arthur Ponsonby, op. cit., p. 172 : "Rich parents are tempted more and more to use their money to withdraw their children more and more from their own supervision."

A DEFENCE OF ARISTOCRACY

This matter of training the will to-day is not taken half seriously enough, particularly in the very class in which long tradition combined with rigorous discipline, and the strong will both impart, are the most essential things of all.

As Kant says: "A common error committed in the education of men of exalted station consists in the fact that, because they are destined to rule, their will is scarcely ever thwarted even in their youth." [1] And Kant was writing in the eighteenth century when some of the best traditions of aristocratic rule and custom were still accepted as law. What would he say to-day? What would he think of the laxity and freedom now allowed in children? His *Pädagogik*, which in many ways is quite the most interesting and most sound little book ever written on the subject of education, shows clearly enough how radically he would have condemned the educational system of the present day, even in its application to the lower and middle classes; how much more radical, then, would his objections have been against the system of education prevailing in the governing caste!

With regard to the matter of marriage; the solemnity of the matrimonial state has been so much degraded and perverted by the notion of the pursuit of happiness, that its duties and the seriousness with which one should enter it have been forced to take an entirely subordinate position. The question asked concerning a newly married couple, nowadays, is not "Are they doing their duty properly to each other, to themselves, to their class and to the institution of matrimony?" but "Are they happy?"

The Hedonistic view of life, backed by the Puritan deprecation of any enjoyment of the bodily lusts outside the married state, throws all the burden of "happiness" upon the matrimonial tie, with the result that men feel justified not only in seeking happiness alone in marriage —which is of course a stupid illusion in ninety-nine cases

---

[1] "*Dieses ist ein gewöhnlicher Fehler bei der Erziehung der Grossen, dass man ihnen, weil sie zum Herrschen bestimmt sind, auch in der Jugend nie eigentlich widersteht.*"—Op. cit., p. 62.

out of a hundred—but also in sacrificing real and solemn duties to themselves, to their class and to their children if the promise of happiness seems to be greater in the direction of a breach of such duties, than in the direction of their observance.

To the man who knows that the matrimonial state is simply the most satisfactory solution of the problem of human propagation within an orderly community, and that it will not necessarily bring him any more joys than his single life has done, but only add to his responsibilities, there is something solemn and serious about this choosing of a mate, and all the consequences it involves, which is incompatible with the frivolous notion of "seeking happiness." Such a man, therefore, sacrifices no duty, either to his class, to himself or to his children, for what he knows to be a mere romantic and stupid will-o'-the-wisp. And although he does not actually court unhappiness when he marries, but regards matrimony as the normal state for an adult of a certain age, and monogamy as the most satisfactory kind of sex arrangement, because it is the only kind in which character can be built up and preserved with any certainty; he approaches the state with a feeling of grave and solemn serenity which is quite foreign to the modern feverish and purely romantic pursuit of "happiness," which so often deservedly ends in total disaster.

There can be no doubt, however, that it is not the middle and lower classes alone who have become infected with this Puritanical and Romantic view of marriage, as indissolubly associated with the pursuit of happiness; and one of the saddest things to be observed among our governing classes is the frivolity with which again and again they sacrifice their duty to their class and their duty to their children by choosing a wife from a lower sphere whom they imagine will bring them "happiness."

Instead of choosing their like—which as I have already shown is essential to the building up or the preservation of character in a family—they very often choose not only their opposites, but actually their inferiors; and they have been

doing this for so long that we have ceased to wonder at it;
just as we have ceased to wonder at the ugliness of our
big cities, the vulgarity of their display and the sickness of
their inhabitants.

No aristocracy that is able to behave in this way and
that does behave in this way, can hope for anything better
than dissolution, decadence and extinction. For, as I have
pointed out before, and here repeat with the utmost emphasis : will-power, virtue and superior character in general,
are not sent down from the clouds; they are not accidental
or miraculous phenomena; they are creations of our own
deeds, of our own strivings, and of our own matings; and
it is not only romantic, it is not only stupid, it is positively
dangerous, foolhardy and madly intrepid, deliberately to
scout the means by which they are produced and preserved.

And now, glancing back upon what has been said, especially as regards its application to the discredited position
in which our aristocracy now finds itself, what is the conclusion we are compelled to draw from the various facts
adduced? What is the conclusion at which in simple
fairness we must arrive, assuming that the principle of
Aristocracy itself has been all this while in the dock
before us?

Is it not obvious, is it not perfectly plain, that if we
condemn and sentence in this case, we shall be subjecting
the prisoner in the dock to a most appalling miscarriage
of justice? For, what have the facts I have adduced, as
advocate for the defence, clearly shown? That the downfall of aristocracies has not occurred in a struggle between
the pure principle of aristocracy and another principle,
superior and more perfect than the former; that it is not
the outcome of a single combat between, say, the aristocratic principle and the democratic, or plutocratic, or
socialistic; but that it is the result of a bitter and cruel war
between the institution of Aristocracy itself, as conceived
and founded by the best of all nations, and the members
of that institution who have been totally unworthy of their

membership, and who, at least in England for the last two centuries, have not even attempted to abide by the essential rules governing their body. In a word, if the principle of aristocracy, which is the principle of life, and the only rational, healthy, practicable and profound solution of the problem of government, seems to have suffered a momentary defeat, a momentary reverse, this has not occurred in a hand-to-hand fight with a superior solution of the problem but in a duel which, for all ordinary purposes, may well be entitled *Aristocracy* versus *the Aristocrats*.

CHAPTER IX

WHAT IS CULTURE?

"Now I understand why the Lords of Life and Death shut the doors so carefully behind us. It is that we may not remember our first and most beautiful wooings. Were this not so, our world would be without inhabitants in a hundred years."—RUDYARD KIPLING: *The Finest Story in the World.*

ONCE to have met, if only for a short minute, some one rare and exceptional, and to have seen him vanish irrevocably from our side while the sunshine of his presence still glowed upon us—this is an experience which, to a person gifted with a fine taste and a good memory in these things, must be the cause of lifelong regret. Such regret may diminish with time; it may cease from being constantly with us; it may tend to return at ever more distant intervals; but on those occasions when it does return, when the name of that rare person is recalled but for one instant it never fails to revive that feeling of profound sadness which was ours at the time of the original loss.

If this is so of one rare man we may have met in the past, to how much greater an extent is it not so of our own rare moments or moods!

Last night suppose that you had a dream! a dream in which a feeling so rare, so prodigiously unusual and exceptional, filled your being, that you woke breathless with surprise, all your nerves still thrilled and titillating from the unutterable beauty of your experience, and you yourself scarcely believing that your inner life possessed anything so exquisitely strange and so wondrously precious. The whole of to-day you have thought and thought, and racked and ransacked your brain, but not a glimmer of

428

that incomparable feeling comes back to you. You know you have had it; you know, therefore, that you are capable of it, and you long either to have it again or at least to be able to enshrine it for good in the jewel-house of your memory. And yet your brain is powerless to recall it, and responds to your untiring efforts, only as the limb of the paralytic responds to his will. It seems to lie very far away, not in your life, perhaps, but in a life extremely remote, buried in ages across which your voice and your will can no longer be heard or felt. The life of one of your ancestors, belike, experienced this joy, the mere reverberation of which across countless generations almost shattered you in your sleep.

Looking around you, looking before you into the future, nothing seems to promise to regenerate that feeling within you, and yet you repeat to yourself half in despair, half in anger: " It was in me, therefore *I* was capable of it." And, just as you may often have wished that the rare man you once chanced to meet might be a more common occurrence in the world about you, so you ask yourself now what you must do, what must be done, what change must come over your world in order that the rare moment you had in your dream may at least enter your waking life and become a more constant feeling either with you or with your children.

And this inquiry pursued with earnestness and courage, and with rapt attention to that inner voice of yours, which is the voice of your ancestors and of their triumphs, will lead you surely and inevitably to a thought upon Culture which, in its vividness, will obliterate with one flash all the meandering gossip, all the irresponsible chatter, all the nonsense and pompous pedantry that you have ever heard pronounced and ever seen written upon that sacred word. Gradually it will dawn upon you that Culture is precisely the object of your once desperate search; you will know that it is that creation of man and subtle contrivance of his genius, whereby he tries not only to perpetuate, not only to enshrine, and not only to multiply his rare and exceptional fellow-men and moments; but that it is also the means whereby he guarantees a crop of these rare and exceptional men and moments to the future and to posterity.

And you will also realise that this same Culture, if it is to be valuable, fruitful and glorious, must be something very different and apart from that idealistic, cowardly and one-sided cultivation of mild, tame, temperate and negative virtues, which is the practice and aspiration of all modern society and civilisation. You will know that an emotion, or a sensation, has not only quantity, but also quality, and that its greatest quality to us feeling natures, and that which seduces us most to the love of it, is undoubtedly its depth. Deep feeling alone can give you that thrill, that titillation of all your nerves, of which the rare and exceptional moment in your dream allowed you to taste. But depth is not to be found in the mild, tame, tolerant and shifting passions or virtues of modern times; consequently there is less joy abroad and a weaker love of life. Only on deep passions and on deep virtues will you therefore wish to base the Culture which is to enshrine your rare men and moments. But you will not hesitate to see, of course, that this love of depth, this enthusiastic rearing of fierce and positive virtues and passions, involves the condonation of much which is not always compatible with peace and with a humdrum existence of back-parlour comfort and propriety. You will know that deep positive virtues, if thwarted, if checked, show the same violence in their obverse manifestations as they do in their unthwarted and unchecked progress. Nevertheless, you are no longer idealistic, you, who have suffered from the irrevocable loss of a rare and exceptional feeling, cannot afford to be idealistic and romantic. You are prepared to face all the evil of your choice in manhood, provided you get what you regard as the good.

Willy nilly you will have beauty back again; you will have beauty a more constant quality in your external world and in the world of your own emotions. And since you want those rare moments again which depend upon positive virtues for their existence, your aim is to rear lofty positive virtues. You see as plainly as if the fact were written in unmistakable letters across your path, that all one-sided breeding and rearing of squeamish ideals of what a man and a woman should be, although it leads to smug security and ease, is steadily eliminating all greatness and all character from your world of friends and companions. Therefore you say, and with a full knowledge of the undoubted risks you run: "In Heaven's name let great omnipotent desire and the great positive virtues it breeds, be once again the aim and justification of Culture; for, even if the recoil stroke of the pendulum bear some men into a kind of perdition, the dire blackness of which even the most adventurous and most intrepid of to-day could not picture successfully, what matters it provided in its upstroke the pendulum of life leads into ecstasies of which no one, not even the best nowadays, can have a remote inkling, save once, perhaps, in a rare and unrepeated dream, which he is subsequently at an absolute loss to recall?"

And, if you are in earnest about this matter; if you feel that mankind, like yourself, will soon have no other alternative than to search with ever diminishing visual power, hungrily, thirstingly, frantically, bravely, for the rich deep beauties it once possessed, simply because, despite the fact that they brought a profounder and cleaner sort of tragedy in their train than present conditions do, they alone made life possible and desirable; your next question will be: What are the values, the particular moral code and table of virtues and vices which are associated with these rich and deep virtues? At what time in the history of mankind have they prevailed? How can they be made to prevail again?

And do not suppose that this is by any means either a hopeless or a fantastic investigation. On the contrary, the material for its accomplishment lies already to hand, all ready garnered and stored safely away. It is even full of the richest rewards for all those who are curious enough, intrepid enough, desperate and sad enough, to undertake it with energy and perseverance. But it demands two qualities that are becoming and will continue to grow ever more and more exceptional and rare as time goes on. I refer to independence on the one hand, and to health on the other : the independence of thought and of deed that does not mind for a while at least incurring the suspicion even of disreputability or dirt; and the health that knows how—that cannot help knowing how—to digest or to vomit up at the right time and in the nick of time.

Those who are young enough and brave enough will understand what I mean. And it is to the young man that I particularly address this treatise. Old men, or men of middle age, already owe a debt of gratitude to their opinions, however erroneous they may be; they already feel that if they have travelled so far, it is to their opinions and to their particular view of things that they owe the successful accomplishment of the stages of the journey. The young, however, have not yet any such bond of gratitude fastening them to their particular views. If these happen to be erroneous, therefore, they can abandon them with more freedom and with less regret. That is why it is to them that I make my appeal; and them in conclusion whom I remind of Disraeli's fine and stirring words : " We live in an age when to be young and to be indifferent can no longer be synonymous. We must prepare for the coming hour. The claims of the Future are represented by suffering millions; and the Youth of the Nation are the trustees of Posterity." [1]

[1] *Sybil*, p. 88.

F F

INDEX

57; Society for the Prevention of Cruelty to, founded sixty years after the Society for the Prevention of Cruelty to Animals, 53 note; harnessed to trucks in mines, at a time when harnessing of dogs to carts was abolished, 53 note; appalling condition of, in factories and mines, 54 note; refusal of Irish to allow them to be employed underground, 55; ale a drink for, 210; John Locke on the best food and drink for, 210 note; cruelty to, 235; used as bucklers by Cromwell's soldiers, 235 note; dogs of more account than, 272 note

CHINA: Government in, always by consent of the people, 14; social grades in, dependent on guidance of Manchu aristocracy, 16, 17; respect for the burden bearer in, 20, 21; execution of six Englishmen in, 20; English missionaries sent to, 53 note, 95; its knowledge of the laws of flourishing life, 53 note; care of the body in, 95; rules for qualities requisite for wet nurse in, 95; permanence of its culture, 254; its aristocratic culture, 257; reverence for ancestors in, 258; consent of the people to their ruler's rule in, 265; popular rebellion in China merely a change of rulers, 268; slow change in, 269; the Chinese mandarinate a repository of taste, 269; the idea of the gentleman a very definite thing in, 274; dislike of the foreigner in, 301; education in, 421, 422

CHRISTIANITY: its contempt for

the body and glorification of the soul, 94, 95; the decay of Christian culture, 99; a negative creed, 195-198

CHRISTMAS: suppressed by the Puritans, 192, 193

CHURCH: its levelling tendency, 25; robbed from European rulers the tutorship of governing, 25, 26; controlled by Venetian aristocracy, 25; its failure to see that fluid population means lax morality, 72; Cromwell a possessor of Church lands, 111; Church lands, robbed by Lords and landowners, restored under Charles I, 128, 138; abuses against Church property punished by Laud, 141; Strafford's restoration of Church lands, 148. *See also* CATHOLIC CHURCH

COBBETT: his opposition to machinery, 36 note; his indictment of the English country gentleman and landowner, 61; his belief in aristocracy, 61; on the misery of the agriculturalist, 63; on factory slaves, 67 note; his disapproval of people travelling, 72 note; on the stages of national degradation, 103; his loathing of the Quakers, 136; on the cowardice of Strafford's friends, 152 note; his hostility to tea and coffee, 224; his dislike of the middleman, 228, 229; his lamentation over the death of spirit in England, 231; on wealth and property, 239; his alarm at innovations, 263

COCKNEY: sterile in three generations, 65

COFFEE: one of the deleterious substitutes for old English ale, 219-226; "Coffee and Com-

438

monwealth came in together,"
219 note; popular petition
against, 223; Women's Petition against, 225; forbidden
in the Koran, 256 note

COLBERT: the people's ingratitude for his championship, 106;
fought greed and opulence for
the sake of the people, 107

COMMERCE : instability of a state
founded upon, 23

COMMERCIALISM : 41, 45; the
advisability of, not questioned
by English rulers, 46

COMPETITION, unrestricted : its
grinding down of the workers,
35; Trades Unions formed
against influence of, 46; definition of, 83; reduces everything
to a struggle for existence, 280;
introduces elements of inter-
herd morality into the herd,
288

CONFUCIANISM : the way of the
superior man, 5 note, 6

CONFUCIUS : on caring for the
heart of the people, 16; on
respect for the burden, 20; a
representative of flourishing
life, 20; his doctrine of the
superior man, 76; a man of
taste, 257; his idea of the
gentleman, 274

CONSANGUINITY in marriage. See
MARRIAGE and INBREEDING

CONSCIENCE : the voice of a
man's ancestors, 11, 28, 277;
reared only by long tradition
and careful discipline and dependent on aristocratic rule,
27; the sick, of the upper
classes, 83; charity, the flower
of an uneasy, 84; charity a
conscience salve, 231; definition of, 276, 277

CONSTANTINE THE GREAT: mixed
marriages proscribed by, 307,

319; knew that all crossing is
not bad, 326

CORN : the repeal of the Corn
Laws defeat of agriculture, 63;
Charles I's prevention of rise
in price of, 135, 136

COUSINS : marriage of, regarded
as the natural thing in modern
Egypt, 332 note. See also DAR-
WIN, George, on cousin marriages

CRAFT of governing. See GOVERN-
ING

CRIMINALS : produced by vile
conditions of labour, 54; their
descendants in Australia probably people of spirit, 54

CROMWELL : his cruelty, 54; the
leader of a race of unscrupulous
capitalistic oppressors, 101; his
Puritanism a conscientious
justification for being in possession of Church lands, 111;
accused Laud of "flat Popery,"
116; acknowledged that England could be properly governed
only by a single ruler, 127, 128
note; his hypocrisy, 171; his
ugliness, 176, 334; a brewer,
184; the diet provided by his
wife, 226, 227; his unseemly
behaviour when signing Charles
I's death-warrant, 232; a man
utterly devoid of taste, 233;
responsible for enslaving his
fellow-countrymen, 233; his
atrocities against the Irish,
234, 235

CROSS-BREEDING : destructive of
instinct, 298, 299, 302, 304, 347;
destructive of race, 302, 320–
323; Theognis on the danger
of, 304, 305, 306; fall of Greece
and Rome due to, 308; breaks
the will, 310, 318, 320; productive of degeneration, 319; destructive of virtue, 319, 320,

INDEX

347, 349; productive of fertility, 321; undermines character, 322, 325, 327; occasional necessity for judicious, 323–326; fatality of tasteless and indiscriminate, 326; with allied races productive of good results, 326; under democracy never salutary, 349; causes disintegration of will and character, 385; leads to reversion to a low type, 388

CULTURE : the building up of, one of the duties of ruling, 98; makes a people, 98; the character of modern, 98, 99; decay of Christian, 99; present day, one of doubt, 99; intellectual, denied to the parvenu, 100; dependent on aristocracy, 248; produced by inbreeding, 299; rapid culture of certain endogamic peoples, 347; transmission of acquired characteristics important to, 395, 397; based on traditional occupations, 399; definition of, 429

DARWIN, Charles : his doctrine of the survival of the fittest, once a conscience salve, refuted, 83; on the incapacity of the Fuegians for civilisation, 297; a fourth child, 376; on primogeniture being opposed to selection, 377 note; his experiments on pigeons, 388; his belief in the transmission of acquired characteristics, 392, 397

DARWIN, George : on cousin marriages not being fraught with evil results, 385 and note

DECADENCE : due to the dictates of mediocrity, 6, 7; a state in which the precepts of flourishing life have been forgotten and the true aristocrat dethroned,

23; due to prevalence of bad taste, 24; democratic revolt and cynical hedonism the fruits of, 73; soon too late to arrest, in Europe, 96; its prevalence in modern times 384, 385; consanguineous marriages as a cause of, only a modern idea, 385

DECLINE : of nations not a necessity, 254; of British Empire preventable, 255; of nations due to disobedience to the voice of flourishing life, 258

DEGENERACY. *See* DECADENCE

DEMOCRACY : dangerous errors under, concerning the importance of the body, 13; unfruitfulness of democratic revolt, 73; political amateurism, 88; demands the existence of the amateur in politics, 89; misery the chief propelling power of, in England, 237, 358; the meaning of, 248–253; *must mean death*, 249–253; political corruption under, 249 note; discards Taste, 250, 251; calls upon the people to weigh principles and policies, 264; in an absolute, the people really govern, 265; calls upon the people to judge on matters of taste, 266; salutary revolution impossible under, 267; neglect of loftier interests of art and science under, 273 note; of uncontrolled trade unfavourable to the production of the gentleman, 282; foreign affairs under, 282; imposes the practice of two moralities on the private citizen, 288; therefore democracy immoral, 288; difficulty of foreign policy under, 291 note; the materialistic doctrine

440

of majority omnipotent under, 292, 293; destructive of will and character and productive of ugliness, 320, 387; increase of vanity under, 320 note; injudicious cross-breeding characteristic of, 325; prejudice of, against close consanguineous marriages, 331; cross-breeding under, simply chaos, 349; undermines conscientious labour, 353; mere wealth as a standard leads to, 365; hostile to heredity, 378; opposed to assortive mating, 384, 387; prejudice against one's like under, 386; dead level established by, 387

DEMOCRAT: a rank blasphemer, 5; Nemesis threatens all societies victimised by the, 49; his mistaken estimate of the people, 74; English Lords democrats at heart, 97; his attack on aristocracy superficial, 239; attitude of various types of, towards private and public morality, 289–291; prefers to ascribe superiority to accident, 379; his dislike of marrying his like the self-preservative instinct of the sick man, 386, 389

DEPOPULATION of country districts: 42; grave consequences of, 58; F. E. Green's warning against the results of, 64; Charles I opposed to, 119; commission appointed by Charles I to inquire into, 129

DEPORTATION. *See* TRANSPORTATION

DETERMINISM: 314–315; from within, 314; from without, 315

DISCIPLINE: necessary for producing example of flourishing life, 362; English aristocracy's lack of internal, 362, 363, 364, 368; among the Brahmans, 366; in the Catholic Church, 366; among the Venetian aristocracy, 367; among the Egyptian priesthood, 368

DISEASE: its prevalence in modern times, 3, 47, 385; modern acquiescence in, 96; spread by modern commercial culture, 98; a breeder of Puritanism, 178, 181; regarded as unclean in the Old Testament, 199, 337; and by the Brahmans, 337; when present multiplied by inbreeding, 385

DISRAELI: on revolutions not being due to economic causes, 10 note; on national character, 24; on the decline of public virtue being due to class hostility, 82 note; on the true greatness of man, 90; on the degeneration of the subject into a serf, 102; on the duty of power to secure the social welfare of the people, 102; on the modern Utopia of Wealth and Toil, 355 note; his appeal to the Youth of the Nation, 432

DISSENTERS: their hatred of life, 55; their impudent effrontery, 112; their impudent assumption of omniscience, 142; the Scriptural warrant for their negative creed, 195; their brutality, 234

DIVINE RIGHT: to rule when the craft and tutorship of governing are both fulfilled by the ruler, 10; to govern ill an absurdity, 10, 14; disbelief of English peerage in their own, 33

the possible longevity of well-ordered states, 16 note; on thraldom depending on benefits received, 25

HOPS: the deleteriousness of, 214-218; petition against, 215; a soporific and an anaphrodisiac, 217; retard digestion, 218; an ingredient introduced in ale to make it keep for sake of shopkeepers, 228 note

HUGUENOTS: their reasons for opposing Machiavelli, 283

ILL-HEALTH. *See* DISEASE

INBREEDING: productive of culture, 299; ancient wisdom in regard to, 301; productive of character, 318; and sterility, 321; can last a long while without evil results, 322; fixes character, 322; in Egypt, 322; in Sparta, 323; preserves virtue, 329; the Jews and, 342; Jewish checks against ill effects of, 346; productive of character and flourishing life, 385; multiplies disease and also multiplies healthy and good qualities, 385, 386 note; not in itself a cause of degeneracy, 386; failure of the House of Lords not due to, 403, 405, 406

INCAS OF PERU: their bloodless victories owing to superiority, 8; their refusal to rule a bestial people, 9; their beauty, 11 note, 333; permanence of their culture, 254; their aristocratic culture, 257; cause of the downfall of their culture, 259; a hereditary caste, 330; brother and sister marriages among, 331; their belief in the value of tradition, 398

INCEST: modern prejudice against, 331; Moses and Aaron the children of, 342

INDUSTRIALISM: never guided by the English ruler, 36; rise of, 41, 42, 45; advisability of, not questioned by English rulers, 46

INSTINCT: definition of, 296; in the production of civilisation, 297; destroyed by cross-breeding, 298, 299, 302, 304, 347; race a matter of, 302; store set by great nations of antiquity on, 309; its importance in the life of a nation, 309, 310; the relation of will to, 311-315; relation of virtues to, 315; preserved by assortive mating, 384; destroyed by democracy, 387

IRISH: their humanity, 55; Strafford's good rule of the, 148, 149; Puritan brutality to, 232; sent into slavery by Cromwell, 233, 235; Cromwell's atrocities against the, 234

JACOB: the father of Levi, 338; his interference with the law of primogeniture, 340 note, 364; his own priest, 341; his taste in men, 377; the patriarch Jacob the best judge of what constitutes the man *who knows*, 414

JAMES I: his regard for quality, 50; his opposition to the interference of Tom, Dick and Harry in State affairs, 88 note; his *Book of Sports*, 130; his opposition to machinery, 132; his proclamation against the clothiers, 135; his dislike of tobacco, 225 note; number of peers created by, 403

INDEX

JAPAN : Japanese gentleman capable of practising two moralities, 287 note; aristocracy in, 365, 366

JESUITS : their reasons for opposing Machiavelli, 283, 289

JEWS : on beauty of body in their priesthood, 12 note; a chosen people, 300, 301; their contempt for the alien, 301, 302, 310; the hereditary character of their priesthood, 330, 339; the rise of their aristocracy traced to a single family, 338; their self-appointed aristocracy, 340; their doctrine of the firstborn, 341, 342, 346; the institution of the Levites as an aristocracy, 339, 342; their aristocracy a select inbreeding caste, 342, 343; strict laws regarding the bodily fitness of their priests, 344; occasional inter-tribe marriages allowed for Levites, 343, 345, 346

JOHNSON, Samuel : his rebuke of Lord Chesterfield, 418, 419

KANT : conceived of education as a matter of discipline and will development, 423, 424

KORAN : forbids coffee to the faithful, 256 note

LABOUR : bodiless abstract concept of, 44; obedience on the part of, implies protection on the part of capital, 47; obedience on the part of, sullen and forced, 48; decline of sense of responsibility on the part of, 48; indirect tax on, first introduced by the Puritans, 214

LAISSEZ-FAIRE : the cruel and lazy principle of, tolerated, 44; capitalistic cry of, 46; *laissez-faire* economists responsible for

the cruel exploitation of women and children, 52; definition of, 83; behest of, obeyed by the Tories, 102; defeat of Charles I an important step in the direction of, 163; labouring proletariat mercilessly exploited under the system of, 175; Puritanism the religion required by the economic school of, 188; introduced by the Puritans, 216, 227 note; wealth and property uncontrolled by, 239

LANDOWNERS : their obligations, 38; their duties in feudal times, 38; their rights qualified in feudal times, 39; the irresponsibility of urban landowners, 39; Kett's demands concerning, 42 note; lust of appropriation on the part of, 43; British landowners responsible for depopulation of country districts, 58; Cobbett's indictment of, 61; F. E. Green's indictment of, 64; upstart landowners introduced by Henry VIII, 59 note, 108

LAUD : no respecter of persons, 110, 141, 143; his impartiality in quelling religious disturbances, 114; accused of Papist leanings by the Puritans, 116; his readiness to spend his private money in the public service, 122; his uprightness, 141; his punishment of abuses against Church property, 141; his struggle against anarchy in religion, 142; his fairness, 143; brutal treatment by the Puritans, 144; his will, 144

LAWYERS : F. E. Green on their cringing cowardice, 64, 65; Strafford foresaw that the rule of Parliament meant rule of

448

INDEX

the landowner and lawyer at expense of the poor, 117; in Parliament, 355; not fit to govern, 408; Strafford's suspicion of, 408; list of some, in the House of Lords, 409, 410

LEVI, the tribe of : their origin, 338, 339; the self-appointed aristocracy of the Jews, 339, 340; inbreeding practised by, 343; strict laws regarding bodily fitness of, 344

LIBERALS : even they believe in government by the few, 14; essentially a capitalistic party opposed to the true interests of the people, 101

LIBERTY : the King's prerogative to defend the people's liberties, 8 note; the so-called English love of, not responsible for the evils of the present day, 60; the cry of capitalistic and unscrupulous oppressors, 101; the specious cry of, raised by Charles I's opponents, 105, 106, 112, 138, 156; the Puritans thirsted for " liberty " to oppress the people, 127; definition of the true liberty of the working man, 159; appalling misery so-called liberty conferred on the masses, 159; Jeremy Bentham on the cant of, 159; cry of, mere cant, 160; the masses lured over to the Puritans by cries of, 267 note; equality opposed to true, 355

LIFE : summed up in the two words *select* and *reject*, 240

LOCKE, John : on the best food and drink for children, 210 note

LORDS, House of : deprived of much power, 31, 32; deserved their fate in 1911, 102; majority of the, joined Charles I reluctantly, 158; contains many elements of sound aristocratic power, 354; criticism of, 354–420 *passim*; its lack of self-discipline, 362, 363, 364, 369; the hereditary principle in, 401; not really a hereditary chamber, 403; Pitt's creations disastrous to the character of the, 404; inbreeding not the cause of the failure of, 403, 405, 406; selective principle more active than the hereditary principle in the, 406, 407, 408; ignoble character of the, 407; list of lawyers in the, 409, 410; list of business men in the, 412, 413; not self-selective, 414, 415

LUDDITES : their movement discussed in relation to machinery, 69; execution of sixteen, for machine breaking, 70; their hostility to machinery, 131 note

LUNACY : increasing in England, 385

LUTHER : his doctrine of the omnipotence of the individual conscience, 88; his ugliness, 334; his son a proof of heredity, 375 note

MACAULAY : his stupid estimate of Strafford, 123; his idea of a gentleman, 280 note; his muddle-headedness, 284

MACHIAVELLI : on the liberty of the Church, 25; on conspiracies being of little account under a good ruler, 34 note; on the Prince being the inspirer of good counsels, 139, 140; on political and private morality being different, 282; on the necessity for a Prince to

GG 449

INDEX

appear to have good qualities, 282 note; his opponents, among others the Jesuits, the Huguenots, Frederick the Great and Metternich, 283; his supporters, among others Charles V, Henry III and Henry IV of France, Bacon, Richelieu and Napoleon, 285; advises princes to patronise ability and those proficient in art, 418

MACHINERY : its degrading effects foreseen by few in England, 36; capital punishment for destruction of, 44, 69; introduced without hesitation, 45; its evils due to lack of control, 49; its introduction a definite act of taste, 49; inseparable from capitalism, 50 note, 133; never "placed" by the English aristocrat, 65, 67; viewed with suspicion by the Tudors and Stuarts, 68 note; Samuel Butler on machinery as a slave-driver, 69 note; rebellion of the workmen against, 69; execution of sixteen Luddites for breaking, 70; poor quality of work done by, 70; Lord Byron's speech against, 70; Charles I's suspicion of, 132, 133, 138; where to draw the line in the evolution of, 134

MAETERLINCK : a Puritan owing to lack of culture, 180

MAHOMMED : a specimen of flourishing life, 257

MANCHU aristocracy : their rule in China, 16, 17

MARRIAGE : Theognis on mixed marriages as a source of degeneracy, 306; Alexander the Great's foolish encouragement of mixed, 306; mixed marriages proscribed by early

Romans, 307; and by Constantine the Great, 307, 319; *mésalliances* condemned by Manu, 319; consanguineous marriages multiply chances of handing on both good and evil qualities, 331; Henry IV of France, his bad, 381, 382; consanguineous marriages a cause of degeneracy, only a modern idea, 385; modern view of, as a road to happiness, 424, 425. *See* INBREEDING and CROSS-BREEDING.—Marriage of cousins. *See* COUSINS and DARWIN, George

MASSES, the : too deeply engaged in the struggle for existence to rule, 38; forced to defend themselves against exploitation, 47; their innate incapacity to rule well, 73, 74, 75; not impressed by plutocratic solutions of social evils, 85; failure of English aristocracy to see that their literature was good, 91; neglect of their bodies in England, 94, 95; the duty of power to secure the welfare of the people, 102; Charles I's rule considered primarily the welfare of, 119 note; the true attitude of, towards Strafford, 154 note; on the side of Charles I, 159, 161 note; misery of, owing to so-called liberty, 159; dehumanised by besotting labours, 235; not necessary for the, to understand and judge their rulers, 264; the sympathetic response of the people the pre-requisite of aristocratic rule, 265; lured over to the Puritans by cries of "Liberty," 267 note; deleterious effects of meddling in foreign affairs on the, in a democracy,

piece of subject meddlesomeness under good rulers, 90; Temperance movement a stupid subject movement, 91; charity a subject solution, 92; inadequate education supplied in England by subject efforts, 94; degeneration of the subject into a serf, 102; never oppressed by Charles I, 120

SUNDAY: strict Sunday observance laws of the Puritans, 129; repealed by Charles I, 129, 130; Sunday amusements granted to the people by James I, 130; gloomy, insisted upon by the Puritans, 189–192

SUPERIOR MAN: his taste the taste of flourishing life, 6; requires people to be ready to recognise him, 7; more likely to appear in ages of order and long tradition, 11, 12, 13; always beautiful, 11; his creation of culture, 98; minor artists dependent on the, 248

SUTTEE: 167, 168 note

TALENT: the obligations of, 7, 27; the production of the man of, not to be ascribed to chance, 361

TASTE: of science too slow and indefinite, 3; the artist the man of, 4; the man of, 5; the rarity of the man of, 7; the man of, sets the tone of his people, 16; of the Venetian aristocracy, 22; bad, leads to decadence, 23; of the people should be founded on higher authority, 24; the possession of the true aristocrat, 24; English aristocrat's lack of, 47, 416, 417; ought to incline those above to cultivate genuine superiority, 80; the power of

wealth over, 106; the treasure of a bygone age, 166; of Charles I in art and literature, 181, 182; the greatest power in life, 241; the importance of, 241–256; conflict of good and bad, in the seventeenth century, 244; Who possesses the touchstone of? 244; the specimen of flourishing life possesses it, 246; imposition of, by the voice of flourishing life the highest altruism, 247; men of, assert their supremacy themselves, 259; necessity for the continual exercise of, 269; leading to hatred of the foreigner among the ancients, 302, 309

TEA: one of the deleterious substitutes for old English ale, 219–226; popular petition against, 223

TOBACCO: an anaphrodisiac, 225 note; dislike of, on the part of James I and Charles I, 225 note; Puritans' appreciation of, 226 note.

TORIES: their stupid theory of class hatred, 34; their missed opportunity, 102; might have taken the place of the Crown as patriarchal rulers, 102; but obeyed the behest of *laissez-faire*, 102

TOWNS: growth of, 42, 43; good enough for sharpers and weaklings, 60; rise of powerful middle class in the, 109

TRADE: the Grand Rebellion fight of, against tradition, 50; intimate connection of Puritanism with, 111, 174; Charles I's constant interference with, 50, 136, 138 note; invention by the Puritans of the religion of, 173; success in, no criterion of the possession of ruler-

INDEX

qualities, 412; list of some peers connected with, 412, 413

TRADESMEN. *See* SHOPKEEPERS

TRADES UNIONS: transportation for forming, 44; created by the people in self-defence, 46; formed owing to bad rulers, 60

TRADITION: favourable to the appearance of the superior man, 11, 12; productive of beauty, 12; necessary for the rearing of Beauty, Art, Will, Conscience and Spiritual Strength, 27; requires stability for its establishment, 28; the Grand Rebellion the struggle of, against trade, 50; rears character, 348; necessary for the production of talent and genius, 361; necessary for producing an example of flourishing life, 362; large families necessary for carrying on a great, 376; believers and disbelievers in the transmission of acquired characteristics united in the word *tradition*, 397, 398; belief of ancient aristocracies in the importance of, 398; value of traditional occupations for both aristocracy and people, 399, 400, 401

TRANSPORTATION: for poaching and forming Trades Unions, 44; to Australia, 54; of English slaves by Puritans, 54; for so-called fornication, 204

TRANSVALUATION OF VALUES: necessary for the revival of aristocracy, 260, 261; accomplished by the Puritans, 262, 263

TRAVELLING: bad for the man without backbone, 72

UGLINESS: its prevalence in modern times, 3, 47, 49, 168; never an attribute of the true aristocrat, 13; demands change, 28; due to Puritans and Nonconformists, 51; prevalence of, owing to guidance of voice of impoverished life, 79

UNIONIST PEERAGE: indignation of some of them over the Parliament Act, 33

VANITY: its increase under democracy, 320 note.

VENICE: the aristocracy of, very nearly the ideal rule of the best, 22; her control of the Church, 25; her tasteful aristocracy, 367; her Watch Committee, 367 note

VIRTUE: decline of public, due to class hostility, 82 note; the rearing of, 275; Aristotle's concept of, 275, 276; the virtues of the gentleman, 277, 278; the virtues, sub-divisions of the instincts, 311, 315, 316; possibility of cultivating, 316, 317; destroyed by cross-breeding, 319, 320, 347; caste virtue, 328; preserved by inbreeding, 329; killed by mixed marriages, 349; killed by modern conditions, 353; preserved by assortive mating, 384; destroyed by democracy, 387; dissipated by besotting labour, 399; the outcome of tradition, 400, 401

WAGES: measures to establish maximum, 43; poor rates in aid of, 44

WATCH COMMITTEE: J. S. Mill on necessity for, 14; in Venice, 367 note.

WEAK: exploitation of the, only justifiable for the sake of true

458

superiors, 100 ; selfishness necessary for the, 278 note

WEALTH : true, beauty and character, 24 note; the responsibility incumbent upon, 38; derived ultimately from the nation, 38; cruel and lifeless notion of the *Wealth of Nations*, 44; present capitalistic system the natural outcome of the *Wealth of Nations*, 66; may be a divine and beneficent power, 237; Egyptian view of, 238 note; divine dignity of, violated in England, 238; Socialist case against abuses of, 238; Cobbett on, 239; superficiality of Socialist attack on, 239; material, regarded as the highest good by modern man, 271, 272; no consideration to-day of how wealth is acquired, 279; Theognis on wealth mixing races, 304; Disraeli on a *Utopia of Wealth and Toil*, 355 note; mere wealth as a standard leads to democracy and ochlocracy, 365; a modern test for promotion to the peerage, 411; the bane of the social and political influence of, dishonestly acquired, 411

WENTWORTH : Sir Thomas. *See* STRAFFORD

WILL : reared only by long tradition and careful discipline and dependent on aristocratic rule, 27; dependent on sound instincts getting the mastery, 28;

the manifestation of instinct, 309; its importance in the life of a nation, 310; the relation of instinct to, 311–315; Free Will and Determinism, only the weak man has Free Will, 314, 315; broken by cross-breeding, 310, 318, 320; decline of, under democracy, 320; rich reproductive powers associated with low order of will power, 322; built up by assortive mating, 384; disintegrated by persistent cross-breeding, 385; destroyed by democracy, 387; modification effected through the, 395; reared by tradition, 401; should be trained by education, 423, 424

WOMEN : the Suffrage Movement a sign of misery, 34, 35; their entry into the ranks of industry and commerce, 42; in factories, 52, 57; appalling condition of, in factories, 54 note; refusal of Irish to allow women to be employed underground, 55; effects of female labour on homes of workmen still to be investigated, 57; the decline of domestic arts among, 57; difficult confinements of, employed in factories, 95; deleterious effects of tea upon, 223 note; Women's Petition against Coffee, 225; discontent among, 235; *laisser-aller* in the treatment of, by men and *vice versâ*, 270

THE END

PRINTED IN GREAT BRITAIN BY
RICHARD CLAY & SONS, LIMITED,
BRUNSWICK ST., STAMFORD ST., S.E.,
AND BUNGAY, SUFFOLK.

ND - #0021 - 010323 - C0 - 229/152/25 [27] - CB - 9781527983007 - Gloss Lamination